Containment
Concept and Policy

Containment
Concept and Policy

Based on a Symposium Cosponsored by
the National Defense University
and
the Foreign Service Institute

Edited by

Terry L. Deibel
John Lewis Gaddis

IN TWO VOLUMES

VOLUME TWO

1986

National Defense University Press
Washington, DC

National Defense University Press Publications

To increase general knowledge and inform discussion, NDU Press publishes books on subjects relating to US national security.

Each year, the National Defense University, through the Institute for National Strategic Studies, hosts about two dozen Senior Fellows who engage in original research on national security issues. NDU Press publishes the best of this research.

In addition, the Press publishes other especially timely or distinguished writing on national security, as well as new editions of out-of-print defense classics, and books based on University-sponsored conferences concerning national security affairs.

NDU Press publications are sold by the US Government Printing Office. For ordering information, call (202) 783–3238 or write to the Superintendent of Documents, US Government Printing Office, Washington, DC 20402.

Library of Congress Cataloging in Publication Data

Containment: concept and policy.

Includes bibliographies and index.
1. United States—Foreign relations—1945–   . 2. World politics—1945–   . 3. United States—Foreign relations—Soviet Union. 4. Soviet Union—Foreign relations—United States. I. Deibel, Terry L. II. Gaddis, John Lewis. III. National Defense University. IV. Foreign Service Institute (U.S.)
E744.C7615 1986 327.73   86–23582

First printing, November 1986

Contents

VOLUME TWO

Part Three: Applications

Containment
Concept and Policy

Part Three

Applications

12

The 'X' Article
and Contemporary Sources
of Soviet Conduct

Jerry F. Hough

E VEN IN THE HINDSIGHT of over thirty-five years, George
Kennan's 'X' article remains a remarkable document.[1] It
was, of course, first of all a political statement—and one with a
message far more complex than many remember. On the one
hand, it offered a powerful argument against the naive assumptions associated with Henry Wallace. Kennan cautioned that we
"must continue to expect that Soviet policies will reflect no abstract love of peace and stability." Soviet "political action," he
warned, "is a fluid stream which moves constantly, wherever it
is permitted to move, toward a given goal. Its main concern is
to make sure that it has filled every nook and cranny available
to it in the basin of world power." The answer that he proposed
was "a policy of firm containment, designed to confront the
Russians with unalterable counter-force at every point where
they show signs of encroaching upon the interests of a peaceful
and stable world."

Jerry F. Hough is J. B. Duke Professor of Political Science at Duke University, and a staff member of the Brookings Institution.

Yet, on the other hand—and given Kennan's subsequent positions, one wonders if this were not a more fundamental purpose of the article than is sometimes assumed—it repeatedly attempted to calm fears that the Soviet Union was "like Napoleon and Hitler," or that it was seeking immediate victory. The "fluid stream" that he warned against was of "political action." Nowhere did Kennan refer to a military threat; instead, he constantly highlighted Soviet weakness. The Kremlin that Kennan described was "basically flexible in its reaction to political reality [and] . . . by no means unamenable to considerations of prestige." Kennan counseled patience and painted a rather hopeful picture of the future if only "the western world finds the strength and resourcefulness to contain Soviet power over a period of ten to fifteen years."

In Kennan's discussion of the subject emphasized in the article's title—the sources of Soviet conduct—it is striking how little attention a man identified with the realist school of international relations paid to such factors as the interests of the Russian state. Indeed, the concept of national interest is totally absent from the piece, as is any discussion of a desire for security as a driving force in Soviet policy. Instead, Kennan found the sources of Soviet conduct in other spheres: first, in communist ideology; second, in the imperatives of maintaining power at home.

On the first point, Kennan emphasized most what he called "the Soviet structure of thought"—"the mental world of the Soviet leaders." He referred to communism as a "mystical, Messianic movement," to the communists' "particular brand of fanatacism," to their assumptions about an "innate antagonism between capitalism and socialism" and about the "infallibility of the Kremlin [as] the sole repository of truth." With this way of looking at the world, he said, "there can never be on Moscow's side any sincere assumption of a community of aims between the Soviet Union and powers which are regarded as capitalist."

"There can be no appeal to common purposes, there can be no appeal to common mental approaches."

On the second issue, Kennan explicitly asserted "that the stress laid in Moscow on the menace confronting Soviet society from the world outside its borders is founded not in the realities of foreign antagonism but in the necessity of explaining away the maintenance of dictatorial authority at home." He placed great emphasis upon "the concept of Russia as in a state of siege" as virtually the sole legitimating mechanism for the dictatorship. "The millions of human beings who form that part of the structure of power must defend at all costs this concept of Russia's position, for without it they are themselves superfluous."

Kennan's view of the future was somewhat ambivalent. Certainly, he gave great attention to the possibility of change in the Soviet Union, if only the communist movement were contained. Through most of the article, he wrote as if he had cataclysmic change in mind. His analysis of the narrowness of support for the Soviet rulers led in this direction. He argued that "the excesses of the police apparatus have fanned the political opposition to the regime into something far greater and more dangerous than it could have been before the excesses began," and he discussed at length the possibility that the succession might lead to an unravelling of the structure of power. "The possibility remains (and in the opinion of this writer it is a strong one) that Soviet power, like the capitalist world of its conception, bears within it the seeds of its own decay, and that the sprouting of these seeds is well advanced."

Yet, in his conclusion, Kennan raised the possibility of a far more moderate kind of change:

> The United States has it in its power to increase enormously the strains under which Soviet policy must operate, to force upon the Kremlin a far greater degree of moderation and circumspection than it has had to observe in recent years, and in this way to promote tendencies which

must eventually find their outlet in either the break-up or the gradual mellowing of Soviet power. For no mystical, Messianic movement—and particularly not that of the Kremlin—can face frustration indefinitely without eventually adjusting itself in one way or another to the logic of that state of affairs.

Kennan and Soviet Thought in the 1940s

The Kennan article was written nearly forty years ago. How does it stand up as an analysis of the Soviet Union of its time and as a prediction of the future? How relevant is the analysis for understanding the contemporary Soviet Union?

In the long debate about the origins of the Cold War, widely differing views have been expressed about Soviet intentions and thinking in the late 1940s. A variety of evidence, including the contemporary statements of Maxim Litvinov about which Professor Mastny has written,[2] suggests that Kennan was basically right in his description of the way that Stalin thought. Stalin did seem to fear that a more open posture toward the West would strengthen liberal tendencies at home. Ideology did increase Stalin's suspicions of the West and his hostility toward it.

Where, in retrospect, the 'X' article stands up less well is in its tendency to overgeneralize about communist thinking, even at that time. In talking about "the powerful hands of Russian history and tradition" sustaining the Soviet leaders in the belief that "the outside world was hostile and that it was their duty eventually to overthrow the political forces beyond their borders," Kennan glossed over the fact that the Great Russian members of Lenin's Politburo—Bukharin, Rykov, and Tomsky—became the core of the Right Opposition, which seemed to have a more relaxed attitude toward markets and the West.

Even in 1947, there is evidence of a debate at the highest levels of the Politburo. There is one curious aspect of the 'X' article that is almost never noted. It was published in the same issue of *Foreign Affairs* that carried an article on Anglo-American competition by Eugene Varga, the director of the main Soviet scholarly institute concerned with the outside world and a man who provided a weekly package of analysis and advice for Stalin on the subject.[3] Paradoxically, as the person chosen to present a Soviet view of the West, Varga had a way of thinking about the subject that was extremely different from Kennan's generalizations about Soviet thinking.

While concluding that Britain and the United States were united in the chief aims of their foreign policy, Varga asserted that "England is trying to pursue a foreign policy of her own." Treating differences between the domestic policies of the British Labor Party and the Truman administration as quite significant, as well as differences in foreign policy between Truman and Roosevelt and between Bevin and the left wing of the Labor Party, Varga implied that Western governments had some independence from their ruling classes.[4]

In the Soviet media, Varga was even more explicit. He denied that governments were subordinated to "the monopolies," and scornfully dismissed the idea that "now in 1947 the working class and the Labor Party has no influence on the policy of England, that the financial oligarchy makes all the policy."[5] He suggested that the influence of the masses on the bourgeois state could become so great that it could serve as the vehicle for the transformation of capitalism and the peaceful transition to socialism, and he spoke of British nationalization as something serious.

> Today, thirty years after the victory of the Great October Revolution, the struggle in Europe is becoming in its historical development more and more a struggle for the tempos and forms of the transition from capitalism to socialism. Although the Russian path, the Soviet system, is undoubtedly the best and fastest path of transition from capitalism to socialism, historical development, as Lenin

had theoretically predicted, shows that other paths are also available for the achievement of this goal.[6]

Varga differed from policy not only on the possibility of different paths to socialism but also in the question of East-West relations. In his book, he had suggested that "the democratic forces in all countries" were so strong and had such a strong potential impact on governmental policy that "the relationship of the capitalist countries to the Soviet Union will not be the same as it was in the prewar period."[7] He argued that Lenin's theory of the inevitability of war between capitalist countries was no longer valid, and that political independence for countries such as India could have real meaning in terms of their foreign policy.

Of course, Varga's institute was closed, and he himself, while not arrested, published little for the rest of the Stalin period. But while the 'X' article was basically accurate in its description of the pattern of thought of Stalin and some other members of the Politburo such as Molotov, it remains a fact that Varga's views could still be published through the fall of 1947. It is difficult to believe that he, too, did not have support in the Politburo. By all indications, one of these supporters was Georgii Malenkov, chairman of the foreign policy subcommittee of the Politburo and the number two figure in the political system after 1949.

I have raised the question of Varga and Malenkov not because I want to engage in revisionism on the origin of the Cold War. I think that Stalin had an impregnable position and a set of views that was not conducive to any very different foreign policy outcome. I emphasize the point, rather, as a reminder that not all Marxist-Leninists thought alike, even in the Stalin period.

Recent Changes in Soviet Thinking

Varga's thought pattern also is important to emphasize because much of it became orthodoxy in the post-Stalin period, and virtually all of it became highly respectable. In fact, on the questions of the inevitability of war, of peaceful paths to socialism, and of the possibility of an independent foreign policy by Third World countries, Varga's position became unchallengeable doctrine in 1956. His denunciation of the proposition that Western governments are subordinated to the "monopolies" of Wall Street has been incorporated in innumerable Party documents and, though challengeable, is accepted by virtually everyone in the Soviet foreign policy establishment. The degree of the impact of the masses on Western foreign policy is the subject of continual debate, but the Varga position is adopted by all the pro-detente forces.

It is now possible to present an image of international relations in the Soviet press that is at the polar opposite from the two-camp image. Thus, the head of the International Organizations Department of the Ministry of Foreign Affairs, V. Petrovsky, has warned against "turning [the concept of] global conflict into an absolute." "The concept of international conflict as an eternal, root category or even essence of international relations . . . in whatever phraseology it is clothed, in practice, ignores the objective fact of the constantly widening collaboration in politics, economics, and science and technology of states of different systems."[8]

The framework in which this point is most frequently raised is in a discussion of "global problems," "general human problems," "global interdependence," and the like. Discussions of these problems usually center on such questions as pollution, food supply, the energy crisis, oceanic issues, and so forth. One such article, written by an official of the Central Committee apparatus, contained a three-page section on "the discontinuation of the arms race as the necessary condition for solving economic problems."[9] On Moscow television in 1982, Georgii Arbatov pointed to yet another common interest when he said that "everybody is dependent on the stability of the international economic system and the international monetary system."[10]

Sometimes this image is simply implied in the use of phraseology far from that of irreconcilable class conflict or "two camps." One scholar writes of the "human association";[11] a foreign ministry official asserts that "mankind continues to exist as a united whole;"[12] a Central Committee official speaks on Soviet television of "we Europeans," linking Russians together with West Europeans;[13] two other scholars refer to "the two lines in world politics—between the proponents of an aggressive policy and the advocates of the preservation and deepening of detente," without suggesting that these two lines coincide with the division between classes or even between the two systems.[14]

The Soviet media also contain views on revolutionary prospects abroad that are far from those of the Stalin era. For example, a number of leading Soviet Latin Americanists have been insisting that the major countries of that region are closer to southern Europe in their socioeconomic development than to most of Asia and Africa, and that their political development is likely to follow the path from military dictatorship to constitutional democracy seen in southern Europe in the mid-1970s. These scholars draw the logical conclusions so far as the proper tactics of the communist parties are concerned. One of the most outspoken, Boris Koval, the deputy director of the Institute of the International Workers' Movement, has contended that "in a whole group of countries, the toilers, in practice, have to select not between capitalism and socialism, but between bourgeois democracy and fascism." Indeed, he went so far as to suggest that the struggle for democracy (in a presocialist system) would be the determining feature of Latin American politics for many years and perhaps decades.[15]

Koval made his opinion clear regarding the position of local communists in this struggle. While maintaining their independence, they should be willing to cooperate with the moderates where there was a coincidence of interests—and the preservation of representative democracy was certainly one such case. In 1982, Koval specifically cautioned against an underestimation of the revolutions in Peru in 1968–1975 and

Zimbabwe in 1980. Although these revolutions did not produce socialism, they did lead to a change in political system, and in his opinion this was not insignificant. He wrote with near contempt of "petty-bourgeois revolutionism" based on peasants and white collar forces,[16] and while he did not say so, it was difficult to forget that the Central American guerilla movements were, first of all, based on intellectuals and peasants.

Similar views are expressed about revolution in Asia and Africa, although everyone recognizes the possibility of radical victories in the most backward countries. Virtually all USSR scholars openly assert in print that the Soviet model, based on internal mobilization of resources and complete suppression of the private sector, is undesirable in the Third World. They believe that outside resources are necessary and that the socialist countries are too poor to provide them in all but a few cases. Hence, Western investment is inevitable and even desirable, and most see political dependence on the West flowing from economic dependence. Privately, many of the major scholars simply state that "the United States has won in the Third World." Many of the scholars of the Institute of Oriental Studies, in particular, have this view.

These statements bespeak a pattern of thought totally different from that depicted in the 'X' article. I do not want to imply that all Soviet citizens think in this way. In the debates in Soviet journals and on television talk shows, other persons continue to insist on the importance of the class factor, on the implacable hostility and expansionism of the United States, and on the possibility of successful revolution in the Third World. Many treat Soviet-American relations as far more a zero-sum game than a realm for possible cooperation.

Yet, at a minimum, the persons on the unorthodox side are not eccentric outsiders. Arbatov is a Central Committee member, and the deputy directors of the Institutes of the International Workers' Movement and of Oriental Studies have posts in the nomenklatura of the Central Committee. Koval, in particular, is very closely associated with Vadim Zagladin, the first deputy head of the international department and a man whose own writings come very close to a revisionistic position. In 1982, a reliable Soviet source said that Zagladin was the one man in the foreign policy establishment with whom Chernenko was consulting during the last year of Brezhnev's life.

Kennan's Predictions of the Future

What, then, are the implications of the opening up of the debate and the spread of the Varga viewpoint through large parts of the Soviet foreign policy establishment? The first implication is that we must be extremely careful before we begin to infer the sources of Soviet behavior from the assumptions of Marxism-Leninism as they were perceived by Stalin thirty years ago—*extremely* careful, and I could make the point more strongly. It simply is illegitimate to say that if we read the 'X' article, if we study and understand the Soviet Union of the forties and the fifties, we can confidently say that we understand the contemporary motivation and pattern of thought of the Soviet leaders at the present or in the future. The fact that men like Gromyko, Ustinov, and Ponomarev already held important posts at that time and have been at high levels for forty years does, of course, imply considerable continuity—although Gromyko and Ponomarev used to be closer in their thinking to Varga than to Stalin—but now that they have lost control of Soviet foreign policy, we may be dealing with people who think very differently.

It is, of course, one thing to say how not to understand the sources of Soviet foreign policy; it is something else to say what those sources actually are. In understanding the sources of Soviet conduct today, it is not only fair but worthwhile to consider how 'X' viewed our own time, that is, Kennan's 1947 projections of the future.

In fact, Kennan's predictions were in many respects quite accurate. He was right that if events stubbornly kept disconfirming the ideological predictions, Messianic communism would begin to mellow. It is fascinating to read the debates of the 1960s and 1970s and watch the impact of events from the Cuban revolution to the internationalization of world production to the Islamic revolution on Soviet thinking—not on everybody's thinking, of course, but on the direction of the debate.[17]

Kennan's predictions were also right about the connection between domestic and foreign policy. A more relaxed attitude toward the outside world and a more relaxed attitude toward unorthodox views *have* gone together in the Soviet Union, most spectacularly during the de-Stalinization of the mid-1950s. The same is true of the relationship between declining support of the Soviet economic model abroad and the deepening belief of Soviet intellectuals that the model needs modification at home.

Kennan's predictions were even right about the instability of the Soviet political system, if one defines that system as the totalitarian model did: an overpowering dictatorship, an absolutely rigid and dogmatic ideology, an irrational terror that arrested totally innocent people as well as those who broke the rules of the system, millions of people sent to camps on various political criteria, a xenophobic reaction to anything Western, and a sheer craziness like that shown in the rejection of great Russian scientific discoveries like the Mendelian theory of genetics. Although some remnants remain, that political system has essentially disappeared. The problem in the Soviet Union in the last decade has not been an overpowering dictator who lashes out at the elite and society on the basis of his dogmatic ideology, but leaders who will not take strong action on any basis, who do not know what they want to do or are afraid to act, who say as Andropov did on economic reform, "I have no recipes."

And yet, one rereads Kennan's predictions with frustration. He correctly stated, as already quoted, that irrational police action was undercutting support more than helping it; but he did not draw the conclusion that the curbing of the police—the transformation of the Soviet Union from a totalitarian dictatorship into an authoritarian dictatorship (if we use the definitions of the fifties)—would produce a regime that has proved very stable for thirty years. He underestimated the sources of support for the basic communist system in the Soviet Union and paid too much attention to the possibility of its collapse in contrast to its evolution.

Similarly, in foreign policy Kennan was right about a mellowing of ideology and about a modification of foreign policy in a more cooperative direction. But whatever he may have thought privately (and Kennan has been a rather pessimistic man about human nature and governments), his article did not prepare the reader for the kind of challenges that a mellower Soviet Union would continue to pose, or for the continuities in many kinds of behavior.

Factors Influencing Soviet Foreign Policy

The basic problem, it seems to me, is that the sources of Soviet foreign policy in 1947 were limited neither to rigid ideological suspicion and hostility nor to Stalin's desire to consolidate his power. A series of other factors were also at work in shaping Soviet policy at the time, which came more into focus when the factors that Kennan emphasized began to fade.

First, ideology is not simply a dogmatic guide to action. It also provides the definition of values on which the legitimacy of a system rests. Two superpowers with competing ideologies would inevitably come into conflict on this basis alone. For example, the United States in all meaningful senses has accepted Soviet control of Eastern Europe. Yet, for reasons of internal legitimacy and human rights, there was no way that the United States could fail to provide moral (and some concrete) support to Solidarity when it arose in Poland. And this produced a strong reaction in much of the Soviet elite.

Similarly, the Soviet Union in all meaningful senses has written off Central America. The Soviets would not react if the United States sent troops to El Salvador or invaded Nicaragua,

and they have been unwilling to bankroll Nicaragua economically, thereby virtually guaranteeing that the Sandinistas or
their successors eventually will have to move toward the right.
Yet, the basic Soviet value structure and the dynamics of competition with the United States makes it inevitable that the Soviet Union provide moral support and small-scale aid to the El
Salvadoran rebels. And this has produced a strong reaction in
the United States.

Second, the momentum of events and past commitments
needs to be emphasized. A "winter Olympics" image of international relations might be useful here, for once a nation pushes
off down the ski jump—frequently without fully thinking
through what it is doing—it picks up speed rapidly and finds it
difficult to change course. This, too, is an aspect of Soviet behavior that we ignore at our own peril. When a radical revolution occurs, it is difficult for the Soviet Union not to become
committed at some low level. When the United States challenges Soviet allies frontally, it is difficult for the Soviet Union
not to increase its support to them. Similar mechanisms operate
on the American side.

Third, any analysis of the factors shaping Soviet foreign
policy that does not prominently include a drive for basic national security and the promotion of a series of innate national
interests seems deeply flawed. Even if Russia became democratic or America became communist, the relationship between
the two superpowers would likely remain one of conflict—at
least until sometime in the twenty-first or twenty-second century
when countries such as China, India, and Brazil become superpowers, leading to new alignments.

Indeed, this point, often ignored by hawk and dove alike,
is the place where any serious analysis of Soviet goals and
intentions must begin. Hans Morgenthau, the leading realist
international relations theorist of the 1950s, was correct in
insisting that international relations always involve a struggle
for power, that all countries are engaged in an attempt to expand
their power and influence. In that sense, all countries, including
even Denmark, are expansionist within their means. Similarly,

all countries are looking for opportunities to make gains and
are, in that sense, opportunistic. And of course, all are attempting to preserve what they already have, and in that sense
they are all defensive. To argue whether the Soviet Union is expansionist or defensive misses the point. It is both. So to suggest that better understanding can produce an era of total good
feeling is to show naivete. But it is just as naive to suggest that
we refuse to cooperate with the Soviet Union on any issue until
it accepts a definition of detente that requires it to stop
promoting its interests, thus preventing cooperation where we
have common enemies (such as Islamic fundamentalism) or
common causes (such as the containment of the Iran-Iraq war).

The crucial questions in international relations are not those
of ultimate goals. They center on the *risks* a leader is willing to
take to achieve these goals. (All Argentine governments have
wanted the Falklands, but none of the others took the risks of
the last military government.) They center on *means* chosen to
achieve goals. (The Japanese are still trying to dominate Southeast Asia, but use economic means instead of military.) They
center on the *priority* assigned to various conflicting foreign policy
goals. (The balance the United States makes between the commitment to Israeli policy and the commitment to the peace process in
the Middle East is always an excruciating choice.) And, above all,
these questions center on leaders' changing *perceptions* of cost-
benefit ratios for different foreign policy options.

It is through such a prism that Soviet foreign policy needs
to be viewed. Soviet policy of the Brezhnev era, especially during its last years, was marked by much less willingness to take
risks than that displayed under either Stalin (in Berlin and
Korea) or Khrushchev (in the Third World or the Cuban missile
crisis). It was marked by a growing pessimism about the
possibility of achieving revolutionary goals in the Third World,
but even more by an unwillingness or inability to make hard
decisions on priorities. The Soviet Union continually pursued a
number of contradictory goals, and would not choose between
them in a way that would have permitted any of them to be
achieved. It courted American allies, but did so through peace-

campaign techniques that had long proven ineffective rather than through the making of meaningful concessions. Similarly, Soviet leaders could not bring themselves to make reductions in secrecy that would have been necessary for real arms control.

Domestic Imperatives in the Gorbachev Era

One looking toward the foreign policy of the Gorbachev era would be wrong to see any basic change in the Soviets' drive to pursue their interests. However, a real change is possible in the way that the Soviet Union defines its interests or priorities, and in its willingness to make hard choices between alternatives.

At the end of his *Time Magazine* interview, Gorbachev added a personal "few words that are important in understanding what we have been talking about all along."[18] He asserted that "foreign policy is a continuation of domestic policy," and then asked his Soviet and foreign readers "to ponder one thing. If we in the Soviet Union are setting ourselves such truly grandiose plans in the domestic sphere, then what are the external conditions that we need to be able to fulfill those domestic plans?"

Gorbachev ended the interview enigmatically ("I leave the answer to that question to you"), but his emphasis on the point was significant. The connection between domestic and foreign policy *has* been a close one in Soviet history. Kennan was right in saying that Stalin was thinking about (and afraid of) the domestic consequences of good relations with the United States. One of the major factors behind the continuation of the bipolar policy throughout Brezhnev's period was his preference for the present Soviet economic system. As long as the Soviet leaders want strict central planning and foreign economic relations limited to centralized bilateral trade (and want the same for Eastern Europe), there are few advantages in this age of unlikely foreign attack to a real multipolar foreign policy.

So to understand the changes in Gorbachev's foreign policy, we must understand the nature of his domestic imperatives. Gorbachev has indicted that his goal is to raise Soviet technology to world levels. He has stated—and he is right—that superpower status in the twenty-first century depends on it. The

Soviet Union faces an enormous window of military vulnerability at the end of the century. If the Western armies and weapons become fully computerized, if contemporary weapons such as tanks become obsolete, if SDI were to work (or simply have important spin-offs for conventional weapons), if China with its billion-plus population were to begin to modernize seriously, if Japan were to have a change of government and return to the foreign policy of the 1930s, an unmodernized Soviet Union could be in enormous danger. With 40 percent of the Soviet army in the twenty-first century made up of Central Asians, the Soviet Union can have a computerized army only if all its population has been brought into the twenty-first century.

Raising Soviet technology to world levels is incredibly difficult. Many Westerners would say that it is impossible, but this is wishful thinking. John Foster Dulles said in 1955 that Japan could never challenge the United States in high technology markets. We should not make similar mistakes with the Soviet Union. Nevertheless, the difficulty remains. Brezhnev demonstrated that the importation of Western technology is no panacea, and something radically different must be tried.

The experience of Japan, Taiwan, and South Korea suggests that one secret for solving the problem of technological backwardness is a policy of exporting manufactured goods. Those countries began to export not when they reached world levels of technology but when they were quite backward. They did so because only such a strategy could subject their manufacturers to foreign competition, forcing them to improve the quality of their exports to world levels. Soviet manufacturers enjoy a level of protectionism unknown in the outside world, and an attack on this protectionism is absolutely vital if the Soviet economy is to be modernized.

Implications for Foreign Policy

If the need to raise the quality of Soviet technology is to be the driving force behind Soviet foreign policy, a number of implications follow.

First, radical revolution in the Third World has been unsuccessful in all but pre-industrial societies—the Afghanistans, the Yemens, the Ethiopias, the Nicaraguas—and the politics of industrializing Third World countries are moving to the center and the right. The number of pre-industrial countries is declining; these countries are by definition not significant economic and military powers; and even radical pre-industrial societies such as China and Mozambique are showing a tendency to moderate their policy. A Soviet foreign policy that focuses on promoting revolution in countries like Nicaragua (with 2½ million people) while neglecting countries such as Mexico (with 79 million) is following a losing strategy.

That strategy becomes even more counterproductive if one considers economic factors. An export strategy will be difficult to pursue in the industrial world because a country with inferior goods must compete by lowering prices, a practice which inevitably runs into protectionist pressures and charges of dumping. The Third World is the natural place for Soviet leaders to begin forcing their manufacturers to compete with Western manufacturers, and only moderate regimes there have the money to buy.

In many respects, a move toward courtship of moderate Third World countries is already under way. The crucial case is the Philippines. Not only is the Soviet Union not supporting the communist revolution materially, but the Soviets gave a medal to then President Marcos for past service as ambassador to the Soviet Union, and the USSR was the only country to send congratulations to Marcos on his fraudulent victory in the February 1986 presidential election. Similar tendencies are seen in the establishment of diplomatic relations with Oman, sports diplomacy with Saudi Arabia, and diplomatic flirtation with Israel.

Second, in the military realm, the logic of Gorbachev's domestic policy is to shift the emphasis from short- to long-range defense needs. Current spending levels on procurement, readiness, and manpower are unnecessary, especially with China reducing its army by a million people. Similarly, with a slow deployment of the mobile SS–25 being the least expensive answer to American development of first-strike weapons, the Soviet Union can reduce its strategic expenditures regardless of any arms control agreement with the United States. By contrast, the Soviet Union has a great military problem in the long-term perspective. To meet this problem, the Soviet Union needs to pour money into research and development, especially in areas (such as computerization) that will be necessary for the military technology of the twenty-first century—and for civilian technology as well. SDI and Chinese modernization are the perfect threats for Soviet leaders to emphasize, because they pose no short-term danger at all but symbolize the long-term danger.

Third, the short-term logic of Gorbachev's domestic needs is to deemphasize relations with the United States—even to stress anti-Americanism—while focusing on relations with Western Europe and Japan. Paradoxically, doves such as Marshall Shulman and hawks such as Richard Perle have been united in a different view of the requirements of Soviet liberalization and modernization. Both assume that such a program requires arms control agreements with the United States. The doves have argued for detente to promote such a development; the hawks have argued for a hard-line policy either to prevent it or to obtain major concessions from the Soviet Union in the process.

This position seems fundamentally wrong, for no Soviet leader can afford to give the USSR's main enemy a veto power over its domestic evolution. In fact, modernization, though it requires an economic opening to the West, is much easier to sell domestically in the name of anti-Americanism than in the context of agreements with the United States. If a Soviet leader says that a more relaxed information policy and opening to the West is possible because the United States can be trusted, Soviet conservatives will think him deeply naive. But if a Soviet leader says this is necessary as the only way to have the computerization that is needed to thwart the American danger, or if he can say that the United States is trying to force the Soviet Union into an arms race to bankrupt the Soviet economy, he can put the conservatives on the defensive. And if he says that the opening to the West can be accomplished through concessions to Japan and

Europe, then he is in a position to defend it as a measure that undercuts American alliances. All the evidence suggests that this is precisely the strategy Gorbachev is following.

For these reasons, Gorbachev is likely to present the United States a challenge it has not seen for years. We have grown used to a Soviet Union that only uses ineffective peace campaigns, that concentrates on (with the exception of India) small, pre-industrial countries in the Third World, and that has allowed its economic system to lose all its attractiveness. As Gorbachev moves to correct these mistakes, the United States, too, will have to develop a new approach. The mellowed Soviet Union that Kennan correctly predicted will be far more worthy an opponent than one hidebound by ideology and the imperatives of conspiratorial rule.

Notes

1. George F. Kennan (writing as 'X'), "The Sources of Soviet Conduct," *Foreign Affairs* 25 (July 1947), pp. 566–82.

2. Vojtech Mastny, *Russia's Road to the Cold War* (New York: Columbia University Press, 1979).

3. Varga was a Hungarian by birth, but he had lived in the Soviet Union for over twenty-five years and was at the heart of the foreign policy establishment. What he was saying in print was that the

basic two-camp image of the world was wrong, that Lenin erred in his argument with Bernstein about the possibility of evolution to socialism under the bourgeois state, and that his own native Hungary should not be subjected to the Soviet model of socialism. (At the time, Varga was supporting Hungarian leader Imre Nagy in his fight against collectivization of Hungarian agriculture.)

4. E. Varga, "Anglo-American Rivalry and Partnership: A Marxist View," *Foreign Affairs* 25 (July 1947), pp. 594–95.

5. "Diskussiia po knige E. Varga 'Izmeneniia v ekonomike kapitalizma v itoge vtoroi mirovoi voiny,' 2, 14, 21 maia 1947 g., Stenograficheskii otchet," *Mirovoe khoziaistvo i mirovaia politika,* No. 11 (November), 1947, Supplement, p. 61.

6. E. Varga, "Sotsializm i kapitalizm za tridtsat' let," in *ibid.,* No. 10, 1947, pp. 4–5.

7. *Izmeneniia v ekonomike kapitalizma v itoge vtoroi mirovoi voiny* (Moscow: Gospolitizdat, 1946), p. 319.

8. V. Petrovsky, "Dogmy konfrontatsii (Ob amerikanskikh kontseptsiiakh 'global'nogo konklikta,' " *Mirovaia ekonomika i mezhdunarodnye otnosheniia,* No. 2, 1980, pp. 21, 22.

9. S. M. Menshikov, "Global'nye problemy i budushche mirovoi ekonomiki," *Voprosy filosofii,* No. 4, 1983, pp. 113–15.

10. Studio 9, May 1982. Translated in FBIS, *Daily Report—Soviet Union,* 1 June 1982, pp. CC6.

11. V. N. Shevchenko, "K kharakteristike dialektiki sovremennoi epokhi (chast' parvaia)," *Filosofskie nauki,* No. 5, 1981, p. 23.

12. V. Petrovsky, "Kontseptsiia vzaimozavisimosti v strategii SShA," *Mirovaia ekonomika i mezhdunarodnye otnosheniia,* No. 9, 1977, p. 71.

13. Vitalii Kobysh, on Studio 9, 24 December 1983. Translated in FBIS, *Daily Report—Soviet Union,* 27 December 1983, p. CC10.

14. D. Tomashevsky and V. Lukov, "Radi zhizni na zemli," *Mirovaia ekonomia i mezhdunarodnye otnosheniia,* No. 2, 1983, p. 10.

15. B. I. Koval' and S. I. Semenov, "Latinskaia Amerika i mezhdunarodnaia sotsial-demokratiia," *Rabochii klass i sovremennyi*

mir, No. 4 (July-August), 1978, pp. 115–30. B. I. Koval', in "Mezhdunarodnaia sotsial-demokratiia v Latinskoi Amerike," *Latinskaia Amerika*, No. 4, 1978, p. 103.

16. See "Revoliutsionnoe dvizhenie v Peru: uroki, problemy, perspektivy," *Latinskaia Amerika*, No. 1 (1984), pp. 162–63; and "Rabochii klass i revoliutsionnost' narodnykh mass: opyt 70kh godov," *Rabochii klass i sovremenny mir*, No. 2 (1983), pp. 8-9, 13.

17. The evolution of the debates on the Third World from the 1950s into the 1960s and 1970s is described in Jerry F. Hough, *The Struggle for the Third World: Soviet Debates and American Options* (Washington: Brookings Institution, 1986).

18. "An Interview with Gorbachev," *Time Magazine*, 9 September 1985, p. 29.

13

Soviet Conventional Power Projection and Containment

Robert E. Harkavy

A CAREFUL RE-READING of Mr. X's "The Sources of Soviet Conduct" may indeed be a salutary and educational exercise beyond mere nostalgia or a twinge of deja vu.[1] Considered in conjunction with some other concurrent writings, as well as with subsequent general critiques and interpretations of the US containment policy, it allows one to reflect upon some very broad, vital, and enduring questions, many of which are closely bound up with interpretations of the recent expansion of Soviet conventional power projection capability.[2] These questions involve the relative validity of ideological versus spatial (or geopolitical) interpretations of Soviet expansionism and the relative weighting of an appropriate Western response. They also involve judgments about the extent to which containment may have succeeded or failed thus far, for what Soviet conventional power projection is all about is the extended leapfrogging of the old "forward" containment ring.

Robert E. Harkavy, Professor of Political Science at Pennsylvania State University, has served with the Atomic Energy Commission and the Arms Control and Disarmament Agency.

Some analysts might claim that the correlation of forces has seriously changed. The scattered red blotches on the map signaling Soviet clients, and the anchors and stars pinpointing associated Soviet naval and air facilities, provide a graphic and depressing scoreboard.[3] Others, however, noting Moscow's internal problems and the obvious Soviet loss of revolutionary elan and cachet, might claim that the game plan of 'X,' however slowly and fitfully played out, has proven its worth. In this view, the United States may be seen—so far—as having played a classic "bend but not break" defense fairly well between the world's twenty-yard lines, while keeping the opponent's score within manageable limits. Whether that—in conjunction with the pressures of SDI on the Soviet economy, the increase of non-Russian groups in the Soviet Union, East European insurrections, and arteriosclerosis in the nomenklatura—will cause the eventual implosion or at least mellowing implied as Kennan's end point remains to be seen.

In the 'X' article and in other related writings by George Kennan, several connected major themes recur with degrees of relative emphasis and critical nuance. First is an insistence on the central role of communist ideology as a driving force in the determination of Soviet foreign policy—from the visceral perspective of Soviet elites, it is said really to count![4] Second, regarding US primary interests—i.e., those most worth defending as the bottom line of a containment strategy—there is an emphasis on the "traditional" heavy industrial regions which provide "sinews" of war production like steel, coal, and autos.[5] In a related vein, there is also a stress on an "asymmetrical" counterstrategy, one hinged upon the "strong points," the industrial cores of Europe and Asia. According to John Gaddis, that strategy "sought to counter the fear brought about by the Soviet military presence in Europe and Northeast Asia after World War II, not by building up countervailing military force, but by relying on US economic aid to rehabilitate war-shattered economies in Western Europe and Japan, thereby creating in those countries the self-confidence that would allow them to resist the Russians on their own."[6] It might be argued, however, that

Kennan's broader imagery of ultimate Soviet mellowing through containment implied a more symmetrical, geographically comprehensive, rimland strategy of the sort later enshrined in NSC–68.[7]

It is intended as no criticism of Kennan's earlier writings to point out that they are, in some crucial respects, reflective of the mood, events, or *zeitgeist* of the immediate postwar period. The assumptions about the visceral hold of Marxist-Leninist ideology on Soviet foreign policy elites were, of course, almost a natural result of the closeness of 1947 to the revolutionary era and its aftermath, to the careers and utterances of Lenin, Trotsky, and their Comintern colleagues. Nowadays, most scholars must strive mightily to find a remnant of visceral ideological belief behind the central realities of Russian nationalism and the self-serving aggrandizement of an almost ascriptively based nomenklatura. Who nowadays would weight an interpretation of Soviet foreign policy so heavily with ideology as did Kennan in 1947?[8]

Kennan's focus on centers of warmaking industrial capacity seems also heavily (and by now anachronistically) concentrated on earlier concerns, events, and somewhat theoretical interpretations of the locus of national rivalries. That focus is above all Eurocentric,[9] redolent of past rivalries over the terrain between the German and French core areas—the *Ruhrgebiet,* Alsace-Lorraine, Belgium's Wallonia, and Luxembourg. One is reminded of Czechoslovakia's inheriting of the Skoda Works from the ashes of the Austro-Hungarian Empire, of reciprocal German and British bombing of Coventry and Essen, of the Soviet rape of industrial Manchuria in 1945 (and Soviet demands for a similar rape of Germany). By contrast, few US security analysts nowadays might couch arguments on behalf of the continued defense of Western Europe in terms of retention of the Dassault or Rhinemetall plants. To the extent that today's concerns echo those of 1947, the worry would rather center on whatever small-scale versions of Silicon Valley or Route 128 may have arisen in Bavaria, the suburbs of Paris, or Osaka.

That shift of focus in turn raises another interesting point of historical analysis. In the late 1940s—indeed, for many years thereafter—the traditional corpus of writings on geopolitics associated with the theses of Mackinder, Mahan, Spykman, and others had been substantially discredited as a result of the geopolitical quackeries of Haushofer and the so-called "Munich school."[10] More importantly, the sudden submergence of political geography as one of the core sub-disciplines of national security was reinforced by assumptions that space, size, and distance would soon be transcended by technology; that indeed was the burden of the prominent contemporary critique of geopolitics by Harold and Margaret Sprout.[11] The United States, after all, was the world's number one power, and it was not a heartland power.[12] Long-range weaponry had seemingly annihilated distance and, with it, age-old nostrums about the difficulties in projecting power over distance.[13] In line with these trends, there was talk about the growing permeability of nation-states' borders. Kennan and others came naturally to focus on industrial warmaking areas as the foci of big power rivalry.

The downgrading of traditional geopolitics, along with concerns about industrial core areas, seems also to have implied a concomitant downgrading of competition for raw materials, another longstanding concern of traditional geopolitics. The near-autarchic resource base of the Soviet heartland perhaps gave rise to assumptions that the USSR would act less forcefully than Germany or Japan to acquire additional mineral resources, and it may further have been assumed that Western colonialism would endure for sometime, or, at any rate, that what would later become the Third World lay well behind the front lines of the containment ring. What later would be a staple concern of analysts of Soviet conventional power projection did not loom large in the writings of 'X.'

If communist ideology and the locales of sinews of war seem from the vantage point of 1985 to be overplayed by Kennan, the advocacy of symmetrical response to Soviet expansionism does not. Recent arguments over horizontal escalation and a new US maritime strategy have merely highlighted continuing uncertainties over the relative advantages of symmetrical and asymmetrical responses, follow-ons to the historical ebb and flow so ably portrayed by Gaddis.

X's Obscure Alter Ego: A Geopolitical Counterpoint

Curiously, while Kennan's 'X' article remains highly visible today—indeed, has provided a point of departure for so much else, not least the endless arguments revolving about Cold War revisionism—another important piece which preceded it by only six months within the same *Foreign Affairs* volume has long since sunk into obscurity. "U.S. Strategic Bases and Collective Security" was written by Hans Weigert, already well known as an important analyst of traditional geopolitics.[14]

Weigert was conscious of the disadvantage under which the United States had labored at the outset of World War II because of the absence of a significant forward basing network, and because of the long-held if seldom articulated doctrine of "hemispheric defense."[15] He was also aware that the United States faced major decisions (and some major political battles with wartime allies like Brazil, Australia, Ecuador, Portugal, Denmark, and Iceland) about how far it might contract the elaborate basing system acquired during World War II. The immediate impetus to his article was the debate over disposition of the former Japanese-mandated Pacific islands—the Marshalls, Carolines, and Marianas. But its focus was also much broader, constituting a global *tour d'horizon* which raised serious questions about the proper scope of America's postwar collective security structure.[16]

Weigert discussed a forward extension of the US basing system from a Soviet perspective as well. In the process, he raised the (polemical) arguments over the relative offensive and defensive motives of Soviet foreign policy which later formed the basis of arguments between traditionalist and revisionist interpretations of the Cold War:

What we regard as bases intended for defense against attack by hostile Powers might, and surely will, be considered by other Powers, e.g. the Soviet Union, as evidence
of a new American belief in Manifest Destiny. In other
words, wherever we maintain a strategic base for defense
purposes, we shall be suspected of harboring aggressive
intentions. (Indeed, some early sponsors of the plan to
erect an American security system upon a strong chain of
fortified bases gave justification for this suspicion by explaining that the purpose was to offset the future power of
the Soviet Union and of China.) A Russian admiral in a
Pravda article of September 12, 1946, described the
United States naval policy as clearly offensive in character. He declared that our far-flung peacetime naval bases
cannot be intended for the defense of the American continent, since some of them are situated at the close approaches to the Asiatic continent (Okinawa) and of Europe
(Iceland and Greenland). In the same vein, on September 13, 1946, the Russian historian Eugene Tarlé attacked
Admiral Halsey's statement that henceforth American foreign policy must be conducted from "aggressive positions." Vice versa, we suspect the Russians of offensive
intentions when they establish advanced bases.[17]

Weigert's work demonstrated that, as early as 1946, some
perceived that the evolving Cold War struggle would take on the
character of a traditional geopolitical contest for access and position, whatever its ideological content. Weigert's view followed the traditional imagery of heartland versus rimland
(continental landpower versus Anglo-Saxon seapower), fundamental images shared by Mackinder and Mahan in spite of their
conflicting views about what would prevail and why.[18] And, of
course, Weigert recognized the fundamentally different requirements of the superpowers for forward access, resulting from
their respective geographic positions:

We would be dangerously mistaken if in analyzing the
strategic bases of Soviet Russia we limited ourselves to a
discussion of the Kuriles, or of her bases in Finland, or of
Kalinograd (the former Konigsberg), or to the appraisal of

her actual or possible demands for bases in the Dardanelles, in Eritrea and Tripolitania, or on Spitsbergen. To
complete the picture of the strategic bases of the Soviet
Union we must include Germany east of the Oder-Neisse
frontier, as well as northern Korea. We must also include
the entire belt of nations within the Soviet sphere of influence, both in Europe and Asia. To fail to perceive the full
meaning of the term "strategic base" is to misjudge completely the relative power positions of the United States
and the Soviet Union. If one should limit one's appraisal
of bases to those which come under the classification of islands or ports, and compare the strongholds of this nature
maintained by the United States with those under the Soviet flag, one would reach the erroneous conclusion that
the Soviet Union has shown considerably more restraint in
establishing bases than has the United States. Henry
Wallace seems to fall a victim of this generous but dangerous error when, in his letter of July 23, 1946, to President
Truman, he claimed that "up to now, despite all our out-
cries against it, their [the Russians'] efforts to develop a
security zone in eastern Europe and in the Middle East are
small change from the point of view of military power as
compared with our air bases in Greenland, Okinawa, and
many other places thousands of miles from our shores."
The Soviet Union, in fact, found ample compensation for
the lack of opportunities overseas by establishing bases in
lands directly adjacent to hers, either by military occupation or by the collaboration of friendly governments in her
spheres of interest.[19]

Weigert anticipated the Soviets' later outward thrust by
referring to "possible demands for bases in the Dardanelles, in
Eritrea and Tripolitania, or on Spitsbergen." That echoes
Mackinder's earlier fears about combined landpower and
seapower emanating from the Eurasian heartland, a view which
sees these two aspects of military power as not necessarily mutually exclusive.[20] Not so easily anticipated from the vantage
point of 1946 were the coming political and economic costs of
military access.

But the development by the USSR of even the beginnings of longer-range conventional power projection capability would take at least a decade. As long as Soviet naval and air transport capability remained limited, it would be suitable for defensive purposes only. But by the late 1950s, several telescoped developments were to signal a far more ominous and determined outward thrust of Soviet conventional power. The accelerated pace of Third World decolonialization provided numerous opportunities. Relaxation, after Stalin's death, of Soviet inhibitions about forming security ties with radical/anti-Western (but formally noncommunist) regimes made it much easier to find and take advantage of such opportunities. And the expanding Soviet arms production base made possible large-scale arms deals such as those with Egypt and Syria in 1955, a precursor of the determined use of arms-for-basing which was to become the hallmark of Soviet access and alignment politics. The stage was set.

Elements of Conventional Power Projections

Soviet conventional power projection capabilities actually subsume several related capabilities and activities, as well as a complex mix of relatively objective and subjective conditions:

- acquisition of external bases or facilities: naval, air, communications, and intelligence;

- development of a more significant navy and long-range air transport capability;

- establishment—in connection with the above—of a "presence" in various areas of the world, as measured by "ship-days" in various ocean areas and by the volume of port visits to numerous hosts of varying political affinity;

- coercive diplomacy: threats, demonstrations, etc., involving both overt acts and a more subjective deterrent effect not easily measured by events data analysis;

- direct military interventions, along a spectrum of involvement;

- indirect military interventions, e.g., use of surrogate forces, arms resupply operations;

- base denial activities, changing the correlation of forces relevant to power projection by subtracting from the foes' access; and

- arms transfers, particularly as they feed into surrogate or other activities acting in lieu of actual Soviet military deployments: the Soviet equivalent of a "Nixon Doctrine."

These large subjects are not discrete, but are interrelated in complex webs of reciprocal causation. For example, the expansion of the Soviet global basing system may be said to have created pressures and rationales for expansion of naval and air forces; in reverse, the latter may be said to have driven the quest for the former. Soviet access to facilities may have helped enable interventions in Angola and Ethiopia; interventions and arms resupply operations helped to open up enhanced access to facilities in Ethiopia, Vietnam, and Syria. Overall, the various components of Soviet conventional power projection capability seem to have advanced together, with successes in one area advancing the prospects in others.

This conclusion is implied in a typology provided by Hosmer and Wolfe in a recent book on Soviet expansionism in the Third World.[21] Under "continuation of already established activities" and in projecting "possible patterns of future Soviet behavior," they list arms transfers, acquisition of additional basing and overflight arrangements, support of selected national liberation movements, support of new "progressive" regimes produced by internal coups and uprisings, low-risk probes by Third World clients, actions to forestall the reorientation of regimes closely tied to Moscow, and protection of clients threatened with catastrophic defeat. Others might prefer to view basing access and some broader concept of combined access or influence as dependent variables in relation to the rest, cumulating to a bottom line of overall military power.

It is worth emphasizing that *neither* the United States nor the USSR possessed a significant external basing system before World War II. External basing was then largely a correlate of colonial empires; hence, Britain and then France had the most extensive oversea access.[22] Further, there was then nothing really equivalent to long-term, durable, ideologically based alliances such as NATO and the Warsaw Pact.[23] Though less so than in the nineteenth century, the international system was characterized by multipolarity, an absence of ideological loci of conflict, limited numbers of sovereignties, and rapidly shifting alliances. That combination tended to limit the extent of basing access extended to some sovereign nations by others.

The USSR had virtually no external basing access before 1945—some apparent forward basing of aircraft in Czechoslovakia before 1938 may have been one exception—and the USSR was a major importer of arms technology rather than an arms supplier during that period.[24] The United States, meanwhile, had some basing assets in the Pacific—the Philippines, Guam, Wake, Hawaii, and American Samoa—as well as the Panama Canal Zone plus considerable access for ship port visits around the Caribbean, even then deemed an "American lake."[25] Only in 1940, as part of the Lend-Lease agreement with the United Kingdom, did the United States establish a more forward presence in the Atlantic, stretching from Labrador to Guyana via Newfoundland, Bermuda, the Bahamas, Antigua, and Trinidad. Even that was more an extension of the hemispheric defense perimeter than a global basing system concomitant to the role of world power.

After 1945, the colonial empires gradually withered, subtracting numerous basing assets from the Western orbit. The United States, however, established an elaborate system of access in connection with NATO, CENTO, SEATO, ANZUS, and numerous bilateral alliances.[26] But many of those alliances later withered in one degree or another, leaving the United States in a global competition for access with the USSR, a competition based on a mix of security assistance and the cement of political ideology.

Expanded Soviet Access to Basing Facilities

The Soviets' gradual expansion of access to external and noncontiguous basing facilities has been central to their building of conventional force projection capability. They started from near zero in this respect, with the minor exceptions of temporary naval bases in Porkkala in Finland and Port Arthur in China. Even up to the early 1960s, the sole significant exception was submarine basing in Albania from 1958 to 1961, preceding the Sino-Soviet split. Throughout the first two decades of the Cold War, the USSR was, thus, at a great disadvantage regarding all the related elements of conventional force projection. Rather, its defense doctrine stressed a massive land army, air defense, and a homebound coastal navy abetted by submarines and land-based naval aircraft. There was little prospect then of long-range projection of power. To the extent there was a "basing strategy," it was for the most part a base denial effort directed against the West's assets through the varied mechanisms of propaganda and the fomenting of internal, anticolonial opposition to Western basing rights. Soviet propaganda during this period stridently advocated "the elimination of all foreign bases," a logical strategy for a nation which possessed none.[27]

But the gradual Soviet acquisition of basing access became one element of a changing global correlation of forces after the Cuban missile crisis. Further, Soviet acquisition of access in various regions of the world—Southeast Asia, North Africa, the Caribbean, West Africa—might be said to have altered somewhat the perceptual basis for the heartland-rimland imagery which has underpinned the containment policy. During the two decades after 1960, the old containment rim was leapfrogged in numerous places by Soviet access and other related criteria.[28] The result had to be a different geopolitical imagery, featuring a more globally dispersed game-board on which the superpowers' rivalry is played out.

The beginnings of the Soviet acquisition of external bases can be seen in the arms transfer relationships inaugurated in the late 1950s and early 1960s. Arms deals with Egypt and Syria in 1955 were the opening wedges, followed by the initiation of other client relationships with North Yemen (1957), Indonesia (1958), Guinea (1959), India (1961), and indirectly with the Algerian rebels in the late 1950s. Shortly thereafter, others were added to the list: Iraq, North Vietnam, Ghana, Sudan, Somalia, Tanzania, and Mali. But the absence of significant blue-water naval capability and of adequate long-range air transport tended to modify the Soviets' drive for facilities from 1955 to 1965. During this period, new Soviet oversea arms and aid recipients did not in most cases provide the Soviets facilities, though political relationships were established which later would allow the Soviets to cash in their chips for military access as growing naval and air capabilities required it.

The major expansion of Soviet basing facilities began around 1964–65, just a couple of years after the Cuban missile crisis. Under Admiral Gorshkov's aegis, the USSR had begun to move in earnest toward global naval capability, so as to offset the local crisis advantage provided by American sea control. The early expansion of basing access was concentrated in the Mediterranean, Caribbean, and Indian Ocean areas, and it was paralleled by rapidly escalating levels of port visits and regional presence.

Still, in this early phase of Soviet naval expansion, fleet support was provided by a mix of shore facilities, auxiliaries, and merchant fleets. Relative to the United States, the Soviet Union relied heavily on "floating bases" in lieu of permanent shore facilities. There was, concomitantly, heavy reliance on off-shore anchorages and in-port use of auxiliaries like repair ships, tenders, and tugs, which provided a high degree of security and self-reliance but involved some serious problems.

Major repairs were difficult to accomplish; there was limited storage for spare parts, material, and food; aerial resupply from Soviet home bases was difficult; and anchorages were subject to inclement weather. For all of these reasons, Soviet naval deployments in the Mediterranean were limited up to the 1967 Middle East war, with ships stationed there for only a couple of months at a time and heavily dependent on auxiliaries shuttling back and forth from the Black Sea with fuel, water, and other consumables.[29] But after 1967 there was significant change: longer deployments and increasing numbers of ships, greater logistical requirements, and much greater access to foreign ports—in Egypt, Syria, Yugoslavia, and North Africa.

Between 1967 and 1972 (peaking in the latter year), the Soviet navy had regular access in Egypt to Alexandria, Port Said, and Mersa Matruh, as well as extensive access to airfields for antisubmarine warfare (ASW), reconnaissance, and fighter aircraft. That access was curtailed in 1972 and virtually ended in 1976, but partially replaced after 1973 by much greater access to Syrian naval and air facilities. Then, too, the Soviet navy was also granted access to several Yugoslav ports, not only for routine port visits but also for maintenance and repairs. Algeria came to allow similar access (including minor repairs for submarines); its airfields were important to the Soviet staging of arms to Angola in the mid-1970s, for supplying Guinea, and for some transits en route to Cuba. Libya, too, provided various types of access beginning around 1975. All in all, by the mid-1970s the Soviets had vastly increased their capacity to project power into and around the Mediterranean. They had also acquired access to numerous facilities in that area useful for staging personnel and materiel further south in Africa.

In the Indian Ocean area, Soviet basing assets were developed a bit later, the major expansion occurring between 1968 and 1974. (Up to the 1973 Middle East war, the closure of the Suez Canal precluded movement of ships to the Indian Ocean from the Black Sea, so Soviet naval deployments had to come all the way from the Siberian naval bases of the Soviet Pacific

Fleet.) But, during this period, in line with a considerable increase in Soviet deployments in the Indian Ocean, access of
greater or lesser degree was achieved or reinforced in Somalia,
Iraq, South Yemen, India, Mauritius, Ethiopia, and Mozambique. Somalia was a particularly critical hub of Soviet air and
naval access between 1972 and 1977. Its port at Berbera was
used for repairs, fueling, crew rest, communications, and storage of naval missiles, its air bases for Soviet reconnaissance and
ASW flights. South Yemen, too, acquired considerable importance, among other things, for the staging of materiel to
Mozambique and to Ethiopia during its war with Somalia.

Though Soviet base expansion was concentrated from 1964
to 1977 in the Mediterranean and Indian Ocean areas, there
were also the beginnings of expansion in other regions. Cuba,
of course, had become a major Soviet base host beginning in the
early 1960s, crucial to a Soviet presence in the Caribbean area
near the United States. In Southeast Asia, the Soviets acquired
some access to Vietnamese facilities in the mid-1970s, after the
fall of Saigon to Hanoi.

In West Africa, Guinea—one of the earliest Soviet arms
client states in Africa—became a significant host for Soviet facilities in the 1960s, allowing the USSR to establish a continuous small naval patrol off the Guinean coast. This Soviet West
Africa patrol, later shifted to Angola, consisted usually of an
amphibious ship and oiler, anchored off Conakry, a port used
for crew rest, minor repairs, and replenishment. The Soviets
also had use of Guinean airfields for reconnaissance and ASW
flights and for staging arms southward to Angola.

All during the 1960s—a period in which Soviet global
basing access remained limited relative to the United States—
the Soviets compensated by making extensive use of surrogates.
Merchant ships and fighting vessels performed functions like
communications relay and satellite tracking in lieu of shore
bases, and the Soviet navy made extensive use of off-shore anchorages or mooring buoys in the Mediterranean, Indian Ocean,

and western Pacific. In the Mediterranean, for instance, these anchorages were located at Kithira (south of Greece), Hammamet (off the Tunisian Coast), Crete East, the Alboran Basin (east of Gibraltar), and off the Chella Bank.[30] There were numerous other secondary anchorages. These interim measures demonstrate the Soviet capacity for using second-best solutions to compensate for lack of basing access.

Today the Soviets have a near-global system of air, naval, and technical facilities, usable over a range of military power projection functions. That system is by no means as elaborate as that availed the United States, but it does not need to be. The Soviets' large land mass and central, Eurasian position, and their use of ships in lieu of what might more efficiently be performed on land, act as compensating factors. And the Soviets' continuing quest for access is underpinned by a very determined, purposeful effort to sell arms to and otherwise support clients and friends in a manner wholly bereft of concern for arms control, human rights, or other idealistic diversions.

In the Pacific, and in consonance with the major, ongoing buildup of Soviet seapower, the primary basing hub is in Vietnam, where the Soviets inherited former US facilities. Vietnam has received over $5 billion in Soviet arms aid since 1978, much of it in connection with Soviet support during and after the PRC-Vietnam conflict.[31] According to *Soviet Military Power,* the USSR has "transformed Cam Ranh Bay into the largest Soviet naval forward deployment base outside the Warsaw Pact."[32] That entails forward deployment of 25–30 ships to the South China Sea, including surface combatants, attack and cruise-missile submarines, and naval auxiliary ships. It also involves a large contingent of reconnaissance and combat aircraft which extend the Soviet reach over Southeast Asia and well into the western Pacific: 8 Bears and 16 Badgers (10 with strike capability) and a squadron of MiG–23 Floggers.

Elsewhere in the Pacific–Southeast Asia area, one may point to reported Soviet naval access to a Kampuchean facility at Ream, extending the Soviet navy's access a bit westward. And in the southwest Pacific, where numerous new sovereign island nations present tempting opportunities (analogous to the Caribbean), the USSR has been reported seeking access for its fishing vessels in places like Tonga, Kiribati, and Vanuatu, presumably as wedges for more overt military activities later on,[33] such as a Soviet air staging base.

In South Asia, the main focus of Soviet base acquisition has been in Afghanistan, in connection with the ongoing war and occupation. The USSR has a force of some 115,000 troops in Afghanistan, itself an aspect of forward conventional power projection which threatens Pakistan and Iran. In addition, the Soviets now have access to several Afghan air bases—Kabul, Kandahar, Bagrame, and Shindand—which put Backfires and other aircraft in range of critical areas around the Persian Gulf, including the Straits of Hormuz.[34]

The Soviet navy reportedly has been given occasional port visit access at several Indian bases: Bombay, Cochin, Vishakhapatnam, and Port Blair in the Andaman Islands. But thus far, the massive long-term Soviet arms supplies to New Delhi—most recently involving MiG–29s, Il–76 transports, and T–72 tanks—has not resulted in permanent basing rights. Soviet aspirations for a naval facility in Pakistan's Baluchistan might come into focus if Pakistan's political situation should change either via realignment or further dismemberment.[35]

Further west along the Indian Ocean littoral, the USSR has acquired important basing assets in the crucial area—referred to by some as an "arc of crisis"—spanning Southwest Asia and the Horn of Africa. This has involved some complex shifting of alignments in recent years. Somalia, North Yemen, and Iraq, along with South Yemen, used to provide access to Moscow, but today Ethiopia has replaced Somalia, while Soviet ties with North Yemen and Iraq have weakened somewhat as these nations have become more pro-Western. Use of Iraqi naval facilities has, at any rate, been precluded since 1980 by the Iran-Iraq war.

South Yemen has been a critical focus of Moscow's attention since the Soviets' expulsion from Somalia in 1977. Underpinned by a massive assistance program and the presence of some 1,000 Soviet, Eastern European, and Cuban advisers, South Yemen has provided the USSR nearly unlimited access.[36] That access has involved use of Aden's port for berthing and anchoring and as a transshipment point for POL and arms en route to Africa. Soviet Il–38 May naval reconnaissance aircraft fly out of Aden and another air base at Al-Anad, and there is also an important high frequency (HF) communications facility at Bir Fuqum.

Important access to naval and air facilities in Ethiopia, which began during the Horn War of 1977–78, has cost Moscow $3–4 billion of military assistance. A key naval base at the Dahlak Archipelago in the Red Sea provides a maintenance and supply depot, including a large floating drydock, floating piers, helipads, fuel and water storage, a submarine tender, and other repair ships.[37] There are regular calls by Soviet guided-missile cruisers, and nuclear-powered submarines operating in the Indian Ocean and Red Sea call regularly at the base. Earlier, Il–38 May antisubmarine warfare (ASW) and maritime reconnaissance aircraft operated out of an airfield at Asmara.

Further south, the USSR has other points of access in sub-Saharan Africa, on both its east and west coasts. Mozambique, Angola, and Guinea provide access, and at times several other African countries have been forthcoming. Mozambique, which in recent years has flirted with closer ties to the West, has provided some access for the Soviet navy at its ports of Nacala and Maputo. In Guinea, the USSR uses Conakry harbor routinely as a facility for its West African patrol. Although access for Tu–95 reconnaissance aircraft was terminated by Sekou Touré in 1977, Conakry airport is still used for staging military transport aircraft. Luanda, in Angola, has now become the most important port for the Soviets' West African naval units. There is a large floating drydock there, and the airfield at Luanda hosts Tu–95 reconnaissance aircraft, which deploy in pairs three or four times a year.[38]

Elsewhere in this region, the USSR has achieved some access to the Seychelles. Transport aircraft stop there en route to southern Africa, and regular access for naval units is being sought. In the past, arms resupply operations to Angola were eased by access to air staging bases in Guinea-Bissau, Mali, and the Congo, among others.[39] Also, Equatorial Guinea, before the revolution overthrowing the Nguema regime, apparently hosted a Soviet communications or intelligence base.[40] Madagascar is reported occasionally to provide access for Soviet ships, as do Cape Verde and Benin. Uganda under Amin may have provided a technical facility, perhaps a space-tracking station.

In the Mediterranean area, Egypt's defection from Soviet tutelage has left Syria, Libya, and Algeria as the most important providers of access to Moscow's forces. Among these, Syria's role is foremost.

The USSR has some 4,000 military advisers in Syria, many in air defense roles; after the 1982 defeat of the Syrian air force by Israel, the Soviets themselves manned SAM–5 Gammon missiles and other command, control, and communications (C^3) and electronic warfare equipment. Soviet advisers are involved in all aspects of Syrian defense activities, and the Soviet navy has access to the port of Tartus and air deployment rights at Tiyas airfield (Il–38's). Tartus is used for submarine maintenance; a sub tender, yard oiler, and water tender are stationed there.

The Soviets have limited, though increasing, military access to Libyan ports and airfields. There have been some port visits and Il–38 May ASW aircraft deployments since 1981. Algeria, now perhaps shifting toward a more pro-West orientation, has in the past reportedly offered transit rights for Soviet aircraft and also minor maintenance for Soviet subs at Annaba.[41]

Finally, Soviet military access in Latin America involves primarily Cuba, but to a lesser degree also Peru and Nicaragua. Cuba has, of course, received massive Soviet economic aid and subsidies (now at the level of about $4 billion a year), military aid ($3 billion in equipment from 1981 to 1984 alone), and some 15,000 military and civilian advisers and technicians. In return, the Soviets have access to naval facilities (Havana, Mariel, Cienfuegos) which allows them to maintain a naval presence in the Caribbean. The USSR also deploys Tu–94/Bear D and Tu–142/Bear F ASW and naval reconnaissance aircraft in Cuba and has, at a complex at Lourdes, several sites devoted to signals intelligence (SIGINT) and communications.[42]

Soviet ships have made some calls to Nicaragua's ports, and new airfields being built there will be able to accommodate any Soviet aircraft. In Peru, the USSR has gained access for logistics support and maintenance for their nearly 200 fishing vessels operating off the coast of South America. Aeroflot uses Lima as a primary hub for rotating merchant seamen and fishermen, whose vessels often have crucial military roles involving intelligence, communications, and space-tracking.

External access—as it relates to conventional power projection—involves not only use of facilities, but also use of overhead airspace. Indeed, the matter of overflight rights has become a very important component of modern security diplomacy, necessary for air staging of war materiel and also—in a less time-urgent manner—for routine movements of cargo and combat aircraft.[43] Its importance derives from present-day tendencies toward "closure" of both the seas and overhead air space, as the newer nations increasingly attempt to dilute the superpowers' traditional prerogatives and freedom of movement.

Permissions for overflights by military aircraft are relatively routine among friends, at least under ordinary circumstances; however, US problems with European allies during the

1973 Middle East war demonstrated the importance of political cross-pressures which may arise during crises. Conditions for overflights by neutrals or political opponents may be far more stringent. Hence, both superpowers must pay attention to various air corridors throughout the world, and their availability in turn depends on networks of allies and friends.

The importance to the USSR of overflights has been repeatedly demonstrated during recent years. Turkey and Yugoslavia allowed Soviet overflight of the arms resupply for Egypt and Syria in 1973. Several West African states apparently permitted Soviet overflights en route to Angola during the intense phase of the conflict there in the mid-1970s.[44] Iraq and India have been mentioned as providers of overflight rights for the Soviet resupply of Vietnam in its war with the PRC in 1979. And, in more difficult circumstances, the Soviets may have overflown several unwilling nations in their resupply operation on behalf of Ethiopia in 1977–78: Pakistani, Iraqi, Sudanese, and perhaps Egyptian airspace may all have been violated. And, of course, Soviet client relationships throughout the world may help preclude US overflight rights for both routine and crisis operations.

The Buildup in Soviet Forces: Expanding
Forward Power Projection Capability

Parallel to the Soviet drive for access in various regions of the world has been the buildup of Soviet forces most germane to conventional power projection. That involves, centrally, naval forces (including their auxiliaries in the merchant marine and fishing fleets), long-range air transport capability, some forward-based combat aircraft and missiles, and limited deployments of Soviet combat troops and advisers, as well as those of surrogates.

The Soviet navy now fields some 289 surface combatants, including four *Kiev*-class carriers, two *Moskva*-class ASW helicopter carriers, some 39 cruisers (of which two are nuclear), 45 guided-missile destroyers, 23 gun destroyers, 32 guided-missile frigates, and 152 gun frigates. In addition, there are some 700 minor surface combatants: guided-missile corvettes, vast numbers of missile patrol boats, minesweepers and minelayers, 79 amphibious ships and 109 additional amphibious craft, and 305 principal auxiliary ships (such as replenishment, tanker, missile support, supply, cargo, submarine tender, repair, hospital, submarine rescue, salvage/rescue, and training ships). There are also some 60 intelligence collection vessels (AGI), 134 naval research vessels, and 350 civilian oceanographic, fishery, space-associated, and hydrographic research vessels. The Soviet submarine force is equally formidable. Aside from 63 SSBNs and 14 SSBs, there are some 213 attack submarines, of which 72 are nuclear-powered, and 66 cruise-missile submarines, 49 of which are nuclear (SSGNs).

The bulk of the naval forces are divided into an Arctic Command comprising the Northern Fleet, an Atlantic Command comprising the Baltic and Black Sea Fleets and the Mediterranean Eskadra, and the Pacific Fleet. The Arctic Command deploys 42 SSB/BNs, 138 other subs, 80 major and 120 minor surface combatants, 15 principal combatants, 22 amphibious ships, and 35 auxiliaries. The Black Sea Fleet fields 30 subs, 78 principal and 160 minor surface combatants, 21 amphibious ships, and 53 auxiliaries. The Pacific Fleet, with its main bases at Vladivostok, Petropavlovsk, and Sovetskaya Gavan, deploys 31 SSB/BNs, 88 other subs, 85 principal and 200 minor surface combatants, 19 amphibious ships, and 98 auxiliaries.

These imposing numbers can, of course, be interpreted for conventional force projection only in various hypothetical contexts. One might, of course, be talking about conventional operations against a Third World state or the PRC without direct US involvement. Or one might be talking about various "conventional" scenarios pitting US against Soviet naval forces; a protracted "conventional phase" escalating toward nuclear war is also a possibility.[45] But, then, one may be talking about coercive actions short of actual combat, involving a form of "deterrence" rather than warfighting. Suffice it to say that the Soviet navy is large and growing, and that its presence does raise doubts about US global sea control. Short of all-out war, maritime supremacy does seem less than indivisible.

Taking a narrow interpretation of the Soviet navy's conventional force projection capability—one measured against either major or minor powers—several recent developments are worth noting. The Soviets are moving, gradually, toward development of large carriers. A 65,000-ton carrier is under construction, along with new fixed-wing aircraft capable of carrier deployment. This hardware will eventually allow the Soviets to extend their operations beyond the umbrella of land-based aviation, improving their distant area power projection capabilities.

The Soviets are also moving ahead with capabilities for amphibious warfare, a domain long dominated by the United States. They now have 16,000 naval infantry forces—7,000 with the Pacific Fleet and 3,000 with each western fleet. These units are highly mechanized, equipped with tracked and wheeled amphibious vehicles including PT–76 tanks and BTR–60 APCs. Meanwhile, the USSR now has two *Ivan Rogov*–class amphibious assault vessels, and the Soviet navy is also the world's largest operator of military air cushion vehicles. These amphibious units are now deployed in the Pacific and Indian Oceans, in the Mediterranean Sea, and off West Africa, and have already been involved for coercive purposes in some crises: for instance, bolstering a friendly regime in the Seychelles.[46]

In each fleet area, the USSR also has some Spetsnaz forces, trained to conduct a variety of sensitive missions including reconnaissance, sabotage, and assassination. These forces could be used in a conventional conflict against a wide spectrum of targets: ship and submarine bases, airfields, C^3 and intelligence facilities, ports, harbors, or radar and SOSUS (sound surveillance system) sites. A brigade-size unit of Spetsnaz forces is assigned to each of the four Soviet fleets.

The maritime capabilities of the USSR cannot, of course, be measured solely by what is formally defined as part of the Soviet navy. Additionally, there are the Soviet merchant, fishing, and research fleets, each of which often has purposes less benign than those advertised.

As pointed out by *Soviet Military Power*, the Soviet Merchant Marine now deploys some 1,700 ships, many of which can be used for military logistics in crisis or war.

> Merchant ships produced over the last two decades increasingly have been constructed to military standards, incorporating such key features as chemical-biological-radiological (CBR) protection, increased endurance and service speeds, improved capability in handling gear and self-servicing features, advanced communications, navigation and electronics, including identification-friend-or-foe (IFF) systems—systems restricted to naval ships in the West. . . .
>
> The operations of the Merchant Marine are closely coordinated with naval requirements from the Moscow level down to the smallest port facility. On a regular basis, a significant amount of logistic support required by the Soviet Navy in peacetime, especially in distant areas, is provided by merchantmen. This flexibility allows Soviet merchant ships to obtain supplies for naval use in ports where warship visits might be denied. In a crisis, the highly organized, centrally controlled merchant fleet can provide suitable military support quickly and effectively, particularly for amphibious operations, troop movements, and arms shipments.[47]

The Soviet fishing fleet has an equally formidable military potential. That fleet has been reported at around 4,000–5,000 vessels or some 60 percent of the world's fishing fleet tonnage, though responsible for a much smaller percentage of the annual fishing catch.[48] Many of these large trawlers are virtual adjuncts of the Soviet navy, carrying sophisticated intelligence-gathering gear, radars, ASW equipment, and so forth. And because of their ostensibly peaceful purposes, they are often able to go where overt military access might be denied (Spain's Canary Islands have been one example). In other cases, the Soviets have apparently requested such access as the opening wedge for later grants of naval access; the recent efforts among the new nations of the southwest Pacific have been good illustrations.

The Soviet fishing fleet, believed coordinated by a centralized command and control system, conducts near-global operations. In the Atlantic, it has concentrated in the North Sea, in the English Channel, in the Great Sole Bank, and off the Shetland Islands; off the United States and Canada in the Grand, Sable Island, and Georges Banks. Other more recent favorite "fishing" grounds have been off the west coast of Africa near Walvis Bay, the Gulf of Guinea, the Cape Verde area, and the Canary Islands. In the South Atlantic, Soviet fishing boats prowl near the Falkland Islands and South Georgia,[49] while whaling fleets operate off Antarctica. In the Indian Ocean, the Soviets exploit fisheries near Farquhar Island, near the Seychelles and Mauritius, near Kerguelen Island, in the Mozambique Channel, and off the Australian North West Cape. In the Pacific, fishing operations used to be concentrated in the Bering Sea and off the US West Coast, but are now diminished.

Concomitant to the Soviets' far larger navy has been the large-scale enhancement of their long-range air transport capability, embodied in the component called VTA. That, in turn, has allowed for large-scale arms resupply operations: to Egypt, Angola, Ethiopia, and Vietnam as primary recent examples. It also provides the basis for large-scale insertion of Soviet forces, as exemplified by the early phases of the Afghanistan war.

VTA has some 750 aircraft—variously, the An–2, –8, –12, –24, and –26, the Il–14, the Il–76, and the An–22. The latter two aircraft, of which the USSR has some 240, are the largest and closest to their American counterparts in capability—the

An–22's payload and range are greater than those of the US C–141B, though still smaller than those of the C–5A/B. But the Soviets also have under development a newer transport, the An–400 Condor, whose capabilities will rival those of the C–5.[50] And, not to be forgotten, some 1,300 medium- and long-range passenger aircraft of the civilian Aeroflot fleet and the 1,250 transports of other services could augment a VTA airlift.

The Soviet army now has seven airborne divisions and, additionally, some 16 brigades and three regiments of Spetsnaz forces. In conjunction with the above-noted airlift capacity, that translates into at least the potential for long-range power projection. The mobilization of Soviet airborne divisions—and the accompanying warnings—toward the close of the 1973 Middle East war showed how such instruments might be used for coercive purposes and might even be read as harbingers of later possibilities.

Of course, it must be stressed that the "facts" of expanding Soviet power projection capability can only obtain real meaning in the perspective of rival US capabilities. That perspective, in turn, presents a host of analytical problems which can here only be mentioned, for instance, the overarching but always speculative question, projection to where and under what circumstances? Rival projections to the Persian Gulf are one thing, to Nicaragua another. But despite the contraction of the US basing structure, American capabilities remain unsurpassed according to the several most commonly used measurements: steaming days in various areas, ship port visits, ratios of combatants to auxiliaries, exercise days in various oceans, and so forth. For most purposes and with regard to most places, the USSR remains unmistakably the second superpower. However, given its proximity to Soviet Central Asia, the balance of projected power at the Persian Gulf remains ambiguous and troubling.

Presence

One often-used measure of growing Soviet conventional force projection capability is that of degrees of "presence" achieved, as objectively measured by port visits in various locales or fleet ship-days in various oceans or seas. Traditionally, such efforts to "show the flag"[51] represent one measure of Soviet capability to sustain forces out of area. And even in the absence of actual or threatened combat, these data do convey something about deterrence, latent coercive power, and regional influence. In a way, they may be said to measure growing confidence, status, or even boldness, particularly as such deployments may become routine over time. One way or the other, they reflect an obvious desire on the part of the USSR to be accepted as a fully equal superpower with global interests and responsibilities.

Though very recent data of this sort are not easily available, pre-1980 data is provided by Bruce Watson and by a team at the Center for Naval Analyses.[52] Both show an ineluctable trend of growing Soviet maritime presence from the 1960s through the 1980s in all three major oceans and the Mediterranean.

Watson provides the data shown in table 1 for "out of area" ship-days by geographical area from 1956 to 1980, beginning near the time of the Suez war and shortly after the Soviet arms deals with Egypt and Syria which kicked off the major burst of Soviet expansion in the Third World.

Several points may be imputed, cautiously, from these data. First, although there was an enormous expansion of the Soviets' global naval presence over the 25-odd years surveyed, most of that expansion came in the period before 1973. After that year, there was a leveling off, and the Soviet presence in the Mediterranean actually declined a bit, a result no doubt of the severing of security ties with Egypt. Not surprisingly, the one area of some post-1973 expansion has been the Pacific, related undoubtedly to the growing Soviet presence in Vietnam as well as to the growth of the Soviet Pacific Fleet. Noteworthy,

Table 1. Out-of-Area Ship-Days—Distribution by Geographical
Area, 1956–1980[a]

Year	Mediterranean Sea	Atlantic Ocean	Indian Ocean	Pacific Ocean	Caribbean Sea	Total
1956	100	500	0	200	0	800
1957	600	1,500	0	200	0	2,300
1958	1,000	1,300	0	900	0	3,200
1959	4,000	2,100	0	900	0	7,000
1960	5,600	1,600	200	400	0	7,800
1961	2,300	2,200	0	700	0	5,200
1962	800	4,300	100	1,400	0	6,600
1963	600	3,600	100	1,800	0	6,100
1964	1,800	5,300	0	2,000	0	9,100
1965	3,700	5,400	0	2,500	0	11,600
1966	5,400	5,500	0	2,800	0	13,700
1967	8,800	5,800	200	3,600	0	18,400
1968	11,700	5,900	1,200	4,200	0	23,000
1969	15,400	9,600	4,100	5,900	300	35,300
1970	17,400	13,600	4,900	7,100	700	43,700
1971	18,700	14,800	4,000	6,200	700	44,400
1972	17,700	14,500	8,900	5,900	1,900	48,900
1973	20,600	13,000	8,900	6,300	1,400	50,200
1974	20,200	13,900	10,500	7,400	1,200	53,200
1975	20,000	13,200	7,100	6,800	1,100	48,200
1976	18,600	14,000	7,300	6,500	1,000	47,400
1977	16,300	15,800	6,700	7,500	1,200	47,500
1978	16,600	16,100	8,500	6,900	1,300	49,400
1979	16,600	16,900	7,600	10,400	1,100	52,600
1980	16,600	16,900	11,800	11,800	700	57,800

[a]Data for the years prior to 1969 have been extrapolated from approxima-tive information and are not considered as valid as those for the years 1969–80. Ship-days in the Indian Ocean prior to 1967 reflect ship transits through the Ocean and are not ships deployed specifically for Indian Ocean operations.

Source: Bruce Watson, *Red Navy at Sea* (Boulder, Colo.: Westview, 1982), p. 183.

too, is the relatively even division of Soviet presence in the four major regions represented: Mediterranean Sea and Atlantic, Pacific, and Indian Oceans.

Watson also presents extensive data on Soviet port visits, by regions and by individual nations and their ports. Some of these data are aggregated in table 2, utilizing the top ten countries—as measured by total ship-days—in each of the relevant regions. Any number of salient, albeit in some cases speculative, points may be imputed from this information, which in Watson's work is supplemented by individual ports data and by appended explanations of what, centrally, was at issue in each case.

Clearly, there are not many surprises in the biggest cases. The Soviet presence, measured in this manner, has largely been concentrated where the USSR has had its most extensive basing access underpinned by major security assistance relationships: Cuba, Guinea, Angola, Syria, Vietnam, South Yemen, Ethiopia, and (earlier) Somalia and Egypt. The seemingly outsized numbers for Albania reflect the Soviet use there of submarine bases from 1958 to 1961. There are, however, a few surprises. Singapore did extensive overhaul and yard work on Soviet ships at least up until 1980, when further access was denied in the wake of the Afghanistan invasion. Yards at Chiba and Yokohama in Japan have done extensive overhaul work on Soviet auxiliary ships. And there has been the surprising level of Soviet access to Las Palmas in Spain's Canary Islands since 1969, used by auxiliary ships to support naval operations in Guinea and elsewhere in the Atlantic. The inclusion of Morocco, Sweden, Senegal, Canada, Tunisia, Greece, Italy, Gibraltar, Fiji, Mexico, and Ecuador on these lists is interesting and gives rise to various political, if not merely commercial, interpretations. Indeed, Watson's longer lists include a plethora of NATO nations and others closely aligned with the United States. But regarding these nations, nothing much more than traditional courtesy visits among nations not at war may be imputed.

Table 2. Cumulative Totals of Soviet Naval Ports Visits: 1953–1980

Atlantic		Mediterranean		Indian Ocean		Pacific	
Country	*Ship-Days*	*Country*	*Ship-Days*	*Country*	*Ship-Days*	*Country*	*Ship-Days*
Guinea	8,488	Egypt	38,966	Somalia	6,199	Singapore	5,078
Cuba	7,781	Syria	13,739	Ethiopia	4,812	Vietnam	2,866
Angola	3,394	Albania	11,283	South Yemen	4,625	Japan	330
Canary Islands	1,011	Yugoslavia	8,062	Bangladesh	3,920	Canada	100
Morocco	666	Algeria	2,252	Egypt (Red Sea Coast)	1,599	North Korea	82
Sweden	540	Tunisia	1,695	Iraq	1,386	Fiji Islands	55
Benin	462	Greece	742	Mauritius	965	Peru	48
Senegal	446	Italy	603	Sri Lanka	548	Mexico	42
Canada	317	Gibraltar	425	India	374	Kampuchea	34
Uruguay	300	Spain	171	Mozambique	261	Ecuador	29

Source: Bruce Watson, *Red Navy at Sea* (Boulder, Colo.: Westview, 1982), tables in Appendix.

Overall, however, the combination of data for ship-days and port calls does portray a significant and expanding Soviet global naval presence, one now made routine at a fairly high level. Though difficult to gauge and interpret, these facts do seem to underscore the extent to which the Soviet navy has leapfrogged the old Eurasian containment ring. The bear not only swims, but swims in a large number of dispersed places, cumulating to a truly global presence. What this might mean if the ancient dictum about the indivisibility of maritime control were really tested is, of course, hard to say.

Coercive Diplomacy

Connected to the Soviet Union's expanding oversea air and naval presence and its associated basing network is the question of the extent to which it has empowered coercive diplomacy, often referred to as "the political use of military force." The massive work of Steven Kaplan and his associates has attempted to conceptualize, measure, and assess this somewhat difficult domain.[53]

Gauging the coercive use of armed force involves some highly subjective, arguable matters—after all, who can say what would have happened if no force had been used or threatened? Nonetheless, it is worth noting that Kaplan, et al. identified some 190 incidents in which Soviet armed forces were used as a political instrument between June 1944 and August 1979, running from Soviet pressures in 1944 on Poland, Finland, Romania, and Bulgaria, to the events in 1979 surrounding the Afghanistan and China-Vietnam wars.[54] These incidents were divided into lists of "major coercive actions by U.S.S.R. forces since Stalin's death," "incidents in which U.S. and major U.S.S.R. armed forces were used," and "coercive activities of Soviet armed forces in the Third World."[55] The lists cross-reference different Soviet orientations to Third World conflicts with various uses of ground, air, and naval units. And some detailed case studies are provided: Soviet interventions in Eastern

Europe, Sino-Soviet border conflicts, the Korean and Vietnam Wars, the Arab-Israeli and other Middle Eastern conflicts, naval diplomacy in African waters, and the conflicts in Angola and the Horn of Africa, to name a few.

Amid the blizzard of detail and the difficulties of drawing conclusions or inferences, a mere scanning of Kaplan's book underscores one general point: that Soviet military power has become a global presence in spite of the US containment policy. Since 1960, when Moscow began to develop conventional power projection capability, Soviet military power has at least been a factor in a lot of places. Kaplan's data include involvement in Iran, Indonesia, the Congo (Zaire), Laos, Cuba, North Yemen, Cyprus, China, the Arab-Israeli conflict, South Yemen, Ghana, Cambodia, Somalia, the Sudan, the Syria-Jordan imbroglio, Guinea, Sri Lanka, Sierra Leone, India versus Pakistan, Bangladesh, Oman, Guinea-Bissau, Iraq versus Kuwait, Kurdistan, Angola, Western Sahara, Lebanon, Ethiopia, Japan, China versus Vietnam, and Afghanistan. Some of these involvements, because they are contiguous or near to the Soviet rimland, concern the older imagery of containment. A scanning of the remainder reinforces the point that the containment ring has long been leapfrogged, that the reach of Soviet power extends well beyond the close-in rimlands.

Much a part of Soviet conventional power projection is Moscow's use of surrogate forces. This development has, of course, received most attention in connection with the crucial role of Cuban forces in Ethiopia's defense against Somalia, and in Angola on behalf of the Neto regime.[56] Numerically smaller efforts have been made by Soviet client forces in Syria versus Israel and in Nicaragua. Whatever the interpretation of the political nature of Soviet-Cuban collaboration in the two major cases, it is clear that Soviet logistics—air and sea transport, use of en route staging facilities, etc.—were crucial. And, of course, the success of the Horn and Angola operations resulted in additional points of access for Soviet naval and air forces, usable for a variety of possible future contingencies as well as for more routine activities.

Thus far, of course, the Soviets have been very cautious about direct involvement of their combat forces outside the USSR, especially in noncontiguous areas. The heavy involvement of Soviet forces in Afghanistan has been one exception, as were the earlier suppressions of revolution in Hungary and Czechoslovakia. In noncontiguous areas, some Soviet forces were involved in the manning of Syrian SAMs in 1982 and as pilots in Egypt's war of attrition against Israel in 1969–70.

Also of note is the use of Soviet aircraft for moving military equipment forward in Vietnam in 1979,[57] and the activities of high-level Soviet officers on behalf of Ethiopia in 1977–78. But with the exception of Afghanistan, use of large-scale Soviet combat units has so far been avoided. And the alerting of a number of Soviet airborne divisions during the 1973 war was the one example of the long-range deterrent or compellent use of Soviet conventional power. Whether the future will see more ambitious and open use of Soviet combat power overseas remains to be seen.

Arms Transfers, Military Aid, Economic Aid

Recent decades have seen the USSR become a major supplier of arms, alternating with the United States in the leading role. The most recent ACDA annual, *World Military Expenditures and Arms Transfers, 1985,* gauges Soviet arms deliveries in the period 1981–84 at 28.4 percent of the world total, ahead of the 24.6 percent credited to the United States. The Soviet lead in deliveries to developing countries was much larger, 31.7 percent to 17.4 percent. And, of course, the USSR was the sole or predominant arms supplier to a number of developing states: North Korea, Vietnam, Laos, Kampuchea, India, Iraq, Syria, Libya, South Yemen, Algeria, Nicaragua, Ethiopia, Mali, Benin, Madagascar, Angola, Mozambique, Zambia, Tanzania, the Congo, and some other smaller states within Africa.

The Soviet arms sales effort was underpinned by a massive arms production base which in some major weapons categories (tanks, artillery pieces, jet fighter aircraft, surface-to-air missiles, and patrol boats) resulted in far larger annual unit production runs than in the United States. These arms sales were accompanied by large-scale military training programs, within the recipient countries, in the USSR, and in other Eastern bloc countries. (According to a CIA publication, training between 1955 and 1979 also involved such countries as Cameroon, Ghana, Nigeria, Sierra Leone, Togo, Zaire, North Yemen, Iran, Pakistan, and Bangladesh, none of them normally deemed Soviet "client states."[58]) During the same period, communist countries' economic aid was extended to a plethora of noncommunist LDCs (some of it admittedly token and near-symbolic). That extended list included Mauritania, Morocco, Tunisia, Botswana, Burundi, Cape Verde, the Central African Republic, Chad, Comoros, even the Philippines, Brazil, Mexico, Uruguay, and Venezuela. While these relationships may not have resulted in base rights or the availability of surrogate forces, they may still be seen as a broader effort at extending Soviet influence and reducing that of the United States. Whether these transfers have had an impact on the overall conventional military balance is doubtful, but there is little question that arms sales, or more broadly, security assistance, has become the major item of quid pro quo in exchange for military access.[59]

Although year-to-year arms transfers are an important aspect of Soviet power projection, arms resupply during conflict constitutes a more salient and visible manifestation of Moscow's support. The Soviets have conducted several successful arms resupply operations in connection with major Third World conventional wars, usually where US interests were engaged on the other side. The examples are well known: the Middle East war of 1973, Vietnam versus the United States, Ethiopia in 1977–78, India in 1971, Angola in 1975, and Vietnam in 1979. And Soviet or client state arms have sustained a variety of lower intensity combat operations by surrogates: e.g., Nicaragua,

Zimbabwe, Western Sahara, Chad, Vietnam, and South Yemen. More protracted and less time-urgent operations have used Soviet sealift, surreptitious and indirect as well as overt. The case of Iraq since 1980 has demonstrated that political-strategic cross-pressures may sometimes cause a more ambivalent Soviet support effort, capabilities notwithstanding.

Addendum: Conventional Power Projection and the Nuclear Balance

While the primary focus of this paper is on *conventional* power projection, a strict separation between it and nuclear power projection is a bit artificial. The link has always been there. The original containment policy was based, if only implicitly, on the assumption that America's disadvantage in conventional forces around the Eurasian rimland could be counterbalanced by a nuclear deterrent. And of course, one lesson the Soviets could not avoid learning at the time of the Cuban missile crisis was the importance of "local" conventional balances on the ladder of escalation to nuclear weapons. At any rate, for both the United States and the USSR, many oversea facilities are usable both for conventional and nuclear-related purposes. Likewise, some weapons systems have dual implications. SSNs can be used in conventional wars but would also be critical in a "nuclear phase" vis-a-vis rival surface or submarine forces.[60]

The expansion of the Soviet naval basing system provides a number of forward positions from which SSNs could operate, either in a nuclear phase or in a lengthy conventional phase during which both sides were seeking to degrade each other's forces so as to increase their relative nuclear advantage. As noted, the Soviets now have numerous oversea airfields from which to fly ASW and ocean surveillance aircraft important to the nuclear equation. SIGINT, space-tracking, and communications facilities likewise have dual functions. Cuban air bases—in part now protected by Soviet conventional deterrent power—could be used as possible recovery bases for Backfire bombers. And the expansion of the Soviet fleet (including its

Merchant Marine and fishing fleet) provides numerous assets relevant to the nuclear equation: communications, ASW, space-tracking, etc. In the future, some Soviet oversea facilities may be used for basing mobile cruise missiles, or perhaps for various functions in relation to strategic missile defense like ground-based lasers or satellite launching.

Summary

What does this development of Soviet conventional power projection capability mean to the original aims of the containment policy? As noted earlier, that policy stressed a more or less symmetrical rimland defense backed by a nuclear deterrent. It appeared to emphasize (in territorial terms) the defense of Western Europe and, with it, the so-called "sinews of war," and re-tention of sea control was a necessary adjunct to these broad aims.

Some forty years later, has that containment policy worked? Western Europe remains outside the bear's grasp not-withstanding "Finlandization," trends toward neutralism, Europessimism, and the resurgent "German problem." And the Sino-Soviet split, US-PRC rapprochement, Japan-PRC rap-prochement, South Korea's tenacious independence, and ASEAN's vitality all have redounded to the advantage of the West even as the economic center of gravity along the Eurasian rimlands has shifted toward the Pacific Basin. (Indeed, it might be argued that containment appears more successful in Asia than in Europe from the perspective of 1985.) The Soviets' develop-ment of heavy industry and weapons production has long since removed the issue of "sinews of war" from center stage, and the Persian Gulf (with its oil) and other raw materials locales have supplanted Western Europe's industries as crucial strategic prizes.

To be sure, containment—in its original sense of contiguity to the Soviet rimland and the associated imagery of falling dominoes—has suffered some setbacks. Vietnam was the prime example. Iran was lost to the West, if not yet gained by the USSR. Turkey, Greece, Spain, and Portugal all seem in recent years to have become less solid members of the Western alliance even if all are still formally within NATO. But aside from the Soviets' precarious hold on Afghanistan, there has been little outward movement of the Red tide. And looked at in other ways, the geopolitics of containment has retained much of its original "shape." Scenarios for protracted conventional phases or for limited nuclear war stress the need for containing Soviet conventional naval power as well as SSBNs inside "the bastions" of the Norwegian and Barents Seas and the Sea of Okhotsk. The Greenland-Iceland-UK (GIUK) gap and the various straits of Northeast Asia have come to represent a strictly military form of containment; by contrast, in many of the land-contiguous areas around the USSR, containment involves application of a mix of military and political measures.

The Soviets' primary gains have occurred—spatially speaking—in the form of the leapfrogging of containment. Solid though perhaps impermanent alignments with client states have been acquired in Vietnam, Laos, Kampuchea, South Yemen, North Korea, Syria, Libya, Ethiopia, Iraq, Mozambique, Angola, Guinea, Cuba, and Nicaragua. Some earlier client relationships, however, have been lost: Egypt, the Sudan, Indonesia, Equatorial Guinea, and maybe North Yemen (Grenada too) head that list. Less solid but significant security ties have existed in many other places: India, Madagascar, Zimbabwe, the Congo, Benin, Zambia, Guinea-Bissau, Algeria, Peru, and Kiribati among them.

In a curious way, the contrasting perspectives of Kennan and Weigert now seem each to capture an aspect of current reality. Kennan's taking Marxist-Leninist ideology very seriously appears apt, retrospectively, in that most of the oversea client states which contribute to Soviet projection capability are, to one degree or another, self-defined Marxist states, though Peru, India, Algeria, and Libya, for disparate reasons, are exceptions. This pattern of alignment persists even as Western writers disparage Soviet ideology as little more than a cover for the tenacious clinging to power of a hidebound party elite, and even as

recent developments in China pose a serious threat to the ideological basis of the Soviet regime. Indeed, the ideological fervor
of some far-flung Soviet client states seems oddly to contrast
with the increasing cynicism and weariness suffusing the Soviet
body politic.

What is clear is that the Soviets have achieved valuable
strategic outposts in several key areas of the world: Vietnam in
Southeast Asia, South Yemen and Ethiopia in the Southwest
Asia/Horn of Africa region, Angola along the African South Atlantic littoral, Mozambique on the eastern African flank, Cuba
in the Caribbean, and Nicaragua with both Caribbean and Pacific coasts. And Soviet military power is such that—with perhaps an occasional odd exception such as Grenada—these
outposts are rendered rather immune from hostile actions to subvert the Brezhnev Doctrine.

Future Policy Implications

American policies dealing with Soviet conventional power projection capabilities can be found in several interlocking dimensions. First, policies aimed at coping with increased Soviet
naval and air logistics capabilities can be distinguished from
those meant to deal with enhanced Soviet basing access. The
former involve, primarily, matching weapons and logistics
capabilities and are primarily within the domain of defense procurement. The latter, by contrast, involve primarily the politico-
military elements of alliance politics, security assistance,
intervention efforts, and related deterrent effects. Within both of
these broad categories, one may discern another spectrum, that
ranging from macro- to micro-level problems; regarding alignments and access, that spectrum runs from general foreign policy orientations or doctrines to ad hoc responses to specific
crises, wars in the Third World, coups, etc. In a significant
way, Gaddis' relative distinction between symmetrical and
asymmetrical responses can be applied across all of these areas.
In a broader sense—as applied to the entirety of containment

policy—others have used a more complex and varied set of concepts, to which we shall return.

Since the late 1970s, and in an accelerated manner since the advent of the Reagan administration, the United States has been moving to counterbalance growing Soviet power projection capabilities. US procurement efforts have included the thrust toward a 600-ship Navy, the expansion of the number of carrier battle groups and the recommissioning of World War II battleships; increased attention to readiness in all three services; expansion of long-range air transport capabilities; development of a roll-on-roll-off (Ro-Ro) fleet; and elaboration of the former Rapid Deployment Force into the Central Command.[61]

In a narrow sense, the Carter-Reagan buildup is designed to match Soviet power projection capabilities in the Persian Gulf region. As such, it fits the model of "symmetrical" strategy geared to meeting potential Soviet expansionism head-on, at the point of attack.

In a broader sense, however, some aspects of evolving US doctrine associated with the buildup (such as the maritime strategy associated with Navy Secretary John Lehman and former Assistant Secretary of Defense "Bing" West) appear more redolent of the alternative tradition of "asymmetric strategy," particularly the concept of "horizontal escalation" made prominent during the early days of the Reagan administration. Although that concept could be applied in a variety of situations, it was most often discussed in relation to Persian Gulf contingencies, where it amounted virtually to an admission that the United States could not match Soviet conventional power.

The budgetary aspect of procurements meant to deal with Soviet conventional power projection can, of course, involve very broad and complex considerations. For instance, current discussion about whether US development of SDI would entail severe economic burdens for the USSR (making Soviet economic reform more difficult) might be extended to consideration of its impact on Soviet conventional force capabilities. Might

aborting of the SALT process and a more serious race to ballistic missile defense affect relative conventional force capabilities
to the detriment of Soviet power projection? Generally, however, it appears there are only limited means available to the
United States for limiting further growth of the Soviet navy and
of VTA's air transport capability. The serious questions have to
do with countervailing US procurement, including endless questions of where and under what circumstances force is to be
projected.

The problem of dealing with Soviet access to basing
facilities—hence, the broader problem of Soviet alignment strategies and clients in the Third World—appears at least to provide
more scope for measurable and visible countermeasures. Generally, this subject leads to considerations of security assistance,
intervention, covert operations, and whatever other instruments
might be available to preempt, forestall, or reverse Soviet access to bases. The question of symmetrical and asymmetrical
approaches is involved here as well as are fundamental questions about acceptable levels of direct or indirect US military intervention and more subtle activities designed to shift the
political orientations of Third World states.

As an illustration of an asymmetrical response, one might
cite the Carter administration's response to the events in Iran
and Afghanistan in the late 1970s. Utilizing the instrument of
security assistance, the United States moved forcefully to acquire and enhance access in Oman, Kenya, Diego Garcia,
Somalia, Egypt, and Morocco, counterbalancing the new Soviet
capacity to project force into Southwest Asia with an increased
US capability to match that projection. Soviet access to
Nicaragua called forth a US effort to secure facilities in
Honduras and Colombia, another example of asymmetrical response. And, when in the later 1970s, Soviet access in Angola
was enhanced, the United States moved to enlarge its access in
Liberia and Ascension Island. Indeed, US acquisition of intelli-
gence facilities in western China to compensate for those lost in
Iran could be cited as another such example, albeit one more

germane to the nuclear balance than to rival conventional force projection capabilities.

One can envisage some emerging situations which may call for asymmetrical responses. The Soviet position in Vietnam—entrenched after the Sino-Vietnamese war in 1979—did not call forth a substantial US response, in great measure because of the already existing US naval and air presence in the Philippines. If the latter should be lost, the presumed subsequent US search for alternatives might be viewed as a belated asymmetrical response to the Soviet capabilities.

In recent months, however, some neoconservatives have given voice to strategic alternatives which come closer to symmetry. It has been suggested that the United States work harder at driving the Soviets out of some of their forward positions: in Nicaragua, Angola, Afghanistan, and Cuba.[62] This newer strategic thrust is not only justified on the basis of eviscerating Soviet forward power projection capabilities and thus preempting the further fall of dominoes; it is also justified as serving to exacerbate *internal* Soviet political disarray by discrediting a Soviet regime which must base its legitimacy on leadership of the international revolution.[63] It is a policy thrust highly reminiscent of the "rollback" emphasis echoing from the Eisenhower-Dulles era, except that what is now to be rolled back is the spread of the Red tide to scattered locales in the Third World. This newer rollback is also suggested, it may be noted, in a period of relative strategic nuclear parity, whereas the older policy of the same name was meant to rely on US nuclear superiority and massive retaliation. Presumably, the newer emphasis banks on a Soviet perception that its interests in places like Cuba, Angola, and Ethiopia are less vital than those in Eastern Europe, with the assumption that dramatic Soviet responses to setbacks in the more distant areas are less likely.

Of course, the history of US containment policy provides some examples of the Soviets being driven from positions of clientship and access, assisted by a mix of active US military intervention, covert political action, and use of economic and other policy tools. Some have involved coups or revolutions, some not. But it is also worth noting that the USSR has always recouped by acquiring substitute positions of influence and access nearby. Vietnam made up for the loss in Indonesia; access in Syria and Libya replaced that in Egypt; Ethiopia replaced Somalia. This suggests that a more maximalist or "rollback" US containment policy must be designed to deal with a flexible and pragmatic Soviet reaction in situations where a superpower's position on one side often almost guarantees an opportunity for the other superpower. The Soviets exploit the Arab-Israeli conflict to gain access to Syria, the South African imbroglio to gain access to Angola and Mozambique, the Indochina conflict for access in Vietnam. In response, one can only point to US opportunities for a more "dynamic containment" policy as advocated by Max Singer and others, one geared to full utilization of all available instruments in a game now expected to be more fluid and dispersed and less dominated by rigid ideological alignments.

The United States may now, indeed, have greater opportunity for utilizing the attractiveness of its economic system to wean away erstwhile Soviet basing clients, if only gradually or in part. Such Western attributes have served to wean Guinea partially away from Soviet tutelage, resulting in restrictions on Soviet use of air bases there. Algeria, Iraq, India, Mali, Mozambique, and maybe others have also moved away from the Soviet orbit in recent years, attracted by a more promising set of economic and cultural relationships. It remains to be seen whether similar inducements might succeed with Soviet client states not now appearing vulnerable to counter-revolution, coups, or regional military pressures, such as Vietnam, South Yemen, and even Cuba.

Aaron Wildavsky, in his summary of *Beyond Containment*, offered five variants of containment strategy, ranged along a continuum from passive to active. Those were (a) minimal containment, (b) a fixed line at borders of the Soviet empire, (c) a fixed line around assets (Western Europe, Israel, North America, and Japan), (d) flexible containment, and (e) containment plus.[64] With narrower application to the problem of containing Soviet conventional power projection capability, the viable options seem to include the last three. The neoconservative movement, installed but not dominant within the Reagan administration, advocates a shot at containment plus. The Carter administration began with a rhetorical commitment closer to minimal containment. Most probably, actual US policy will continue to oscillate around an ad hoc, but not always forcefully applied, version of flexible containment.

Notes

1. George F. Kennan (writing as 'X'), "The Sources of Soviet Conduct," *Foreign Affairs* 25 (July 1947), pp. 566–82.

2. See, in particular, George F. Kennan, *Memoirs: 1925–1950* (Vol. I) (Boston: Little, Brown, 1967), esp. chaps. 10–15.

3. See, for example, US Department of Defense, *Soviet Military Power, 1985* (Washington: US Government Printing Office, 1985), especially chap. VII under "Global Ambitions," and therein, the map on pp. 116–17, headed "Soviet Global Power Projection."

4. Hence, in the 'X' article, p. 572:

The first of these concepts is that of the innate antagonism between capitalism and Socialism. We have seen how deeply that concept has become imbedded in foundations of Soviet power. It has profound implications for Russia's conduct as a member of international society. It means that there can never be on Moscow's side any sincere assumption of a community of aims between the Soviet Union and powers which are regarded as capitalist. It must invariably be assumed in Moscow that the aims of the capitalist world are antagonistic to the Soviet regime, and therefore to the interests of the peoples it controls. If the Soviet Government occasionally sets its signature to documents which would indicate the contrary, this is to be regarded as a tactical manoeuvre permissible in dealing with the enemy (who is without honor) and should be taken in the spirit of *caveat emptor*. Basically, the antagonism remains. It is postulated. And from it flow many of the phenomena which we find disturbing in the Kremlin's conduct of foreign policy: the secretiveness, the lack of frankness, the duplicity, the weary suspiciousness, and the basic unfriendliness of purpose. These phenomena are there to stay, for the foreseeable future. There can be variations of degree and of emphasis.

5. See Kennan, *Memoirs* I, p. 359, wherein he writes,

A third great deficiency, intimately connected with the one just mentioned, was the failure to distinguish between various geographic areas, and to make clear that the "containment" of which I was speaking was not something that I thought we could, necessarily, do everywhere successfully, or even needed to do everywhere successfully, in order to serve the purpose I had in mind. Actually, as noted in connection with the Truman Doctrine above, I distinguished clearly in my own mind between areas that I thought vital to our security and ones that did not seem to me to fall into this category. My objection to the Truman Doctrine message revolved largely around its failure to draw this distinction. Repeatedly, at that time and in ensuing years, I expressed in talks and lectures the view that there were only five regions of the world—the United States, the United Kingdom, the Rhine valley with adjacent industrial areas, the Soviet Union, and Japan—where the sinews of modern military strength could be produced in quantity; I pointed out that only one of these was under Communist control; and I defined the main task of containment, accordingly, as one of seeing to it that none of the remaining ones fell under such control.

This is also discussed in Marvin Kalb, "The Vital Interests of Mr. Kennan," *The New York Times Magazine,* 27 March 1966, pp. 31 ff. According to him:

> Kennan sees the world in terms of "prime" (sometimes he uses the word "vital") and "secondary" areas of concern. There are to him a finite number of "vital" concerns for every nation (for the U.S. the number is five) and an infinite number of "secondary" concerns. Any self-respecting state must learn to distinguish between the two, never allowing itself the luxury of human beings: to be swept along by emotional or legalistic considerations toward major commitments that hold the promise of only minor rewards.

For an excellent review of definitions and analyses of a spectrum of national interests, see Thomas W. Robinson, "The National Interest," *International Studies Quarterly* 11 (June 1967), pp. 137–51.

6. John Lewis Gaddis, "Containment: Its Past and Future," in Richard Melanson, ed., *Neither Cold War nor Détente? Soviet-American Relations in the 1980s* (Charlottesville: University of Virginia Press, 1982), pp. 1–33, quote from p. 8. These issues are also discussed in several chapters of Howard Bliss and M. Glen Johnson, eds., *Consensus at the Crossroads* (New York: Dodd, Mead & Co., 1972).

7. A symmetrical strategy is strongly implied in at least two places in the 'X' article. On p. 576: "Soviet pressure against the free institutions of the western world is something that can be contained by the adroit and vigilant application of counter-force at a series of constantly shifting geographical and political points, corresponding to the shifts and manoeuvres of Soviet policy...." On p. 581: "This would of itself warrant the United States entering with reasonable confidence upon a policy of firm containment designed to confront the Russians with unalterable counter-force at every 'point' where they show signs of encroaching upon the interests of a peaceful and stable world."

8. After having drafted this paper, this writer admits to having been chastened somewhat by the press coverage of some of Mr. Gorbachev's remarks during the November 1985 summit meeting in Geneva, some of which hinted at just such deep-seated visceral beliefs regarding the power of the US "military-industrial complex." Generally in this regard, see William Safire, "Yes, the Soviets really do be-

lieve in Communism," *Pittsburgh Post Gazette*, 26 November 1985, p. 11.

9. One work which reminds us of the tenacious hold of Eurocentric perspectives beyond the point their validity had clearly faded is Hajo Holborn, *The Political Collapse of Europe* (New York: Knopf, 1960), esp. chap. VII.

10. Among numerous general works on this subject, probably the best review is Saul Cohen, *Geography and Politics in a World Divided* (New York: Random House, 1963). More specifically, on the discrediting issue, see Robert Strausz-Hupé, *Geopolitics: The Struggle for Space and Power* (New York: G.P. Putnam's, 1942).

11. See Harold and Margaret Sprout, "Geography and International Politics in an Era of Revolutionary Change," in W.A. Douglas Jackson, *Politics and Geographic Relationships: Readings on the Nature of Political Geography* (Englewood Cliffs, New Jersey: Prentice-Hall, 1964), esp. p. 47.

12. On behalf of an altered geopolitical imagery centered on US primacy, see Alan K. Henrikson, "America's Changing Place in the World: From 'Periphery to Centre,' " in Jean Gottmann, ed., *Centre and Periphery: Spatial Variation in Politics* (Beverly Hills: Sage, 1980), pp. 73–100.

13. See Albert Wohlstetter, "Illusions of Distance," *Foreign Affairs* 46 (January 1968), pp. 242–55, for the view that distance factors applied to power projection had declined in importance.

14. Hans Weigert, "U.S. Strategic Bases and Collective Security," *Foreign Affairs* 25 (October 1946), pp. 250–62. Prior to this article, see Weigert and V. Stefansson, eds., *Compass of the World: A Symposium on Political Geography* (New York: Macmillan, 1944). Later on, appeared Weigert, et al., eds., *Principles of Political Geography* (New York: Appleton-Century-Crofts, 1957).

15. These matters were also ably covered in George Weller, *Bases Overseas* (New York: Harcourt, Brace, 1944).

16. This controversy, largely pitting the State Department against the Pentagon, is discussed in T. Campbell, "Nationalism in America's U.N. Policy, 1944–45," *International Organization* 27, (Winter 1973), pp. 25–44.

17. Weigert, "U.S. Strategic Bases and Collective Security," pp. 251–52.

18. Later on, this theme would be picked up by Robert E. Walters, *The Nuclear Trap* (Baltimore: Penguin, 1974).

19. Weigert, "U.S. Strategic Bases and Collective Security," p. 254.

20. Halford Mackinder, *Democratic Ideals and Reality* (New York: Norton, 1962), pp. 62, 70. In the latter: "What if the Great Continent, the whole World-Island or a large part of it, were at some future time to become a single and united base of sea power? Would not the other insular bases be outbuilt as regards ships and outmanned as regards seamen?"

21. Stephen T. Hosmer and Thomas W. Wolfe, *Soviet Policy and Practice Toward Third World Conflicts* (Lexington, Massachusetts: D.C. Heath, 1983), in chap. 14, under "Future Soviet Involvement in the Third World."

22. The long-term development of the British imperial basing system is described and analyzed in P.M. Kennedy, *The Rise and Fall of British Naval Mastery* (New York: Scribner, 1976). See also D.H. Cole, *Imperial Military Geography,* 12th Edition (London: Sifton Praed, 1956).

23. This point is elaborated upon in R.E. Harkavy, *Great Power Competition for Overseas Bases* (New York: Pergamon, 1982), chaps. 1, 2, and 4.

24. Information on interwar basing facilities may be gleaned, on a country-by-country basis, from the files of Navy and Old Army Branch, National Archives, Record Group 165 (Records of the War Department, General and Special Staffs), Military Intelligence Division (MID).

25. See Richard Millett, "The State Department's Navy: A History of the Special Service Squadron, 1920–1940," *The American Neptune* 35 (1975), pp. 118–38.

26. This is best outlined in Roland Paul, *American Military Commitments Abroad* (New Brunswick, New Jersey: Rutgers University Press, 1973).

27. See Alvin Cottrell, "Soviet Views of U.S. Overseas Bases," *Orbis* 7 (Spring 1963), pp. 77–95.

28. See Bradford Dismukes and James McConnell, eds., *Soviet Naval Diplomacy* (New York: Pergamon, 1979), particularly app. D under "The Politics of Soviet Access to Naval Support Facilities in the Mediterranean," by Richard B. Remnek; and Barry M. Blechman and Robert G. Weinland, "Why Coaling Stations Are Necessary in the Nuclear Age," *International Security* 2 (1977), pp. 88–89.

29. R.G. Weinland, "Land Support for Naval Forces: Egypt and the Soviet Escadra 1962–1976," *Survival* 20 (1978), pp. 73–79.

30. Charles C. Petersen, "Trends in Soviet Naval Operations," in Dismukes and McConnell, eds., *Soviet Naval Diplomacy*, pp. 65–66.

31. US Department of Defense, *Soviet Military Power, 1985*, p. 131. Similar information can be gleaned from *The Military Balance* (London: International Institute for Strategic Studies), annual publication.

32. US Department of Defense, *Soviet Military Power, 1985*, p. 131.

33. Regarding Kiribati, see "Micronesia Resents a Far Land Called Washington," *New York Times*, 25 October 1985, p. 2.

34. This possibility is discussed in "Moscow's Spring Offensive: Two Afghan Options?" *New York Times*, 10 March 1980, p. A12.

35. See, for instance, T.H. Moorer and A.J. Cottrell, "The Search for U.S. Bases in the Indian Ocean: A Last Chance," *Strategic Review*, Spring 1980, pp. 36–77.

36. US Department of Defense, *Soviet Military Power, 1985*, p. 128.

37. Ibid., p. 123.

38. Ibid.

39. Abram Shulsky, "Coercive Diplomacy," in Dismukes and McConnell, eds., *Soviet Naval Diplomacy*, pp. 144–45.

40. "Spain Rushes Aid to New Regime in Equatorial Guinea," *New York Times*, 12 September 1979, p. A5.

41. Remnek, "The Politics of Soviet Access," p. 386.

42. US Department of Defense, *Soviet Military Power, 1985,* p. 120.

43. P.M. Dadant, "Shrinking International Airspace as a Problem for Future Air Movements—A Briefing" (Santa Monica, Calif.: RAND, 1978), Report R–2178–AF.

44. Shulsky, "Coercive Diplomacy."

45. Douglas Hart, "Soviet Approaches to Crisis Management: The Military Dimension," *Survival* 26 (September/October 1984), pp. 214–23.

46. US Department of Defense, *Soviet Military Power, 1985,* p. 123.

47. Ibid., pp. 105–06.

48. Michael D. Davidchik and Robert B. Mahoney, Jr., "Soviet Civil Fleets and the Third World," in Dismukes and McConnell, eds., *Soviet Naval Diplomacy,* pp. 324–30.

49. Ibid.

50. US Department of Defense, *Soviet Military Power, 1985,* p. 83.

51. Charles C. Petersen, "Showing the Flag," in Dismukes and McConnell, eds., *Soviet Naval Diplomacy,* chap. 3.

52. Bruce W. Watson, *Red Navy at Sea: Soviet Naval Operations on the High Seas, 1956–1980* (Boulder, Colo.: Westview, 1982).

53. Stephen S. Kaplan, *Diplomacy of Power* (Washington: Brookings Institution, 1981). The earlier effort was Barry M. Blechman and Stephen S. Kaplan, eds., *Force Without War: U.S. Armed Forces as a Political Instrument* (Washington: Brookings Institution, 1978). See also Alexander George, et al., *The Limits of Coercive Diplomacy* (Boston: Little, Brown, 1971).

54. Kaplan, *Diplomacy of Power,* chap. 2, under "An Aggregate View," and app. A, pp. 689–90.

55. Ibid., pp. 43, 53, 59.

56. Steven David, "Use of 'Surrogate' Forces by Major Powers in 'Third World Wars,' " in R. Harkavy and S. Neuman, *The Lessons of Recent Wars in the Third World: Comparative Dimensions* (Lexington, Mass.: D.C. Heath, forthcoming in 1986).

57. This is noted in Harlan W. Jencks, "Lessons of a 'Lesson': China-Vietnam, 1979," in Harkavy and Neuman, *The Lessons of Recent Wars in the Third World: Approaches and Case Studies* (Lexington, Mass.: D.C. Heath, 1985), pp. 139–60.

58. US Central Intelligence Agency, National Foreign Assessment Center, "Communist Aid Activities in Non-Communist Less Developed Countries, 1979 and 1954–79" (Washington: 1980).

59. See R.E. Harkavy, "The New Geopolitics: Arms Transfers and the Major Powers' Competition for Overseas Bases," in Stephanie Neuman and Harkavy, eds., *Arms Transfers in the Modern World* (New York: Praeger, 1979), pp. 131–51.

60. This is expanded upon in R.E. Harkavy, "The Evolving Geopolitics of Nuclear-Strategic Basing for the 1990's," paper presented at the annual meeting of the American Political Science Association, New Orleans, Louisiana, 29 August–1 September 1985.

61. In addition to sources previously cited, see Harlan K. Ullman and R. James Woolsey, "Seapower and Projection Forces," in George E. Hudson and Joseph Kruzel, eds., *American Defense Annual* (Lexington, Mass.: D.C. Heath, 1985), chap. 6.

62. By late 1985, there were even references in the press to a (non-formal) "Reagan Doctrine" to describe this new policy thrust, as per George Will, "Reagan Doctrine: Conservatism in the true sense of the word," *Centre Daily Times*, 12 December 1985, p. A4. This is also discussed under the heading of "the new globalism" in Anthony Lewis, "The Urge to Intervene," *New York Times*, 9 December 1985, p. A23.

63. See "Push the Russians, Intellectuals Ask," *New York Times*, 25 November 1985, p. A9.

64. Aaron Wildavsky, ed., *Beyond Containment* (San Francisco: Institute for Contemporary Studies, 1983). The typology is contained in the conclusion, "From Minimal to Maximal Containment," pp. 231–37; see also, in particular, the chapters by Charles Wolf, Jr., "Extended Containment," and by Max Singer, "Dynamic Containment," chaps. 8 and 9.

14

Containment and the Future: A European Perspective

Francis Pym

E VERY CENTURY THROUGHOUT HISTORY can be characterized by the changes that took place within it. And the scale and pace of change have been gathering momentum continuously over time. The twentieth century thus has seen by far the greatest changes ever known. Of these, the most profound are the changed pattern of world power, the invention of nuclear weapons, and the revolution in communications. All are relevant to our subject.

For several centuries, Europe was the dominating influence and power in the world. The seeds of its decline were sown in 1914. World Wars I and II did more than direct European energies to a destructive and introverted end: they caused Europe to forfeit its moral capacity and strength to direct the affairs of the world.

The Right Honorable Francis Pym, M.C., M.P., former British Secretary of State for Foreign and Commonwealth Affairs, is the Member of Parliament for South East Cambridgeshire.

Out of these conflicts has developed the situation in which America and Russia bestride the world as two superpowers. The existence of two nations, both incomparably more powerful than any other, acting out their rivalry on the canvas of the world is a new phenomenon. The irony is that both these nations used to be, and perhaps inherently still are, more isolationist than expansionist in temperament. They have very different histories and occupy different continents, but they are now vying with each other in the far reaches of the universe, only seventy years after the old powers of Europe plunged themselves into a war which brought about a huge change in the pattern of world power.

That pattern today is something of a paradox. Power is at the same time more concentrated and more diffuse. Europe's withdrawal from its colonies and the spread of economic growth have created scores of new and independent nations. These countries may not possess much power, but they have the means—and some have used them—to cause great instability in the world. In this way, as the dominance of the superpowers has grown, their control has diminished. These contradictory developments add up to one of the profound changes of all time.

Containment: The Early Years

The concept of containment was the first policy response by the United States and the West to the expansionist aims of the Soviet Union. After Russia's heroic fight with the Allies to defeat the Hitler regime, the peoples of the West greeted the aggressive attitude of the Soviet Union with deep dismay. Hardly was the ink dry on the Yalta agreement when the need to draw the lines round the Soviet Empire became clear. The Soviets advanced into Eastern and Central Europe, attempted to swallow up Berlin, and tried to take over Greece. The Cold War had arrived with a vengeance.

To the West, the idea of another conflict after World War II was unthinkable. A new Western alliance was essential, and NATO has indeed been successful in its task. The only practical policy was that of deterrence and containment, a policy which also had an idealistic side to it. It was hoped—indeed, half expected—that a combination of understanding cooperation, patience, and firmness would lead sooner or later to a less aggressive and more reasonable stance by the Soviet Union. Unfortunately, this proved to be wishful thinking.

In Europe, the demarcation lines became firmly drawn. Both sides understood the severe penalties that would be involved in infringing them. In Asia, on the other hand, containment proved a more difficult policy. Soviet expansion through subversion was arrested, but at great sacrifice. The Korean War was the first conflict fought to hold expansion in check, followed in due course by Vietnam. The costly failure in Vietnam showed that the gains made by the communists could not be rolled back by military or any other means. The objective was, literally, to contain the situation as it was.

Unfortunately, the NATO pattern was not successful in Asia. The defensive pacts of CENTO and SEATO failed because, first, the perceived threat was neither obvious nor direct enough to many of the countries involved, and second, the resources committed by the West to these organizations were not adequate to enable the Asian member countries to feel that sustained military effort against the Soviet Union was worth the risks. The alternatives of nonalignment or some kind of accommodation were more attractive. In the event, the results have been mixed. What is certain is that US naval power in the Indian Ocean, the South China Sea, and the Pacific is crucial to the continued Western alignment of many countries, such as those in ASEAN.

In the rest of the world, the situation is even more blurred. No clear spheres of influence were established and neither side admits to the other the existence of such spheres. But the early postwar years brought considerable successes for the Soviet Union. Soviet propaganda was effective, aided by the Third World's attitude towards decolonization. In addition, Marxist economic doctrines sounded attractive, particularly as there was so much ignorance and naivete about the true nature of the Soviet system. But over time the reality became clearer, the invasion of Afghanistan finally causing the last scales to fall from people's eyes. In the Third World, neither the political nor the economic models of the Soviets have shown themselves to have lasting appeal. Over the last fifteen years or so, it is Western influence that has steadily grown, which is a success story for us. That growth could not have been achieved without the power of the United States and the West, but it certainly was not achieved by the use of our military power. Our success here derived essentially from the inherent superiority of our system and our policies of enlightened self-interest.

From this success flows an important lesson. Military containment is indeed necessary, but it is very expensive. And there is a limit upon the resources our electorates are prepared to devote to the military, for there are many other more productive and desirable ways of using those resources. Furthermore, the uncommitted countries do not want to have the East-West conflict fought out on their soil; they know where their true interests lie. So the task of providing economic and developmental assistance is of the first importance. We neglect it at our peril. The lesson is that military containment alone is not enough: a more comprehensive strategy is required—concerning not only countries outside the Soviet bloc but also the Soviet Union itself.

The Process of Detente

It is not surprising that the search for a more cooperative working relationship with the Soviet Union began in Europe, for Europe is a continent artificially split by the imposition of the communist system on its eastern half. This division does great violence to the historical, cultural, and political traditions of Europe. No European accepts that such a legacy can be natural or permanent. There is a deep urge in people to have greater contact across the barriers and not always to sacrifice the interests of the individual to the dictates of the state. It could be said that the emergence in Western Europe of something like the

Conference on Security and Cooperation in Europe was almost inevitable once the military situation seemed to be stabilized and the Soviet threat under control. After all, we are all Europeans, on whichever side of the divide we live.

The United States, though, took the lead in moving toward detente. It proposed a collection of economic inducements which Americans believed could be a primary agent in changing political behavior. Ironically, the Europeans were initially suspicious of this action: it was not the sort of proposal they themselves would have made. Nevertheless, there were high hopes for the process, and the Europeans played their full part.

In the end, the process floundered for several reasons. First, because the agreement meant completely different things to the two sides, the West perceived the Soviet Union to be in breach of it, certainly in spirit if not in word. Second, the economic inducements offered by the West were offered on over-generous and unsustainable terms. And third, in the spirit of the agreement, the West stayed its hand on any military buildup or significant modernization of its weapons, while the Soviet Union continued its military program unabated. The result was the perception of an ever-widening gap, not only in intermediate and strategic missiles and in conventional weapons, but also in the interpretation of responsibilities in relation to human rights.

The practical failure of detente became more and more apparent over time. With the invasion of Afghanistan, the process fell into total disrepute. At that time, there was a widespread feeling that East-West relations were back to square one. But in fact, some important lessons were there to be learned, and another attempt is now being made to breathe life back into the process.

Trends in Soviet Policy

The core of the problem of East-West relations is the fundamental difference of aims, interests, and philosophies between the two sides. These differences flow from the incompatibility of Marxist-Leninist ideology with democratic ideals. Neither is going to change in the foreseeable future. But circumstances and conditions do change, all the time. The Soviet Union can learn new ways of attaining its ends, and so can we.

The central fact about the Soviet Union is the relative failure of its economy. Across the board, the Soviet government fails to get a reasonable return on its investment, and the standard of living of the Soviet people is pitifully low. Since 1945, the Soviets have been unable to introduce desperately needed economic reforms because of the dead weight of bureaucracy, entrenched interests, and ideology. But now the new leadership is showing itself fully aware of the problems and their long-term consequences. Like Mr. Andropov before him, Mr. Gorbachev shows he understands what has to be changed and intends to make a major effort to change it. There must be doubt about the extent to which he will succeed. His present approach appears conventional, calling for more discipline, more productivity, and better management, but all within the current centralized system. No method of motivating people has been proposed, nor any inducements for individual enterprise. But if he can bring about a significant improvement in the economy, he will achieve a big change in the balance of strength between East and West. Indeed, nothing else could bring about so great a gain for the Soviet Union.

This sort of change is his top priority, and, when coupled with his new-found flair for public relations, it is possible to foresee a partial turning of the tables in the overall balance between East and West. Space does not permit me to analyze that balance here, but my conclusion is that it has always been—and is today—strongly in favor of the West in spite of the Soviet Union's military strength, which is the basis for its status as a superpower. But there is no law of nature that makes the balance in favor of the West inevitable or permanent. Who knows? One day the Soviet Union may even become self-sufficient in agriculture. But the Soviets will have their set-backs too. They have many social, ethnic, and political problems that are likely to frustrate any dramatic improvement in economic performance.

On security issues, the Soviet Union is likely to remain paranoid for a long time to come. The Soviets will continue to build "defenses" in the absence of arms control agreements. Some Americans have argued that greater confidence and trust between the United States and the Soviet Union is not necessary if agreements that are verifiable and enforceable can be obtained. I do not agree, for two reasons. First, such agreements will never be arrived at, let alone kept, without a minimum level of confidence and trust that agreements can reinforce; the history of the ABM treaty seems to demonstrate this truth. And second, a feeling of security—which the Soviet Union so badly needs if it is not to depend solely on excessive military might—must have some foundation of confidence in a predictable and sustainable relationship with the United States. In my view, therefore, the Europeans are right to have limited faith in military might alone and to attach importance to agreements and to the confidence which must necessarily underlie them.

So far as Soviet satellites are concerned, the Soviet Union now appears to understand that overt invasion is not the best way to secure submission: the price in the hostile reactions of the rest of the world is unacceptably high. As we have seen in its handling of Poland, the Soviet Union is now adopting more indirect and subtle methods. This is an important change, which emphasizes the thought that military containment from the West is by itself inadequate to meet the challenge.

Yet another potentially dramatic change would occur if Russia were to achieve significantly better relations with China. This plainly is a major policy objective. It will be difficult for them to succeed because China is not likely to play second fiddle to anyone. China will continue to keep its distance from the Soviet Union, but we would be wise to reckon with the possibility of something approaching normal relations between China and the Soviet Union coming about over time.

Choices for the West

In these circumstances, there are essentially two choices. The first is to use the dynamic of the much stronger Western economy to "confront" the Soviet Union, to try to bury its more feeble economy and to beat it into the ground. One way of bringing about such a contest would be an unbridled arms race.

The advocates of this approach seem to be confined to the United States. None of the Allies would be likely to agree: they have neither the appetite nor the resources for such a knock-out competition. They would not believe in it in principle anyway, nor wish to rely on its succeeding. Deliberate antagonism is not part of their outlook. Japan would be likely to be of the same mind. Such a policy would result in an enormous increase in international tension and cause stress in the Alliance that might prove impossible to contain. Probably all political parties in Europe would disassociate themselves from such a concept.

So this plan seems a non-choice. The United States might attempt to go it alone, but if it loses its allies it has lost the war. To be successful, any strategy vis-a-vis the Soviet Union must take account of the views of the Allies. What does America stand for if it ceases to stand for a free Alliance of free nations willingly accepting US leadership? Military containment by itself is an inadequate policy for the Allies and an inadequate response to the growing sophistication of Soviet diplomacy.

The second choice is some form of cooperation with the Soviet Union. The question is how far this should go. What is plain is that the megaphone diplomacy of the early 1980s, if an inevitable by-product of Afghanistan, brought no progress in East-West relations. Rather, it enabled the Soviet Union to buy time for aging leaders to be retired or to die. Whatever may have been the original reasons—and there were good ones—the period marks a low point in East-West relations which should be seen as abnormal rather than the norm. The early 1984 shift to a policy of greater dialogue, based on sound premises, came as a great relief in Europe.

There must be some basis for coexistence. It could be argued that a distinctly wary coexistence is the right posture, at least until there is evidence of good behavior from the Soviet Union. But how is that better behavior going to be induced? There is no point in going back to the kind of negative linkage which was found impossible in, for example, Poland. It is unrealistic to expect the prodigal to reform in any substantial way, and if that is a condition of expanding the relationship, there will be no progress. What is needed is the establishment of the broadest possible working relationship and the prospect of conditional cooperation over a wide range of issues.

What I have just said would not seem relevant to those who believe, mistakenly in my view, that we—either Americans, or Europeans—can live without agreements with the Soviet Union, or worse, that it would actually be better to do so. It should be obvious by now that we are better off with agreements with the Soviet Union than without them, and that the pursuit of them should be a central objective of Western policy. And agreements can only be reached between parties that have a basic working relationship. It is a precondition. The agreement the Europeans attach most importance to is one on arms control, but arms control progress is going to be extremely difficult given the Soviet attitude. To reduce the constant spotlight on this issue by expanding the scope of other multilateral or bilateral relationships would be valuable. For this reason, among many others, President Reagan's initiative in raising regional issues with Mr. Gorbachev is extremely welcome.

On the assumption that the case for building a more cooperative East-West relationship has been accepted, the next step is to consider the requirements that need to be satisfied if the policy is to succeed. These requirements fall under three broad headings: consistency of policy, with which should be coupled cooperation between the Allies; ground rules for relations; and the allocation of resources in support of the policy.

Consistency of Policy

Consistency of policy springs out of a sustained purpose, matched with the appropriate means to carry out the policy. The Soviet Union has a better record here than the West, because of the simplicity of its purpose and because that purpose is pursued with the ruthlessness of a military dictatorship. The West has an equally clear purpose: to contain Soviet expansionism, prevent the spread of communism, and convince the Third World of the superiority in every way of our system. In other words, our policy—in part, at least—is reactive to another's initiative. By definition, that is a more difficult hand to play. The task is complicated further by the fact that the West comprises a widely varied collection of independent countries.

But that very diversity is one of the West's greatest assets. The pooling of different perceptions is a source of great strength. Unlike the Warsaw Pact, the West does not function on the basis of a subservient conformity. On the contrary, the Alliance is a democratic organization in which all views count. Certainly, that makes it more difficult to manage, but it also adds strength. Western values based on freedom of speech, freedom of choice, and the importance of the individual are closer to human nature, more deeply rooted, and more appealing. The Soviet Union fears the contagion of liberty. The moral and spiritual bankruptcy of Marxism is a continuing pressure on the fiber of the Soviet Union and its satellites, and will sap their strength over time.

To achieve consistency of policy in the West, the vital need is for improved coordination between us. And there are genuine difficulties to be overcome here. We are proud of our democratic ideals and the power and influence wielded by our informed electorates. But these very strengths impose political constraints on all governments. Often, there can be a conflict of interest between the political needs of the domestic national scene on the one hand, and the international situation on the other. In recent years, the tendency has been to respond more readily to national needs than international ones.

"It is in the national interest" is a cry to which people readily respond, especially in the television age when political leaders can make a direct and personal appeal to their electorates. But of equal importance to the national interest of each country is the international interest. Sometimes this aspect is not given the weight it warrants. The spirit of internationalism has taken some knocks recently. After forty years of peace for the Alliance, the reality of interdependence is inevitably less obvious. The failure to solve a number of international problems and conflicts has led people to lose faith to some extent in international institutions. But internationalism must be revived and nourished and nurtured, for there can be no prosperity or happiness for any nation except in the context of a world that is in some degree in harmony.

There is a particular threat to internationalism at this moment: protectionism, in itself an expression of nationalism. Politicians must have the vision and the will to resist the sirens of protectionism. I salute President Reagan's firm stand here. In theory at least, the option of autarchy exists for the United States, but certainly not for the rest of us. Even for the United States, a lapse into protectionism could only lead to impoverishment and the undermining of its security as well as ours. We have to convince our electorates that problems such as unemployment and slow economic growth can best be tackled in cooperation. My generation learned through the 1930s depression and the 1939–45 war that nations with a devotion to freedom must work together for the preservation of peace and for the prosperity of our people. Indeed, the indispensable work done today by major international institutions like the GATT, the IMF, and the EEC has been made possible only by the confidence in international solutions shown in the postwar period. We must not allow the populism of narrow nationalism or beggar-my-neighbor policies to take hold in the international system.

Upholding internationalism is a priority responsibility for Western leaders. And there is an added reason for emphasizing it now. In Mr. Gorbachev, the Soviet Union has acquired a forceful leader who has established his authority immediately. The imagination he has brought to his role is dramatic, and his skill at presenting himself and his country is already legendary. A couple of weeks ago, the British press were reporting a campaign by the White House to wrest the public relations initiative away from Mr. Gorbachev and back to President Reagan!

This advantage, if in fact it exists, is likely to be only temporary. But there is a further advantage the Soviet Union enjoys which could be more enduring. Mr. Gorbachev is likely to stay in charge for many years to come. Consequently, continuity in the conduct of Soviet foreign policy will be maintained. This is not so evident in the West. Although no sudden or sharp change in foreign policy is likely, the fact is that before very long a new president will be campaigning in the United States. No one knows who he will be or what foreign policy prescriptions he may have, but it is certain that he cannot be Ronald Reagan. Therefore, as the American election approaches, an element of doubt about US foreign policy must exist. The summit and its aftermath clearly have a bearing on this, but as 1988 draws nearer there is a danger that no new initiatives will be taken. Soviet leaders could use such an interlude to strengthen their economy and put themselves in as strong a posture as possible, ready to do business with the next occupant of the White House. To the extent they succeed, they would be in position to conduct a more forceful foreign policy and drive a harder bargain.

Finally, we can anticipate that the new Soviet leader will try hard to devise better techniques than his predecessors for dealing with the satellite states. Whether he will make communism any more acceptable to them in the long run is very doubtful. But it may well be that Mr. Gorbachev, using all his personal skills and the power of the Soviet Union, can strengthen the cohesion of the Warsaw Pact, at least in the short and medium term. That would be yet another change on the international landscape. And all the time the Soviet Union will be playing on Western differences and trying to divide the United States from its allies by every subtle means.

The extent to which this analysis is valid is a matter of opinion, but, however measured, it conveys a loud signal to the West. For as far as we can see, the Soviet Union will be just as strong an adversary as in the past; and in some ways, because of the ability of its new leadership and the lessons learned from the past, it may become an even greater challenge to the West than ever. To counter that effectively requires the West to get its act together more positively, coherently, and consistently than it does today. Such consistency demands courage, strong leadership, and hard work. But without it, we shall have difficulty in convincing our electorates that their security is assured, or that our leaders have a clear view of where they are taking us. In my view, the most potent constraints upon consistency are the national political pressures that bear upon all heads of government. Those pressures have to be responded to, but they must be responded to in a way that ensures consistency of policy by the West as a whole. That is the real challenge that faces Western leaders today.

Ground Rules for Relations

The second requirement for building a more cooperative East-West relationship is adherence to the ground rules that have been established. Here the most important field is arms control, the immediate issue both between the superpowers and within the Western alliance being the ABM treaty.

Existing arms control agreements are based on the principle of mutual vulnerability, which is written into the linkage between the SALT agreement and the ABM treaty. As envisaged, SDI clearly does not infringe that treaty, but the research could not be carried into deployment unless the treaty were renegotiated. The administration recognizes this, as the 4-point agreement between the president and the British prime minister of December 1984 demonstrates.

Nevertheless, in Europe we hear and read of the continuing argument about SDI issues in the United States. European anxiety will remain until there is unchallenged acceptance of the proposition that SDI-related deployment would have to be a matter for negotiation. This is a good example of an issue that causes uncertainty and nervousness in the West. It can best be coped with by the United States continuously consulting its allies on the important and difficult issues surrounding the ABM treaty—issues which ultimately affect their security just as much as that of the United States—and by taking positions in negotiation with the Soviet Union that are consistent with Western standards of political behavior and do not descend by "counter-cheating" to the standards of the other side.

The Europeans are well aware that the Soviet Union has taken full advantage of the provisions of the ABM treaty that permit research. It is perfectly possible that the Soviet Union signed the treaty because it feared that otherwise the United States would gain a lead in missile defense. What then happened was that the Soviet Union forged ahead with its research program, quietly but resolutely, while the United States largely halted its activity in this field. During the ten years after the treaty, there seemed to be insufficient evidence to challenge the Soviet Union on violations, but the deployment in 1983 of the Krasnoyarsk radar indicated the creation of a missile defense system on an altogether new scale. It is even possible that their ABM system (together with their air defense programs) could give the Soviet Union a capability to break out of the ABM treaty altogether. Protecting the West against this danger is the most important argument in favor of SDI.

The United States has an invaluable asset in its superior technology, which the Soviet Union perceives as a real challenge if not a threat. This is so despite the fact that the Soviet Union is the only country with a deployed antisatellite system.

Soviet leaders show every sign of developing that system further, but they fear that the United States has embarked on a massive research project into space-based systems that would be capable of overtaking what they can do. No wonder they reacted so vehemently against SDI! They will campaign vigorously against it while saying nothing about their own capabilities.

The manner of SDI's launching was unfortunate, because the reserved or even hostile reception accorded it in Europe made fertile ground for Soviet progaganda. But without developing this argument here, Europeans must accept that the United States is not inclined to give up its technological advantage merely as a bargaining chip for Soviet cuts in offensive weapons. At the same time, the United States must grasp the fact that unregulated competition in space is not seen by Europe as better—in any sense—than the threat of nuclear retaliation, especially since Europeans do not believe that SDI will enable nuclear systems to be dispensed with anyway. This attitude should not be confused with opposition to SDI, but it does mean that the United States must make good its professed aim of discussing with the Soviet Union the relationship between offensive and defensive weapons, and of negotiating in due course—if this is the way things begin to go—a regulated transition that would govern anything going beyond research on defensive systems. Such a regulated relationship on defensive systems should be accompanied by, if it cannot be preceded by, deep cuts in offensive systems. The United States is, of course, trying to achieve all this.

My view is that it would have been preferable for the United States to have had deep discussions with the Soviet Union on the whole question of defensive systems *before* launching SDI. The Soviet Union might have rejected such discussions out of hand, but at least the attempt would have been made to pursue "Star Wars" and all its potential implications with consultations between the superpowers instead of with maximum antagonism. If we are going to succeed in preserving peace and security at a lower level of armaments, *agreements* have to be *reached.*

The Camp David 4 points are essentially about establishing and observing ground rules. Doing so is crucial, not only to progress in improving East-West relations, but also to the maintenance of confidence within the Alliance. These considerations apply also to honoring existing agreements. The United States has full European support for its interim adherence to the restraints of SALT II, and the Soviet Union is sharply criticized for its SS–25 deployment in breach of the ground rules.

The lack of any ground rules in other parts of the world is a serious problem. Nor will it be easy to create them. Because neither superpower admits the notion of spheres of influence, demarcation lines scarcely exist. The efforts being made by President Reagan and Secretary of State George Shultz to find a way forward here are much to be welcomed. Both superpowers have legitimate interests in the rest of the world, and a valuable start could be made by recognizing these.

The United States seems to lack consistency on this issue. Naturally, the Americans are very angry when the Soviet Union interferes in their Central American "back yard." Yet, at the same time, they do not admit of a Soviet role in the Middle East, despite the fact that that region lies on the USSR's borders and the United States is the party operating "out of area." The analogies here are not exact, but it is obvious that the Soviet Union cannot accept—any more than the United States can—the notion that it has no interests or rights beyond its own boundaries. In any case, it has a capacity to disrupt and exploit, and puts it to effective use.

What is required is some code of conduct for those parts of the world where no ground rules now exist. The inherent difficulty of this objective is complicated by the issue of surrogates. If it is thought that the Soviet Union is pursuing its nefarious aims with greater expertise and subtlety than before, the question arises as to how far countries like Cuba and Nicaragua are tools of the Soviet Union and how far they are free agents. They are certainly not cost-free for the Soviets, for they have need of a great deal of aid which can come only from communist sources. But the revolutionary zeal they exhibit cannot be manufactured by Moscow: there is an indigenous element.

Whether putting the squeeze on the United States by causing disruption or conflict at its vulnerable points is part of Soviet policy is a matter for conjecture, but it could not be done in practice unless there already existed indigenous causes of discontent that can be exploited successfully. The notion that all the subversion is being done by surrogates is misleading because it obscures the fact that a momentum to cause revolution must already exist at home. A more realistic appreciation of such conflicts is that not only are they aspects of East-West competition, but they also have indigenous causes and consequences.

The policy objective therefore is to deny the Soviet bloc any targets of opportunity. That is a formidable task, perhaps impossible. It encompasses all aspects of international relations. To leave the debt crisis unresolved and allow it to go on festering, for example, would be contrary to the policy objective. The recent moves in US policy made by Treasury Secretary James Baker at Seoul are clearly directed at this problem.

When a target of opportunity—such as Nicaragua—has been captured and is being sustained by communist aid, the problem becomes acute. Democracies have the right to help friendly neighboring countries to resist the export of revolution. But do democracies have the right to intervene internally to reverse the revolution itself? Every case is different, but the judgments required are extremely difficult. Only a minority of countries are democracies, and to impose such a system by force from outside would constitute counterinterference, with unforeseeable consequences. Such action would, as a general rule, fall outside most people's definition of the call to "make the world safe for democracy." The problem is one of damage limitation: better by far to have prevented capture of the target in the first place.

Allocation of Resources

The third and final requirement for success in building a better relationship concerns the allocation of resources. Preventive action to reduce the risks of subversion or conflict demands a commitment of sufficient resources. It is easy to make the charge that the Western world collectively has been guilty of short-sightedness here. Finance and aid and loans have been provided on a massive scale, but often without foresight as to the consequences. The most important consequence, of course, is that most of the countries aided have no means or scope for repayment. Another consequence is often a substantial rise in population. So it is no wonder that in recent years the emphasis has been on economic discipline in debtor countries. The debt crisis has led to an insistence on sterner discipline, but clearly the political limits to austerity have already been reached in some countries. It is hard to avoid the conclusion that the only way to attain more economic discipline is by accompanying it with rather more help. No doubt, such action might be highly self-interested in a narrow sense; but in a broader and more important sense, it serves the West's long-term self-interest in creating an environment that denies opportunities for subversion.

Every country is experiencing the enormous cost of defense. The Soviet Union is under pressure no less than the rest of us—a different sort of pressure, but still pressure. The United States, too, is under pressure. Within the West, our total defense could be bought at a lower cost if the political constraints against much closer integration could be overcome. But even so, the allocation of resources will remain a key issue. Britain, like the United States, accords a top priority to defense. We cannot, and we will not, take risks with the security of our countries. But we also know the other claims upon our limited resources. There is a need for all of us to reappraise what our present needs are, where our money can be most effectively spent, and whether the overall balance between competing claims is the best that can be devised to attain our international objectives. Of course, a whole range of vested interests are involved, but the task of statesmen is to cut through those constraints and lead their countries along the route most likely to fulfill their people's aspirations. The deepest of those aspirations is for a calmer, more stable, more peaceful world.

Conclusions

In this essay I have sought to give a European perspective, but it is also a British perspective and a personal one. It reveals the issues that are of great importance to Europe and indicates the kind of approach to East-West relations that many of us believe most likely to succeed in present conditions. It has also spelled out some principles and guidelines that I believe should be followed, and which are already embodied in British policy without—as recent events have shown—there being any question of sacrificing our national security.

My main thoughts are these:

- We are likely to see some enhancement of Soviet strength militarily, in the sophistication of their foreign policy, and perhaps economically. Unless the West matches that enhancement with greater cohesion, the overall balance between East and West could move unfavorably for us.

- The maintenance of fully adequate defenses and an effective deterrent is indispensable: without them there will be no arms control agreements.

- But containment alone is an incomplete strategy, and defenses alone are not enough; we need arms control agreements, too.

- The terrain of working cooperation with the Soviet Union must be identified, however limited; this means consistency of policy and adherence to ground rules.

- The Soviets' methods are becoming more subtle and less confrontational, aimed at the long term. They will try to recover their position with the Third World.

- The West needs to provide more positive policies and more resources for the Third World, and to demonstrate to Third World nations by example, by economic success, and by enlightenment that it pays to stay with the West—of their own free will.

A formidable task, maybe. But I have every confidence that between us all, under US leadership, we have the determination and the depth of experience to match up to it.

15

Containment in Europe: The Critical Context

Catherine McArdle Kelleher

A NY SUMMARY EVALUATION of containment policy faces an analytic conundrum. Like deterrence, containment's impact is a Holmesian "dog that does not bark." Evidence of its success is at best negative (the absence of continued Soviet expansionism in Europe) and limited in time (up to today). The causal chains are far from conclusive: one must ask whether the Soviet Union really ever intended to expand west of the demarcation line agreed to at the end of World War II. And, again in striking parallel with deterrence, the instruments and measures of containment's success center on psychological and political processes far more than on indicators of military capability or doctrine.

Catherine McArdle Kelleher is Professor, Head of the National Security Studies School of Public Affairs, and Director of the Maryland International Security Project, Bureau of Governmental Research, at the University of Maryland.

Yet for all the difficulty, assessment of the goals and accomplishments of containment in Europe remains the central task for an analyst of postwar American foreign and defense policy. Measured in terms of time, money, manpower, and policy consistency, NATO-Europe is the key area of American postwar commitment: it contains two of the four non-American military-industrial centers that Kennan and successive American political elites saw as vital to American security; it is an area where containment has always been the domestic rallying cry for continued American involvement, and where critics of that involvement are asked for credible alternatives. And given the questioning of NATO's political texture that surely lies ahead, it is essential to sort out the critical requirements and limits of American's containment strategy.

The Origins of Containment in Europe: Kennan's View

Kennan's notion of containment in Europe was based on a number of fundamental assumptions about the nature of the international system and the requirements of American national security in the postwar era. His perspective was that of the quintessential "realist," interpreting the postwar distribution of power in terms of the rules and prerequisites of the nineteenth-century diplomatic tradition. American national security after World War II depended more than ever on the maintenance of a favorable international balance of power. The United States had global interests and numerous traditional commitments, but in the century of total war, the balance of industrial-military power was the crucial determinant of influence and authority. According to Kennan, there were five vital centers of such power: the United States, Great Britain, Germany and Central Europe, Russia, and Japan. Only one of these areas was under Soviet control, and the task of American national security policy—in 1947 and thereafter—was to prevent Soviet expansion into the others. Consonant with the limited nature of American resources, Kennan advocated a strategy that concentrated on defending these vital centers in the global balance.

Europe in 1947 was an optimal target for Soviet pressure. The political and economic chaos of war's end left the Continent vulnerable and exposed. The Red Army had advanced well into Central Europe and functioned as a prop for communist parties and factions in both Western and Eastern Europe. The vacuum left by Germany's collapse was only partially filled by temporary Allied occupation forces and commitments. And the objective political and economic weakness of Europe, especially in the bitter winter of 1947, resulted in a climate of subjective, psychological weakness.

Accordingly, the Soviet threat, in Kennan's eyes, was not primarily military but rather political and psychological. Russian expansion was largely driven by internal causes with roots in historic Russian feelings of insecurity and inferiority toward the West, together with the contemporary urges of a totalitarian system. Kennan's famous 'X' article, "The Sources of Soviet Conduct," appearing in *Foreign Affairs* in 1947, prescribed the appropriate American response. The Soviet Union's efforts to expand its influence into additional areas of industrial capacity could be thwarted by "the adroit and vigilant application of counter-force at a series of constantly shifting geographical and political points. . . ."[1]

But counterpressure was to be primarily political, with military capability a decidedly secondary element. Writing in his *Memoirs* twenty years after the fact, Kennan maintained that his notion of containment had been broadly misunderstood, and that the 'X' article must be viewed against the background of events that had preceded it.[2] In 1947, Kennan was concerned over what he perceived as a series of concessions made by the United States to Russian expansionism. At the same time, he wanted to dispel the notion that war between the United States and the Soviet Union was inevitable. Kennan acknowledged that the 'X' article had failed to make it clear that the containment of Soviet power was "not the containment by military means of a military threat."[3] In addition, it failed to spell out the geographic bounds of containment: the article did not show that Kennan assigned priority to Europe or the other vital regions of military-industrial capacity.

A number of authors have tended to confirm Kennan's interpretation of himself. John Lewis Gaddis argues that one must go beyond a reading of the 'X' article to understand Kennan's vision of containment.[4] Through an examination of the doctrine as it was originally expounded in various Policy Planning staff studies, speeches to the National War College, and numerous other notes and memoranda, Gaddis reconstructs Kennan's diagnosis of the postwar situation in Europe, the nature of the Soviet threat, and the appropriate American response.

According to Gaddis' analysis, Kennan's notion of containment in Europe had three phases, each with distinct objectives. The first task of American policy was to restore both Europe and Asia as independent centers of power, thus restoring international equilibrium. Instrumental in achieving this goal would be the bolstering of European self-confidence, the promotion of economic recovery, and—a crucial point—German recovery and rehabilitation. The principal levers would be political and economic assistance, an American military presence in the short term, and an American commitment to the security of democratic European regimes. In May 1947, as Director of the Policy Planning staff, Kennan put these ideas into practice by recommending an American program for European recovery that would aim to combat "the economic maladjustment which makes European society vulnerable to exploitation by any and all totalitarian movements and which Russian communism is now exploiting."[5] But the danger was still primarily potential Soviet political influence; as Kennan later remarked, "It had been primarily the shadow, rather than the substance, of danger which we, in contemplating a European recovery program, had been concerned to dispel."[6]

Germany played a pivotal role in this scheme. Kennan's attitude toward Germany was always ambivalent; even as a student, he had doubts about the German capacity for political stability and the destabilizing potential of Germany in any Central European equilibrium, given the country's raw potential and "egocentrism."[7] Yet Germany's defeat left an alarming power vacuum in the European order; its division was now both the precondition for the establishment of a conditional European balance and the central question which an enduring political settlement between East and West would have to address. But in the immediate postwar period, the issue was German economic potential. The restoration of German productivity was essential to the rehabilitation of Europe. In a speech before the National War College on 6 May 1947, Kennan urged action to secure this goal: "In my opinion it is imperatively urgent today that the improvement of economic conditions and the revival of productive capacity in the west of Germany be made the primary object of our policy in that area and be given top priority in all our occupation policies. . . ."[8]

Restoration of the political and economic balance was a precondition to Kennan's second containment phase: the reduction of the Soviet Union's ability to project influence beyond its borders. The principal new channels of Soviet influence were also primarily political: first, the dependent communist governments of Eastern Europe; second, the broader network of Moscow-dominated communist movements and partisans. Kennan argued that the strategy of the United States should be the encouragement of diversity and tension within the international communist movement, leading to the fragmentation of Moscow's overriding influence and "colonial" control. The methods must be indirect and patient, dependent on the Soviets' basic inability to tolerate divergence over the long term and on the potent forces of national identity, interest, and tradition.

In many respects, Europe would be the primary testing ground for this phase as well. The Soviets would, Kennan thought, have grave difficulties sustaining their domination of Eastern Europe, even with the Red Army in place. The economic rehabilitation of Western Europe would only make Soviet hegemony more difficult. The magnetic power of a "vigorous, prosperous and forward-looking civilization" in Western Europe would make unfavorable comparison inevitable, and that comparison would "be bound in the end to have a disintegrating and eroding effect on the communist world."[9]

The third phase would be the modification of Soviet international behavior through a strategy of deterrents and inducements that Kennan subsumed under the term *counterpressure*. The goals should be to acknowledge but not defer to the internal roots of Soviet behavior, to provide both the circumstances and the conditions for modification of Soviet expansionist tendencies. The last would be accomplished not by means of global confrontation, but through a strategy of "strongpoint defense": the United States would focus its application of counterpressure at vital points of its choosing, including Europe. Counterpressure was to employ both political and economic instruments and would be followed by negotiations to overcome the postwar status quo on the European continent. Above all, Kennan did not expect containment to continue indefinitely, nor did he foresee a long-term American involvement and presence in Europe:

> The purpose of "containment" as then conceived was not to perpetuate the status quo to which the military operations and political arrangements of World War II had led; it was to tide us over a difficult time and bring us to a point where we could discuss effectively with the Russians the drawbacks and dangers this status quo involved, and to arrange with them for its peaceful replacement by a better and sounder one.[10]

As the Soviet threat was primarily political and psychological, Kennan foresaw only a limited role for strictly military defense. Consequently, he greeted the call for the formation of a North Atlantic defense pact with reservation. His concerns were outlined in a 1948 memorandum of the Policy Planning staff which insisted, "Basic Russian intent still runs to the conquest of Western Europe by political means. In this program, military force plays a major role only as a means of intimidation." Military defense would be of limited utility in countering this threat:

"A North Atlantic Security Pact will affect the political war only insofar as it operates to stiffen the self-confidence of the western Europeans in the face of Soviet pressures." While such support might be necessary, the United States would run the danger of becoming preoccupied with military affairs; valuable resources would be diverted from economic recovery. Rather than a defense pact, "the best and most hopeful course of action . . . remains the struggle for economic recovery and for international political stability." Moreover, Kennan had reservations about the geographic scope for such an alliance and the danger of global overcommitment.[11]

Kennan's basic concern was neither with eventual European or even German rearmament nor with the continued, conditional presence of American military forces as a deterrent to Soviet adventurism. His objection was rather to what he saw as the inevitable consequence of a military alliance—the final cementing of the postwar division of Europe. In a theme more clearly expressed in his Reith lectures of 1957, Kennan feared that NATO's consolidation would mark a point of no return. Soviet insecurity and traditional American concern with the mechanics of the military balance would hinder any eventual withdrawal of Soviet and American forces from Central Europe. The grounds for negotiation of mutual disagreements would be undercut, the opportunity to construct a new intra-European settlement on terms favorable to broad US security requirements, lost.

In Kennan's view, the only proper function for NATO would be as a psychological shield for the Europeans, bolstering their self-confidence and allowing them to proceed with the more urgent task of political and economic recovery. If such a shield were truly necessary, then Kennan favored an alliance organized according to the "dumbbell concept." A European end based on the Brussels Pact would be mated with a US-Canadian end, each separate in identity but linked by a unilateral American guarantee of European security. Kennan later wrote: "Even for this, I saw no real necessity; but I was prepared to see us accept such an arrangement if this was the only way the Europeans could be given the reassurance necessary for them to proceed confidently with the task of economic and domestic-political recovery."[12] Elsewhere, Kennan admitted,

> The Western Europeans, in particular, have a *maime d'invasion,* and I suppose it is true that if we had not eventually created some sort of compensatory ground forces, they would—in political terms—have tended ultimately to "commit suicide for fear of death." I concede, therefore, that there was a need for the creation of something resembling NATO in Western Europe.[13]

Evaluation: The Kennan Measuring Stick

Most analysts, with Gaddis, maintain that the architect and implementers of containment subsequently parted company. How, then, is one to evaluate the success or failure of containment in Europe some three decades after the doctrine's formulation? How does the implementation of containment measure up against Kennan's own standard for success, or, alternatively, against the interpretation of others?

In Kennan's terms, the broad outcome in Europe has been a mixture of resounding success and qualified failure.

> It was not a failure in the sense that it proved impossible to prevent the Russians from making mortally dangerous encroachments "upon the interests of a peaceful world" ... nor was it a failure in the sense that the mellowing of Soviet power ... failed to set in. The failure consisted in the fact that our own government, finding it difficult to understand a political threat as such and to deal with it in other than military terms ... failed to take advantage of the opportunities for useful political discussion when, in later years, such opportunities began to open up, and exerted itself, in its military preoccupations, to seal and to perpetuate the very division of Europe which it should have been concerned to remove. It was not "containment" that failed; it was the intended follow-up that never occurred.[14]

In his BBC Reith Lectures of 1957, Kennan suggested that mutual withdrawal of Soviet and American forces from Europe would not place the West at a great military disadvantage. He implied further that another solution to the German problem might be possible, but never specified whether it would take the form of a neutralized or demilitarized Germany or occur in the context of a general European security pact. But he did perceive disengagement as compatible with the continued existence of NATO in some form, for NATO's real strength rested not in its military forces but "in the appreciation of the member nations for the identity of their real interest, as members of the Western spiritual and cultural community. If this appreciation is there, NATO will not be weaker, as a political reality, just because it may be supplemented or replaced by other arrangements so far as Germany is concerned."[15]

Kennan's continuing concern—reflected in the Reith lectures and elsewhere—focused on the militarization of the European division and on the central role played by Germany. "Strongpoint defense" necessitated drawing the line to contain Soviet expansionism at the inter-German border. The postwar Atlantic as well as European system necessarily turns on relations between the two Germanies; changes in the inter-German dialogue or tremors along its internal border reverberate through both alliances. Containment placed heavy political and psychological burdens on German leaders on both sides of the front line, as well as on the populations most directly affected by a militarized division of Europe. In this context, as the popular mobilization surrounding the INF episode aptly illustrates, changes in the military balance (or indeed in the broad outline of the status quo) are fraught with political symbolism and profound psychological impact.

Containment may fare better when measured against standards of success other than Kennan's own. Gaddis' analysis of containment suggests measurement along the continuum of successive steps, as each postwar phase had distinct goals and created new political conditions for what followed. The first goal was to restore the European and Asian balance of power. Economic and technological means, selectively and appropriately applied, were to promote European self-confidence and allow political and economic recovery to proceed apace. Today, political and economic recovery on the European continent is an uncontestable fact. Germany, albeit in a truncated form, has been fully rehabilitated and integrated into the Western community of states. Soviet expansion into this vital center of industrial and military power has not occurred. As Gaddis concludes, "One need only compare the configuration of power in Europe and Northeast Asia today with that established over three decades ago to realize the impressive success this particular strategy of containment attained."[16]

Similarly, phase two—the reduction of Soviet control over the international communist movement—can be said, on balance, to have been implemented successfully. It is only with regard to the third goal—what Gaddis called "behavior modification" of the Soviet Union—that containment has fallen short. Ultimately, the outcome in Europe is a far cry from Kennan's vision of an independent center of power in the multipolar balance. Kennan's world of many power centers has not yet been restored; Europe's divisions are still to be overcome. Perhaps, as David Calleo argues, the creation of a multipolar balance was unrealistic given the need for a hegemonic US role to regulate the new liberal world order. But many of Kennan's fears on the consequences of NATO seem to have been borne out: with the rearmament of both Germanies into two military blocs, the Alliance did in fact contribute to a militarization of the European division and the perpetuation of the postwar status quo. Phase three—a negotiated peaceful replacement to postwar division—never materialized.

Still, to regret NATO's contribution to Europe's continued division hardly constitutes proof that there was any viable alternative. Gaddis identifies Kennan's reliance upon psychological means to achieve containment's ultimate objectives as the doctrine's fundamental flaw. Rational decisions can be the source of irrational fears, and, as he points out (appropriately for the European case), "dismissing irrational fears for what they were was not enough to make them go away."[17] In this

view, Kennan failed to address the fact that psychological uncertainty could effect changes in the balance of power. At best,
Kennan drew the necessary policy conclusions reluctantly. The
"gap between the desirable and practicable" left few alternatives
to NATO, given the psychological uncertainty that reigned in
the Europe of 1947. The United States was in a dilemma from
which there was no best way out. As Kennan described the
situation,

> By asking the Europeans to go in for economic recovery
> before achieving military security, we were in effect ask-
> ing them to walk a sort of tight-rope and telling them that
> if they concentrated on their steps and did not keep look-
> ing down into the chasm of their own military helplessness
> we thought there was a good chance that they would arrive
> safely on the other side. And on this basis we made our
> economic aid available.
>
> Now the first of the snags we have struck has been the
> fact that a lot of people have not been able to refrain from
> looking down.[18]

NATO, with all its shortcomings, helped the Europeans not to
"look down."

A second, related point turns on the desires of the Europeans themselves, largely treated as background in Kennan's conception. As events after the Korean invasion of 1950 amply
demonstrate, European elites of the center-right were at least as
concerned with external Soviet pressure as they were with internal subversion. Moreover, they feared that the United States
would withdraw to its own predilections as it had in 1919. Now
more than then, the United States was strong enough to hold the
balance of Europe's economic and military fate, but inaccessible
to European influence and determinedly innocent of European
domestic constraints and international fears. It was therefore the
Europeans as well as the Americans who, in Kennan's later
judgment, made the instruments of containment into ends in
themselves.[19]

Kennan's answer to European fears was the evolution of a "third force Europe," one capable of integrating its political and economic potential in order to itself contain the Soviet Union. But at no point from 1949 onward did the political preconditions for such a Europe exist. The available evidence suggests that American preferences and interests played an important role in the failure to unite Europe at some historic points—perhaps most vividly in 1956 and again in 1963. But the principal source of failure has been the continuing unwillingness of European elites and populations to make the hard choices needed to construct such a Europe. What, for example, is to be the role of a West Germany no longer balanced or guaranteed by a direct American presence? What is the appropriate role of the smaller states in the direction of European foreign policy? What is to be their role in the control of what would still remain the national nuclear forces of Britain and France? And what will be the form of intra-European relations, even with attenuating links between the two superpowers and at least different ties between the two Germanies?

Futures

Measured against many standards, NATO may be termed both a necessary and a sufficient condition for implementing postwar containment—at least in its first stages. But the American security agenda under which Kennan first proposed his policy of counterpressure has evolved with major discontinuities. Although not an independent center of power as envisioned by Kennan, Europe is nevertheless an economic and political power in its own right, increasingly critical of American leadership and somewhat restive in the intra-West dialogue. Soviet military capabilities are considerably greater than in 1949, though the actual nature of the Soviet threat is open to dispute. Many would argue, moreover, that foreseeable direct threats to American national security exist outside of Kennan's five vital centers of power. A changing security environment calls attention to American and European vulnerabilities to the interruption of vital resources and to the dangers inherent in international economic disruption. Further, NATO itself has evolved into a form that would have been unrecognizable in 1949: increased size and scope have transformed the Alliance both geographically and functionally.

In spite of these changes in the global environment, however, the policy questions for the United States remain remarkably constant. Can containment, and more specifically NATO, effectively preserve the Atlantic balance of power in the coming decade? Is there, indeed, any realistic alternative to NATO as an instrument of containment?

Events of the past decade emphasize that NATO's future effectiveness as an instrument of containment will depend not only on what it does vis-a-vis its adversaries but also on how well it manages relations among its members. The maintenance of adequate military forces must be complemented by sufficient attention to intra-Alliance relations. Both are central to Kennan's strategy:

> The problem of containment is basically a problem of the reactions of people within the non-communist world. It is true that this condition depends upon the maintenance by ourselves and our allies, at all times, of an adequate defense posture, designed to guard against misunderstandings and to give confidence and encouragement to the weak and fainthearted. But so long as that posture is maintained, the things that need most to be done to prevent the further expansion of Soviet power are not ... things we can do directly in our relations with the Soviet government; they are things we must do in our relations with the peoples of the non-communist world.[20]

In the coming decades, NATO will face many challenges to the management of its internal relations. As an organization, the Alliance will repeatedly be called upon to coordinate policies on arms control and out-of-area issues, to balance defense and economic concerns, and to reevaluate the structure of risks and benefits. The domestic link is equally critical. On both sides of the Atlantic, the national costs of containment—both political and economic—will become increasingly clear in a period of competing claims on an ever-smaller pool of funds. At the same time, domestic political support must be maintained at a time when many in a post-INF era are questioning the risks and benefits which accompany Alliance membership. Faced with these many challenges, both domestic and within the Alliance structure itself, NATO's utility as a psychological shield or as a military sword will be severely tested.

All of these forces for change, however, relate to the future, not the present. In one sense, they are anticipations of problems, projections perhaps of "worst-case scenarios." At the most, carried to their logical extremes, they point toward gradual attrition of present relationships, a gradual decline of the value and the burden assumed by the European-American link. However unsatisfactory and worrisome the Alliance link appears, the degree of popular support for the European-American connection and for sharing the security burden is, and appears likely to remain, remarkably high. There is, of course, no dearth of proposals for either radical or piecemeal reform of NATO. Most are unlikely to be implemented, given the natural conservatism of decisionmakers and their propensity to settle on a known quantity, no matter how severe its faults. The present pattern, therefore, appears a good bet for at least the next five to ten years, perhaps the only relevant horizon for present Western political leaders.

Only one European factor, not really new, points in the direction of fundamental change: the evolving relationship between East and West Germany. The present limits to this development are clear: in anything that matters, both superpowers reassert alliance priorities and receive eventual compliance. It is also not certain what either Germany's leaders really want from their mutual relationship in the short run: a sound show for domestic publics, a testing of their political maturity, a handy bargaining lever vis-a-vis their principals, or hostages taken against an uncertain or "inevitable" future. Given the many suspicions and constraints surrounding it, the impact of their relationship may well stem from the perceived potential for change rather than from its realization.

The "democratization" of the American defense debate is a second new factor. The nuclear freeze campaign's momentum has disappeared; its efforts to reach institutionalized status, either alone or in concert with other groups, have decisively failed. There remains far more political discussion and information about nuclear policy and arms control than before, but without an effective active program or discernible continuing political impact (e.g., contrast arms issues in the 1982 congressional election with those in the 1984 presidential race). SDI is accepted as "worth trying" despite the doubts of scientists and arms controllers. The need to be seen as "strong on defense" continues to be the touchstone for Democratic political candidates.

Even greater democratization in the United States would almost certainly have a fragmenting impact on the Alliance. The significance of American deployments in Europe has never been widely perceived by the electorate; it has symbolic support under the NATO umbrella but little else. Greater economic necessity, forcing a true choice between guns and butter, would arouse national sentiments akin to present protectionist outpourings. Moreover, a move toward conventional defense would raise the neuralgic issue of burden sharing and the unmentionable prospect of a return to the draft. Indeed, it may now be dangerously easy to advocate a return to Kennan's original notion of a disengaged America, broadly supportive of but not directly involved in the management of the European balance of political, economic, and eventually military power.

But the question still remains as to whether, if the United States does not completely go home and the American political system continues to support a broad NATO commitment, it is possible that there are alternative options for the organization of Atlantic security consistent with the goals of containment. One option—around for some time but a subject of renewed interest, particularly in the last year—is a revival of a European framework for defense. It would involve not Kennan's dumbbell or the European Defense Community concept of the 1950s but rather something closer perhaps to President John F. Kennedy's "two-pillar concept," with a loose European organization linked to something similar on this side of the Atlantic. These two pillars would be sufficient for deterrence and would coalesce into a single integrated organization in event of war.

Here one stumbles into the same kinds of problems which were critical in the 1950s. What is the basic willingness of Britain and France to accord Germany a full role in such an organization, unbalanced by an equalizing American weight? What new problems of nuclear control would arise and assume ever-increasing importance as the British and French forces modernize toward the 1990s and toward a third, significantly different stage of nuclear weapons development? How would these forces be coordinated with the American guarantee? And would all these arrangements allow Germany and the smaller states a direct role in deciding whether or not nuclear weapons are used in their defense? Or indeed, could they permit these states to develop nuclear weapons of their own, however unrealistic that now seems?

A second set of options, more consistent with the severe economic and demographic constraints Europe will increasingly face, emphasizes a drastic change in the kind of defense organization and level of effort European states would undertake. It might be a force structure "made in Europe" rather than in the United States. It might involve cadre divisions which could be filled out given sufficient warning, or greater emphasis on the use of reserves along the lines of that faded Swiss model of the gun in the closet. NATO as an overarching organization would be of lesser importance, while bilateral (especially US-German) ties would be crucial. But however attractive, such concepts include a formidable set of political responsibilities and would require a willingness to go beyond some rather bad memories of the past. The use of reserves—not just by Hitler, but indeed by the German leadership in the 1920s as well—suggest one unpleasant potential. Again, the question of the confidence of others—Europeans, Russians, and Americans—is paramount.

A third alternative is one barely outlined in Egon Bahr's catch-phrase, "mutual security through security partnership." Alluded to in the alternative strategy debates in Germany during 1983–84, this concept is one which takes account of the special security responsibilities borne by the two halves of Europe (and especially the two Germanies) toward one another. Some versions also include a closely connected set of responsibilities toward all targets of Nazi aggression, particularly "the Soviet people." At issue is not only the rethinking of present doctrine and force employment guidelines but also the development of a "non-provocative defense" in structure and operation. Remaining to be considered are the implications this arrangement would have on the stationing of other forces on German territory (East as well as West) or on the future conduct of the European-American alliance.

These are but three alternatives; there are many others that could be and have been considered. To most conceivable Atlantic leadership groups over the next decade, all of them will probably look less attractive than the basic NATO framework. This celebration of the status quo may be simply a tribute to our failure to imagine the full scope and impact of coming events. It certainly reflects the basic continuity of European and American interests, the set of beliefs and calculations which have always made the Atlantic tie the cornerstone of postwar foreign policy. Although dissatisfactions have grown, the probabilities for startling future achievements or new initiatives now seem very low. Along the crucial dimensions, it will almost certainly continue to seem the safest bet to stick with policy stances which promise the fewest risks and preserve the greatest number of future options while assuring present benefits.

Still open, however, are major questions which turn on the degree of attention given to European issues by future American administrations. How much strain will there be in normalization and adaptation? And will the containment bargains struck in the 1950s be fully understood by the political leaderships that will come to power in the United States during the 1980s and the 1990s?

Epilogue

Ten years after his first exposition of the containment doctrine, Kennan returned to the issue of NATO in a 1957 Reith lecture entitled "Strengthening NATO—To What End?" Kennan recalled his notion of NATO as a "military shield" to stabilize the situation in Western Europe and reassure the European people. "Strengthening NATO," he argued, must be not a military end in itself but the means to an end: "the piecemeal removal, by negotiation and compromise, of the major sources of the military danger, particularly, the abnormal situation now prevailing in Central and Eastern Europe, and the gradual achievement of a state of affairs in which the political competition could take its course without the constant threat of a general war." He concluded that NATO would also be ill-advised to "put all our eggs in the military basket and neglect the positive things" which Alliance members could do. The latter included cooperation on economic and technological issues and attention to domestic problems in each member country that undermined NATO's overall strength and utility. Kennan's words reflected an oft-repeated concern for the internal vitality and health of Western societies.[21]

Written over two decades ago, these words seem relevant to the world of the 1990s. Because radical departures from NATO as an instrument of containment seem unlikely, today's task is one of assuring that NATO can continue to function. The greatest danger lies in Soviet exploitation of internal weaknesses and divisions within countries and among Allies. Here Kennan's caution against becoming wholly fixated on the military aspects of containment is particularly pertinent. "Let us, then, while keeping our guard up and while never ceasing to explore the possibilities for progress by negotiation, not neglect those undertakings that are necessary for the spiritual and economic advancement of Western society."[22] In 1957 these undertakings included greater Western European integration, attention to the pound-dollar division, and establishment of common policies "in those areas where our concerns and responsibilities are common." Today the list would be somewhat different and far longer. But, as Kennan observed then, these things must not be "lost in the military shuffle." In fact, the future of even military containment may depend on making them the subject of sustained and common Atlantic effort.

Notes

Cathleen Fisher provided expert research assistance for the preparation of this paper.

1. George F. Kennan (writing as 'X'), "The Sources of Soviet Conduct," *Foreign Affairs* 25 (July 1947), p. 567.

2. Kennan, *Memoirs: 1925–1950* (Vol. I), (Boston: Little, Brown & Co., 1967), pp. 364–65.

3. Ibid., p. 358.

4. John Lewis Gaddis, *Strategies of Containment: A Critical Appraisal of Postwar American National Security Policy* (New York: Oxford University Press, 1982), chap. 2.

5. Kennan, *Memoirs* I, p. 336.

6. Ibid., p. 351.

7. Ibid., chaps. 1 and 2.

8. Ibid., p. 334.

9. Kennan, quoted in Gaddis, *Strategies of Containment,* p. 45.

10. Kennan, *Memoirs* I, p. 365.

11. Gaddis, *Strategies of Containment,* chaps. 3 and 4.

12. Kennan, *Memoirs* I, p. 407.

13. " 'X' Plus 25: Interview with George F. Kennan," *Foreign Policy,* No. 7 (Summer 1972).

14. Kennan, *Memoirs* I, p. 365.

15. Kennan, *Russia, the Atom and the West,* the BBC Reith Lectures (New York: Harper and Brothers Publishers, 1957), p. 46.

16. Gaddis, *Strategies of Containment,* p. 65.

17. Ibid., p. 88.

18. Kennan, quoted in ibid., pp. 73–74.

19. Kennan, quoted in ibid., p. 79.

20. Kennan, *The Realities of American Foreign Policy* (Princeton: Princeton University Press, 1954), p. 87.

21. Kennan, *Russia, the Atom and the West,* pp. 96–97.

22. Ibid.

16

Kennan, Containment, and Crises in Eastern Europe

Karen Dawisha

S TATIONED IN MOSCOW as second-in-command of the US
embassy at the end of World War II, George Kennan reflected pessimistically on the new global order. He not only saw
around him the total devastation of victors and vanquished alike
across the entire Eurasian continent, but he also attributed much
of the cause for the outbreak of the war to the failure of diplomacy as an instrument and the balance of power as a system.
Europe too, he calculated, had in its brutal division become the
subject rather than the object of global competition—and so he
feared it was likely to remain for decades to come.

Like Churchill in his 1946 speech at Fulton, Missouri,
Kennan warned that the West might be defeated even in the absence of war if it failed to recognize the threat to Western
values, interests, and ultimately Western territory posed by the
Soviet Union's subversive intent, the phalanx-like purposive-
ness of its internal order, and the expansionist aspirations inherent in its ideology.

Karen Dawisha, a Soviet policy expert, is a Professor of Government and Politics at the University of Maryland.

Kennan's "long telegram" from Moscow in February 1946 alerted US decisionmakers to the fact that the world was going to be bipolar for the foreseeable future, and global politics were going to be shaped by intense rivalry between two powerful and mutually antagonistic blocs. Soon after, in the USSR, Party Secretary Andrei Zhdanov enunciated the "two-camp" theory, dividing the world into implacably opposed ideological blocs.[1] And in the very same issue of *Foreign Affairs* in which Kennan published his famous 'X' article on "The Sources of Soviet Conduct," the noted Soviet economist Evgeni Varga published an article that forecast the further demise of European, and particularly British, influence over world affairs, leaving a vacuum which increasingly would be filled by the United States and the Soviet Union.[2] By the beginning of 1948, therefore, each side saw the other as its primary opponent in the next phase of global struggle.

Ideological Deviation and Nuclear Division

The 'X' article unquestionably helped to shape the basic concept of containment which underlay American policy during the 1950s. How ironic it was, therefore, that when he came to write the first volume of his memoirs in the mid-1960s, Kennan should "emphatically deny paternity of any efforts to invoke that doctrine today in situations to which it has and can have no proper relevance."[3]

Kennan was referring here to two major situations. One was the growth of fissiparous tendencies in the international communist movement, which had led by the mid-1960s to the Soviet rift with Yugoslavia, the Sino-Soviet conflict, and the beginning of reform movements in a number of Eastern European countries. When he wrote those memoirs, he had good reason to hope that Eastern Europe might yet emerge from the system of firm control imposed by Stalin. Although Hungary had been kept within the Soviet orbit (though only by force) in 1956, the balance sheet for the West in 1967, when the first volume of Kennan's memoirs appeared, was not without promise. The Yugoslav "deviation" had survived, the 1955 Austrian State Treaty had produced a Soviet troop withdrawal in return for neutralization, and the Chinese stand against Moscow had drawn Albanian support and spurred Romanian defiance. Intellectuals in Budapest, Warsaw, and most of all in Prague were talking about the need for the reform of the socialist system.

Kennan had good reason, therefore, to hope that the need for containment of Soviet communism in Europe would diminish as a result of the internal transformation of the socialist bloc, brought about by the gradual de-Stalinization of the Soviet system and the redefinition of Soviet vital interests away from Eastern Europe. Nevertheless, the invasion of Czechoslovakia in 1968 sadly diminished the grounds for Kennan's optimism. Improvements made in Eastern Europe during the 1970s were once again jeopardized by the Polish crisis in 1980–81, and it would now appear that the cycle of reform and reaction in Eastern Europe at best promises an evolutionary process of "two steps forward and one step back," and at worst, during periods of crisis, threatens to destroy the delicate fabric of postwar security arrangements.

The second situation which Kennan felt had undermined containment was the development of nuclear weapons by the United States and the USSR, spurring an uncontrolled, and indeed perhaps uncontrollable, arms race in the fields of nuclear weapons, delivery systems, and space technology. So George Kennan, who in 1946 hoped for a restoration of the balance of power and advocated a multidimensional policy of containment to meet the challenge of Soviet expansion, saw instead the birth of the balance of terror. The transformation of the international system by nuclear arms was complete: not only did nuclear weapons revolutionize the waging of war, they also transformed the waging of peace.

And nowhere did this transformation in warfighting technology intermingle with mutual suspicion more than in Central

Europe. By 1955 the North Atlantic Treaty Organization and the Warsaw Treaty Organization had already begun the process of militarization and rearmament in the name of mutual deterrence which continues today. Even as early as 1948, Kennan had serious reservations about the wisdom of both the division of Germany and the creation of security systems in Europe: he warned, "from such a trend of developments, it would be hard ... to find 'the road back' to a united and free Europe."[4] As he was to observe in his memoirs, the major difficulty posed by the creation of NATO and the Warsaw Pact was that although both pacts were formed as *instruments* of policy they inexorably became *ends* of policy, with questions of alliance cohesion and military preparedness taking precedence over reunification and genuine security in Europe. He regarded the stationing of Soviet and American forces in Europe as unnatural, and he hoped it would be temporary.[5]

Of course, Kennan's hopes have not been realized. Not only has the division of Europe continued, but the recent deployment of Soviet and American intermediate-range nuclear forces in Central Europe has increased doubts of its rationality on both sides of the Iron Curtain. Additional voices have been raised challenging the *raison d'être* of the bloc system in Europe, maintaining that the division of Europe is artificial and dangerous: far from guaranteeing its continued security, Europe's division has become its major source of insecurity. The over-reliance on the military instrument, it is argued, has created an unnecessary intrusion of security interests into political and economic debates. This intrusion has occurred to some extent in Western Europe (as in American concerns over the security implications of socialist or communist party electoral victories in Italy or France), but it takes on a much sharper and even qualitatively different significance in Eastern Europe.

There, local regimes have struggled to increase the viability of their own rule against the backdrop of widespread unpopularity, brought about largely by the universal perception that local leaders serve Moscow's interests, particularly in the security field. The unity and cohesion of the Warsaw Pact is an inalienable principle of socialist construction, and any indigenous reform in Eastern Europe will be allowed only to the extent that it is thought to enhance and not detract from adherence to this principle. Leeway is greater when Moscow feels itself to be less under external threat, as during both the mid-1960s and mid-1970s, but maneuverability is more limited when the Soviet Union is challenged either by unacceptably subversive reforms in Eastern Europe or by changes in the military balance of power on the central front. Such changes have occurred on several occasions. The entry of Germany into NATO in 1955 triggered the formation of the Warsaw Pact and contributed to the Soviet Union's sharp response when Hungary tried to leave the Pact in 1956. In the mid-1960s, the NATO doctrine of "flexible response" produced great Soviet military pressure on Czechoslovakia to accept the permanent stationing of Russian troops, and Czech refusal to agree was one important reason for the Soviet invasion of August 1968.[6]

Beginning in the late 1970s, the gradual shift in both Soviet and American strategic doctrine produced the deployment in European Russia of SS–20s targeted on Western Europe, and the counterdeployment of Pershing–II and cruise missiles in Western Europe targeted on the Soviet Union. The Soviet response included the stationing of SS–22 missiles in Czechoslovakia and East Germany; and by mid-1985, despite various proposals for arms limitations and reductions, there appeared little prospect of "turning back the clock." This latest round of the arms race, involving the European members of the two blocs as never before, put great pressure on Eastern European states already reeling from the effect of the Polish crisis. Leading politicians in Hungary, Romania, and East Germany, supported to a certain extent by some sympathetic commentaries in the Soviet press, insisted that the "small states" in Europe have a significant role to play in preserving the achievements of detente, irrespective of their bloc affiliation.[7] This debate has continued despite the failure of these states to wrest significant concessions from Moscow in return for the extension of the Warsaw Treaty, and there is obviously considerable hope in Eastern Europe that the new Soviet leadership will allow reform to continue. But, as repeatedly emphasized in Eastern Europe, the collapse of Soviet-American detente in the early 1980s certainly has decreased the scope for maneuver.

The point that needs underlining here is not that the West was in any way responsible for the original division of Europe. That came about as the result of Stalin's own designs. Nor is it being suggested that if NATO were unilaterally to disappear there would be no Soviet impediment to European unification and independence. On the contrary, the Soviet Union will not peacefully relinquish fundamental control over Eastern Europe, taken to mean the member states of the Warsaw Pact. What is being argued is that the record of Soviet behavior shows Eastern Europe to be the geopolitical area in which the most vital Soviet external interests are engaged, but that problems inherent in the structure of Soviet control and the legitimacy of these regimes make Eastern Europe potentially more crisis-prone and therefore more dangerous than any other area where Soviet and Western interests collide.

Soviet Reactions to Crises

Three crucial elements create and define a crisis condition for decisionmakers: (1) a threat to basic values, (2) high risk of involvement in military hostilities, and (3) finite time for response—not necessarily a short time, but a specific situation which obliges decisionmakers to operate under the pressure of a perceived deadline.[8] The theoretical literature assumes that as a crisis escalates, the stress on individual decisionmakers becomes more intense and impairs their capability to cope with the situation effectively or rationally. In particular, studies have shown that American policymakers tend in crises to rely on stereotypes and rigid images of the outside world.[9]

Although in normal times Soviet decisionmakers since Stalin have held an extremely complex and differentiated image of the outside world, during crises there is also in the Soviet Union a marked tendency to rely on stereotypes. Kremlin leaders, according to almost all the literature on Soviet crisis behavior, revert to "two-camp" images and see the source of the crisis as being the undifferentiated and unending hostility of the imperialist world toward the very existence of socialism, even though in their management of the crisis they may continue to show caution and avoid risks.[10]

This tendency has, however, been most evident in Soviet handling of the crises in Central Europe, ranging from Hungary in 1956 to Berlin in 1961, Czechoslovakia in 1968, and Poland in 1980–81. For example, in each of these four crises, Soviet leaders appreciated and acted on the specific internal source of the crisis, whether it was the actual uprising in Hungary, the Rupublikflucht in Berlin, the ambivalence of Dubcek in preventing the institutionalization of the reform movement in Czechoslovakia, or the dislocation of Polish society produced by economic and other failures. Nevertheless, as these crises escalated, Soviet alarm was magnified by a tendency to perceive wider sources and repercussions.

Elsewhere, the Soviet Union has shown itself capable of managing crises without reverting to these base stereotypes. During the four most obvious cases—the Cuban missile crisis, the mining of Haiphong harbor, the October 1973 Middle East war, and (to a lesser extent) the 1979 invasion of Afghanistan—Soviet statements did not reflect the image of an absolutely undifferentiated and total attack by imperialism on the socialist camp, even though US military forces were actually involved in Vietnam and Cuba. Although important issues and interests were at stake, the Soviet response to these crises was nevertheless cooler, more complex, and able to differentiate between the local Soviet-American rivalry and the wider demands of superpower cooperation. Thus, at the height of the Cuban missile crisis, Khrushchev was able to appeal directly to Kennedy for a deescalation, saying that "we argue with you, we differ on ideological questions. But in our conception of the world, ideological questions and economic problems should not be resolved by warfare but in peaceful . . . competition."[11] In 1973, during the October Middle East war, the Soviets never blamed the United States for Israeli activities and ambitions, seeking throughout to maintain the distinction between Israeli actions, supported though they were by the United States, on the one hand, and Soviet-American efforts to find a ceasefire, on the other. In Afghanistan, the Soviet leadership seems to have calculated, wrongly as it turned out, that they would be able to isolate the invasion from their wider rivalry with the United States. And in Vietnam, the Soviet leadership, against some internal opposition from Alexander Shelepin and Piotr Shelest (who was demoted the day before Nixon's visit to Kiev), decided to distinguish US involvement from the wider opportunities for cooperation between the two countries in other areas, including arms control.

As with all generalizations, there are exceptions. For example, in 1968 Prime Minister Kosygin was particularly keen to decouple the negotiations with the United States on strategic arms limitation from the negative effects of the harder line which emerged in Soviet policy toward the Czechoslovak reform movement. Although he succeeded, he did so only by making arms talks a private negotiation, inevitably subservient to the gradual hardening of the general line. By midsummer, there were Central Committee declarations and top leadership statements that imperialist subversion had become the major front in the struggle between socialism and capitalism. As the crisis in Czechoslovakia escalated, therefore, it became impossible for Kosygin or anyone else to oppose the hard-line view of the Prague Spring as an attack by imperialism and counter-revolution on the very basis of socialism in that country, and as an attempt to change the borders of the socialist bloc, repeatedly referred to in the Soviet press as "our" borders.[12]

However, attempts by hard-liners like Shelest and Shelepin to draw similar analogies between crises in Eastern Europe and the war in Vietnam failed. Although there were differences in their views, hard-liners were again united in seeing the bombing and mining of Haiphong harbor as proof of the unending hostility of imperialism toward socialism as a whole, and as reason not to improve Soviet-American relations. The difference between the Czech and Vietnam crises was that in 1968 the hard-line opposition prevailed but in 1972 it did not; the reason it failed was partially the much more positive anticipated gain in 1972 but also, even more importantly, the permanent obsession of the Soviet leadership with crises in Eastern Europe.

The Dangers of Superpower Confrontation

The implications of these experiences are twofold. First, Soviet leaders objectively place the security, cohesion, and control of Eastern Europe above their other global objectives. Although they would not wish any crisis in Eastern Europe to harm their relationship with the United States, they will protect their interests in Eastern Europe if forced to choose, as in 1980–81. Second, such is the centrality of Eastern Europe to Soviet security and ideological interests that, whatever receptivity Soviet leaders may exhibit toward reform in Eastern Europe during non-crisis periods, crises almost inevitably trigger misperceptions, distortions, and ideological rigidity that end, at least temporarily, any chance for reform. It took the Hungarians over a decade to recover from the effects of the 1956 rebellion; the Czechs have yet to emerge from the after-effects of the 1968 invasion; and the Poles may have to wait even longer before they can retrieve any of the gains made before the imposition of martial law.

The situation in East Germany is even more delicate because of firm Soviet resistance to any reform which might hint at national reunification. The divisions both of Germany and of Berlin are the most visible expressions of the contradictions inherent in a divided Europe. Thus, in ordinary times, the prosperity of both Germanies and the loyalty of each to its own bloc are apparent testimonies to the vitality and viability of postwar security arrangements. However, every time there is a crisis in Central Europe—East or West—that crisis touches the nerve of the German question, reminding everyone that it is still unanswered. And it is significant that both East and West Germans have been at the forefront of efforts to shield their own "special relationship" from any new phase of Soviet-American confrontation. They reject containment and suggest that the only way to change the status quo is, ironically, to accept it. As a result, there are many high officials even in the Federal Republic who now call for a peace treaty and the formal exchange of ambassadors between the two German states. Such actions, it is argued, would further stabilize the previously uncertain situation in Central Europe, reassuring Moscow and thereby creating a climate for gradually improved links between Eastern and Western Europe outside the security field.

The threat to world peace from crises in which US and Soviet interests compete has never been greater. The avoidance of nuclear war over the past forty years can be attributed to equal measures of design and luck, to largely fortuitous imbalances between superpower capabilities and interests. It will not always be possible to depend on the coincidence of activity on the part of one superpower with passivity on the part of the other. Circumstances which were fortuitous in the past may not continue into the future, particularly in an era of nuclear parity and under conditions in which crisis escalation may result from internal political pressures as much as from rational calculation of outcome and risk. Because the Soviets have shown a propensity toward caution and risk avoidance, such danger as exists in the Third World lies in the sheer number of conflicts that have become globalized and the extent of arms supplies. In Eastern Europe, the danger lies rather in the extent of Soviet vital interest, combined with the fragility of nonmilitary methods of control and the fundamental illegitimacy of many Eastern European regimes.

The West may be able to contain and challenge Soviet opportunism in the Third World without great danger to global peace, but in Eastern Europe such challenges are hardly realistic. There, the USSR has shown increasing willingness to use overwhelming force to protect its interests, despite the fact that efforts to reassert short-term control undermine the long-term domestic viability of socialism among Eastern European populations. Reflecting on the reasons for the West's failure to prevent the division of Europe, George Kennan concluded some twenty years after the 'X' article that responsibility lay not in the injustice of American ideals but in the overwhelming and therefore self-defeating American reliance on the military instrument to achieve Western goals. To the extent that containment had failed, he wrote, "the failure consisted in the fact that our own government, finding it difficult to deal with it [the Soviet threat] in other than military terms . . . exerted itself, in its military preoccupations, to seal and to perpetuate the very division of Europe which it should have been concerned to remove."[13]

In conclusion, therefore, the incredible sensitivity of the Soviets when dealing with crisis in Eastern Europe is likely to continue, and as George Kennan has long maintained, the West should not hope or expect that a direct or indirect military challenge to Soviet hegemony there will produce anything but the most negative results. Order might appear to have triumphed over justice in this argument, but attempts to balance the two recall the debate between the Athenians and the Melians described by Thucydides. The Melians, whose neutrality in the Peloponnesian war was being challenged by the stronger Athenians, pleaded for justice at the expense of order; but the Athenians responded that international relations is the domain of necessity and that there are times when "justice and honor cannot be followed without danger"; after which they proceeded to conquer and kill the Melians. At a time when Europeans, both East and West, are trying to preserve a tentative detachment from the Cold War, these words maintain a poignant, if mournful, appropriateness.

Notes

I would like to thank Raymond Garthoff for valuable comments on an earlier written draft of this paper. John Steinbruner, Michael McGwire, and Richard Betts also provided useful comments during a seminar presentation at the Brookings Institution, where I was a guest scholar in 1983–84. Portions of this paper are drawn from the draft of my forthcoming book on *Eastern Europe In Between* for the Council on Foreign Relations.

1. The two-camp theory had its roots in Party resolutions and articles by Zhdanov on "Survivals of bourgeois ideology" among Soviet intellectuals who expressed "servibility" toward the West while ignoring the decisive role of Russian ideas. See, for example, his sharp denunciation of G.F. Aleksandrov's book, *History of West European Philosophy* in *Bolshevik*, No. 16 (August 1947), p. 22. Aleksandrov at that time was the head of the Propaganda Department of the Communist Party.

2. E. Varga "Anglo-American Rivalry and Partnership: A Marxist View," *Foreign Affairs* 25 (July 1947), pp. 583–96.

3. George Kennan, *Memoirs, 1925–1950* (New York: Bantam, 1967), p. 387.

4. *PPS 37*, "Policy Questions Concerning a Possible German Settlement," 12 August 1948, FR: 1948, II, 1287–97, quoted in John Lewis Gaddis, *Strategies of Containment: A Critical Appraisal of Postwar American National Security Policy*, (New York: Oxford University Press, 1982), p. 75.

5. Kennan, *Memoirs, 1925–1950*, pp. 477–81.

6. See Karen Dawisha, "Soviet Security and the Role of the Mil-

itary: The 1968 Czechoslovak Crisis," *British Journal of Political Science* 10 (1980), pp. 341–63.

7. Matyas Szuros, secretary of the Hungarian Socialist Workers' Party Central Committee, has been a consistent promoter of these views. For a collection of his speeches and the debate between Moscow and the East Europeans, see Ronald D. Asmus, *East Berlin and Moscow: The Documentation of Dispute* (Munich: Radio Free Europe, 1985). The Soviet reaction to this debate has continued with a hard-line denunciation by a top Soviet official in *Pravda* on 21 June 1985 of East European mediation between Moscow and Washington. In an apparent response, two articles appeared in the July edition of *Kommunist* (No. 10, 1985, pp. 70–81, 82–93), one by the deputy general secretary of the Hungarian Socialist Workers' Party and one by the director of the Soviet Institute of the Economics of the World Socialist System. They argued that Soviet control cannot be achieved at the expense of viability of local regimes, since to ignore local national interests would not further the goals of bloc unity and strength.

8. Michael Brecher, *Decisions in Crisis: Israel, 1967 and 1973* (Berkeley: University of California Press, 1980), p. 1.

9. See Davis Bobrow, et al., "Understanding How Others Treat Crisis," *International Studies Quarterly* 21 (March 1977), pp. 199–224; Joseph De Rivera, *The Psychological Dimension of Foreign Policy* (Columbus, Ohio: Charles E. Merrill, 1968); Robert Jervis, *Perception and Misperception in International Politics* (Princeton: Princeton University Press, 1976); and Richard S. Lazarus, *Psychological Stress and the Coping Process* (New York: McGraw-Hill, 1966).

10. See Hannes Adomeit, *Soviet Risk Taking and Crisis Behavior* (London: Allen and Unwin, 1982); and Stephen S. Kaplan, *Diplomacy of Power: Soviet Armed Forces as a Political Instrument* (Washington: Brookings Institution, 1981).

11. Herbert S. Dinerstein, *The Making of a Missile Crisis: October 1962* (Baltimore: Johns Hopkins University Press, 1976), p. 274.

12. Analyzed in depth in Karen Dawisha, *The Kremlin and the Prague Spring* (Berkeley: University of California Press, 1984).

13. Kennan, *Memoirs, 1925–1950*, p. 385.

17

An Arab View of Containment

Rashid Khalidi

IN CONSIDERING A DOCTRINE as important as containment, it is useful to reflect on both the circumstances in which it was first enunciated and the original ideas from which it grew. For the major gap in time between the writing of "The Sources of Soviet Conduct" in 1947 and the actual application of containment theory to the Middle East in the following decade was accompanied by major transformations in regional and world realities.

Most of these changes had taken place by the mid-1950s, the heyday of containment in the Middle East, when plans were formulated first for a Middle East Command, then for a Middle East Defense Organization, and finally for the Baghdad Pact (or Central Treaty Organization, as it came to be known). In the intervening period, the line between East and West had hardened in Europe, two wars had been fought in Asia, and the principles of "firm containment, designed to confront the Russians

Rashid Khalidi is Associate Professor in the Political Science Department at Columbia University.

with unalterable counter-force at every point" had become articles of faith in the United States, embodied in a chain of alliance systems around the USSR.

Changes occurred in the Soviet Union as well, following
the death of Stalin. These were profound changes, which
George Kennan himself foresaw in part in his seminal article,
but whose scope and significance surpassed the comprehension
of most Western policymakers at the time. Changes also
occurred in the Middle East. The most notable of these were the
rise of local nationalism, the eruption of the Arab-Israeli conflict as a primary focus of regional tension, and the arrival of
the Soviet Union on the scene as a major power, beginning with
the now-famous Egyptian and Syrian arms deals of 1955.

Two interesting points emerge from a consideration of the
central premises of Kennan's thesis in relation to the Middle
East. The first is the rigidity with which these ideas were applied, often in simplified and unrealistic form, to the Middle
Eastern reality of the 1950s. The alliances, pacts, and military
commands which were proposed then have resurfaced in slightly
different forms at various times, most recently in former Secretary of State Alexander Haig's 1981 call for a regional "strategic
consensus" against the Soviet Union.

In making such proposals, Western policymakers have paid
little attention to regional configurations. In the 1950s, countries
which had been involved in decades-long struggles to free themselves of foreign bases were asked to accept such bases on their
soil in the name of a conflict with the Soviet Union which most
did not consider a priority. Furthermore, the sensitivities of the
states of the region were often ignored in such planning, which
at times called for strategic coordination between the Arab states
and Israel despite the absence of a settlement between them, or
similarly asked other traditional regional rivals to work together.
Finally, sensitive nationalist regimes were told that they could
not obtain Western arms or aid unless they accepted such
unpalatable arrangements.

In fairness to Kennan, it should be recognized that the almost mechanical way in which containment was put into practice in the Middle East during the early fifties had little relation to the ideas he had actually expressed. Specifically, alliance systems were created or projected in this region in circumstances quite different from those which he described as necessitating a policy of firm containment wherever the Soviets showed "signs of encroaching upon the interests of a peaceful and stable world." Clearly, the Baghdad Pact and its predecessors were put forward at a time and place where few such signs existed.

This consideration brings us to the second striking feature of the application of Kennan's ideas to the Middle East. Historically, before 1955, there was no Soviet push in this region, no "unceasing, constant pressure" as in Europe, Asia, and Southeast Asia. Indeed, the Soviet Union was hardly a major regional player, and the area was almost completely free of Moscow's influence before the dramatic chain of events of 1955–56 brought a massive Soviet presence in several Arab countries. It is true that Iran, Turkey, and Greece were all subjected to just such pressure in the mid-1940s. But these events occurred in the two years immediately after World War II and form part of another story, that of the resolution of issues left over from wartime dispositions and from the Yalta and other great power conferences. Moreover, this pressure came at the height of the Stalin period and was characteristically heavy-handed, an example of the very conduct Kennan was trying to explain in his essay. By contrast, in the years following 1947, the USSR adopted a distinctly lower profile in the Middle East, even as the Korean War and events in Europe seemed to confirm the validity of the Kennan thesis.

Indeed, far from there being Soviet pressure in the core countries of the Middle East, 1948 saw the United States and the Soviet Union on the same side of the Palestine dispute, competing with one another to be the first to recognize the new state of Israel. And when the Soviets did enter the region in the mid-1950s it was *not* as a result of ceaseless, unremitting pressure, but rather because they were invited in by Arab nationalist regimes like that of Abd al-Nasser. The Egyptian leader and others like him had sought Western aid and arms, but they were infuriated by the demands made upon them as quid pro quo in line with the containment policies of the United States and the neocolonial posture of its British and French allies. Primary Egyptian sources make it quite clear that, in his initial contact with Chou En Lai at the Bandung Non-Aligned Conference in April 1955, it was Abd al-Nasser who sought out the Soviets rather than vice versa. Moreover, it was only intense frustration with the strong pressure being put on Arab states to join Western alliance systems, combined with an escalation of tension on the frontiers with Israel, which drove both Egypt and Syria to take such a radical step in 1955. In this sense, the heavy-handed implementation of containment in the Middle East produced the very danger it was meant to contain!

Ironically, at the same time that the USSR was moving away from the rigidly bipolar "two-camp" theory associated with Andrei Zhdanov, enabling it to benefit from the growing trend of neutralism and nonalignment in the Third World, the United States was moving in just the opposite direction. Under the vicarship of John Foster Dulles, US foreign policy took on a Manichean cast, transforming containment into a rigid doctrine.

Though based on extensive first-person observation at the height of the Stalin era, Kennan's theory on how to deal with the Soviet Union nonetheless included crucial elements of flexibility. In the hands of Dulles, much of this flexibility disappeared at a time when Soviet policy was much more able to capitalize on American inflexibility. The resulting enunciation and application of this form of containment in effect isolated the United States from those who failed to perceive the world in strictly bipolar terms. Thus American friendship was extended only to the Camille Chamouns and Nuri Sa'ids, who were overtly anticommunist and closely aligned with the United States in international affairs, even when this orientation was considered inappropriate or even harmful by the polities they led. The end result was a diminution of US influence in the Middle East.

Things became worse in the following decade, when the Arab-Israeli dispute became increasingly polarized along East-West lines. In the 1960s, American policymakers—preoccupied with the Vietnam War—were naturally inclined to see the Middle East in the same East-West terms that dominated their view of Southeast Asia. They thus accepted the assurances of those who argued that American interests against the Soviet Union were served when Israel successfully confronted the Arabs.

This patently false argument, first trotted out in the period following the 1967 war, has had a long shelf-life; it was revitalized early in the Reagan administration after a blessed period of dormancy. But like the Middle East containment policies of the 1950s, it almost totally ignores regional realities. These include the non- or anticommunist nature of regimes in virtually all the Arab states since they gained their independence, the enormous scope for active Soviet involvement in the region provided by absolute if not unquestioning American support for Israel, and the basic desire of most Arab states involved in the confrontation with Israel for good relations with the United States, notwithstanding the need of many of them for Soviet arms.

Most important among these realities, however, is the direct link between anti-American feeling in the region and perceived American bias in favor of Israel, particularly in times of crisis over the past two decades. A recent example was the aftermath of the 1982 Israeli invasion of Lebanon, when the most virulent and destructive wave of hostility toward the United States in the history of the Arab world was unleashed as a direct result of perceived American-Israeli collusion. The United States and the region will continue to pay the price for such perceptions, not so much in strategic terms, where much damage can yet be done, as in terms of the American cultural, educational, and humanitarian presence in Lebanon, which is much more significant in the long run and is now being rapidly eroded.

Moreover, the much-touted strategic advantages for the United States of close alignment with Israel were proven hollow by the end results of the Lebanese war. It may have brought joy to the hearts of the short-sighted to witness the spectacle of F–15s and F–16s shooting down MiG–23s and MiG–25s, or to contemplate the acquisition of some choice intelligence data. But the Soviets simply upped the ante in terms of both hardware and their own direct military commitment, backing the winning Syrian horse in the Lebanese conflict with the consequent humiliation of both the United States and Israel.

As a result, an ill-thought-out attempt to reduce Soviet influence has again led instead to its increase. Following the advice of those who believe that sowing suspicion and distrust between Americans and Arabs will lead to defeats for the Soviet Union has served neither the interests of the United States nor those of the region itself.

By now it should be clear that the Middle East is not among those regions where there is a significant constituency for a policy of containment of the USSR. Of course, such an assertion must be qualified by events like the invasion of Afghanistan, a matter of some regional concern. But the limits of this concern can be seen in the fact that it has not been strong enough to cause Iran to abandon its nonalignment between the two superpowers or Saudi Arabia to align itself overtly with the United States against the Soviet Union. Although the latter course was urged by Secretary Haig on his April 1981 tour of the region, the Saudis and their Gulf allies seem to be edging in the opposite direction. Just as in the 1950s, the Soviet Union today is not seen by public opinion or by most leaders in the Middle East as the most serious threat to their security.

The perception of many in Washington—that some states aligned with Moscow (like Libya and South Yemen, or even Syria) are no more than regional proxies for the Soviet

Union—is clearly not shared by their local rivals. Saudi Arabia, the Sudan, Morocco, Tunisia, Jordan, and Egypt—all good friends of the United States—generally try to restrain the Soviet Union's friends in the Middle East by improving bilateral relations with those countries, by improving their own ties with the Soviet Union, or by creating countervailing local alignments and axes. They are very unlikely to see local conflicts as primarily East-West issues and act accordingly.

Only Israel claims to be wholly in favor of such an approach, and its posture seems mainly designed to appeal to American preferences. In practice, Israeli governments have shown themselves willing to be most pragmatic and unideological in their dealings with Moscow, *if* there is a possibility of their benefiting. Israeli reiterations of the danger of the Arab-Soviet axis notwithstanding, Israel has consistently operated with a full awareness of the contradictions between Soviets and Arabs and the inherent limitations and constraints in their relations.

Thus we are left with a most pernicious outlook—an American preoccupation with the USSR in the Middle East to the exclusion of far more important regional considerations, and a consequent reliance on Israel as the only reliable American regional ally, the unsinkable Eastern Mediterranean aircraft carrier. This extremist outlook is grounded not in reality but in ideology, and serves neither the interests of the United States nor those of the Arab nations, nor even those of the Israeli people.

To be sure, Arab extremists have played their part in regional polarization. But sadly, it has been those in Israel, many of them in what is conventionally considered the mainstream, who have done the most to perpetuate a simplistic Cold War view of Middle Eastern conflicts. They have only succeeded in doing so, however, because of the lack of clarity of those in the United States, and in Washington in particular, who have failed to take account of changes in the realities of world and regional politics since George Kennan set pen to paper nearly forty years ago.

18

Strategies for Containment in the Middle East

Bruce R. Kuniholm

I N APRIL 1945, HARRY S TRUMAN became President of the United States. World War II was not yet over, but the world power balance had already been radically altered and the loci of world power had shifted to Washington and Moscow. Within a year, Stalin was exploring his options along the Soviet Union's southern borders and, it appeared, would continue to do so unless resisted. The British empire, meanwhile, was disintegrating. By 1948, the British would be forced to withdraw their forces from Greece, Turkey, India, and Palestine. The combination of the rise of Soviet power and the demise of British influence presented the United States with new responsibilities and difficult choices.

Bruce R. Kuniholm is Associate Professor of Public Policy Studies and History at Duke University.

From British to American Containment

In the nineteenth century, the expanding Russian and British empires had played for high stakes. A consequence of their rivalry from the Balkans to India was the creation of a zone of buffer states between their two empires. The rulers of these buffer states traditionally opposed the ambitions of both empires and sought to survive by playing one off against the other. At the end of World War II, this game became more difficult, and the survival of Turkey and Iran was threatened by the relative disparity between Soviet and British power. Of the thirteen noncommunist states that bordered Russia before the war, only five were independent when it was over. Norway seemed secure, Finland was neutralized, and Afghanistan retained its traditional role as a buffer state, but Turkey and Iran were in serious jeopardy of being drawn into the Soviet fold. While almost all of the states in the Middle East welcomed the decline of British influence, those on the periphery of the Soviet Union recognized the need for a countervailing force to balance Soviet influence. Invariably, they asked the United States for help.

President Truman's response to Soviet pressures on Iran and Turkey in 1946 was a gradually increasing commitment to the two countries' territorial integrity and sovereignty. Events in those countries during the early postwar years schooled the administration in balance of power politics and the fundamentals of containment—even before the containment thesis was consciously propounded. Had the United States failed to confront Soviet pressures in Iran and Turkey, it is likely that Marshal Stalin would have been able to expand his sphere of influence in the Near East as he did in Eastern Europe and the Far East. The administration's policies, in short, put Stalin on notice that expansion to the south could be carried out only at the risk of confrontation.[1]

When Whitehall found itself unable to continue supporting Greece and Turkey in 1947, President Truman, in the first of a series of postwar doctrines that would define US commitments to the Near East, responded by asking Congress to assist the two states. The president's commitment to maintain the balance of power in the Near East was articulated publicly in March 1947 in the Truman Doctrine, and his determination to sustain that commitment throughout the early postwar period served to undergird his administration's policies in the Middle East. Their primary objective was to contain Soviet influence through economic, political, and military support for the sovereignty and territorial integrity of the Middle East's "Northern Tier." Implicit in the notion of containment was the idea of an equilibrium of forces; it had been a cornerstone of British diplomacy in the Near East for over a century, and would come to play the same role for US diplomacy in the postwar era.

In the early 1950s, the United States strengthened its commitments to the defense of the Near East when the enormous increases in defense expenditures associated with the Korean War appeared to obviate the necessity of distinguishing between peripheral and vital concerns. Making such distinctions had always troubled the Joint Chiefs of Staff, who disagreed among themselves over the relative importance of the balance of power in Western Europe and the Near East. When difficult choices were no longer required, Turkey's strategic contribution to the NATO alliance and the fact that the Middle East was supplying 75 percent of all European oil requirements led the Joint Chiefs to view the balance of power in the Near East as directly related to the balance of power in Europe and to see Turkey as the linchpin.[2] As a result, President Truman supported the incorporation of Greece and Turkey into NATO.

The role played by Turkey in containing Soviet influence in the Middle East was, and continues to be, critical. In addition to serving as a threat to the Soviet Union's southern flank and, hence, as a deterrent to a Soviet attack on NATO's central front, Turkey has the potential to block the projection of Soviet naval power in the Aegean, and to detect, intercept, and limit the intrusion of Soviet land-based aircraft into the Mediterranean and the Middle East. Turkey also provides facilities that are crucial to NATO security concerns and fortify an important land barrier to Soviet influence in the region.[3] "It is only behind [the] solid Turkish shield on the northern edge of the Middle East," Dankwart Rustow has pointed out,

> that governments in Cairo, Baghdad, or Damascus can afford to play their precarious balancing acts by leaning toward Moscow one year and toward Washington the next without incurring the fate of governments in Warsaw, Prague or Kabul. Only behind that Turkish shield can Israel effectively cope with the intermittent hostility of the surrounding Arab countries without having to confront Soviet armies on the Golan Heights.[4]

The Persian Gulf region, meanwhile, with the important exception of Saudi Arabia, was regarded during much of the postwar era as a British preserve. This was true from World War II, when the Persian Corridor played an important part in the supply of lend-lease goods to Russia, until 1971, when the British withdrew. Nevertheless, the steady decline of Britain's position in the Middle East gradually led the United States to assume Britain's role in maintaining the balance of power along the Empire's old lifeline—first, as we have seen, in Greece and Turkey, next in the eastern Mediterranean, and eventually in the Persian Gulf as well.

In the mid-1950s, Britain's reluctant decision to leave Egypt and look instead to Iraq as a secure alternative for maintaining a political-military presence in the Middle East led Secretary of State Dulles to encourage development of a regional defense arrangement—the Baghdad Pact—among the Middle East's Northern Tier states. President Eisenhower, meanwhile, following the debacle over Suez in 1956, promulgated the Eisenhower Doctrine—an attempt to fill the new void created by Britain's withdrawal and to serve notice that the United States would defend the Middle East against a perceived Soviet threat.

The Eisenhower Doctrine extended the containment policy from the Northern Tier states to the Middle East in general.

Congress, in turn, authorized the president to use armed force to assist Middle Eastern states threatened by armed aggression from any country controlled by international communism. Rooted in a misperception of regional problems and a mistaken assumption of the preeminence of the communist threat, the Eisenhower Doctrine ultimately foundered: instabilities in the region were neither caused by the Soviet Union nor capable of being deterred by presidential pronouncements. These facts were brought home by the revolution in Iraq in 1958 and Iraq's formal withdrawal from the Baghdad Pact in 1959. The Soviet Union, meanwhile, was able to circumvent the Northern Tier and establish close relations first with Egypt, later with Iraq and Syria, and after Britain's withdrawal from Aden, with the People's Democratic Republic of Yemen (PDRY). The initial American response was to restructure the Northern Tier concept of buffer states by negotiating executive agreements with Turkey, Iran, and Pakistan in the Central Treaty Organization (CENTO). US obligations were to take such action, including the use of armed force, as was mutually agreed upon—and as was envisaged in the Eisenhower Doctrine. Although not constituting a treaty guarantee of their security, these bilateral agreements effectively institutionalized American military support to the CENTO countries.

However ineffective American policies were in the 1950s, the problems that they confronted appeared minimal compared with those posed by the British decision in 1968 to withdraw from the area East of Suez in 1971. By then, global commitments and the Vietnam War precluded the kind of substantial commitment that had been possible in the 1940s. Shortly after taking office, the Nixon administration initiated a major review of US policy in the Persian Gulf; its focus was the question of how the Nixon Doctrine, first enunciated in June 1969, could best be applied to the region. The Doctrine specified that the United States would furnish military and economic assistance to nations whose freedom was threatened, but would look to those nations to assume primary responsibility for their own defense.

The result of the review was the president's endorsement in November 1970 of what became the "twin-pillar" policy. Its rationale was that the United States had strategic interests in Iran and Saudi Arabia. Despite their mutual mistrust, which meant that support for either would alienate the other, cooperation between the two was felt to be essential in the face of growing Arab radicalism. Britain, US officials believed, would retain much of its political presence and influence in the Gulf. The United States, for its part, would ensure stability through cooperation with Iran (which American officials recognized as the region's predominant power) and Saudi Arabia.

This framework, in conjunction with the Nixon administration's increasing emphasis on the Iranian "pillar," served as the basis for US policy until 1979, when the Iranian revolution forced the United States to reexamine its priorities and reformulate its policies. The revolution undermined the twin-pillar policy followed without change by both the Ford and Carter administrations, and it raised serious questions about the very idea that regional states could assume primary responsibility for their own defense. A Marxist coup in Afghanistan in April 1978, meanwhile, was followed by a Soviet-Ethiopian treaty in November 1978; by early 1979 the PDRY was creating problems in the Yemen; and in March, following the crumbling of the Iranian "pillar" and the reorientation of Iran's geopolitical posture, Turkey and Pakistan withdrew from CENTO. As a result of these adverse regional developments, American officials were left without a strategic conception of how to contain Soviet influence and protect their regional interests.

In this conceptual vacuum, the Carter administration began to develop a security framework for the region. Meanwhile, the Iranian hostage crisis that began in November 1979, and the Soviet invasion of Afghanistan in the following month, underscored the limitations of US ability to project military power in the region and revolutionized the geopolitical picture there. If the invasion of Afghanistan had a defensive quality about it, it also presented possibilities that were offensive. As such, the invasion was clearly opportunistic: the United States could not prevent it; it put the Soviets in a position to provoke and exploit the region's instabilities; and, ultimately, it provided the Soviet Union with strategic advantages—even if those advantages had not been part of the original calculation.

Events in Afghanistan made more urgent the development of the strategic framework that had been under discussion since the fall of the Shah. That framework was now fleshed out and expanded after its rationale was articulated in President Carter's State of the Union message in January 1980:

> Let our position be absolutely clear: an attempt by an out-side force to gain control of the Persian Gulf region will be regarded as an assault on the vital interests of the United States of America, and such an assault will be repelled by any means necessary, including military force.

In spite of assertions to the contrary, the Carter Doctrine was carefully considered. Its intent was to put the Soviets on notice that the Gulf region was of vital importance to the United States and, in a departure from the Nixon Doctrine, to make clear that the United States assumed ultimate responsibility for regional defense. Less clear was the extent of the area included in "the Persian Gulf region." Pakistan, for example, sought but received no clarification as to whether it was included under the Doctrine. The president's lack of precision, however, was not ill-considered; it *was* advisable to be wary of undertaking a commitment that could not be met. If something like the Carter Doctrine was required, moreover, there was no sense in being too specific about US commitments and by implication spelling out (as Secretary of State Acheson did in 1950 with regard to East Asia) what the United States would not do—particularly since the nature of many contingencies (such as the invasion of South Korea in 1950) made it virtually impossible to know ahead of time how vital a particular area was and what an appropriate response to a particular contingency might be. The Doctrine did not write off countries whose loss was less than vital, and it kept options open with respect to contingencies in others. Thus, until the security framework was broadened, the Carter Doctrine served a useful deterrent function.

Whatever its merits and shortcomings, the Carter Doctrine defined a US stake in the Persian Gulf region. During the remainder of the Carter administration, defense capabilities in the regional states were improved; access to facilities was acquired in Oman, Kenya, Somalia, and Egypt; US force capabilities were enhanced; and NATO allies were pressed to specify shared responsibilities. In spite of more ambitious goals and a change in rhetoric ("strategic consensus" for a time replaced "security framework"), the Reagan administration in its first years essentially continued and consolidated the approach initiated by Carter. In conjunction with the problems posed by the onset of the Iran-Iraq war, it also encouraged a closer relationship with Saudi Arabia and the smaller Gulf states. The Saudis, in turn, emerged as a cornerstone of US policy in the Gulf and became the focus of the Reagan corollary to the Carter Doctrine (i.e., the United States will not permit Saudi Arabia "to be an Iran").

In the early 1980s, if it was still unclear *what* countries in the Persian Gulf region other than Saudi Arabia were vital to the United States or *how* vital they were, and if a *political* strategy for the region was lacking, it was in part because of the first Reagan administration's ideological predisposition to focus on East-West issues and in part because of conceptual inertia. Strategic thinking about the region initially ignored regional priorities. It also continued to consist of what Gary Sick has characterized as "post-hoc adjustments to unanticipated and largely unwelcome developments." Once such adjustments were made, they tended to become mired in the status quo. Administrations which understood the inadequacy of military power alone to influence political events in the region nonetheless tended to rely on arms sales, military deployments, and occasionally economic assistance as the bedrock of their policies.[5]

The Soviets in the Middle East

The challenge to the second Reagan administration, then, and the problem in containing Soviet influence in the Middle East in the future, is to articulate and implement a viable strategy for the region that can integrate the evolving military posture of the United States in Southwest Asia into the broader political objectives and purposes of US interests in the Middle East as a whole. In addition to the containment of Soviet expansion and influence, those interests include the independence of key states, regional stability, and peaceful change; access to oil (on reasonable commercial terms); prevention of arms imbalances, nuclear proliferation, and nuclear war; the security of Israel; and advancement of the Middle East peace process. Although the focus of this paper is on containment, it is important to keep in mind that this complex of interests, some of which are occasionally at odds with each other, operates as a *gestalt*.

Before attempting an assessment of how to go about containing Soviet expansion and influence in the Middle East in the years ahead, it may be instructive to examine briefly the context of successes and setbacks experienced by the Soviet Union in the postwar Middle East. Except for Afghanistan, the Soviets have generally exercised their influence by economic and military assistance, infiltration, and subversion. The results, clearly, have been mixed. Arab-Israeli differences, US support for Israel in general, and a host of other factors have created a myriad of opportunities for the Soviets to exploit. The impediments posed by a lack of contiguity with most of the countries of the Middle East, however, have also made it possible for such countries as Egypt and Somalia to throw the Soviets out. Other countries in which Soviet influence has been considerable, such as Iraq, have become more wary of the Soviets in the wake of the invasion of Afghanistan; while Syria and the PDRY, in which Soviet influence is still powerful, have created as many problems for Soviet interests as opportunities.

What can be learned from observation of Soviet successes and setbacks, and indeed from the successes and setbacks of all great powers in the Middle East, is best articulated by L. Carl Brown. What has emerged in the Middle East, he has argued, is a distinctive system of international politics—what he calls "the Eastern Question system." This system is characterized by an intense interaction between an international and a regional power system, each composed of a multiplicity of autonomous political entities. Efforts by one or another of these entities to attain hegemony over the region have provoked counter-balancing efforts whose structural similarities illustrate the system's "homeostatic quality" and the region's "stubborn penchant for kaleidoscopic equilibrium." In fact, Brown contends, no outside power has been able to dominate and organize the Middle East, no state within the Middle East has been able to establish regional predominance, and neither the victories nor the losses of outside powers seem as impressive in the long run as they might first appear. According to this interpretation, since no great powers have been able or are likely to dominate the Middle East, and since they can generally maintain a minimal position in the system at a relatively limited risk and cost, they should recognize the limitations on their influence and maneuverability and act accordingly. In short, Brown suggests, they could benefit if they followed more circumspect foreign policies and sought more limited diplomatic commitments.[6]

The "correlation of forces" in the Middle East described by Brown is similar to that in the rest of the world as a whole, which, as John Gaddis has observed, "favors the hegemonial aspirations of no one." To the extent that US and Soviet forces balance each other (and this, it seems, should be the thrust of any containment policy), another of Gaddis' observations is also pertinent: "the superpower that can bring itself to accommodate diversity now will be the one most likely to maintain its status and position over the long haul."[7] The West, Gaddis argues, is in a better position to accommodate diversity than the Soviet Union; he also asserts that the real threat to diversity is not communism but the Soviet Union. If he is right, then the central thrust of any containment policy in the Middle East should be a capacity to deter the Soviet military from imposing its will on others. The key is to ensure that others have a choice, and that we can distinguish those situations in which ensuring such a choice is vital to our interests. In this regard, a comparison between recent US-Iranian relations and Soviet-Afghan relations may be instructive.

Soviet capacities to undertake military options in the region, it should be recognized, are far superior to those of the United States. Twenty-eight divisions in the southern USSR are supported by over 800 aircraft. The Soviet Fifth Eskadra (which includes combatants, submarines, and auxiliaries) deploys approximately fifty ships in the Mediterranean; approximately thirty ships from the Pacific Fleet are deployed in the Indian Ocean, where they serve mainly a monitoring function (only about a third are combatants).

As the Soviet experience in Afghanistan has evidenced, however, there are problems with all of these indices of Soviet power, from quality to readiness, not to mention the obstacles that terrain, weather, and indigenous forces all pose to the projection of Soviet power. Then, too, the capacity to undertake military options must be distinguished from the intention to exercise them, which in turn is likely to be profoundly influenced, particularly after the Soviet experience in Afghanistan, by an increasingly realistic appraisal of the results that military actions are likely to effect. The Soviets, as always, are prepared to take advantage of opportunities, but only when the risk is small.

Threat Scenario

In light of postwar developments and current constraints on the exercise of Soviet influence, Soviet threats to American interests in the region can be grouped in three general categories: direct attacks, support for one country against another in the region, and support for one or another faction in a civil war or insurrection within a particular country.

The most realistic direct-attack scenario is a limited invasion into northwest Iran. Such a move would require little mobilization time and could be easily resupplied and covered by Soviet aircraft. It would also extend the Soviet air umbrella to the head of the Gulf. The importance of this point is that the use of Soviet airborne units, which would be required for a thrust toward the Gulf itself, would be contingent (according to Soviet doctrine) upon air superiority.[8] However, while the logistical difficulties and military costs of a limited attack would be minimal compared to more ambitious undertakings, the economic and political costs of even a limited attack would probably be prohibitive, making such a course extremely unlikely.

One analyst has observed that the Soviet Union's "coalition maintenance" decisionmaking environment tends to discourage bold departures and high-risk actions. A direct attack, he has surmised, would be conceivable only in circumstances that the Soviets perceived to be defensive or extreme: if the costs of inaction were high (as in Afghanistan) or if the stakes were high (for example, if the United States were to attempt to re-create the Northern Tier or re-establish Iran as a strategic barrier to the projection of Soviet power).[9] Indirect means of achieving Soviet objectives, in short, are much more likely than the direct use of force.

Regional conflicts that can threaten US interests are limited only by the imagination. Posing difficult problems by themselves, these conflicts become even more problematic if the Soviet Union is directly involved. Such problems include—

  ● the historical conflict between Arabs and Israelis, which gave rise most recently to the war between Israel and the Palestinians in Lebanon and the subsequent confrontation between Israel and Syria;

- historical differences between Arabs and Persians, exemplified by the Iran-Iraq war and complicated by differences among Shia and Sunni Muslims;

- Iraqi desires for hegemony in the Gulf, evidenced by threatening maneuvers against Kuwait over the last two decades, and more recently by Iraq's ill-considered attack on Iran;

- long-standing tensions between India and Pakistan, which have led to three wars since World War II;

- attacks on the Yemen Arab Republic (YAR) by the PDRY, and PDRY-supported attacks on Oman;

- YAR-Saudi border differences; and

- border conflicts between Afghanistan and Pakistan.

All of these problems derive from historical regional differences. While they may be *influenced* by outside powers, they are much less susceptible to outside *control*. This lesson, well corroborated by history, may have been learned most recently by Israel and the United States in Lebanon. The problem with these regional conflicts is that almost any of them could develop into a major war—a war which, in the event of superpower involvement, could escalate out of control. With the exception of a war between two important oil-producing states such as Iran and Iraq, or a threat to Saudi Arabia (whether from Iran, Iraq, or the PDRY), regional conflicts, while serious, pose much less of a threat to US interests than a Soviet attack, *provided* that the Soviets are not or do not become directly involved. If the Soviets were involved, much would depend upon the proximity of the area to their borders, how vital the issues were to them, and whether or not the United States were to be involved. If, in the Iran-Iraq war, the Soviets were to use troops in support of either country, they would precipitate a serious contingency with all the trappings of a direct Soviet attack. Soviet intervention in noncontiguous states, on the other hand, would be risky and difficult, and hence unlikely, although any buildup of intervention forces and staging areas in the PDRY could make it costly for the United States to combat a Soviet-supported attack.

Coups, terrorism, insurgencies, and revolutions stem from complex political, economic, and social problems for which military responses are often inappropriate and counterproductive. Given the rapid pace of modernization in the region, historical ethnic and religious differences, and discrepancies between rich and poor that exist among and within countries, challenges to established authority are likely. To the extent that challenges endanger regimes friendly to US interests, US options are limited by an inability to confer legitimacy on any regime. American policymakers, in most cases, should favor preventive measures (including security assistance and, possibly, prudent support for the creation of structures for political participation) over reactive ones, since the latter have often proved counterproductive or even disastrous.

If the Soviets were "invited" to intervene in a civil war in Iran (to support Kurdish or Azerbaijani separatists or a rump Tudeh faction) or in Pakistan (to support Baluch or Pushtun separatists), the problems posed by a direct Soviet attack would again arise. For this reason, military strategists cannot be too cavalier in dismissing the possibility of a Soviet attack.

US Responses and the Issue of Strategy

Devising appropriate responses to these Soviet threats is difficult. The most serious threat (a direct Soviet attack) is the least likely, while the more likely threats (Soviet support for or exploitation of developments within the region) are least responsive to military influence. These threats, moreover, are not mutually exclusive; one can easily lead to or be part of another.

American efforts to contain these threats confront a basic dilemma. On the one hand, preparation to counter the most serious threats may encourage and even precipitate other problems. The United States could, for example, attempt to establish a ground presence in the Gulf region in order to give real as well as symbolic support to the region's "moderate" regimes and thereby strike a credible deterrent posture. Such a course, however, could foster the development of a radical, anti-American opposition in those countries or in the region as a whole, undermining rather than supporting regional stability. Depending on the circumstances, such policies could also result in Soviet pressures on Iraq, Iran, or even Kuwait to establish a countervailing presence in the region, thus bringing great power rivalry to the head of the Gulf. In the eastern Mediterranean, it should be noted, massive US support for Israel has led the Soviets to undertake enormous resupply efforts on behalf of Syria, including the stationing in Syria of at least 2,000 air defense specialists.

If, on the other hand, the United States discounts the use of military force in addressing these problems, downplays the Soviet threat, and maintains a low profile out of sensitivity to the vulnerability of the Gulf's fragile regimes, it would leave the Gulf states open to intimidation, coercion, and even attack. Such actions could contribute to a perception that US influence is waning and to a belief among the local states that they should reckon with the Soviet Union. In so doing, the United States could encourage regional initiatives that increase a destabilizing Soviet influence to the detriment of American interests.

A further constraint on efforts to contain Soviet influence in the Middle East is the fact that, in the event of a great power confrontation in the Gulf, it would be infinitely more difficult for the United States or the Soviet Union to ensure access to and control over the oil fields than it would be for either to deny the other such access and control, an important limitation on any military strategy in the Gulf. This constraint underscores the current asymmetry between US and Soviet interests: the United States must ensure access and control; the Soviet Union, which in the short run does not need the oil, has only to deny it to the industrialized nations of the West to have a major impact on their economies.

At present, the United States can deploy a battalion of the 82d Airborne Division to an airfield near the Gulf in forty-eight hours, and, although estimates vary, initiatives currently underway are expected by 1986 to give the commander of CENTCOM the capability of deploying the equivalent of four to five divisions (or 80,000–100,000 combat troops) to the Persian Gulf in thirty days.[10] Beyond these initiatives, some have proposed pre-positioning stocks and equipment for a light infantry division in Saudi Arabia, together with the development in Saudi Arabia of a capacity for a region-wide, integrated defense network, to support the projection of US tactical air and ground forces. Development of a similar infrastructure in eastern Turkey will give the United States even greater flexibility in the region and, by its very existence, serve to deter Soviet adventurism in Iran. In principle, these developments are clearly desirable; in conjunction with other initiatives already undertaken and assets potentially available in Israel, they give the United States access to considerable resources in the region. The only real requirement lacking, all things considered, may be an enhanced sealift and airlift capacity.

The Reagan administration, however, must be sensitive to regional limitations on its policies, being careful not to let design considerations (based in part on a worst-case analysis of the threat to be confronted and in part on interservice rivalries within the Pentagon) confuse the strategy that the United States pursues. At present, in spite of improvement in the United States' *capacity* to deal with military contingencies in the Persian Gulf, debate continues over the military *strategy* that undergirds American military readiness.

At a minimum, most analysts agree that the United States must be capable of "beating" the Soviets to the Persian Gulf if the Soviets are to be deterred from adventurism there. They disagree, however, on whether possessing that preemptive capacity is sufficient to safeguard US interests.

A few who minimize the Soviet threat believe that a US capability for quick preemptive intervention would effectively prevent Soviet adventurism.[11] Since a Soviet attack would result in direct conflict with the United States and since the costs of such a venture would clearly outweigh the gains, they argue, the Soviets would back away from any situation where the United States has established a trip-wire. A variant of this argument is that a relatively limited, "over-the-horizon" sea-based force (with land-based air support) is sufficient to establish such a trip-wire, and that a more elaborate force is not only unnecessary and costly but also counterproductive. According to this interpretation, the asymmetry of the two countries' interests in the region renders this kind of capability sufficient to underscore US determination and dictate Soviet caution.

Critics have pointed out that preemptive intervention is a theory of deterrence, not a strategy, since it fails to address the question of what to do if deterrence fails.[12] If deterrence should fail (and it could, they argue, because most Western nations don't *act* as if their vital interests are at stake), fairly elaborate conventional forces would be essential to back up the trip-wire force. Without such a back-up, the United States would have recourse only to a nuclear threat, which lacks credibility unless the United States has previously committed sizable numbers of troops whose lives are jeopardized. The Soviets, recognizing Western impotence, might be prompted to disregard problems posed by a small conflict with the United States, particularly if they could outmaneuver American forces and establish themselves in some trouble spot before the United States could get there. The Soviets could also provoke the United States to move preemptively in response to a Soviet feint, and then use US intervention as justification for actions elsewhere.

As a result, most analysts see the need for an American strategy that goes beyond a capacity for preemptive intervention. Some have advocated a direct theater (or regional) defense by the United States with a view to entangling Europe, either through Turkey or through requirements of US operations in Southwest Asia that are contingent upon allied assistance.[13]

A strategy of direct regional defense relies on quick reaction to Soviet initiatives. In the event of a Soviet move into Azerbaijan, for example, it requires early intervention such as the insertion of airborne troops in the Zagros Mountains as a means to buy time. Simultaneously, it seeks to create a buffer between Soviet forces and the Gulf through more elaborate military operations, with a view to building a coalition of allies that would make it very difficult for the Soviets to succeed in any aggressive action in southwest Iran. The operating assumption of this strategy is that the Soviets' most significant advantage is not strategic but tactical, and that theater linkage (i.e., a linkage between the Middle East and Western Europe), with its escalatory risks, is necessary to counter that advantage. A corollary to this coalition politics approach is that a more elaborate regional framework (including facilities and pre-positioned material) is necessary if a deterrent strategy is to be credible. How elaborate the regional framework should be depends on an interpretation of the magnitude and likelihood of the Soviet threat, and those who seek the military capacity to counter a sizable Soviet attack generally argue for more elaborate and expanded facilities, discounting the political costs in regional stability associated with an increased US presence.

Which of these perspectives provides the surest guide to the future? Given the political context within which the United States must operate in the Persian Gulf, the most sensible military strategy would seem to be one consistent with current American military capabilities and plans to enhance sealift and airlift. This strategy should allow for a conventional force sufficient to—

- *assist* American allies (e.g., Saudi Arabia);

- *help defend* them against threats from other regional forces (e.g., Iran, Iraq, or the PDRY); and

- *deter* a Soviet attack.

The strategy would be supported by means of—

- a capacity to deploy a *preemptive force* in readiness;

- a capability to transport (by air and sea) *conventional reinforcements* that would serve as a significant obstacle to Soviet aggression in the unlikely event it were to occur; and, ultimately,

- the uncertain threat of *vertical and horizontal escalation.*

The level of forces required to throw back, rather than impede, a determined Soviet attack on the Gulf would be far in excess of what is required to accomplish these three goals. A sizable ground presence would also be politically counterproductive, and it is not at all clear that sizable forces could prevent the Soviets from destroying the oil fields and terminals or denying the United States access to Gulf oil anyway. As a result, the strategy recommended here eschews a ground presence. Rather, it relies initially on airborne divisions and sizable sea-based capabilities that could react quickly, secondly on airlifted and sealifted forces, and ultimately on the uncertain threat of nuclear weapons and war-widening capabilities (both at sea and on the ground) to deter a Soviet attack. Should deterrence fail, a full range of options would still be available to decisionmakers.

The military strategy outlined above would have several virtues:

- While it recognizes that the United States must improve its capacity to move tactical air and ground forces rapidly, it directs attention to regional and lesser threats, both of which are much more likely than a worst-case Soviet attack.

- A sea-based force and a rapidly deployable airborne force, supplemented by an increasingly developed infrastructure (i.e., overbuilding, enlarged airstrips, and prepositioned material in selected locations), would afford the United States the option to intervene but would also allow American decisionmakers the choice of avoiding situations that would engulf a land-based American force in hostilities.

• The Soviets, who currently do not have a capacity equal to that of the United States to project force without bases, would have greater difficulty (politically and militarily) matching a US presence.

• As a result, the proposed strategy, while giving the United States a qualified capacity to respond credibly to a Soviet attack, and hence the ability to deter one, would also be more responsive to the internal problems of countries in the region and to the fact that American forces stationed there would be a serious liability to both their interests and those of the United States.

• A corollary is that the strategy would allow for greater receptivity to the needs and concerns of the regional states, and greater flexibility in American dealings with those states.

Alternative Political Strategies

A military strategy toward the Persian Gulf region, of course, is meaningless unless it is conceived in the context of a political strategy. As Rouhollah Ramazani has observed, the United States must share with the region a policy based on a common vision of its priorities and stability; in short, the soldier must remain the servant of the diplomat.[14]

The imperatives that condition the development of a political strategy deserve some elaboration. Washington must acknowledge that relations with the Middle East are symbiotic; regional imperatives must have equal footing with US concerns (not always shared) about the Soviet threat. US officials must also recognize that although there are no reliable substitutes for America's military power, political constraints nonetheless limit its use and efficacy. Finally, they must accept the uncertainties that attend the development and maintenance of a flexible political strategy toward a rapidly changing region.

The range of viable political options for the United States in the Middle East depends upon certain implicit operating assumptions. First among these is that a Soviet (or other national) threat must anticipate the possibility of a credible conventional response by the United States. Second, because conventional US forces are constrained both in size and in manner of deployment by costs at home and regional sensitivities abroad, the United States in confronting a Soviet threat can rely on them only to a certain point, beyond which the United States must rely on the *uncertain* threats posed by horizontal and vertical escalation. Such reliance does not imply that the United States would definitely resort to either course; in fact, the United States may never intend to do so. Rather, it recognizes that the Soviet Union could not ignore US capabilities, especially if non-nuclear deterrence were to fail and American conventional forces were on the verge of defeat. Public declaration of non-intent to resort to either kind of escalation would eliminate whatever deterrent effect those capabilities might have.

Another important consideration, at least in the Gulf, is the balance between Soviet land forces (in the Transcaucasus and Central Asia) and the US Central Command (operating out of the Indian Ocean). This equilibrium, if appropriately nurtured, could foster the gradual creation of what should be a primary objective of any strategy toward the region: *a de facto buffer zone between East and West*—a zone for which there is historical precedent. It is reasonable to assume that Iran and Afghanistan would be amenable to a code of conduct agreement between the United States and the Soviet Union about their policies in such a zone. Iran has already chosen to follow a nonaligned role, evident in the slogan "neither East nor West," which follows traditional policies and currently characterizes its foreign policy. Afghanistan's traditional policy of *bi-tarafi* (without sides), which seeks to balance external influence, is one of the few policies that most Afghans could agree upon. In the context of such an understanding, regional states could be relatively free of great power influence and pursue nonaligned policies to the benefit of all parties.

In the context of an entente, Soviet military capabilities could impede regional adventurism against vital Soviet interests, as US military capabilities could impede regional adventurism against vital Western interests. If properly deployed, US forces could also stimulate regional cooperation. Secure from pressures to accommodate Soviet demands (though still vulnerable to situations that excite great power rivalry), regional states would have a strong incentive to head off troubling situations through regional cooperation.

The military balance would also make it possible for Gulf states to control their own destinies, so long as their policies do not directly threaten vital US or Soviet interests. Ultimately relying on the balance of power between the United States and the Soviet Union, regional states could and would have to play a primary role in the management of regional conflicts.

This development would in turn make it easier for the United States and the Soviet Union to accommodate political change within the region, as long as neither country seeks to change the status quo by drastic measures. Although the United States could support particular states within the broader region, especially Turkey (which is, after all, a NATO ally), Saudi Arabia, and Pakistan, it would have to be sensitive to the various regional contexts within which those nations operate. Accordingly, the United States would have to anticipate changes, constantly evaluate the significance of changing circumstances, and develop adjustable policies. To facilitate the process, policymakers would have to think in terms of cooperating with, and encouraging, sub-regional groupings of states: for example, a nonaligned "Northern Tier," the Gulf Cooperative Council, or a bloc of states on the subcontinent. These sub-regional groups would constitute discrete if not always cohesive sources of political, economic, or military strength; they could address collective problems and advance common interests.

The role of America's NATO allies and Japan in such a strategy would have to be carefully thought through and closely coordinated. Operational problems and political concerns associated with joint military responsibilities might lead the United States to rely essentially on its own reaction forces in the Indian Ocean, although it would continue to coordinate with France, Britain, and Australia on naval deployments. The United States could explore a division of labor with its NATO allies and Japan, whereby they increase their defense responsibilities in Europe and in the Pacific, respectively, to balance increased American efforts in the Persian Gulf and Indian Ocean. The United States could also encourage its NATO allies to exercise their influence in particular countries of the region (e.g., Germany in Turkey, France in Iraq, Japan in Iran, and Britain in Oman).

If European commercial ties with the Soviet Union improve (a development which the gas pipeline will encourage), the Soviet Union might be more amenable to allowing European influence to serve as a "third alternative" to that of the two superpowers. The Germans and the Japanese saw themselves providing Turkey, Iran, and Afghanistan with an alternative to Soviet and British influence earlier in this century, and the French, certainly, aspire to such a role in the Gulf in the 1980s. Though the rest of the European countries and Japan have been more reserved about playing such a role, they, too, may seek to develop special relationships with individual countries in the region.

Were the United States to encourage a third alternative to US and Soviet influence in the Gulf, the Soviet reaction would be difficult to predict. Implementation of the strategy could result in the creation of a buffer zone there between East and West, and would encourage the region's developing and nonaligned countries to use their collective influence to restrain the Soviet Union and the United States from taking risks. These developments would lessen the chances of confrontation between the United States and the Soviet Union, encourage regional stability, reassure the Soviet Union of American interest in amicable relations *if the Soviets desire them,* and perhaps even facilitate a resolution of the Afghan problem.

Although outside the purview of this paper, the situation in Afghanistan deserves brief comment because it suggests the desirability of thinking across regions when exploring the problem of containment. To effect Soviet departure from Afghanistan, it is clear that more than US support for the resistance will be required. Political pressure on the Soviet Union from India is also necessary and can occur only in a regional context in which India feels secure. For this reason, it is important to keep in mind the relationship between the two primary policy options in South Asia.

One option is an attempt to separate Cold War issues from regional tensions and to encourage local initiatives that promote regional cooperation in the context of nonalignment. This option would be consistent with support for the general strategy of a nonaligned buffer zone across the Northern Tier. It is constrained, however, by a number of factors: the present impasse in US-Soviet relations, persistent and deep antagonisms between the states of the area, Indian and Pakistani nuclear policies (which may seriously compromise American relations with both countries, Indian suspicions of China and Pakistan, and Pakistani fears of an Indo-Soviet pincer. Such a policy may overestimate India's capacity and will to play a key role in deterring Soviet hegemony in Afghanistan and could, if poorly managed, lead Pakistan to accelerate rather than delay its acquisition of nuclear weapons. A conjunction of adverse events involving these constraints could undermine the ability of the United States to influence *either* India or Pakistan, to the detriment of US security interests in the region. As a result, implementation of this approach would depend on an improved dialogue among the United States, India, and Pakistan, and on a willingness by all parties to take the initiatives necessary for their long-term interests.

A second option would continue the US commitment to bolster Pakistan's standing in the region. This option responds to Pakistani as well as regional fears of steadily increasing Indian military power and domination of the subcontinent, and lays the groundwork for a more balanced relationship between India and Pakistan. Excessive support for Pakistan, however, risks undermining long-term US interests by antagonizing India. Insofar as US support for Pakistan is accompanied by significant aid to Afghanistan, it will also antagonize the Soviet Union. India could compensate by moving closer to the Soviets, calling a halt to its gradual rapprochement with China, and beefing up its forces along Pakistan's border. Depending upon the threat that India perceives, a number of worrisome scenarios are imaginable: a preemptive strike against Pakistan's nuclear facilities; a military move against the territories of Azad Kashmir; or, in conjunction with the Soviet Union, and in support of Pushtun, Baluch, and Sindi separatist movements, an attempt to dismember Pakistan. As a result, a strong American commitment to Pakistan should be pursued with caution.

The key point, here, is that neither option, by itself, can address all US concerns in South Asia. Flexible application of both options, on the other hand, may create an environment that is conducive to many of the interests that we have in common with the states of the region. Finally, it is clear that what happens in South Asia is intimately related to what happens in Southwest Asia and the Persian Gulf. The relationship between containment policies in one region must be integrated with those in other areas and cannot be pursued in a vacuum.

Comprehensive US Strategy for the Middle East: "Strength through Respect"

The positive effects of the political strategy described above would be far more convincing if presented along with other initiatives in the context of a thaw or a least a "tough-minded" detente in US-Soviet relations. If the Soviets reacted cooperatively, Moscow and Washington might agree to take advantage of this opportunity to reach a modus vivendi and go back to some of the rules of the "Great Game" that the great powers have played in the region since the eighteenth century.[15] Such a trend could even prove promising for a constructive Soviet contribution to the Middle East peace process—a contribution which may be necessary to obtain Syrian cooperation (which in turn seems essential to any progress at all). If the Soviets believed US initiatives were a guise for re-creating a pro-US Northern Tier barrier, on the other hand, Moscow would probably attempt to subvert them. The strategy's success would then depend on the extent to which countries of the region believed US policy to be in their best interests, and the degree to which they could be convinced of the strategy's efficacy and US determination to carry it through.

A comprehensive strategy that builds on such assumptions would provide convincing evidence of American support for the sovereignty and territorial integrity of existing states and would best safeguard US interests in the region. The policy would address realistically the regional constraints on American policies. It would be consistent with American ideals, would be more acceptable to states of the region, and would provide a potentially significant and politically effective voice against aggression from any front (especially the Soviet Union). At the same time, the strategy would avoid repetition of the American experience with other formerly conservative regimes (Libya, Iraq, Ethiopia, and Iran)—all of which established close military cooperation with the United States, all of which were overthrown, and all of whose successors are among the more rabidly anti-US regimes in the world. Oman may one day experience a similar fate, and Russia's experience in Egypt should be instructive. The comprehensive strategy proposed here could be characterized as one of "strength through respect," for it acknowledges that pluralism has come of age, and that support for regionalism is in the security interests of all countries.[16] It could signal the beginning of a constructive and fruitful US policy toward the Third World.

To safeguard the interests of the industrialized countries while respecting the flux in the Gulf region, the strategy of "strength through respect" would have three elements. The first would be to give US support to a *de facto* regional coalition of old CENTO countries (an aligned Turkey, a nonaligned Iran, and a quasi-aligned Pakistan) which would constitute a buffer zone between the Soviet Union and the Gulf states. The aim in Turkey would be to maintain the linchpin of the Northern Tier barrier whose role has been so effective in the postwar era. If a real thaw in US-Soviet relations were ever to take place, Turkey might once again gravitate toward nonalignment. Until such time, however, Turkey will continue to be a key ally of the United States.

The difficulty with formulating a policy toward Iran and Iraq is that long-term US interests preclude support of, or opposition to, either country, while demanding better relations with both. Future US relations with Iran and Iraq will be determined to a great extent by the interplay between internal and external factors: between Iranian politics in the wake of the Ayatollah Khomeini's demise, the ability of the Ba'athist regime in Iraq to survive the war, and traditional geopolitical realities that will continue to operate in the region long after the Iran-Iraq war winds down.

In Iran, the comprehensive strategy's aim would be to support (through Turkey and Pakistan) the country's independence from Soviet pressures and influence without suggesting that the Iranians should participate in a military association aimed at Moscow. An active US policy toward Iran could result in undesirable consequences such as the partition of Iran, which would be extremely destabilizing for the region, or Soviet intervention, which would be catastrophic. Instead, the strategy would encourage Pakistani and Turkish cooperation with Iran in security areas that are of concern to Iran, thereby attempting to minimize short-run conflict with other US security interests in the Gulf.

If the Iraqis are severely threatened by an Iranian offensive or the Soviets move closer to Iran, the United States could, and perhaps should, move closer to Iraq. In conjunction with NATO allies such as France, the United States could play a more supportive role in helping the Iraqis to resist continued Iranian attacks and consolidate local resistance to Iranian aggression in the Gulf. Better US relations with Iraq, if handled with care, are not necessarily harmful to or incompatible with an improvement in US-Iranian relations, particularly if US support for Iraq is solely defensive. If Saddam Hussein survives and can reach a modus vivendi with a post-Khomeini Iran, better relations with *both* Iran and Iraq would be consistent with American support for nonalignment in the region—a policy position to which both states subscribe. Overzealous pursuit of US-Iraqi relations, of course, would jeopardize American interests in Iran. Support for Iraqi defensive efforts against Iran, however, is less dangerous. The normalization of US-Iraqi relations is not especially harmful to US interests in Iran and is welcomed by the Gulf states, who remain concerned about Saddam's aspirations to play an important regional role but are more concerned at present about ' his survival.

The Gulf's littoral states pose major problems for any comprehensive strategy toward the region. Efforts to safeguard US interests in the Gulf are complicated by three separate sets of problems: the historical animosity between Iran and some of the Arab states, particularly Iraq, which are now exacerbated by Sunni-Shiite differences; the possible disintegration of either Iran or Iraq, which could make the regional role of one or the other inordinately significant; and the ideological differences exemplified by Iraqi-Saudi relations. These threats to regional stability suggest the practicality of a policy whose essential thrust is to prevent domination of the Gulf by any single power (i.e., Iran or Iraq) while fostering a sense of cohesion among Saudi Arabia and the states of the Arabian Peninsula littoral. As a result, the second element of the three-pronged strategy would be to support a regional coalition of Arab Gulf states such as the

Gulf Cooperation Council (GCC), under Saudi leadership, whose defense systems the United States could help to integrate.

The Arab Gulf states are growing more confident of their international influence in economic matters and are beginning to establish closer economic, political, and military ties with each other. The key for the United States, in addition to supporting Gulf security by maintaining a balance among the region's three centers of power, is to respect the Saudis' instinct for survival.[17] To push the Saudis beyond what that instinct tells them is acceptable can only invite failure and lead to damage to the interests that the United States and Saudi Arabia have in common. In the event of serious differences between the United States and Saudi Arabia, the United States might be forced to rely on Turkey, Israel, and Egypt as its only important allies in the region, with Oman being America's primary Gulf partner. American options would be extremely grim in this scenario, and the United States cannot afford the kind of deterioration in US-Saudi relations that might result from a repetition of recent Saudi inability to purchase forty-eight F–15s and spare parts from the United States.

The third element of the proposed comprehensive strategy would be quiet US support for the Islamic Conference (IC). The IC is the best forum for subsuming the interests of the buffer zone and Gulf littoral groupings described in the first two elements of the strategy. It makes the Soviets uncomfortable because of its religious focus and its possible effect on the Soviet Muslim population. It would also keep Afghanistan in the public eye and undercut the influence of secular radical coalitions.

Former Ambassador Hermann Eilts has urged that we avoid misguided efforts to harness the Islamic world to the American bandwagon. He has underscored our poor understanding of it and emphasized that tying it to superpower policies taints the limited moral effectiveness it may have.[18] The argument here is not to tie the IC to our policies, but to make it possible for the IC to support them. Since Islam is the single most important cultural and political fact in the region, one of those universal movements which can mobilize human energy in a devoted and concentrated way, it is advantageous to focus its negative attention on our adversaries.

To do so, however, the United States must make a real effort to alleviate Islamic concerns by addressing the Palestinian problem. In this regard, it is important to acknowledge that while Israel may be a regional asset because of its military capability and apparent reliability, it also constitutes a *strategic* liability. The close association between Israel and the United States, to the extent that it leads the United States to ignore the Palestinian problem, to disregard other important US interests, and to alienate many of the states within the region, has the clear potential for undermining regimes that cooperate with the United States and creating inroads for Soviet influence. Although this argument has been voiced since 1948, developments of the last decade and a half make it more plausible today than it was two or three decades ago. The financial power of the Gulf states is a mixed blessing in that it makes them vulnerable to the charge that they have done nothing to resolve the Palestinian issue—and in fact have helped to prevent its resolution.

Whether or not the Palestinian question is resolved, serious problems will continue to develop in the Middle East—the Iran-Iraq war has made that clear. What seems equally clear, particularly in the aftermath of the Israeli invasion of Lebanon, is that until there is progress in the peace process, American efforts at security cooperation in the Middle East will be at best impeded and at worst fundamentally challenged. As a result, the United States must continue to make a determined effort to reconcile the conflict between Israeli security concerns and the Palestinian quest for self-determination.[19]

To complement this three-pronged strategy, the United States might also wish to support Egyptian, Jordanian, Pakistani, or possibly Turkish troops with US airlift capabilities, and build closer ties between those Muslim countries and the Gulf states. Because it relies on Islamic states to protect mutual interests, this concept would be more acceptable than the introduction of American forces into the region or closer strategic cooperation with Israel. It would also facilitate a mutually beneficial arrangement between countries rich in manpower but poor in oil, and those that have small populations but are oil rich.

Such a strategy could, however, commit the United States to greater involvement in the Gulf or cause it to incur more far-reaching responsibilities in the region (especially to Pakistan) than presently envisioned. These are all desirable options only to the extent that some regional power, perhaps Iran, poses a serious threat to regional security or gravitates toward the Soviet Union. Such a shift would change the political and strategic contexts within which US forces operate and create the opportunity to change policies in response to regional "shocks."[20] In the absence of such an opening, these options must be developed cautiously because of the consequences that a heavy-handed American influence could have on the often tenuous power bases of leaders in the region. The extent of Gulf cooperation would hinge on a number of variables, including perceptions of the Soviet threat, Soviet relations with Iran, progress on the Palestinian question, the role of Israel in America's strategic posture, the relationship at the time between Iran and Iraq, and the climate of opinion within the Gulf region.

Notes

Portions of this analysis, in different form, have appeared in my book, *The Persian Gulf and U.S. Policy: A Guide to Issues and References* (Claremont, Cal.: Regina Books, 1984), and in *Security in the Middle East: Prospects and Problems in the 1980s,* edited by Samuel F.

Wells, Jr., and Mark A. Bruzonsky (Boulder, Colo.: Westview Press, 1986).

1. Bruce R. Kuniholm, *The Origins of the Cold War in the Near East: Great Power Conflict and Diplomacy in Iran, Turkey, and Greece* (Princeton: Princeton University Press, 1980).

2. Bruce R. Kuniholm, *The Near East Connection: Greece and Turkey in the Reconstruction and Security of Europe, 1946–1952* (Brookline, Mass.: Hellenic College Press, 1984).

3. Bruce R. Kuniholm, "Turkey and NATO: Past, Present, and Future," *Orbis,* Summer 1983, pp. 421–45.

4. Dankwart Rustow, "Turkey's Liberal Revolution," *Middle East Review,* Spring 1985, pp. 5–11.

5. Gary Sick, "The Evolution of U.S. Policy toward the Indian Ocean and Persian Gulf Region," n.d., in the author's possession.

6. L. Carl Brown, *International Politics and the Middle East: Old Rules, Dangerous Game* (Princeton: Princeton University Press, 1984).

7. John Gaddis, "Containment: Its Past and Future," *International Security,* Spring 1981, pp. 74–102.

8. Thomas L. McNaugher, *Arms and Oil: U.S. Military Strategy and the Persian Gulf* (Washington: The Brookings Institution, 1985), pp. 35, 45–46.

9. Dennis Ross, "Considering Soviet Threats to the Persian Gulf," *International Security,* Fall 1981, pp. 159–80.

10. The Reagan administration apparently intends to double the size of the 220,000-man RDF to 440,000 by the end of the decade. For further details, the policy implications of alternative RDF levels, and the budgetary implications of such levels, see *Rapid Deployment Forces; Policy and Budgetary Implications* (Washington: Congressional Budget Office, February 1983).

11. Christopher Van Hollen, "Don't Engulf the Gulf," *Foreign Affairs* 59 (1981), pp. 1064–78; Stanley Hoffmann, "Security in an Age of Turbulence: Means of Response," *Third-World Conflict and*

International Security (Part II), Adelphi Papers, No. 167, September 1980.

12. F. J. West, "NATO II: Common Boundaries for Common Interests," *Naval War College Review* 34 (1981), pp. 59–67.

13. Interviews with officials in the Department of Defense; see also John Hackett, "Protecting Oil Supplies: The Military Requirements," in *Third-World Conflict and International Security* (Part I), Adelphi Papers, No. 166, September 1980, pp. 41–51; Albert Wohlstetter, "Meeting the Threat in the Persian Gulf," *Survey* 24 (1980), pp. 128–88; W. Scott Thompson, "The Persian Gulf and the Correlation of Forces," *International Security* 7 (1982), pp. 157–80.

14. Rouhollah Ramazani, "Weapons Can't Replace Words," *Newsweek* (International), September 1980, p. 23.

15. The "Balkan Problem," the "Eastern Question," the "Persian Problem," and the "Great Game," all refer to different geographical foci of the rivalry between East and West (initially between Russia and Great Britain and later between the Soviet Union and the United States) that began in the area stretching from the Balkans to India as long ago as the eighteenth century. The term "Great Game" was used by Rudyard Kipling to describe what he saw as Britain's attempts to contain Russia's expansion southward into Southwest Asia. J. B. Kelly, "Great Game or Grand Illusion," *Survey* 24 (1980), p. 118, argues that "over the past decade, through inattention rather than design, the West has failed to abide by the rules of the Great Game as it is played in Persia, thereby inadvertently paving the way for the Soviet Union, in their turn, to break them in Afghanistan."

16. An essential component of this strategy, which should be underscored even during the current oil glut, is a comprehensive energy program. Such a program is necessary—and will be increasingly so in the 1990s—if we are to reduce our vulnerability to OPEC and convince the countries of the Middle East that the strategy is more than a ruse to trick them out of their oil.

17. Bruce R. Kuniholm, "What the Saudis Really Want: A Primer for the Reagan Administration," *Orbis,* Spring 1981, pp. 107–22.

18. Hermann Eilts, "Security in the Persian Gulf," *International Security,* Fall 1980, p. 112.

19. For elaboration on this issue, see Bruce R. Kuniholm, *The Palestine Problem and U.S. Policy* (Claremont, Cal.: Regina Press, 1986).

20. This is what economists call "the displacement effect." Examples of past "shocks" would be the fall of the Shah or the Soviet invasion of Afghanistan. An example of a future "shock" would be an Iranian decision to mine the Strait of Hormuz or, less likely, a Soviet decision to send troops (invited or otherwise) into northwest Iran. The latter decision clearly would affect the magnitude of our relationship with Turkey as well as Gulf attitudes toward US bases in the Gulf, and would open up an entirely different set of options for the United States in the region. Planning for such options, of course, must anticipate their likelihood.

19

Containment and the Soviet Union in Afghanistan

Selig S. Harrison

T HE INABILITY OF THE UNITED STATES to contain Soviet political and military expansion in Afghanistan has been rooted
in two principal factors. The first and foremost of these is timing. During the decades when the monarchy provided a focus of
political legitimacy for Afghanistan, the United States made little or no effort to compete with Moscow. The United States has
now entered the fray at a time when noncommunist Afghans no
longer have any symbol of legitimacy around which they can
unite. Second, both the limited efforts to compete that were
made prior to the Soviet occupation and the more intensive attempt now being made to recover lost ground have reflected
insensitivity to the internal power realities of Afghan society.

In the early years, the United States underrated the strength
of irredentist claims made by Afghanistan's Pushtun majority. It
was American military support for Pakistan and the concomitant

---

Selig S. Harrison, a specialist in South Asian affairs, is a Senior Associate of
the Carnegie Endowment for International Peace.

American alignment with that country on the critical Pushtunistan issue that opened the way for Soviet military aid to Afghanistan, Soviet penetration of the Afghan armed forces, and the development of an Afghan communist movement. More recently, the United States has overrated the strength of pan-Islamic fundamentalist elements of the Afghan resistance, ignoring the basic conflict between fundamentalist concepts of a centralized theocratic state and deep-rooted Afghan traditions of tribal, ethnic, and religious diversity and autonomy. By helping to build up fundamentalist groups, the United States has reinforced factionalism within the resistance, especially the divisions between tribally based commanders in the countryside and fundamentalist leaders based in Pakistan.

This paper begins by analyzing the roots of the American failure prior to the communist coup of 1978. It then focuses on the critical 1978–79 period, assessing the American posture toward the new communist government. It examines both the initial US attempt to contain Soviet influence by encouraging the national-communist tendencies personified in Hafizullah Amin, and the subsequent, fateful decision in early 1979 to support the destabilization of the Amin regime. Finally, it discusses the current political and military environment in Afghanistan and the increasingly limited policy options still open to the United States.

1953: The Cost of the Pakistan Alliance

Recalling a meeting in 1951 with the Afghan ambassador, Prince Mohammed Naim, former Assistant Secretary of State George C. McGhee has conveyed the full flavor of the indifference that marked American policy toward Afghanistan throughout the early years of the Cold War. Prince Naim "said that he had come to discuss American military aid," McGhee writes, "and hinted that if it were not forthcoming the Afghans might have to talk to the Russians. Sensing that he was bluffing . . . I picked up the phone and asked my secretary to get me the telephone number of the Russian Embassy. I wrote it on a piece of paper and handed it to the Prince, whereupon we both laughed."[1]

The consistent failure of the United States to concern itself with the containment of Soviet influence in Afghanistan during the "years of opportunity" has been perceptively recounted by Leon B. Poullada, a former South Asia specialist in the State Department who attempted unsuccessfully to sound the alarm during the fifties and sixties.[2] The United States ignored King Amanullah's request for recognition in 1919, rebuffed his offer to visit Washington in 1928, rejected an Afghan bid to purchase surplus US military equipment after World War II, refused Afghan requests for a development loan in 1949, and spurned a series of overtures for economic aid during the fifties. Above all, the United States dismissed repeated Afghan efforts to buy military equipment, including a personal appeal from Prince Naim to Secretary of State Dulles in October 1954. It was just one month after Dulles formally turned down this request that Kabul started negotiations on the $25 million Soviet military aid offer that opened the way for $1.25 billion in Soviet military aid and another $1.265 billion in economic aid prior to 1978.

It is worth recalling that the United States was seeking to apply the containment concept to South Asia as a region even when failing to do so in Afghanistan. As interpreted during the Dulles period, containment of the Soviet Union also required containment of suspect noncommunist countries that were unwilling to align themselves militarily with Washington against Moscow. In the case of South Asia, Pakistan thus had a dual value in American eyes as an anti-Soviet and an anti-Indian ally. Richard M. Nixon, then vice president, spelled out this interpretation explicitly in an off-the-record briefing that I attended at the American Embassy in New Delhi in December 1953. Explaining the projected American decision to provide military aid to Pakistan, Nixon observed that it would, among other things, "help to keep Nehru in line." One of Nixon's early biographers noted that he had pushed for aid to Pakistan both as a direct deterrent to Soviet expansion and "as a counterforce to the confirmed neutralism of Jawaharlal Nehru's India."[3]

In contrast to India, which had aroused American antipathy, Afghanistan was largely ignored in the formulation of the Pakistan aid decision. The American refusal to sell military equipment to Kabul did not result only from Afghan-specific considerations, though some were involved. Equally important was a single-minded American focus on Pakistan and a consequent American identification with the Pakistani stance on the Pushtunistan issue. The United States was afraid that Afghanistan might use American weaponry to pursue its irredentist territorial claims, endangering American interests in Pakistan. American policymakers were only dimly aware of the historical dimensions of the Pushtunistan conflict and its emotional meaning to Afghanistan's dominant ethnic group, the Pushtuns. Taken forcibly by the British Raj and handed over to the new state of Pakistan in 1947 over the protests of Afghanistan, the lost Pushtun territories embraced nearly half of the Pushtun population. It was this issue that led Kabul to oppose Pakistan's admission to the United Nations. As Poullada has observed, "the Pushtunistan dispute, which the United States ignored as a minor annoyance, became the key to Soviet success. It led to Afghan humiliation, bitterness and thirst for revenge. It blinded Afghan leaders into accepting Soviet military aid, which the U.S.S.R. used to create the subversive infrastructure for conquest."[4]

It should be emphasized that most of Kabul's overtures for military equipment envisaged the purchase of weaponry on a concessional commercial basis. Afghanistan wanted to remain nonaligned. It was not ready to join the Baghdad Pact, adopt an anti-Soviet declaratory posture, or provide any direct and visible quid pro quo for its American arms. Pakistan, by contrast, while seeking American equipment to bolster its balance of power with India, was prepared to assume a nominal anti-Soviet stance. More important, as it happened, the Pakistan military regime that took over in the late fifties proved ready to offer U–2 bases and electronic intelligence facilities to the United States for use in monitoring Soviet missile testing sites in Central Asia.

Even in 1953, it was not difficult to foresee that the short-term benefits of the Pakistan alliance would carry with them high long-term political and military costs for the United States in India and Afghanistan. In a letter to Secretary Dulles on 20 December 1953, Chester Bowles, who had just retired as ambassador to India, warned that a US arms aid agreement with Pakistan would "almost certainly" give Moscow the opening in Kabul that it had sought for more than a century. Given Afghanistan's land-locked position, he pleaded that the United States should not go ahead with the aid unless Iran agreed to lease Afghanistan the Chah Bahar harbor just west of the Pakistan border, and unless Pakistan agreed to grant special transit facilities for Afghan exports via Karachi harbor.[5] As the US commitment to Pakistan deepened with the acquisition of intelligence facilities during the late fifties and Moscow began its penetration of the Afghan armed forces, my own writing focused on the danger of placing immediate intelligence objectives above long-term strategic considerations. In a 1961 article on the Pakistan aid program, I asked, "How are assets like a radar intercept facility or a missile-tracking installation to be measured in U.S. security calculations against built-in political liabilities? An airfield or a radar station has an incontestably tangible importance and a visible presence on a Pentagon map, but what is the unit of valuation for national emotions? . . . How would one assess the cost to U.S. security of a Soviet-controlled Afghanistan?"[6]

Similarly, there is currently a danger that the US pursuit of short-term military objectives in Pakistan will push India into a Soviet-oriented security posture.[7] But the danger arising from India's Soviet links does not result from the degree of its dependence on Moscow as such. It arises from the Indian perception of a geopolitical community of interest with the Soviet Union, resulting from the US policy toward Pakistan. As experience has shown, India, a subcontinent-sized state with a demonstrably strong political fabric and a broadly based nationalist elite, has been able to absorb its degree of dependence on Soviet aid with little lasting impact on its freedom of action. In politically undeveloped Afghanistan, where social mobilization is limited and nationalism has had an unusually narrow base even by Third World standards, the impact of a more far-reaching dependence was predictably more significant and is likely to be more enduring.

Even after Soviet penetration of the Afghan armed forces started in the fifties and sixties, the opportunity to contain Soviet influence in Afghanistan remained until the destruction of the monarchy in 1973. The polarization of Afghan political life after that critical event led to a cycle of challenge and response between the Soviet Union on one side and the United States, Iran, and Pakistan on the other.[8] It was a bitter irony of history that the American effort to reverse Soviet inroads in Kabul after 1973 merely served to aggravate the process of polarization, culminating in the assassination of President Mohammed Daud and the emergence of a communist regime. The USSR, for its part, moved aggressively after 1973 to prepare for the possible necessity of an eventual communist takeover. As events developed, Moscow found itself confronted with a free-wheeling Afghan communist party dominated by leaders who were not its most trusted Afghan agents and who acted prematurely by Soviet standards in staging their coup. Once the coup was underway, however, Moscow helped to make it successful and to underwrite the new regime financially and militarily in the apparent belief that "a failed socialist revolution would be worse than none at all."[9]

1979: The Cost of Backing the Afghan Rebels

American policy toward the Democratic Republic of Afghanistan has evolved in three distinct stages. The United States recognized the communist government when it was established in April 1978 and conducted normal diplomatic relations with the new regime until the asassination of Ambassador Adolph Dubs in February 1979, maintaining but not extending existing economic aid links. Dubs met with Foreign Minister Hafizullah Amin fourteen times during his brief tenure. This posture of active dialogue reflected his privately expressed hope that the United States could forestall the complete dependence of the regime on the Soviet bloc and encourage it to move in a national-communist direction.[10]

The Dubs assassination, together with the Khomeini revolution in Iran, marked the start of a second, transitional stage in the development of American policy, which continued until the Soviet occupation of Afghanistan in December 1979. The United States did not send a new ambassador during this ten-month period, but it continued to conduct normal diplomatic relations with the DRA government. At the same time, against a background of growing insurgent activity based in Pakistan and covertly aided by the Pakistan government,[11] the Carter administration began to identify the United States with the insurgent cause.

Former National Security Adviser Zbigniew Brzezinski states in his memoirs, "in April 1979, I pushed a decision through the SCC [Special Coordinating Committee of the NSC] to be more sympathetic to those Afghans who were determined to preserve their country's independence. Mondale was especially helpful in this, giving a forceful pep talk, mercilessly squelching the rather timid opposition of David Newsom, who was representing the State Department."[12] Brzezinski is deliberately opaque with respect to the ways in which American sympathy was to be expressed. Nevertheless, he invites speculation as to whether covert American weapons or other aid to the insurgents began during this period. He notes that in early September he "consulted with the Saudis and the Egyptians regarding the fighting in Afghanistan," and that on 28 December, immediately following the Soviet occupation, "plans were made to *further enhance* our cooperation with Saudi Arabia and Egypt regarding Afghanistan."[13] Alluding to this disclosure,

Raymond L. Garthoff comments that "while Brzezinski does not note what this decision entailed, it clearly went beyond a sympathy card."[14] Zalmay Khalilzad writes that the CIA smuggled tapes of speeches by anticommunist insurgent leaders into Afghanistan during 1979; Pakistan provided "some weapons"; and Saudi Arabia, Iran, Libya, and Egypt also gave "some aid."[15]

In any event, the April decisions included active worldwide US government dissemination of detailed information concerning insurgent activity and atrocities committed by Soviet-assisted DRA counterinsurgency forces. Initially, this took the form of media background briefings. On 26 September 1979, Assistant Secretary of State Harold Saunders told a congressional committee that the United States was "especially disturbed by the growing involvement of the Soviet Union in Afghan affairs" and had "important differences with the Afghan government, including our deep concern about the human rights situation in Afghanistan." While the United States had reduced its embassy staff and withdrawn the dependents of US government personnel from Kabul, Saunders said, "we have continued to express to the Government of Afghanistan our desire for normal and friendly relations."[16] On 1 October 1979, the American aid program was phased out.

The third stage in American policy toward the DRA began with the Soviet occupation in December 1979 and has continued into the Reagan years without any basic change. Although continuing to recognize the DRA, it is officially explained, "the U.S. does not conduct normal relations with the Kabul regime. The small U.S. Embassy in Kabul, headed by a Charge D'Affaires, deals with the Afghan Government on the administrative and consular level only."[17] The DRA embassy in Washington must transact business through the protocol section of the State Department, and the US Embassy in Kabul must deal with the protocol section of the Foreign Ministry.

The Soviet occupation immediately produced a powerful upsurge of nationalist feeling among Afghans and an expansion of what had hitherto been scattered pockets of insurgent activity into a broader national resistance to the Soviet presence. Prior to the occupation, the United States did not directly question the legitimacy of the DRA. However, since the killing of Hafizullah Amin, coincident with the arrival of Soviet forces,[18] and his replacement as president by Babrak Karmal, the United States has regarded the DRA regime as a Soviet puppet.

During the first stage of American policy, the United States was notably successful in opening up a positive dialogue with Amin. Indeed, the possibility of a Soviet hand in the Dubs assassination cannot be completely discounted, despite considerable evidence to the contrary, since it was clearly in the Soviet interest to frustrate the evolution of the DRA in a national-communist direction. The Carter decision in April 1979 to identify the United States with anti-DRA insurgents came at a time when tensions between Amin and his Soviet patrons was growing. These tensions culminated in the clumsy Soviet attempt to overthrow Amin in September, resulting in President Nur Mohammed Taraki's death and leading in turn to serious factionalism in the regime during October and November. Yet as a result of the April decision, the United States was unable to test the Dubs strategy effectively during this critical and fluid period, even though some evidence suggests that Amin appealed for Western help up to the eleventh hour.

On the basis of the limited information so far available, it is difficult to judge with certainty the impact of the April policy reversal on the complex chain of events that culminated in the Soviet decision to intervene in December. However, it may be that US identification with the insurgents accelerated this chain of events and thus did not serve US interests.

To be sure, a wide range of global and Afghan-specific factors appear to have figured in the Soviet decision.[19] Soviet distrust of the independent, nationalistic Amin was probably the critical factor governing the Soviet calculus. Contrary to much tendentious analysis, the Amin regime was not about to fall in late 1979. The USSR exaggerated the extent of external support then being given to the insurgency, while officially stimulated American accounts depicted the degree of indigenous resistance in inflated, propagandistic terms. Moscow did not intervene to save the DRA from an imminent insurgent takeover but, rather, to replace an Afghan communist leadership and an Afghan military command structure that it could not control and no longer trusted. Amin's doctrinaire, repressive policies, in disregard of Soviet wishes, had fueled significant insurgent activity; the fact that this insurgency had attracted growing external sympathy and support no doubt accentuated Soviet concern. Moscow might well have concluded that the United States had embarked on what would be an increasingly determined effort to supplant the DRA with a Western-oriented, Islamic fundamentalist regime. A *Washington Post* Op-Ed article in October had explained that a successful insurgency would enable the United States to replace its lost electronic monitoring facilities in Iran with even more advantageously situated facilities in Afghanistan.[20] Moreover, as Garthoff has observed, "the Soviets may well have believed there was more outside assistance than was in fact the case, especially as they (and the Afghan regime) were loath to accept that indigenous popular discontent was rising."[21]

Anthony Lake, former director of the Policy Planning Council of the State Department during the Carter period, has argued that "it became harder for the United States to avoid choosing between the rebels and the Marxist regime" as the insurgency grew. He speculates that a more active American effort to make Amin into a Tito during 1979 "might only have led the Soviets to intervene sooner."[22] But why did the United States have to choose? Dubs had not envisaged such a choice, though no one can say how his views might have evolved. In a conversation in Kabul in August 1978, he spoke of a formative period for the communist regime of some "five to ten years" during which the United States would have to tread with consummate care, helping Amin or his successors reduce their

Soviet dependence in carefully calibrated stages while avoiding a direct challenge to Moscow.

The issue is not whether the United States should have done more to support Amin, but whether a detached posture toward the insurgency would have better served American interests. In my view, based on my study of the Afghan communist regime, including visits to Kabul in 1978 and 1984, the prospects for a national-communist evolution of the DRA would have been favorable even if Amin had been removed or replaced by Moscow by different means—that is, without the necessity of a large-scale Soviet occupation.

The Party and the Resistance

Once Soviet forces did intervene, the Carter administration responded appropriately by initiating its program of covert weapons assistance. What had previously been a significant but limited insurgency, based on local resistance to centralized rule and religious and ideological opposition to a Marxist-Leninist regime, soon became a broader nationalist resistance against a foreign occupation force. From the start, however, the US government has been broadly divided into two camps with respect to the purpose of the covert aid program: those who view aid to the resistance as part of a two-track policy in which the United States simultaneously pursues a Soviet combat force withdrawal through a negotiated settlement, and others who discount the possibility of a withdrawal but support the aid program as a means of raising the costs of the occupation. Those who want thus to "bleed" the Soviet Union have clearly been stronger in the Reagan administration than they were during the Carter period. Yet while the quantity and quality of US weapons aid has steadily escalated, the American role in the Afghan struggle has been marked by continuing conceptual confusion.

Apart from the lack of a clear sense of purpose, the Reagan administration has based the implementation of its aid effort and its approach toward a negotiated settlement on a fundamental misperception of the political and social environment in Afghanistan. In the prevailing American image of the war, the resistance "controls" 80 percent of the Afghan countryside. Kabul has never published a precise figure concerning the extent of its administrative network, but the head of the powerful *Khad,* or secret police, told an Indian journalist in September 1984 that the DRA "controls" 7,000 out of 26,000 villages in addition to the capital and most other urban areas. What such figures actually mean in the present turbulent atmosphere of the war is highly debatable.

In reality, most of Afghanistan is governed today, as in past decades and centuries, by local tribal and ethnic warlords. While most of these warlords would like to get Soviet forces out of their areas and out of Afghanistan, relatively few of them are firmly committed to the resistance. Some of them are opportunists who take payoffs from both sides, smuggle narcotics, and sell weapons in the black market. Others cooperate with one or another of the resistance factions but are constrained by fear of Soviet reprisals. Still others, smaller in number, are trying to come to terms with the Babrak Karmal regime but are afraid that helping Kabul would bring punishment from the resistance. For most villages, trapped between increasingly efficient Soviet-cum-Afghan forces and increasingly well-equipped resistance fighters, the issue is simply how to survive.

In numerous conversations on my visit to Kabul in 1984, I was reminded that dedication and a patriotic self-image are not a monopoly of the resistance fighters. The Afghan communists see themselves as nationalists and modernizers in the reformist tradition of King Amanullah, who ruled from 1919 to 1929. The People's Democratic (communist) Party is clearly much stronger now than it was in 1978, even if one assumes that many of the new Party recruits are ideologically unreliable job-seekers. While the official claim is that there are 95,000 Party members, the truth may be closer to the estimate of 15,000 hard-core activists given to me by Brigadier Abdul Niazi, the principal Afghan specialist at the Inter-Services Intelligence Directorate in

Islamabad. But even 15,000 reliable Party activists would make a big difference for the Soviet Union in holding together an Afghan network of some 375,000 military, secret police, and civil service employees. The Party is no longer incapacitated by factionalism as it was when the Russians first arrived, and the Afghan communists are slowly but steadily consolidating their political and administrative infrastructure under the Soviet aegis in their Kabul city-state and in scattered enclaves around the country.

Far from offering an effective rallying point for Afghan nationalism, the resistance groups are fragmented along ethnic, tribal, and personality lines. More broadly, the divisions in the resistance reflect a growing polarization between Islamic fundamentalist exile forces, based in Pakistan, and many of the local field commanders and their followers, who are bearing the brunt of the fighting inside Afghanistan. Inspired by the Pan-Islamic Moslem Brotherhood, with its roots in Egypt, and by orthodox Wahabi groups in Saudi Arabia, the Pakistan-based fundamentalists had a negligible organization in Afghanistan prior to 1979. They were arrayed against the monarchy, against the entire traditional Moslem clergy, which rejects fundamentalist teachings, and against both Western-oriented and communist modernizers. Above all, they had alienated the powerful tribal hierarchy among the Pushtuns by calling for the abolition of tribalism as incompatible with their conception of a centralized Islamic state.

Although the advent of the communist regime aroused widespread alarm throughout the Moslem world, it was the fundamentalist elements in the Persian Gulf region and the Middle East who reacted most purposefully and made the Afghan issue their own. The fundamentalists saw the war as a golden opportunity to build up organizational cadres among the Afghan refugees in Pakistan, with an eye to eventually supplanting the entire pre-existing social and political hierarchy of the country. Their enemies thus were not only the Soviet troops and Afghan communist infidels, but also most of the nonfundamentalist resistance elements, led by Pushtun tribal dignitaries, Sufi and Hanafi clerics, Westernized ex-bureaucrats and military men, and other elements identified with the monarchy and the traditional social structure.

Most US and Saudi aid to the resistance is dispensed under the control of Pakistani officials who are beholden to the fundamentalist *Jamaat Islami* of Pakistan, a key ally of the Zia Ul-Haq regime. The *Jamaat,* in turn, works closely with the powerful leader of the orthodox Wahabis in Saudi Arabia, Abdul Bin Baz, who has long supported its political activities in Pakistan. The Wahabis and the *Jamaat* channel aid largely to like-minded exile groups in the refugee camps. Moslem Brotherhood elements in other areas around the Gulf and the Khomeini regime in Iran also have direct contacts with some of the fundamentalist groups.

The fundamentalists do dole out some weaponry, money, and supplies to selected local commanders inside Afghanistan who are already trusted ideological allies—such as Ahmed Shah Massoud in the Pansjer valley—or who are regarded as potential allies. But they keep most of it to develop their own Pakistan-based paramilitary cadres. These are partly for use in missions in Afghanistan and partly to provide a reserve gendarmerie for the Zia regime in the unsettled Northwest Frontier Province.

The fundamentalist paramilitary cadres have proved useful for carrying out commando missions in cooperation with locally based resistance fighters. As outsiders operating out of base camps in Pakistan, however, they are inherently disqualified from playing a follow-up political role that could translate military successes into lasting control of the countryside. Indeed, they have no desire to see an underground political infrastructure established under the control of the nonfundamentalist tribal leadership that prevails in most parts of Afghanistan.

The seven feuding fundamentalist factions have periodically made token efforts under American and Saudi pressure to establish a unified organization. But the unity they envision would be limited to the leaders of the seven exile factions based in the refugee camps. It would not extend either to the three traditionalist, nonfundamentalist exile factions or to the estimated sixty-five field commanders leading tribal bands in scattered parts of Afghanistan. In the spring of 1985, fundamentalist and traditionalist leaders in Pakistan formed a paper organization in the hope of obtaining recognition in some international bodies, but the new grouping did not significantly improve the military or political unity of the resistance.

Opposition from Pakistan-based fundamentalist groups and like-minded elements in Riyadh was directly responsible for frustrating the promising effort to unify the resistance made during the past two years by former King Zahir Shah. Ruling out the return of the monarchy or any personal role for himself, the ex-King has been attempting to create an Afghan National United Front in which the field commanders inside Afghanistan, the seven-party fundamentalist grouping, and the traditionalist exile factions would all be represented.

His initiative aroused considerable enthusiasm both inside the country and among the refugees. It was viewed as a hopeful opportunity to achieve greater military cohesion while providing a vehicle for negotiations with the USSR and the Afghan communists. At first, King Fahd of Saudi Arabia was prepared to extend quiet Saudi financial support so that Zahir Shah could convene a meeting of resistance leaders in Paris or Geneva to organize the Front. But Prince Abdullah and others in the royal family linked to Bin Baz and the orthodox Wahabis scotched this idea, and the fundamentalist exile leaders passed the word that no further funds or weaponry would be supplied to any field commander or refugee leader associated with the ex-King's effort.

In part, the bitter fundamentalist antagonism toward Zahir Shah reflects the strength of Tajik elements in fundamentalist ranks, who blame him for repression of the Tajiks and other ethnic minorities by his Pushtun-dominated monarchy. But a deeper explanation lies in the fact that the former King sees the proposed Front as a step toward some form of accommodation with Moscow and the Afghan communists that would lead to a Soviet withdrawal. For the fundamentalists, the goal of the war is the complete destruction of all Soviet and communist influence in Afghanistan and its replacement with a fundamentalist brand of Islamic polity, even if this takes several generations. They are banking on a protracted struggle and are seeking long-term foreign support to set up schools and even a university in Pakistan for the training of future Afghan leaders. By contrast, many of the field commanders and others inside the country who are suffering most directly from the war are more disposed to compromise with the Afghan communists and the Russians, so long as Soviet forces withdraw. They are prepared to consider some form of coexistence with a more broadly based Kabul regime in which tribal autonomy is honored and noncommunist elements have a greater share of power. Zahir Shah has not ruled out such a compromise. His refusal so far to lend himself to the idea of a government in exile appears to reflect a belief that a Soviet withdrawal can only be achieved through a face-saving accommodation in which the Democratic Republic of Afghanistan would at least nominally continue to exist.

Negotiations and Soviet Withdrawal

The basic issue in the stalemated UN negotiations, which are nominally between Pakistan and the Soviet-sponsored Democratic Republic of Afghanistan, continues to be the nature of the regime that would be left behind following a Soviet withdrawal. The keystone of the UN approach is that it would legitimize the DRA while leaving the door open for the removal of Babrak Karmal as president and for other changes in the make-up of the communist regime. Two of the key draft agreements that would give formal legal effect to the settlement would be between Islamabad and the Kabul regime. Much to the distress of Washington, Pakistan has recently gone along with language in these draft agreements specifically naming the DRA.

The Reagan administration professes the goal of an Afghan settlement in accordance with UN General Assembly resolutions, based on "a Soviet withdrawal, a return to the independent and non-aligned status of Afghanistan, self-determination for the Afghan people and the return of the refugees with dignity and honor." However, the administration rejects the premise of UN mediators that a Soviet withdrawal alone would satisfy the self-determination criterion of the General Assembly resolutions. Under the UN scenario, the DRA would be left in place at the outset of the withdrawal process and would have a chance to survive, if it could, through either a political accommodation or military struggle with its opponents, or both. The DRA argues that it could, in fact, survive without a Soviet force presence if US and other aid to the resistance were stopped in accordance with the terms of the draft settlement. Administration officials ridicule this claim, but in any event, the American position has consistently been that the replacement of the DRA by a more representative regime should be agreed upon as a precondition for concluding the UN agreement.

At the beginning of the hopeful interlude from April to June of 1983, when the UN negotiations showed promise, Pakistan adopted a more flexible posture than the United States. However, lacking the heart for diplomatic brinkmanship in the face of American, Saudi Arabian, and Chinese disapproval, Islamabad backed off at the eleventh hour. In the April round of the 1983 negotiations, Moscow indicated that it would agree to Islamabad's demand for the replacement of Karmal as a prerequisite for concluding an agreement. Pakistan's President Zia Ul-Haq had firmly declared that he would "never deal with the man who rode to power on Soviet tanks." At Geneva, the late Yuri Andropov's "observer," Stanislav Gabrilov, promised that Moscow would replace Karmal with Prime Minister Sultan Ali Keshtmand in time for the conclusion of the settlement. Pakistan agreed to proceed on this basis, thus signalling its willingness to legitimize the DRA regime. Islamabad also agreed to categorical language in the UN draft text that would have required cutting off support for the resistance coincident with the start of a Soviet force withdrawal. These Pakistani concessions had produced Soviet assurances in April that Moscow would propose a specific time frame for the projected withdrawal at the next round. By the time negotiations resumed in June, however, Islamabad had become equivocal on both key concessions; therefore, Moscow's pledge was never put to the test.[23]

As the UN dialogue has dragged on, the Soviet Union has grown more confident that it cannot be dislodged from Afghanistan and has progressively hardened its terms for a settlement. In 1982 and early 1983, Moscow was worried about factionalism in Afghan communist ranks. Soviet negotiators did not rule out a restructuring of the DRA regime through talks with moderate elements of the resistance in parallel with the UN dialogue. But Soviet staying power has progressively solidified since then as the regime has settled down in its Kabul enclave and as efforts to unify the resistance have repeatedly failed.

Moscow is more reluctant now to replace Karmal or to negotiate major changes in the DRA structure that would weaken communist control. Another key example of the hardened Soviet stance in the UN negotiations has been Soviet insistence on a basic change in the form of the settlement. What was originally to have been an agreement between the United Nations and the contending parties is now to be a set of bilateral treaties that would commit Pakistan more explicitly to recognition of the DRA. In 1983, Moscow and Kabul were negotiating on the basis of a UN draft text expressly providing for a Soviet withdrawal within a defined time period, though the length of this time frame was never settled. By contrast, in the August 1985 round of UN negotiations, DRA spokesmen refused to present their version of the treaty provisions governing Soviet force withdrawals until Islamabad agrees to replace the present UN mediation process with a direct, face-to-face dialogue.

The United States opposes direct talks at any stage of the negotiations, while Pakistan says that it will accept such talks at the "appropriate time" in the negotiations' closing phase. In June 1985, Islamabad and Kabul agreed on a proposed endorsement of the settlement by Moscow and Washington, and the UN presented this draft to both governments for their approval. Moscow responded in the August round with detailed proposals for revision, and the United States formally accepted the UN draft in December, following the Geneva summit, stressing that it would only sign an endorsement if the negotiations produced a "balanced and comprehensive" settlement.

The Reagan administration makes no pretense that the Russians are on the run. As Pentagon intelligence specialist Elie D. Krakowski has observed, despite improvements in the combat effectiveness of the resistance, "the Soviets have widened the (performance) gap in their favor."[24] Krakowski and like-minded observers argue that more and better weaponry for the resistance will in time force Moscow to abandon the DRA regime. But this roseate assessment ignores the depth of the historically rooted cleavages between resistance groups, divisions that make it difficult for them to follow up their military victories by establishing secure liberated areas. Moreover, experience suggests that for every improvement in American-supplied weaponry, Moscow would be likely to counter with its own escalation, as it has done for the past five years.

The stated reason for American coolness toward the UN scenario is that the DRA could not survive in the absence of Soviet forces and that chaos would result, compelling the Russians to return. But behind this rationale lies an unstated concern that the communist regime just might survive. It should be remembered that the UN concept is inherently asymmetrical: it would permit the DRA to continue receiving Soviet economic and military aid while precluding further outside aid to the resistance. Although intermittent fighting would no doubt continue between DRA forces and some resistance factions, the level of conflict in the countryside would be likely to subside over time as tribal and ethnic warlords make their uneasy peace with Kabul in return for local autonomy. The United States and other noncommunist countries should not prejudge whether the Russians could, or would, withdraw under this scenario, but should focus instead on the quid pro quos that would make such a scenario acceptable.

The governing criterion for American support of the UN settlement should be not whether it provides for dismantling the DRA but whether it assures that Moscow would not add strategic bases in Afghanistan to its other military capabilities adjacent to the Persian Gulf and Southwest Asia. At present, the Soviet air bases at Bagram, Kabul, Kandahar, and Shindand have runways long enough to receive a limited number of Bisons and other long-range strategic aircraft, but most Western intelligence sources agree that Moscow has not yet attempted a full-scale conversion of these facilities into strategic or offensive tactical bases. If satisfactory assurances can be obtained circumscribing the further development of these facilities and their use as Soviet bases, the United States should be prepared to support the UN model for a Soviet force withdrawal even if it leaves behind a communist-controlled Soviet client state in Kabul.[25]

It is not entirely clear that the Russians are prepared to make such a deal. My impression during a 1984 visit to Kabul was that they would like to alter the projected terms of the settlement in order to keep a reduced force of 15,000 to 30,000 troops in the country for an indefinite period. Such a caveat would reduce the risks of the UN scenario for Moscow by fortifying the DRA politically as well as militarily during the withdrawal process. Here the United States and Pakistan cannot compromise. No significant section of the resistance is likely to stop fighting unless the Russians commit themselves to a complete withdrawal within a specific time frame. At the very least, Moscow would have to accept a withdrawal in clearly defined stages, with the bulk of Soviet forces removed within a short period and final withdrawals left to a later terminal date.

Even at this late hour, the containment of Soviet military expansion in Afghanistan might still be possible. It should be pursued through a combination of stepped-up military pressure and a more realistic diplomacy. The price for achieving this goal would be initial acceptance of the significant political inroads made by Moscow during the past three decades in building an Afghan Communist Party. Once Soviet forces left, however, Afghan nationalism would gradually reassert itself, shaping the character of Afghan communism as well as the larger future of the overwhelmingly noncommunist Afghan majority.

Notes

1. George C. McGhee, *Envoy to the Middle World* (New York: Harper and Row, 1983), p. 304.

2. Leon B. Poullada, "Afghanistan and the United States: The Crucial Years," *The Middle East Journal*, Spring 1981, pp. 178–90. See also Poullada, "The Failure of American Diplomacy in Afghanistan," *World Affairs*, Winter 1982–1983, pp. 230–252.

3. Ralph De Toledano, *Nixon* (New York: Henry Holt and Company, 1956), p. 164.

4. Poullada, "Afghanistan and the United States: The Crucial Years," p. 190.

5. Cited in Selig S. Harrison, "Case History of a Mistake," *The New Republic*, 10 August 1959, p. 12.

6. Harrison, "South Asia and U.S. Policy," *The New Republic,* 11 December 1961, p. 11.

7. Testimony before the House Foreign Affairs Committee, Subcommittee on Asian and Pacific Affairs, 27 February 1985, and House Appropriations Committee, Subcommittee on Foreign Operations, 2 May 1985.

8. Harrison, "Dateline Afghanistan: Exit Through Finland?" *Foreign Policy,* Winter 1980–81, pp. 164–68.

9. Raymond L. Garthoff, *Detente and Confrontation* (Washington: The Brookings Institution, 1985), p. 916.

10. Harrison, "Dateline Afghanistan: Exit Through Finland?" pp. 170–72.

11. As one example of first-hand accounts of the Pakistani role, see Peter Niesewand's article in the *Washington Post,* 2 February 1979, p. A23.

12. Zbigniew Brzezinski, *Power and Principle* (New York: Farrar, Straus, Giroux, 1983), p. 427.

13. Italics added. Ibid., pp. 427, 429.

14. Garthoff, *Detente and Confrontation,* p. 942.

15. Zalmay Khalilzad, "The United States and the War in Afghanistan," unpublished, pp. 7, 9.

16. Department of State Bulletin, December 1979, p. 53.

17. *Background Notes: Afghanistan,* Bureau of Public Affairs, US State Department, April 1983.

18. It is not definitively established whether Amin was killed by Soviet forces, as is generally believed, or by factional rivals in the PDPA, acting at the instance of Soviet authorities or, as some evidence suggests, acting on their own initiative in the belief that the Russians would not object to their action.

19. Harrison, "Dateline Afghanistan: Exit Through Finland?" pp. 172–75.

20. Khalilzad, "An Ounce of Prevention," *Washington Post,* 10 October 1979, p. A21.

21. Garthoff, *Detente and Confrontation*, p. 921.

22. Anthony Lake, *Third World Radical Regimes: U.S. Policy Under Carter and Reagan,* Headline Series, The Foreign Policy Association, New York, No. 272, January 1985, p. 15.

23. Harrison, "A Breakthrough in Afghanistan?" *Foreign Policy,* Summer 1983, p. 13.

24. Elie D. Krakowski, "Defining Success in Afghanistan," *Washington Quarterly,* Spring 1985, p. 42.

25. This view is spelled out in Harrison, "The Afghanistan Stalemate: 'Self-Determination' and a Soviet Force Withdrawal," *Parameters,* Journal of the US Army War College, Winter 1984–85.

20

Asian Perspectives on Containment

Akira Iriye

T HE HISTORICAL SIGNIFICANCE of containment as formulated by George Kennan seems quite clear in the perspective of nearly forty years. It was a strategy designed to stabilize international order in the aftermath of a catastrophic war and in a period of unprecedented social and technological change throughout the world. As such, it was not a unique phenomenon. We read in Mr. Kennan's majestic study of Bismarck's foreign policy that European statesmen in the 1870s similarly tried to reestablish stability in the wake of the Franco-Prussian war. One may also add Metternich's Vienna structure of European peace, the Versailles peace conference, and other attempts at redefining international affairs. All wars, it would seem, are followed by a period of attempted restabilization. Whether or not such efforts succeed, they at least indicate an awareness that the state of war and destruction is not something that can perpetuate itself, and that mechanisms must be found for reestablishing some sense of order. Containment fits into the same pattern.

Akira Iriye is Stein-Freiler Distinguished Service Professor of History, Professor of American Diplomatic History, and Chairman of the Department of History at the University of Chicago.

Like other similar mechanisms, containment consisted of several ingredients, of which three are particularly important. One was the definition of a new status quo. The old status quo had been destroyed—that is what war means—and some powers had emerged victorious. It was up to them to determine, if they could, the postwar shape of the world. A new balance of power had to be defined and maintained on that basis. Containment, in this sense, was merely another term for the preservation of the new status quo.

Second, like Bismarck's European order, containment aimed at preventing another war, at least on the scale of the one just fought. It was a strategy for upholding the global balance by means short of war. As Kennan envisioned it, containment was not exactly a blueprint for eternal peace, but neither was it intended as a strategy for a third world war. It was, rather, a call for preparedness and mobilization—more spiritual and economic than military—in order to prevent such a war.

Third, the idea of containment assumed, just as did Metternich's and Bismarck's conceptions of order, that there was a symbiotic relationship between international stability and domestic stability. Internal forces of radical change would somehow have to be contained, just as forces of disorder in external affairs had to be contained. This was, on the one hand, because radical developments domestically would have serious external repercussions, and, on the other, because unstable international relations would abet domestic tensions and upheavals. Although social change would be difficult to control, especially in the aftermath of a bloody conflict with tens of millions of casualties, it at least ought to be prevented from developing into a global revolutionary force which might upset the incipient status quo, from expressing itself as a belligerent, chauvinistic force toward other countries, or from being taken advantage of by governmental leaders so as to justify their adventuristic foreign policies. Thus, the strategy of containment should aim at encouraging orderly change within each country as well as in international relations as a whole.

This was a colossal undertaking, but by no means unique, as I have tried to suggest. An assessment of it should, I think, be built on some knowledge of history, so that the achievements as well as the frustrations of the containment strategy may be better evaluated.

The Asian Territorial and Economic Status Quo

How does containment look in the perspective not of European but of Asian history? Of course, it is possible to dismiss such a question by saying that containment as originally formulated was intended as a strategy for checking the spread of Soviet power in Western Europe, and that it was never meant to be applicable to other regions of the globe. Thus narrowly constructed, the success of containment was already apparent by the end of the 1940s. The problem with this interpretation, obviously, is that neither the Soviet Union nor the United States was purely a European power. Both geographically and historically, Russia had been involved in the Middle East, Central Asia, and the Far East, while America had steadily extended its sway over the Pacific Ocean and the Asian continent. Moreover, the Western European countries which were America's main concern were also colonial powers in Asia, from which they were in the process of extricating themselves but in which they had, for centuries, established their vested interests. For all these reasons, containment, even if it had been aimed primarily at Western Europe, would have had implications for Asia. In fact, as we know, it was in Asia that the strategy was to meet its severest challenges.

To understand this situation, it may help to go back to the three aspects of containment mentioned above and see how each of them worked or did not work in East Asia. First of all, what was to be the new status quo that would provide the point of departure for containment? It was fairly explicitly defined at the wartime conferences in Cairo, Tehran, Yalta, and Potsdam. According to the agreements made at these conferences, the postwar Asian status quo would see Japan being reduced to the four home islands, China regaining full sovereignty with the retrocession of Taiwan and Manchuria, the Soviet Union regaining Sakhalin and the Kurile Islands (plus some railway and harbor rights in Manchuria), Korea being promised independence in due course, and the European nations returning to their colonial possessions. The United States would establish control over the formerly Japanese-mandated islands in the western Pacific, while the Philippines would become independent.

This was a reasonably specific definition of the new Asian status quo, and to the extent that containment was aimed at preserving regional stability, this definition provided the point of departure. It is interesting that the Soviet Union, as well as the United States, was involved in defining this status quo through wartime meetings and agreements. By the time of Japan's surrender, the two powers had come to a rough understanding about their respective spheres of influence, on the basis of which a new stability would be established to replace the system of regional order which Japan had tried to create. America and Russia would be the principal powers upholding the postwar regime, but acceptance by China, Japan, and Britain, as well as such other parties as Korea, France, and the Netherlands, would also be required. Much as Bismarck's European diplomacy aimed at maintaining a balance among five major powers by associating Germany with at least two others, so American policy initially needed the support at least of Russia and Britain, or Russia and China, or China and Britain, to prevent Japanese revanchism. Such an undertaking did not require a *new* "containment" strategy; some sort of balance of power in the region was implicit in the wartime agreements. At the same time, these agreements would be still relevant even after Soviet power was perceived to be expansive, undermining the new stability. Containment of Russia would mean, as far as Asia was concerned, making sure the Soviet Union was kept within the bounds it had helped define at Tehran and Yalta. It is for this reason that some historians have argued that there was no drastic shift from wartime collaboration to a Cold War in Asia.[1] Containment, in other words, was implicit in the wartime agreements.

Nevertheless, the strategy of containing Russia ultimately had the effect of significantly altering the Asian status quo. There was no change, to be sure, as far as Japan was concerned. After 1948, Japan came to be seen as a country with which the United States and Britain would form a tripartite association to uphold the regional balance, then viewed as being threatened by Russia and China; but that did not mean the United States would agree to any change in Japan's territorial limits. With China, the story was different. Although the policy of keeping Taiwan separate from mainland China did not become fixed until after 1950, already in the late 1940s officials in Washington talked of detaching the island from China proper to make use of it strategically to contain Russian and Chinese communism. In Korea, in the meantime, the status quo came to mean a division of the country into two halves, another departure from the wartime formulations. Elsewhere, in the colonial region of Southeast Asia, the status quo grew progressively more difficult to define, with European powers either in retreat before indigenous nationalism or engaging in wars with nationalistic forces. The well-known difficulty of where to draw the defensive perimeter in Asia—a prerequisite for an effective implementation of containment—reflected a situation in which no line was likely to remain fixed. There seems little doubt, however, that American policy was often ambiguous and even contradictory regarding the status of Korea and Taiwan, and because of this it was not always clear what the United States was supposed to be containing. The sole exception was Japan, to which Washington came to assign, at least by 1949, a role in upholding regional order.

In understanding how this came about, it will be useful to recall that, in addition to providing for postwar territorial dispositions, the wartime conferences had also formulated an economic agenda. The main purpose was to find an alternative to Japan's autarkic regional system, which had been destroyed and discredited. That country would now be directed to find its salvation in multilateral patterns of trade throughout the world, and Asia would be linked to other regions in the regime of open economic transactions defined at the Bretton Woods conference. The European colonial governments would be expected to offer their Asian resources and markets to the whole world, thereby to promote indigenous economic growth. American officials viewed such a system of economic internationalism as an important counterpart to the territorial settlements; together, they would contribute to postwar peace and prosperity. It is true that the Soviet Union was not as deeply involved in the economic regime as the United States, but at least until the end of 1945, Moscow was engaged in various negotiations to implement the Bretton Woods decisions. In any event, the economic scheme implicitly assigned a role to Japan in postwar Asia which became more explicit after 1949. Although at that time (and indeed for several more years) Japan was viewed as militarily vulnerable, its economic potential was clearly recognized. If some sort of stability were to be maintained in Asia in the face of possible Soviet expansionism, then it was believed of crucial importance to combine Japan's industrial power with the resources of Southeast Asia so as to contribute to Asian economic development and deny the area to hostile forces. Japan could easily play this role for the simple reason that it had already done so, in the 1920s and 1930s.

In other words, the status quo to be contained in Asia had both territorial and economic aspects. The former had been defined at Cairo, Yalta, and other wartime conferences, but had already begun to be modified. The latter, envisaged at Bretton Woods, reached back to the Washington Conference of 1921–22, for it was there that the principles of economic internationalism and political cooperation in Asia were first formulated. To schematize the postwar developments a bit simplistically, it may be said that the Asian status quo meant the replacement of the Japan-imposed "co-prosperity sphere" with the Yalta and Washington frameworks. There was a tension between the two definitions, but both persisted in modified form throughout the postwar years. Japan was one country that fit well into, and benefited from, this turn of events. Its territorial limits were clearly demarcated and were not subject to change; at the same time, by going back to the principles of the 1920s, the nation could once again seek economic security through integrating itself into an open international system. The emphasis on Japan's economic potential, rather than on its military position, was an important part of the containment strategy. In that sense, containment meant going back to the prewar framework of cooperation among the United States, Britain, Japan, and other industrial powers. It was a signal success precisely because it placed less stress on Japan's military capabilities and more on the contributions it could make to regional economic development. In other parts of Asia, however, containment was less successful because of the difficulty of defining the status quo, and because other nations there were less developed economically and more unstable socially.

Containment, War, and Civil War in Asia

My second point about the containment strategy concerns the implicit assumption that it was a policy of utilizing all means short of war to maintain the balance of power. In other words, containment must be judged a failure if it could not prevent the outbreak of wars. In this regard, containment in Asia did fail. The Cold War in Asia lasted but briefly before it led to hot wars in Korea and Vietnam, costing hundreds of thousands of lives. These wars can be judged in many ways, but in the context of our discussion they signaled an outcome very much in contrast to that in Europe, where no comparable wars would take place.

In writing of Europe before the First World War, Mr. Kennan has noted the failure of European statesmen "to grasp the subtleties of a policy that aimed to handle the Russian problem by means short of war." Can we not say the same thing about the postwar containment policy in Asia? It could be argued, of course, that there has been no war with the Soviet

Union in Asia or anywhere else, and in that sense containment has been a success. Even the wars in Korea and Vietnam could, presumably, be said to have contributed to containing Russian power. At the other extreme would be the view that the very nature of containment was such as to make local wars inevitable; the United States was committed to upholding the status quo, and therefore it would have to wage wars once the status quo became threatened. Such views miss the "subtleties" of the original containment doctrine, for its essential objective was not war preparedness but prevention of war. Although that doctrine was invoked to justify American involvement in Korea and later in Vietnam, fighting such wars had not been an integral part of the original policy itself. The concept was more "subtle," aimed at "handling the Russian problem" not by going to war at the Soviet periphery but by diplomacy and through economic and spiritual mobilization. At this level of analysis, then, it may be said that Asian wars broke out in spite of, not because of, the containment strategy.

But why did such wars break out? Volumes have been written about the origins of the Korean and Vietnam Wars, but here it should suffice to list three well-known factors. First, postwar Asia, like the Balkans before 1914, was an area where the clash of imperial and nationalistic forces created an extremely volatile situation. Just as the internal tensions of the Ottoman, Austrian, and Russian empires created chronic instability in the Balkans, in postwar Asia the collapse of the Japanese empire and the weakening of the European empires brought about a situation in which it was virtually impossible to produce any clearly recognized sense of regional stability. Under the circumstances, it would have been next to impossible to know what the containment strategy was supposed to contain. Most critical would be the absence of a unified government in Korea, China, and Vietnam. All these were anticolonialist countries, but the indigenous leaders were seriously divided over the character of post-independence government, and civil wars were unavoidable.

Whether the containment policy was meant to apply to civil wars was thus the second difficulty it faced when applied to Asia. By 1950, it is true, the United States had taken steps to assist the noncommunist regimes in South Korea, South Vietnam, and Taiwan. But at the same time Americans had ruled out massive intervention in China, applying containment there only partially. In fact, some officials in Washington argued that it made more sense to contain Russian power by encouraging Chinese unification under the communists. The often acrimonious debate about China policy revealed the difficulty of implementing containment in a serious civil war situation. The absence of a clearly articulated policy regarding civil wars may explain the fact that American interventions in Korea and Vietnam were justified not as interventions in civil wars but as police actions to repulse external aggression. The fact remains that there had been no clear articulation of a containment strategy toward civil wars, even though in Asia civil wars were far more likely to develop than interstate wars. By the same token, the success of containment in Japan may be attributed to the fact that that country was in no danger of civil strife.

The third factor in accounting for Asian wars is the fact that after 1950 containment tended to be seen in Asia as applicable to the People's Republic of China rather than the Soviet Union. China appeared to be more expansive than Russia, willing to engage in propaganda and subversive activities to undermine the regional order sustained through American power. The Soviet Union, on the other hand, appeared less aggressive and more willing to observe the status quo, especially after the death of Stalin. Russia, after all, had not intervened militarily in the Korean War, whereas China had. In the Khrushchev period, Moscow stressed the theme of peaceful coexistence, which could be interpreted to mean an acceptance of regional stability. Beijing, in contrast, actively pursued a policy of coalescing Third World countries against American imperialism, eventually breaking with Moscow on the issue of peaceful coexistence. How could such a country be contained, if not by being willing to match Chinese initiatives with American ones? Thus reasoning, the United States sought to establish a network of military alliances throughout Asia to keep China in check and to strengthen the military capabilities of noncommunist states. Even more critically, Washington intervened in Southeast Asia so as to maintain the region's stability against revolutionary forces which were, so it was believed, backed by China. The US government also contemplated the use of force against mainland China during the offshore crises of 1955 and 1958 in order to protect Taiwan. Such readiness to consider, and in some instances actually resort to, the use of force in Asia was in contrast to the extreme caution of Washington's policy in Eastern Europe. Any military intervention in Eastern Europe would have risked Soviet retaliation, whereas military measures taken against China did not appear to carry such a risk.

This contrast was most clearly revealed during the 1960s and the early 1970s, when the United States was engaged in war in Asia while pursuing a detente with the Soviet Union. It may be said that containment took two different forms: toward China it envisaged military action, whereas vis-a-vis the Soviet Union it called for measures short of war. It is interesting to note that since the early 1970s the United States has reverted to emphasizing nonmilitary means of containing the People's Republic. American policy was focused on incorporating China into the regional order and on ensuring that country's good behavior through economic and technological assistance. Today, the Chinese leadership no longer speaks of inevitable war with forces of imperialism; instead, it daily reiterates its interest in global and regional stability. Whether the destruction of Vietnam was a precondition for such a state of affairs will long be debated, but in the history of containment the Vietnam War could be said to have been a success only in the twisted sense that it coincided with a rapprochement between America and China. Even so, thirty years of enmity between the two countries would appear to have been a wasteful way of bringing about Asian stability. It would have been better if containment had been interpreted, in the 1950s and the 1960s, so as to justify resumption of diplomatic and economic ties between China and the United States. At the same time, one also should not forget that China today still remains divided between the mainland and Taiwan. In other words, the status quo defined during the war remains unfulfilled, and there is always a danger of civil war. This weakness of the containment policy—namely, its initial commitment to a divided China—is likely to remain for years to come. It remains to be seen whether a more developed China, committed more to stability than to revolution, will be willing to wait patiently for an ultimate reunification with Taiwan by peaceful means.

Containment, Revolutionary Change, and Development
This mention of economic development leads to the third and final aspect of containment: its concern with containing revolutionary change and encouraging gradual evolution. The assumption was that social upheavals and political turmoil in any country would create a situation which would tempt communists and subversive elements to try to seize power. Such a society might fall into the Soviet orbit even without Russia's firing a shot. In the aftermath of the war, this appeared a genuine possibility in the devastated countries of Europe, the principal target of the containment strategy; but, in time, the same thinking was applied to Japan, leading to the adoption of a policy aimed at promoting its economic recovery so as to ensure political stability. Historians have characterized this development as a "reverse course," since it modified the initially more punitive policy of the American occupation.

It may be pointed out, however, that the coupling of domestic stability and international security was nothing new. Even during the war in the Pacific, some segments, at least, of the government in Washington strongly contested the notion that Asian security could be guaranteed only through revolutionary changes in Japan. On the contrary, they asserted that a moderate and reformist Japan, not a radical one, would make a better contribution to regional peace, and that, therefore, the United States should not try to eradicate the country's economic and political leaders, except those who had been explicitly tied to the military. Although the initial guidelines for the occupation went much beyond such an objective and called for far-reaching reforms in land tenure, the family structure, civil laws, and the like, these changes did not quite amount to a social revolution or a political upheaval. Many aspects of Japanese society and politics remained little changed from the prewar years, and in other respects the postwar reforms merely accelerated changes that had already begun to take place. Pre-1945 social institutions and political frameworks continued to function, in modified fashion, so that there was little likelihood of a revolution. Most important, the bureaucratic apparatus was not dismantled, so the civil servants provided an essential link to prewar Japan. Their top leaders were purged by the occupation authorities, enabling younger officials to play an active role in postwar affairs. And there is little doubt that the new leaders were more interested in preserving social order than in revolution.

Even so, postwar shortages of food and shelter, as well as an unceasing inflation, could have led to a serious crisis, especially in view of the fact that the occupation was promoting an ideological transformation of Japan through the rewriting of textbooks and press censorship. With a population becoming increasingly aware of its rights and freedoms, and attuned to a wide range of foreign ideas, Japanese politics might have become much more radicalized if the US government had not shifted its emphasis to economic recovery and reindustrialization. As it turned out, new measures such as controlling radical labor movements, de-purging businessmen and politicians, and allowing the country to rebuild its export-oriented industries paved the way for Japan's reintegration into the world economy, an essential condition for domestic stability.

Although the Japanese economy was still vulnerable and required the massive infusion of American funds during the Korean War to begin to play an active role in Asia, its internal politics came to be characterized by a stability unprecedented in the country's modern history. Socially, too, changes would come slowly and in such a way as to accommodate all segments of the population into a consensus-oriented, middle-class community. (Ironically, this basic stability was, in time, to give rise to complaints by Americans, particularly businessmen, frustrated by the very slow pace of change in Japanese societal institutions and practices.) In any event, to the extent that the original containment policy sought by promoting domestic stability to prevent communist penetration and expansion, Japan was an almost complete success. Today, opinion polls invariably report that the majority of the Japanese people are content with themselves and with things as they are at home; and these people also indicate their support of the postwar structure of US-Japanese relations. In other words, here is a good example of the symbiotic relationship between domestic order and international order.

Japan, however, has been the exception in Asia. In other countries, political upheavals and social turmoil have been the rule since 1945. In China, Korea, Vietnam, and elsewhere, revolutionary developments had already begun to take place before the Pacific war. Historians have pointed to such indigenous factors as population growth and commercialization of agriculture to account for those developments, which had been going on for over a century. It would seem that in many parts of Asia traditional social systems were bound to be destroyed sooner or later. But the Japanese war accelerated the process by dividing local populations into collaborators and resisters, by conscripting and removing native workers, by forcing industrialization, and, most obviously, by driving out Europeans and Americans who had occupied privileged positions in colonial communities. Nationalism or anticolonialism is too loose a term to describe what was happening. These forces merely exacerbated social cleavages by pitting collaborators against resisters, and even among resisters there was often conflict between moderates and radicals. The division was not just political and ideological, but reflected social interests as well. The result, as many well-documented studies of China, Korea, and Vietnam after 1945 show, was that anticolonialism combined with revolution to create extremely volatile situations throughout Asia. To make matters more serious, contending groups often turned to outside forces for support, thereby enhancing the chances for international crises.

Clearly, it would have been extremely difficult to "contain" such a situation. The original containment doctrine did not try to do so. It was aimed primarily at ensuring order in the more advanced countries of Europe and in Japan. By the late 1940s, however, containment came to be applied, at least conceptually, to non-Western countries. Containment became a strategy of development, or liberal developmentalism. It was held that all countries went through similar stages of modernization, and that economic development would result in enhanced social integration and political stability, which in turn would make those countries less vulnerable to outside pressures. It seemed obviously in the interest of the United States to encourage this process. With respect to countries that were being liberated from Japanese imperialism and European colonialism, it was thought that American policy should aim at assisting their economic and political modernization. One practical way of helping them achieve economic change, officials in Washington believed, was to link Japan closely with other Asian countries through trade, making use of its technology and potential industrial capacities. A triangular relationship among Asia, Japan, and the United States would bring benefits to Asian countries as well as to Japan. As some historians have shown, this strategy was most clearly articulated with respect to Southeast Asia,[2] for by the late 1940s China was in the throes of a civil war and Korea was divided, whereas there still seemed to be an opportunity to salvage Indochina, Indonesia, the Philippines, and others through Japanese trade.

The strategy encountered numerous obstacles. The US Congress was not prepared to vote the enormous sums of money that would have been required to promote Asian economic development, so instead it gave priority to military aid. More crucially, revolutionary movements in many of these countries precluded any effective program of economic development through external assistance. After all, such a program would have had to be channeled through some legitimate local government, but legitimacy was in question throughout Asia. Only after the establishment of a recognizable and recognized government would it become possible to give developmental aid. The United States, however, refused to recognize the legitimacy of the governments in Beijing, Pyongyang, and Hanoi, and instead tried to turn Taiwan, South Korea, and South Vietnam into showcases of liberal developmentalism. It could be argued that, at least in Taiwan and South Korea, American economic assistance coupled with military aid did contribute to development and stability, although domestic politics remained in a state of tension because of the possibility of an armed conflict with mainland China and North Korea, respectively. In South Vietnam, on the other hand, a stable society never emerged and, after its unification with North Vietnam in 1975, American attention shifted to ASEAN, a group of Asian countries intent upon promoting internal economic development and regional stability.

In a way, the triangular economic relationship that was envisaged earlier among the United States, Japan, and Southeast Asia thus seems finally to have emerged, thirty years after its conception. The same may be said of American relations with the People's Republic of China, which became "normalized" in the 1970s. American technology and capital have been made available to China, in a belated attempt at helping its modernization. Although there is today much less optimism than earlier that economic development will lead to political democratization, at least the same emphasis on stability is evident. It is expected that as China modernizes its economy, its politics will become less subject to waves of extremism, and at the same time, that a stable political system will in turn facilitate economic transformation. All of this will, it is assumed, help build

up that country as a bulwark against Soviet expansion. To this
extent, America's China policy since the 1970s would seem to
have harked back to at least one strand of the containment
doctrine.

The Spiritual Dimension of Containment

To sum up, containment in Asia has evolved in rather unex-
pected ways. Initially, as I have suggested, it was little more
than a continuation of the wartime agreements on territorial and
economic arrangements. The former, often called the Yalta system, was soon modified, so there was confusion as to where to
draw the line. This situation was due fundamentally to social
unrest and political turmoil in most parts of Asia, resulting in
civil wars. It was extremely difficult to apply a territorial concept of containment to such a situation. Only in Japan, initially,
did the strategy work, because all powers, including the United
States, accepted the wartime territorial decisions and also because, more importantly, the economic aspect of containment
also was successfully applied to Japan; the Bretton Woods
scheme went back to the principles of the Washington Conference, so that all that was needed was to restore the earlier
framework and encourage Japanese reintegration into the regional and global economies. But the successes in Japan were
not enough to create and preserve regional stability, or to define
a well-balanced status quo. Civil wars broke out in Korea and
Vietnam, which the United States viewed as international wars
that could result in the expansion of Russian and Chinese
power. America intervened to restore the balance, but ironically, some sense of stability was established only after a rapprochement with the People's Republic of China. China became
incorporated into the regional order, something that had been inherent in the Yalta system. But Asia has not gone back to Yalta.
China and Korea remain divided, and Southeast Asia is also divided between a unified Vietnam on one hand and the ASEAN
countries on the other. In the meantime, Soviet power has been
far from contained. The Soviet Union has increased its naval

and air presence in the region, and it has established influential positions in North Korea and in Vietnam.

So, overall, the record of containment in Asia is a mixed one. Defined as a strategy for restabilizing international order, it has been more successful in the economic than in the military and territorial spheres. There have been wars and constant redefinitions of territorial boundaries, but at the same time, the whole region has achieved spectacular economic gains. If, as assumed by the architects of the containment strategy, economic development and well-being ensure stability and security, then it may be expected that Asia will come to enjoy a peaceful international order. However, continued division of China and Korea, as well as increases in Soviet military power, militate against stability.

In a sense, a significant gap has existed between economic and military affairs: on one hand, the region has seen economic modernization and integration, but on the other, it has been plagued by territorial division and military imbalance. Japan may best exemplify this gap; its overwhelming economic position has not been matched by a corresponding military role. For this reason, critics have called on Japan to do more to contribute to a regional balance of power, in a sense to revitalize the containment strategy from which it has benefited so much. But it may be doubted whether Japan's increased military power will really help in promoting regional stability. If it should generate fears on the part of other Asian countries, or if it should become so powerful as to encourage a revanchist sentiment toward lost territory, it would become a destabilizing force. On the other hand, if Japan should simply persist in self-enrichment through trade and investment but do little to contribute to the peace and security of Asia, it could risk international condemnation. So the dilemma will persist, at bottom a dilemma of the concept of containment itself, with its dual emphasis on military-territorial affairs and economic-social affairs.

There was, however, something else in the containment strategy as it was originally formulated. In addition to military defenses and economic recovery, it stressed the importance of spiritual mobilization. As Mr. Kennan pointed out on numerous occasions, the strength of citizens' commitment to certain values is the ultimate weapon against totalitarian regimes. It made no sense to turn free societies into garrison states to maintain the balance of power, for then there would be little reason for the protection it offered. The essence of containment was to coalesce the forces of freedom and democracy against those of closed societies. In this regard, the story of containment is not a very happy one in Asia, where freedom, democracy, and openness have more often been an exception than the rule.

Is it not possible to argue that, today more than ever before, regional peace and welfare depend on the spread of those values, and that without them any regime of stability will remain precarious? If so, then it seems clear that the future of containment lies in a return to its original conception, and in a spreading of universal values throughout Asia. Japan will have to take the initiative because it is so powerful economically but without much influence in other areas. It will have to open up its society to others, stop discriminating against Asian residents and against American goods, and develop a much firmer commitment to cultural internationalism. But other countries will also need to change, to democratize their politics and liberalize their societies. And the United States will have to support all such efforts. This may sound too utopian, but as Regis Debray has written, the history of an epoch is revealed as much in its utopias as in its discoveries. In a world too often defined in terms of trade figures and military strategies, Asians as well as Americans may be well advised to consider visions of the future in which they will define stability as much on the basis of shared values as on the maintenance of the balance of power and economic prosperity.

Notes

1. Akira Iriye, "Continuities in US-Japanese Relations," in Yonosuke Nagai and Iriye, eds., *The Origins of the Cold War in Asia* (New York: Columbia University Press, 1977).

2. William Borden, *The Pacific Alliance* (Madison: University of Wisconsin Press, 1984).

21

Containment and the Northeast Asian Triangle

Guo-cang Huan

T HE INTERNATIONAL SYSTEM in Northeast Asia is structured
by two superpowers, the United States and the USSR; two
regional powers, China and Japan; and two local powers, North
and South Korea. This power structure has four characteristics.
In the first place, its dynamics are largely determined by the triangle among the United States, the USSR, and China. Second,
although Japan has great economic power and potential political
influence, it has limited influence on security issues in the region. Third, the two Koreas, especially the North, have relative
freedom of action in both political and security affairs, while
room for them to make significant compromises to each other is
limited. Moreover, there are strong interactions between the relationship of the two Koreas on the one side, and the dynamics
of the triangle on the other. Fourth, all major powers, though
competing with one another (especially the United States and
China with the USSR) for influence over the region, are now

Guo-cang Huan is a Senior Fellow at the Atlantic Council of the United States
and a Research Fellow at the Brookings Institution.

committed to maintaining its stability. This is so because any serious military confrontation or rapid shift of the power balance might escalate to a regional war involving all major powers. Such a war would not be easily limited to the region nor controlled at the conventional level.

The US containment strategy toward Northeast Asia has undergone dramatic changes during the past four decades. These changes were primarily due to the dynamics of the triangle among the United States, the USSR, and China, relations among countries in Northeast Asia, and the development of the power structure in the Asia-Pacific region as a whole. At present, this strategy faces a number of serious challenges. First, although the triangle among the United States, the USSR, and China appears to be more stable than before, Soviet-American competition both in and outside the region has intensified, while there has been a process of limited relaxation between China and the USSR. Second, the military balance in the region has continued to favor the USSR over the United States and its allies, a situation likely to continue in the years ahead. Third, the deep distrust between North Korea and South Korea remains strong, although political tensions between the two sides have declined. Moreover, South Korea's internal political stability has been challenged by opposition forces, while North Korea may experience a succession crisis in the foreseeable future. These developments are likely to affect relations between the North and South and may even jeopardize the stability of the region. Finally, Japan has already begun the process of transforming its economic power into political power, and its effort to rearm has had and will continue to have a significant impact on the dynamics of the power balance of the region, if not of the world as a whole.

These developments raise several questions. What are the key security issues in Northeast Asia? What are the future dynamics of the triangle among the United States, the USSR, and China? What are the trends of Soviet expansionism in the region? And what is the most desirable strategy to contain such expansionism? In order to answer these questions, this paper will briefly review changes in the US containment strategy toward the Asia-Pacific region, then define the key security issues in Northeast Asia and examine the nature and trends of these issues in the years ahead, and finally propose the most desirable American strategy for containing Soviet expansionism.

US Containment Strategy in the Asia-Pacific Region

There have been three different US strategies of containment in the Asia-Pacific region since World War II. The first, dominant roughly through the early 1970s, based US security interests in Asia on bilateral ties with America's noncommunist allies—Japan, South Korea, the SEATO nations, and Taiwan. This model viewed China as the main regional enemy to be contained and was based on direct US military involvement in the region. This strategy did not take the internal political, economic, and social problems of US allies in Asia fully into account. Under this strategy, the United States fought two wars in Asia and froze its ties with China for more than twenty years.

This strategy became increasingly unsuitable near the end of the 1960s. While the United States tied itself down in Southeast Asia, the Soviet Union rapidly strengthened its economic and military power and began its global competition with the United States. Meanwhile, the deepening Sino-Soviet split escalated into a military confrontation between the two communist powers. The triangle among the United States, the Soviet Union, and China thus began to move in a new direction: both the United States and China began to view the Soviet Union as the principal threat to their national security.

At the regional level, the ongoing Vietnam War and later withdrawal of US forces from the Asian mainland further weakened Washington's strategic position in the Asia-Pacific region, leaving US allies in Asia in a vulnerable position—both militarily and psychologically—vis-a-vis Moscow and its allies. Facing the rapidly expanded Soviet military presence in the Far

East and Moscow's efforts to encircle China strategically, Beijing felt more insecure than ever. Moreover, developments in the Vietnam War by the early 1970s and the shifts in Washington's strategic perspective on the Asia-Pacific region gradually changed Beijing's view: the United States seemed no longer the primary threat but rather a potential strategic partner to counter Moscow's political and military pressure.

Henry Kissinger's first trip to China in 1971 began a gradual shift in US security strategy toward the Asia-Pacific region. Under the second strategy, the key enemy to be contained was the Soviet Union, in the Asia-Pacific region as well as elsewhere. China, in turn, was viewed as a potential strategic partner of the United States against the Soviet Union. This strategy reached its high point at the time of Sino-American normalization in 1979. It never actually led to concrete strategic or security cooperation between the two countries, but rather projected a strategic posture on the part of Beijing and Washington vis-a-vis Moscow.

The new approach finally ended a history of more than twenty years of Sino-American confrontation and dramatically changed the triangular relationship among the United States, the Soviet Union, and China. It also restructured the international system in the Asia-Pacific region and moderated the psychological and political crisis of US withdrawal from the Asian mainland. In addition, this strategy created the possibility of a broad strategic alignment against the Soviet Union, including the United States, Western Europe, Japan, and China. In the long run, it thus forced Moscow to face the real danger of fighting a two-front war. In sum, this strategy strengthened the American strategic position vis-a-vis the Soviet Union, both globally and in the Asia-Pacific region, and contributed to preventing further shifts in the power balance between the United States and the Soviet Union.

However, this strategy also had its weaknesses. In the first place, it did not fully take into account the possible political differences between Washington and Beijing, both in their bilateral ties and in their positions on political issues outside the Asia-Pacific region. As a result, when the two countries had disagreements or conflicts, such as on the Taiwan issue or US policy toward the Third World, this strategy immediately became difficult to implement.

Second, although based on the common security interests that Washington and Beijing share in the Asia-Pacific region, this strategy was not fully combined with the cultural, economic, and other political interests that the two countries share. Moreover, Sino-American cooperation was never joined in a concrete way; Washington and Beijing did not work closely to further their common security interests in the region. Consequently, this strategy was not very effective in containing Moscow's and its allies' expansionism.

Third, this new strategy of containment did not fit well with Washington's ties to Indonesia and Malaysia, two ASEAN states which view China, not the Soviet Union and Vietnam, as their long-term threat. It thus constrained Washington's ability to act positively in Southeast Asia.

Fourth, this strategy did not define the differences between Beijing and Washington in their policy toward Moscow, nor did it take a dynamic perspective of developments in the Washington-Beijing-Moscow triangle. Domestic political developments in post-Mao China led to a slow and limited process of relaxing tensions between Beijing and Moscow. In contrast, even within the Asia-Pacific region, Moscow has gradually and increasingly shifted its main strategic target from China to the United States and its allies. Such a tendency has created differences between Beijing and Washington about how to contain the expansionism of Moscow and its allies. Unless Beijing and Washington define their own and common interests and responsibilities carefully and specifically, it is difficult for the two countries to further their cooperation on concrete subregional security issues. Given the changes in international politics and in

American global and regional security interests, both these strategies have now been rejected as US approaches to containment in the Asia-Pacific region.

The Reagan administration came into office with the goal of reversing the perceived decline in the US global position. This decline was attributed both to Moscow's expanding influence and to the general diffusion of political and economic power in the international system due to the emergence of strong regional actors. To make the United States "strong again," the government took "tough" stands in favor of US global interests. It moved sharply away from the policy of detente, which had dominated throughout the 1970s, to a policy of "pushing back" Soviet influence. The level of hostility which this policy engendered made many fear a destabilizing change in the "rules of the game" between the two superpowers and an increased chance of global conflict. Gorbachev's accession brought new opportunities for Soviet-American relaxation and arms negotiations, but deep distrust and sharply conflicting interests remain between Washington and Moscow.

US foreign policy toward the Asia-Pacific region has also undergone important changes. There has been a perceptible shift in American focus—in political as well as economic terms—from the Atlantic to the Pacific. The current administration has identified Moscow as a growing threat to the security of the Asia-Pacific region. The Soviet Union's occupation of Afghanistan, its increased presence in Vietnam, and the buildup of the Soviet naval fleet in the western Pacific are seen as moves to change the balance of power in the region and as threats to US security interests. The administration's response has been to strengthen its political support of America's "old friends" and allies in Asia while at the same time applying pressure on them to do more for their own security. Washington's pressure on Tokyo, for instance, has been the most intense. The United States has advocated the transfer of advanced aircraft to South Korea, Thailand, and Pakistan. In Southeast Asia, Washington has given greater political and diplomatic attention to

ASEAN, although it has moved reluctantly to match this with military support.

The current administration's China policy has sought to find a stable middle ground between the two models described above. Washington regards China as a regional power. Nevertheless, despite the initial shakeup caused by Reagan's 1980 campaign, Washington moved quickly to recognize China's key importance in the Asia-Pacific region and the need for good Sino-American ties. Since the latter half of 1982, when the second Shanghai communique was signed, Washington has improved bilateral relations with Beijing: it defused tensions over Taiwan, expanded economic and cultural ties rapidly, and moved toward low-level military cooperation. Diplomatically, the United States has made efforts to encourage its allies—including Japan, South Korea, and ASEAN—to develop their cooperation with China.

For the most part, this strategy has been effective. Japan has speeded up its process of rearmament and played an increasingly influential role in the region's political affairs. Washington's strategic position in the Asia-Pacific region has been strengthened by better coordination of its security strategy with its allies, by its increased military forces, by its expressed willingness to act in the region, and by its expanded cooperation with Beijing. Moreover, China has supported continued US-Japanese security ties and increased Japanese military spending, while Japan has been supportive of China's modernization program and the US role in it. In addition, relations between China and ASEAN have improved. In general, the countries of the region view stable and friendly Sino-US relations as in the interests of peace and stability in Asia and as an important factor in deterring Moscow's and its allies' further expansion.

Nevertheless, this third strategy of containment is facing a number of important challenges. In the first place, none of the US allies in the region have sufficient military forces to protect themselves; all of them continue to depend heavily on the US security umbrella. The current military balance between the two Koreas still favors the North; Vietnam is militarily much stronger than ASEAN—its army, for example, is four times the size of Thailand's; Pakistan is weak compared to its neighbor, and its security is also increasingly threatened by the Soviet Union from the north; and Japan feels more insecure than ever, given the rapidly expanding Soviet military presence nearby. In addition, domestic tensions and political instability in a number of key US allies—especially in the Philippines, as well as in Pakistan and South Korea—pose a serious challenge. At this stage, Washington has little leverage on the situation in the Philippines, and serious political instability there could eventually lead to a change in regime, the loss of US bases, and a dramatic shift in the region's strategic structure.

Second, Moscow has rapidly improved its strategic position in the Asia-Pacific region. Moscow does not have strong economic and political ties there, so it has concentrated on building up its military presence, most notably in the northern Sea of Japan, and at Cam Ranh Bay and Danang. Although the Asia-Pacific region is not the top global priority for either the United States or the Soviet Union, the latter has recently placed greater strategic importance on the region and channeled more resources to it than the United States. The Soviet Union significantly strengthened its position by enlarging its Pacific Fleet, deploying SS–20 missiles, bolstering its air forces, and cooperating militarily with Vietnam. In contrast, Europe, the Middle East, and Central America continue to take top priority in Washington's global strategy and resource allocation. In addition, the deepening political crisis in the Philippines, the weakening security of Pakistan, and Washington's unwillingness to become directly involved in Southeast Asia have already weakened the US position and hurt American credibility in the region. This tendency is likely to continue.

Third, the US containment strategy in the Asia-Pacific region has responded slowly to changes brought about by improved US ties with China. The United States is still faced with the task of more thoroughly integrating its relatively new (or re-found) friendship with China into its overall containment strategy in Asia. This requires not only stable Sino-American relations, but also progress in Sino-American cooperation on subregional security issues. Furthermore, it requires better mutual understanding between China and US allies in Asia.

Containment and Northeast Asian Security

There are four basic interrelated security issues in Northeast Asia: Soviet-American competition, Sino-Soviet conflicts, confrontation between the two Koreas, and the security of Japan. During the past few years, the nature of these issues and their interrelationships have undergone gradual and important changes. These changes have created the necessity for Washington to adjust its containment strategy accordingly.

The dynamic of Soviet-American competition in Northeast Asia is a part of the superpowers' global competition. It is therefore largely determined by the general trend of Soviet-American relations. However, the development of this competition is also strongly affected by local politics. This result is primarily because of the complexity of political structure in the region and the heavy weight of other international players in its military balance.

Moscow's strategic goals in the region are to develop its military capability to fight a "two-front war"; to compete with US naval forces for control over the western Pacific; to maintain strong military pressure on both China and Japan, thereby deterring any possibility of an anti-Soviet "united front" including the United States, China, and Japan; and to compete with China for dominant influence over North Korea without jeopardizing existing stability on the peninsula.

During the past decade, Moscow has rapidly enlarged its Pacific Fleet, expanded its air force, and increased SS–20 missiles deployed in the Far East. More importantly, while the military balance between China and the Soviet Union has remained roughly unchanged and Moscow has not increased its ground forces along the Sino-Soviet and Sino-Mongolian borders, the Soviet Union has gradually changed the priorities among its strategic targets from China to the United States and Japan. In addition, its strategic position has been strengthened by its increased military presence in Southeast Asia.

For its part, since Ronald Reagan came to office in 1980, Washington has made great efforts to increase its naval and air forces in the region. Washington has not only pushed Tokyo even harder to speed up its rearmament program, but has also encouraged it to play a greater role in regional political and security affairs, including the security of South Korea. The United States has transferred a great deal of sophisticated weaponry to the South Korean army. Further, Washington has developed a low-level Sino-American exchange program and stabilized its ties with Beijing. All these efforts have been effective in countering Moscow's expansion.

Nevertheless, the general trend of this competition has not yet favored the United States. This is primarily because Moscow has invested more resources in the region than Washington. In addition, Moscow's strategic position in Northeast Asia has been supported by its military presence in Southeast Asia, while Washington faces the danger of losing its military bases in the Philippines. Moscow's political and military pressure has been somewhat effective on both Tokyo's and Beijing's policymaking: both have been more cautious than before in dealing with Moscow.

The Soviet-American competition in Northeast Asia is likely to intensify in the years ahead. Globally, the chance to bring about a new detente is slim. Even if Soviet-American relations were improved, it would little affect the power structure and Soviet-American competition in Northeast Asia. The US-Soviet arms control negotiations, for instance, even if they reach new agreement, will have only a limited impact on the nuclear balance in the Far East; an arms negotiation concerning the

Far East including the United States, the Soviet Union, and China is unlikely in the foreseeable future. The Soviet Union, furthermore, is unlikely to slow down its military buildup and expansion in the western Pacific, even though a successful US-Soviet summit might reduce Moscow's drive to change the military balance in Europe. To develop the capacity to fight a "two-front war," militarize its Far East territory, undermine the US position in the western Pacific, and pressure both Japan and China to distance themselves from the United States are Moscow's long-term strategic objectives. Moscow is unlikely to alter these objectives because of possible relaxation in its relations with Washington.

During the past few years, Sino-Soviet relations have also experienced gradual and significant change. The border tensions between the two countries have been reduced, economic and cultural ties have been expanded, and high-level officials have increased their visits. Internationally, both Beijing and Moscow have been less critical of one another's foreign policy outside the Asia-Pacific region. Beijing has significantly improved its relations with most Eastern European states and communist parties in Western Europe, and has taken a more "neutral" position between the two superpowers on the issue of arms control.

On the other hand, however, the basic strategic relationship between the two countries has not changed significantly. Moscow has not appeared willing to meet any of the three preconditions that Beijing put forward for normalization between them: to pull back its troops substantially from both the Sino-Soviet and Sino-Mongolian borders, to cut back its support to Vietnam's occupation of Kampuchea, and to withdraw its armed forces from Afghanistan. Instead, the Soviet Union has rapidly increased its military presence around China as noted above. In sum, the relaxation of tensions between China and the Soviet Union has not altered Moscow's long-term strategic objective: to contain China strategically through increased military power around China's periphery, and to push Beijing away from Washington and Tokyo.

For its part, Beijing continues to view the Soviet Union as the primary threat to its national security. Though Beijing has adjusted the three preconditions it demanded for further improvement of Sino-Soviet ties, its basic security and strategic interests have not changed. These are to reduce Moscow's political and military pressure and to break down what China sees as its strategic encirclement by the Soviet Union. Beijing continues its efforts to develop political and military cooperation with the United States, especially with regard to the security of the Asia-Pacific region. Beijing also plays the major role in supplying weapons to the resistance forces in Kampuchea and Afghanistan, and in maintaining strong military pressure on Vietnam. In addition, Beijing continues its efforts for greater cooperation with ASEAN, especially Thailand. China has repeatedly expressed its interest in maintaining stability on the Korean peninsula and conditionally supporting Japan's rearmament and US-Japanese security ties. In Southwest Asia, the PRC has continued full support for the security of Pakistan, while making efforts to improve relations with India. Beijing has been strongly critical of Moscow's proposal for a "collective security" arrangement in Asia. Taken together, the sharp conflicts in security and strategic interests between Moscow and Beijing have not been reduced significantly and will continue to strongly influence the dynamics of Sino-Soviet relations in the years ahead.

The third security issue in Northeast Asia is the stability of the Korean peninsula, threatened by the possibility of military confrontation between North and South. As mentioned above, the three major powers involved in this region—the Soviet Union, China, and the United States—have shown themselves committed to the maintenance of the status quo on the peninsula. Yet the conflict between North and South Korea is still the irreducible element which structures the dynamics of the region. Generally, their relations have been stable during the past two years. Pyongyang has expressed its willingness to increase contacts with the South and to adopt an "open door" policy for attracting Western investment and technology, and contacts between the two sides have recently been expanded. Nevertheless, the potential for confrontation still exists.

For a number of reasons, the North would be more likely to initiate a conflict than the South. The military balance, which has favored North Korea, may begin to shift in the near future because of South Korea's stronger economic capacity and US support for its military buildup. South Korea also seems to be gaining favor in world opinion. The upcoming succession after Kim Il-sung's death is a further factor of uncertainty in the North. Moreover, the ongoing political struggle between the authoritarian regime on the one hand and opposition forces on the other may be exploited by the North. For all these reasons, the danger of heightened tensions between North and South is real. The North has in fact been the one to push hard for reunification talks while the South has reacted coolly.

Support from the major powers for inter-Korean talks is aimed at reducing tension on the peninsula and stabilizing the existing situation rather than at peaceful reunification. Reunification in the near future seems unlikely in any case given the political, economic, and ideological differences between the two sides. And it appears fairly evident that none of the major powers would welcome the geopolitical changes that a unified Korea might provoke.

Tension on the peninsula has a broad international background. North Korea takes advantage of Sino-Soviet conflicts to serve its own interests. Nor is it in the interest of either China or the United States for North Korea to become a second Vietnam. The new Soviet leadership has already shown its strong interest in increasing its influence in Pyongyang: it has provided the latter with MiG–23 fighters, a Soviet fleet has visited a North Korean harbor for the first time in two decades, and Moscow has given its support to Kim Il-sung's succession arrangement.

At present, China is in a relatively weaker position to compete with the Soviet Union for influence over North Korea.

During the past ten years, Beijing has adjusted its previous policy toward the Korean peninsula. Beijing has announced that it will not support an attack by Pyongyang on the South, although it would help Pyongyang if the South were to attack. With support from Washington, China has also encouraged Pyongyang to open its doors to and increase its contacts with the West. Beijing has received Kim Il-sung's son, while at the same time it has developed ties to South Korea.

All these moves helped to reduce tensions between North and South, but they do not necessarily strengthen Beijing's capability to compete with Moscow. Technically, Beijing is unable to provide Pyongyang the sophisticated arms that Moscow has supplied. More importantly, Pyongyang may view Moscow's strong opposition to the West (especially to the United States) more favorably than it does Beijing's ongoing cooperation with the West, including Japan. In addition, the increased Japanese involvement in the peninsula's political and security affairs may put Beijing in a difficult political position, pushing Pyongyang even closer to Moscow.

Fourth, in the long run, Japan's security policy will have a major impact on the balance of power in Northeast Asia if not the globe itself, for it is quite likely that Japan will eventually reassert its independent political and strategic power. The key questions are how fast, and in what direction, Japan will rearm, and what the new orientation of its security strategy will be. These are questions which should concern both the United States and China, questions they should think about in long-term perspective.

Prime Minister Yasuhiro Nakasone has played a major role in postwar Japanese history by being the first leader of this period to push Japan to assert its political and military role in international affairs. He has stressed the importance of US-Japanese security ties while at the same time emphasizing that Japan should play a more active role in regional political and security affairs. In 1984 Japan's military spending rose 6.9 percent from US$11.5 billion to US$12.3 billion, a figure likely to exceed the self-imposed limit of 1 percent of Japan's GNP.

At present, Japan's security objective is to counter Soviet expansion in the region, but its plan to protect its supply line up to a radius of 1,000 nautical miles has made its neighboring countries uneasy. Moreover, Japan has been more active diplomatically in transforming its economic power into political influence. It has offered large amounts of economic aid to South Korea and is regularly engaging in security consultations with Seoul. As for Indochina, Japan has offered economic assistance to Kampuchea and Vietnam if the latter withdraws its troops. Japan has also significantly increased its aid to the ASEAN states and developed its economic and political ties with China.

However, there are powerful domestic and international constraints on Japan's efforts to expand its political and strategic role. At home, Japan's rearmament process has been limited by budgetary constraints and by mainstream political opinion that still opposes the idea of assuming an independent strategic posture. In the region, Japan has been constrained by the threat of an increased Soviet military buildup in reaction to a more assertive security strategy. ASEAN has already shown concern about the direction of Japan's security orientation.

Beijing and Moscow have different views about Japan's rearmament and US-Japanese security cooperation, although neither of them wants to see Japan become an independent military power. Beijing will not oppose Japan's rearmament as long as Japan's security strategy against the Soviet Union remains unchanged. US-Japanese security cooperation is therefore essential, for such cooperation can help guide Tokyo's strategic intent. In the long run, if US-Japanese security ties fail to prevent Tokyo from becoming an independent military power and altering its military strategy against the Soviet Union, Beijing may have little alternative but to turn to Moscow.

For its part, Washington is facing two tough questions in the short run. The first is how to coordinate its security ties to

Japan with its political and low-level military cooperation with Beijing. Given the constraints on the process of Japanese rearmament discussed above, it is unlikely in the short run that Japan's contribution will help significantly to counter the regional military imbalance between the United States and the Soviet Union. As a result, China will continue to play a key role in this matter. Second, Washington has already been facing criticism from ASEAN on Japan's rearmament and the possible revival of Japanese militarism. Such criticism will continue to restrain Washington from pushing Japan to speed up its rearmament. Moreover, in the long run, Japan's rearmament will destabilize the political structure of the region and severely hurt fundamental US interests there.

Containment in Northeast Asia—What Can Be Done?

In the years ahead, the main objective of the US containment strategy in Northeast Asia will continue to be to counter Soviet expansionism. In the first place, it is in Washington's interest to continue its competition with Moscow and to prevent any further shift of the regional power balance toward the Soviet Union. Second, a relatively stable political and strategic triangle among the Soviet Union, China, and the United States can best serve US interests. A profound Sino-Soviet relaxation would give Moscow the option of transferring forces from its eastern border to its western border, or of concentrating its resources on competition with the United States and Japan in the western Pacific. Third, the US-Soviet competition in the region has increased, while US resources there remain limited. This state of affairs has made the United States increasingly dependent on its allies—especially Japan—to take on more responsibility for regional security. Nevertheless, in the long run it will not be in the US interest if Japan moves in the direction of security independence, for such a development would threaten other countries in the region, create tension between Japan and other US allies in Asia, provoke Sino-Japanese competition, destabilize the region's power structure, and perhaps even pose a direct challenge to US regional interests. Washington's fourth security interest lies in keeping the Korean peninsula relatively stable and preventing North Korea from coming under the Soviet Union's dominant influence. Tensions between the North and South leading to open confrontation would risk involving the United States and China on opposite sides of a conflict and tilting the regional power balance in Moscow's favor.

To further these basic security interests, the US containment strategy in Northeast Asia should include the following elements:

- The United States should continue its efforts to restore the regional military balance. Without equilibrium, there will be no peace. To maintain the US military presence and to counter the Soviet Union's increased military activities, especially its navy and strategic air force, is therefore essential.

- Diplomatically, the United States should further develop political, economic, and low-level security cooperation with China. Such cooperation can reduce Beijing's incentive to reach a rapid reconciliation with Moscow, thereby continuing to tie down Soviet troops along the Sino-Soviet and Sino-Mongolian borders (roughly one-quarter of the total Soviet armed forces) and deterring Moscow's further efforts to change the balance of power. This policy will also help to stabilize the triangle among the United States, the Soviet Union, and China.

- The United States should encourage Japan's rearmament, but it must guide the direction and orientation of Tokyo's security strategy. In the short run, this policy will prevent possible tensions between US allies in Asia (including China) and Japan. In the long run, this policy will prevent a fundamental change of the power structure in the Asia-Pacific region and the danger of Japan hurting US interests.

• On the Korean peninsula, it is important to reach and maintain military balance between the two sides. The United States should not, however, encourage Japan to deepen its involvements in the Korean peninsula's security affairs. At the same time, the United States, together with other nations (such as China, Japan, and the Western European states), should help North Korea increase its political, economic, and cultural ties with the outside world, especially the West. Further, the United States should encourage the two Koreas to expand their contacts and to reduce mutual tensions. Such efforts can deter a possible offensive by the North while reducing Pyongyang's incentive to lean on Moscow, and they might even gradually change North Korea's attitude toward the South and its behavior in the international community.

22

Southeast Asia in Containment Strategies for the 1990s

Ulrich A. Straus

W HEN GEORGE KENNAN FORMULATED the doctrine of containment to deter and restrict Soviet expansionist tendencies in the postwar period, he assuredly did not have Southeast Asia in mind. Controversy still surrounds the question of just what Kennan meant by his article in *Foreign Affairs* and the extent to which containment could be applied to areas outside the main arenas of conflict with the USSR in the mid-1940s, but Southeast Asia was then a political hinterland struggling with very different problems and issues—such as colonialism.

The application of the containment doctrine to East Asia in the late 1940s and early 1950s was unique in that it was directed, in its early stages, not against the USSR but against the People's Republic of China. The communist takeover of the Chinese mainland was viewed in Washington not only as a threat to the Nationalist forces on Taiwan, but also as the start of a general communist offensive against the West, its

Ulrich A. Straus is a Foreign Service Officer currently serving as Professor of International Relations at the National War College.

remaining colonial possessions in East Asia, and the stability of the nascent, often neutralist regimes of the area. In this, the PRC was viewed as the junior partner of the USSR and as a state which, with fresh victories under its belt, was the more radical and the more aggressive of the two. China's subsequent entry into the Korean War removed whatever doubt may have remained about China's designs. Beijing, with Moscow's blessing and support, was seen as determined to undermine peace, security, and the West's position wherever it could. Southeast Asia was its prime target.

The Manila Pact (forming the Southeast Asia Treaty Organization), signed in September 1954, was the US response to the perceived threat. Negotiated shortly after John Foster Dulles had forged similar pacts with Australia and New Zealand (the ANZUS states), the Philippines, and Japan, it was the initial expression of American containment policy in Southeast Asia. In testimony before the Congress in 1974, Assistant Secretary of State Robert Ingersoll described the objective of SEATO as both "to contain the PRC" and, through linkages of bilateral and multilateral defense arrangements, to "serve as a shield behind which the Asian countries . . . could become strong and capable of resisting communist aggressiveness."[1]

Unlike in Europe, where the main threat was perceived in terms of massive armies crossing well-defined borders, in Southeast Asia the chief danger was seen as subversive activities against weak governments. Many of the dissident subversive groups were ethnic Chinese minorities that had not been integrated into the body politic of the emerging new countries. At one time or another there were serious armed uprisings against the governments of Thailand, Burma, Malaysia, Indonesia, and the Philippines. The PRC, voicing a radical doctrine of revolution, was supporting, if not orchestrating, these antigovernment activities.

Against this kind of threat, SEATO's value appeared marginal at best. Southeast Asia then completely lacked the cohesiveness that Europe was displaying on the security and economic fronts. As a result, only two Southeast Asian nations—Thailand and the Philippines—could be persuaded to join the organization at a time when anticolonial feelings were still running high. Moreover, the degree of commitment expressed in the treaty was quite modest.

SEATO was essentially moribund by the time the Vietnam conflict ended. Overtaken by a series of events such as the enunciation of Nixon's Guam doctrine, the dismemberment of Pakistan, the UK's decision to withdraw from commitments east of Suez, the advent of detente, and the emergence of a new US relationship with the PRC, SEATO died a quiet and generally unlamented death in 1977.

The Stakes and the Parties in Southeast Asia

In the aftermath of Vietnam, Southeast Asia rapidly dropped out of sight as an area of active US policy interest. The American public paid scant attention to the region, in a more or less deliberate effort to forget a bad experience, and turned its attention to other places. Meanwhile, ironically, the past decade has witnessed a rapid increase in US economic and national security interests in the area. Two-way bilateral trade with the states of the Association of Southeast Asian Nations (ASEAN) has increased 245 percent from $7.6 billion to $26.3 billion, making ASEAN as a whole America's fifth largest trading partner. Attracted by a benign political, economic, and security climate, US investment has climbed from $4.7 billion to over $10.0 billion in just the past five years. Rising living standards, some of the world's fastest economic growth rates, and sustained political stability have made Southeast Asia a most attractive region for US business.

Strategically, two factors have accounted for a revival of US interests after it was assumed, some ten years ago, that the United States was well on its way toward military retreat from that part of the world. In the latter part of the 1970s, the Indian

Ocean became a more important area for US fleet operations as a direct consequence of the aborted Mecca attack on the Saudi monarchy, the collapse of the Shah and the Iranian hostage crisis, and the Soviet invasion of Afghanistan. All of these events called for a US response in terms of a projection of naval power into the Indian Ocean. This projection in turn required increased use of our long-term military facilities in the Philippines, which then presented the fewest problems of those facilities available to US decisionmakers. The second development, of course, was the Soviet conclusion of a Friendship Treaty with Vietnam in 1978.

The Soviet use of naval facilities in Cam Ranh Bay and air facilities at Danang has permitted the USSR to project its military power into the South China Sea at a relatively short distance from the US bases in the Philippines. Soviet exploitation of these facilities has been slow but steady; their existence has unquestionably complicated the tasks of the US forces charged with keeping track of Soviet ships and planes and with responsibility for the security of the vital sea lines of communication in East Asia. However, given the vulnerability of these facilities to interdiction from US or Japanese forces, their value appears to lie principally in a peacetime rather than wartime situation. They might eventually become useful to the Soviets in applying pressure on Southeast Asian countries, but thus far they have hindered rather than advanced Soviet political interests in the region by raising alarms as to Soviet intentions.

In December 1979, the ASEAN foreign ministers declared as their objective the establishment of a Southeast Asian region free from outside influence or the involvement of great power rivalries. This remains the Southeast Asians' long-range goal, but they know that they are powerless to effect it now and that, for the foreseeable future, there is some merit in having the major powers contend in the region. The ASEAN states tend to see the various outside powers quite differently. They view the US military presence as contributing to the peace and security of the region, but regard the activities of the other powers with varying degrees of apprehension. Moreover, the Southeast Asians see the threat to their security not in terms of aggression across frontiers, but in terms of externally supported violence on the part of dissident domestic groups. ASEAN's steady economic growth and political stability offer the best insurance against these threats, with the Philippines a notable exception to the region's record in that respect.

While ASEAN has not been considered a military alliance, it has served to mitigate intraregional tensions and has contributed to limited military cooperation among several states outside its auspices. Confidence in their ability to deal with the remote possibility of external aggression has also been heightened by the regional powers' beefing up of their military forces following the American withdrawal from Vietnam.

There are currently two external threats to the ASEAN states, both of which could well remain unresolved into the 1990s. The one of greatest immediate concern locally involves the ambitions and ultimate intentions of Vietnam. The earlier hope that Vietnam might eventually become integrated in a Southeast Asian regional organization dimmed considerably when, shortly after establishing a firm Soviet connection, the Vietnamese invaded Cambodia in an effort to establish hegemony over the Indochinese peninsula. Vietnam has termed its goal of dominating Cambodia and eliminating the buffer between itself and Thailand "irreversible." As a result, Thailand has become a "front line" state, subjected to occasional border crossings during Vietnam's annual dry season offensives against anti-Heng Samrin guerrillas. The hard line espoused by Vietnam's leaders in foreign policy recalls the tenacity and determination of wartime Vietnam, and suggests that the wartime generation may have to pass from the scene before an accommodation with the other parts of Southeast Asia will be possible. Such an accommodation seems quite unlikely in the foreseeable future. Meanwhile, the Cambodian issue has served to rally ASEAN to a common cause and contributed to the growing degree of unity in the organization.

The second security issue of local prominence is, of course, the political instability of the Philippines and the associated issues of presidential succession and the future viability of the US bases there. Southeast Asians generally approve of the American presence in the archipelago, even if in some countries it is not politic to be very public about it. The Thais in particular view the bases as a concrete manifestation of US interest in the region, adding credibility to the American security commitment to their country.

Southeast Asians view the home-grown Philippine instability with alarm but feel impotent to affect its outcome. They are quite aware of public US discussions on whether the time may not have come to begin preparations for an eventual military pull-out and to check out possible relocation sites. Opposition politicians in Manila, and even the Marcos government, indicated a desire for a large-scale revamping of the base agreement when it becomes subject to amendment or termination in 1991. These uncertainties have not led any of the Southeast Asians to volunteer their own soil as relocation sites. However, if relocation becomes inevitable, it is conceivable that some US forces might find a new home in one or another of the ASEAN states, especially if the regional security climate had worsened by that time.

Philippine bases play an important global and regional containment role that permits the United States to "balance" Soviet forces and project its power effectively into all of Southeast Asia as well as into the Indian Ocean. Their value is appreciated not only by the Southeast Asians, but by the Japanese and Chinese as well. Relocation to more distant facilities in such places as Guam or Japan could create uncertainties in Southeast Asia which, assuming there is no deterioration in the Vietnam-Soviet relationship, would then include only the Soviet facilities. If there were no compensating increase in US forces, relocation of the bases would result in a thinner US military presence in the region. Aside from affecting Southeast Asian attitudes, such a development could well influence Japanese and Chinese decisions as well.

The Soviet Union and Southeast Asian Containment

Soviet interests in Southeast Asia have been derivative of the USSR's relations with its principal global adversaries, especially the PRC. The USSR would probably endorse the concept of containment, at least as applied to the PRC through the Soviet position in Vietnam. The Vietnam connection has also allowed the USSR to support its pretensions as a global power, and to make some points in its competition with the United States and China.

Soviet policy in Southeast Asia has essentially been one of low risk, low gain. It backed away from the risk of conflict with the United States at the time of the 1972 Hanoi bombing and Haiphong mining operations, when detente was in bloom. Faced with growing Sino-US strategic cooperation, it confronts growing risks in Southeast Asia if it tries to break out of Vietnamese bases for more adventurist schemes. Although the introduction of Soviet forces into Danang and Cam Ranh Bay has clearly raised the Soviet stake, the Soviets are still playing a relatively weak hand in this area. Economically, their interests are negligible. There is only the barest trickle of Soviet economic aid and trade to the ASEAN states; these countries take less than 0.5 percent of their imports from the USSR. In Indonesia, where Soviet political, military, and economic investments during the Sukarno Era were heavy, Soviet policy failed completely. The Soviets' influence over indigenous communist parties is virtually nil; communist movements in the region, to the extent they have taken guidance from abroad, have tended to look more to Beijing than to Moscow.

Moscow's Vietnam connection is proving to be a costly undertaking, and it remains somewhat questionable whether over the long run the Soviets will believe they have struck a good bargain. Vietnam has required massive infusions of Soviet assistance, estimated at close to one billion dollars annually. In return, the Soviets gained only domination of the Vietnam market, the cheap products of Vietnam's light industry, and the importation of Vietnamese labor under the socialist equivalent of the "gastarbeiter" system. Moreover, despite Vietnam's dependence on the USSR, the Soviets can never be entirely certain that Vietnam might not play its "American card" or gain its objectives in Laos, Cambodia, and Southeast Asia by striking a deal with ASEAN.

Of course, the acquisition of Vietnamese military facilities has helped the USSR's strategic posture vis-a-vis the PRC and the United States, and this is probably of overriding importance to the USSR. However, it has had a counterproductive effect on Soviet relations with ASEAN. While some Southeast Asians may see a marginal degree of merit in a Soviet role as a balancer of Chinese ambitions in the area, most view the USSR with suspicion bordering on apprehension. In this view, the USSR's advance into Vietnam could be seen as a real impediment to improved relations with ASEAN.

Ideologically, too, the Soviets are at a distinct disadvantage in the area. As examples of some of the most successful private enterprise economies of the world, the Southeast Asians are hardly susceptible to the siren songs of Soviet socialism. In addition, although as newcomers to the Southeast Asian scene the Russians may not be burdened by the historical baggage carried by the Chinese and Japanese, they have not hit it off well at the personal level. The Russian bear does not easily acclimate to the jungles of Southeast Asia, and the Southeast Asians will likely prefer to avoid a close relationship with the Soviet Union as long as almost any other options are open.

Thus far, Soviet wooing of the Southeast Asians has produced little in the way of positive results. The countries of Southeast Asia, with the notable exception of the Philippines, have stabilized and become internally strengthened to a remarkable extent. The establishment and steady growth of ASEAN institutions have contributed to a regional outlook on many key issues, which makes it more difficult for the Soviets to play off one nation against another. The Soviet civilian economy has faltered while Southeast Asia as a whole has made significant developmental strides. Whatever allure the USSR might have had as a role model in the heady post-colonial days has become badly tarnished. The Soviet invasion of neighboring Afghanistan has damaged the USSR's image with the predominantly Muslim populations of Indonesia and Malaysia; ASEAN, as an organization, took an uncharacteristically strong and unequivocal stance against this big power action against a small neighbor.

Against a weakly perceived threat from the USSR, the countries of Southeast Asia will likely continue to believe that their best defense lies in stability at home and unity and cooperation with their neighbors to avoid giving the Soviets an opportunity to fish in troubled waters. On the global scene, they have a strong interest in having deterrence remain credible. While a significantly increased Soviet military presence in the region would stir concerns, the ASEAN response would not be in the form of a militarization of the area; the relative strengths of the protagonists is too unequal. Rather, ASEAN would seek to counter the Soviet threat by encouraging a more active military role by the United States, and eventually perhaps even by Japan. The recognition that this could well be the ASEAN reaction might suffice to cause the Soviets to restrain any adventurist ideas.

China and Southeast Asian Containment

Southeast Asia has historically been an area of strong Chinese political and cultural influence. Beijing has traditionally considered the area one of legitimate Chinese interest. China's objective in the region has been to avoid superpower domination of Southeast Asia in order to preserve its freedom of action. Having failed to exclude either the United States or the USSR from the region, the PRC has worked at various times with either power to contain the other. A stable Southeast Asia where

Soviet penetrations are kept to a minimum is clearly an important strategic objective for the PRC, which hopes to avoid having to fear a "second front." This consideration no doubt played a key role in the Chinese desire to teach the Vietnamese a "lesson" in 1979, with promises to repeat the lesson if it were not adequately understood.

For almost a decade now, the PRC has endeavored to maintain good relations with the ASEAN countries. These efforts have not been easy, as they have had to overcome historical fears of Chinese big power domination and the more recent Chinese support of revolutionary movements bent on toppling the existing regimes. The presence of large Chinese minorities in several Southeast Asian countries has made this task of reconciliation that much more difficult. Another potential irritant in mutual relations has been the existence of overlapping claims to specks of land in the South China Sea (for example, the Paracel and Spratley Islands), which have already led to clashes between China and Vietnam. The same areas are also claimed by the Philippines and Malaysia, but for the moment the PRC has seen it in its interests to play down such differences and to concentrate on more positive aspects of the relationships. Economically, there is a potential for increased rivalry between the competitive products of Southeast Asia and China in Western markets. Thus far, this rivalry has been kept in check, and Chinese strategic and political interests seem likely to constrain PRC policies in this respect.

Indications are, therefore, that it will remain in the PRC's long-term interests to play a responsible role in Southeast Asia. It has not attempted, for example, to exacerbate the internal instability in the Philippines; indeed it has, if anything, gone out of its way to emphasize its state-to-state ties to the Marcos government, while resisting temptations to establish a relationship with the New People's Army.

For the Chinese, containment in Southeast Asia means preventing the emergence of another nation allied to the Soviet Union, and it means preventing Vietnam from gaining regional

influence. Thus far, PRC policy has worked well. Vietnam remains virtually isolated from its Southeast Asian neighbors. The
price of greater acceptance would be abandonment of its aggressive designs on Cambodia and, perhaps, a weakened relationship with the USSR as well. Containment will also entail
Chinese support for smooth transitions of power in the ASEAN
states, closer state-to-state relations with the countries of
ASEAN, and the availability of access enabling the PRC to
warn all and sundry about Soviet machinations in the Third
World.

For the foreseeable future, then, it seems that China can
play its most significant containment role via the restraint it
imposes on Vietnam. It will no doubt continue to look for opportunities to strengthen anti-Heng Samrin forces in Cambodia
in an effort to avoid the Vietnamization of that state, and it will
try to weaken Vietnam's embrace of Laos as well. Thus sufficiently occupied, and given its enormous domestic problems,
Vietnam should not be in a position to seriously threaten
Thailand, let alone the other ASEAN countries. However, it
should be noted that China's credibility has been somewhat
dimmed by its failure to react when the recent Vietnamese dry
season offensive in Cambodia spilled over into Thailand.

Given the necessarily tenuous state of the PRC's relations
with most of the ASEAN nations, it would not be politic to urge
a more active Southeast Asian role on the PRC. If Soviet sabre-
rattling or a substantial increase of Soviet military force in the
area should create a climate of fear and apprehension, then it
might become more appropriate for the PRC to assume a more
active role. But that would probably occur well after fears of
China's ambitions have eased and after the Southeast Asians
have had a chance to assess how the PRC manages its own leadership succession problem.

Japan and Southeast Asian Containment

Southeast Asia has been an important, perhaps even vital, area
of Japanese national interest in modern times. Although

Southeast Asia may be of less importance strategically than the surrounding areas of Northeast Asia, Japan recognizes that its vital sea communications inevitably flow through the south. Japan therefore cannot be indifferent to political and military developments in the region.

In the postwar period, Japan moved cautiously to refurbish its image while building in some countries on contacts developed during the Second World War. Japan's interests have been primarily commercial. Reparations and trade credits provided the means for Japan's reentry into the countries that had formed a part of Japan's Greater East Asia Co-prosperity Sphere. However, the anti-Japanese riots in Jakarta over a decade ago provided evidence that Tokyo could not afford to move precipitously as it gained influence in Southeast Asia.

Nevertheless, by the mid-1980s Japan had consolidated its position as the unchallenged economic colossus of the area. Japan is the leading trading partner of most of the noncommunist countries of Southeast Asia, excepting the Philippines and Singapore. Japanese direct investment in the area last year amounted to $12.6 billion, heavily concentrated in Indonesia. Japan has become the single largest donor to the Asian Development Bank and of bilateral assistance to Southeast Asia. Japanese official assistance to the area is running at a rate of around three-quarters of a billion dollars annually.

The countries of Southeast Asia are not happy with this degree of economic dependence on one country, but the power of Japanese capital and the excellence of Japanese products and servicing leaves them little choice. Even more than Americans, the people of Southeast Asia now live in a world of Japanese consumer products, and they like it. Like Americans too, the Southeast Asians complain about restrictive Japanese trade practices which have contributed to slowly rising trade deficits. There is also considerable unhappiness about Japan's slowness in facilitating technology transfer to this region of potential competition.

Japan's security interests clearly have not kept pace with its economic penetration. Tokyo readily acknowledges the importance of Southeast Asian raw and semiprocessed materials; disruption of Middle East oil supplies would make delivery of Indonesian oil that much more important. However, the very closeness of the economic ties linking Japan with Southeast Asia militate against the emergence of a real Japanese security role any time soon. Southeast Asians are not particularly eager to add military dependence on Japan to their existing economic dependence, especially if that implies any diminution of the US military presence. In response to US pressures, the Japanese government has indicated a determination to work toward assumption of responsibility for the security of Japan's southern approaches out to 1,000 miles from Tokyo. Effectuation of the policy would bring Japanese sea and air power as far south as the Bashi Channel separating Taiwan from the northern tip of the Philippines, but not beyond it into the Southeast Asian region. The degree of Japanese military buildup now seems quite acceptable to ASEAN, so long as the United States continues to provide the main external military forces in the region.

It seems clear that Japan sees the primary regional threat in terms of political instability and economic malaise, not military aggression. Its policies are designed to contribute to political stability and economic development. It has maintained very close ties with ASEAN states and been a major participant in annual meetings at the foreign minister level in Southeast Asia. Japan has strongly supported the ASEAN line on Cambodia while keeping its lines open to Hanoi with a small but judicious aid program and the maintenance of a resident ambassador there. It seems clear that Japan would welcome a process of weaning Vietnam from its Soviet dependency and would contribute significantly to such a process. But it is not prepared to cross ASEAN interests or US sensitivities on the subject, or to adopt a "high posture" in this respect.

The Philippines represent a special case of incipient instability, one that concerns Japan a great deal. Among Southeast

Asian states, the Philippines is geographically closest to Japan. The US bases at Subic and Clark form the southern anchor of the chain of US bases in the western Pacific. While recognizing the gravity of Philippine events, Japan regards them as primarily an internal crisis; to the extent that external influences can help ameliorate the situation, it believes that the United States must take the lead. Japan has cooperated with US efforts to stabilize the economic slide. Its leading banks have joined US and other banks in turning over the Philippine debt and in providing new credits. Moreover, the Japanese government has recently extended various types of special financial and commodity assistance to the Philippines, despite difficulties created by objections from the left-wing opposition in the Diet. It also indicated a readiness to hold Japanese government assistance hostage to needed reforms of the Marcos government.

ASEAN and Southeast Asian Containment

Of course, ASEAN is by no means united in its perception of the region's security problems. By and large, the fault line occurs over the putative role of the People's Republic of China, with Indonesia and to a somewhat lesser extent Malaysia viewing the PRC as the primary long-range threat to the region, while Thailand and Singapore are inclined to evaluate the PRC's security role somewhat more positively, for the "balance" it provides to Vietnam's ambitions. By extension, countries such as Thailand, which are most concerned about Vietnamese incursions into their territory or Vietnam's control over Cambodia, tend to view the USSR as a potential menace in the region. Indonesia, on the other hand, sees some benefit in a moderate Soviet regional role as a check on the PRC. The Philippines, geographically more removed and preoccupied with its deepening domestic problems, has not come down hard on this particular issue. However, if concern about foreign assistance for the New People's Army (NPA) should mount, it would seem likely that the Philippines will see the USSR as a growing threat.

Currently, the countries of Southeast Asia do not perceive direct threats from the great powers. Their security interests, understandably, are focused on the more immediate instability arising from Vietnam's efforts to consolidate its control over the Indochinese peninsula. The USSR is far away; it is not a credible protagonist in Southeast Asia, except through the medium of an ally such as Vietnam. In terms of a direct conflict with the Soviet Union, Southeast Asia is fortunate in having the PRC, Korea, and Japan as a "buffer" between itself and the Russian bear.

The next fifteen years will be a critical time of transition in Southeast Asia, a period when the region's still fragile political institutions will probably be severely tested. Within this decade and a half, the leadership of all the ASEAN states seems likely to change. Long-term leaders such as President Marcos of the Philippines, President Suharto of Indonesia, and Prime Minister Lee Kuan-yu of Singapore seem destined to pass from the political scene. These men are the founders and strongest supporters of ASEAN and all it stands for. Thailand and Malaysia, both less identified with a particular leader, will also undergo changes at the top. Much will depend on how well these fast-maturing states can solve their individual problems of succession.

The uncertainties created by such internal shifts of power could create opportunities for the Soviets to broaden their presently limited sphere of influence. The opportunity could present itself in the most acute form in the Philippines, where presidential succession seems likely to play itself out against the backdrop of a growing insurgency. Moscow's relations with the government of the Philippines have been correct, and at times it has pleased both sides to hint at possible improvements should there be a marked cooling of the traditional US-Philippine ties; accordingly, Moscow has thus far not become involved with the NPA. However, neither side will ever forget that if the NPA should ever require an infusion of arms, Moscow would be a logical source of supply.

Fortunately, the Philippines is currently the only Southeast
Asian country with a serious insurgency. However, the Southeast Asian societies and economies remain somewhat fragile,
despite recent evidence of growing robustness. In particular, racial issues could again become inflamed in both Malaysia and
Indonesia. To avoid such dissension, all the countries of Southeast Asia are banking heavily on a continuation of the favorable
economic trends of the past decade (and a reversal of the decade's trends in the Philippines). Economic growth will in turn
depend significantly on the continued good health of the Western economies, led by those of the United States and Japan. A
marked decline in market access to the West occasioned by
growing protectionism, or a significant slowing of the availability of new Western capital, could cripple the region's boot-strap
effort and bring about social unrest. Such an atmosphere would
provide opportunities for Soviet adventurism and penetration,
despite the poor image and reputation of the Soviets today.

Although the USSR is viewed as the primary, if remote,
external threat to the region, underlying uneasiness about China
remains. Southeast Asians are unsure how long the present Chinese reforms will endure; moreover, they believe that the PRC,
far more than the USSR, is in a position to take advantage of
disunity and instabilities in the region. Thus the Southeast Asian
perspective on containment necessarily includes an element of
caution with regard to China's long-term ambitions and
capabilities.

The United States and Southeast Asian Containment

As the discussion above makes clear, the Southeast Asian scene
of the mid-1980s is profoundly different from that of the
mid-1960s when, in the name of stopping a "communist tide"
threatening to engulf the region, the United States became engaged militarily. China, no longer a treaty ally of the USSR,
has greatly moderated its ideological fervor of the 1960s and
strengthened its state-to-state ties to ASEAN; it is now regarded
as a protector of the status quo. Its contribution to regional

stability is considerable, based on its appreciation of securing a stable south while it confronts its chief protagonist in the north. Japan, too, has emerged as an economic giant and a growing regional power, profoundly concerned about its economic lifelines and conscious of its responsibilities for world and regional stability. Accordingly, Japan can be expected to play an increasingly active and responsible role politically, if not militarily, in the defense of its very great economic interests in the region.

With the notable exception of the Philippines, the countries of ASEAN have used the past twenty years wisely and productively. Their political institutions have gained much greater legitimacy over that time span and their economic policies have brought tangible benefits to their populations. Both trade and investments are expanding at a far more rapid pace than elsewhere on the globe. Politically, the area has been largely stable and Western-oriented despite some ritual obeisance to neutralist concepts such as ZOPFAN (the Zone of Peace, Freedom, and Neutrality). These countries have dealt well with potentially divisive racial and communal issues to forge new and beneficial nationalisms. At the same time, they have achieved a degree of regional cooperation which few had expected, though more needs to be done. Their international voice has grown remarkably as a result of all these positive developments.

The remarkable development of Southeast Asia has been testimony to the US vision of free and independent nations with essentially capitalist economies pursuing their interests in an international climate of openness and opportunity. Southeast Asia is a good example of where our vision for the future has been seen to work. For the United States, Southeast Asia has thus become an area of substantially greater national interest than a generation ago when we expended so much blood and treasure to maintain the status quo. The region is a part of an East Asian sphere that is now the most dynamic region of the world, where our major interests are inescapably engaged. What we do or fail to do there will have consequences for our ties with the PRC and Japan.

For the remainder of this century, the United States seems likely to play an important role in Southeast Asia, a role that is generally, if quietly, welcomed there. How we play our role will largely be shaped by our perception of the threat. Chastened by our Vietnam experience, it seems likely that we will pay more heed to the views of the Southeast Asian states and our friends and allies in the area. Moreover, we will, I trust, analyze the problem in far broader than simply military terms.

Southeast Asia remains an area where the interests of the superpowers clash, and will likely continue to clash into the 1990s. The lines between the US and Soviet spheres and interests are not sharply drawn here. Moreover, perhaps more than in any other region of the world, the growing interests of a number of other major powers are also importantly involved. Still, the Soviet Union, together with its sometimes unruly Vietnamese ally, will doubtless constitute the key threat to the area through the end of this century. One can further assume that the Soviet military presence will expand at a steady pace in East Asia and will remain the key instrument of Soviet foreign policy, but that Moscow will continue to have great difficulty in translating its military strength into political influence.

Barring some kind of bilateral agreement covering the deployment of US and Soviet forces to Southeast Asia—an arrangement for which one suspects there would be little enthusiasm in Moscow or Washington, or perhaps within ASEAN as well—there is probably little or nothing the West can do to discourage the Soviets' increased use of their military facilities in Vietnam. In the 1990s, as the Soviet military buildup continues worldwide, we can expect to see more Soviet warships in the area, and greater aerial surveillance of US and allied forces. But the Soviet forces will still have to operate at the end of tenuous supply lines stretching back to their Siberian bases, requiring them to pass through narrow straits and air space controlled by the United States and its allies.

One suspects that the USSR will be characteristically cautious in exploiting its growing military force potential in Southeast Asia. The Soviets are almost sure to engage in low-risk probes in this area of considerable sensitivity for the PRC, Japan, and the United States, but geographical constraints will virtually ensure that these probes are of a political, not military, nature. To deter such moves, the United States can do no better than to contribute to the political and economic health of the region while maintaining its own military presence as a stabilizing factor.

The USSR's one ally in the region poses a threat of another order. With the backing of the region's largest, well-tested military force, Vietnam threatens not only continued domination of Cambodia and Laos but eventual domination of Thailand as well. This threat may well be contained by Thailand's reliance on US material and political support, as it has in the past. It will remain important to sustain US credibility in this respect. However, Thailand can also look to the immediate presence of the PRC, which it could not do twenty years ago. China's interest in containing the USSR and in curbing Vietnamese expansion should ensure that Thailand does not bend before a Vietnamese attack.

In the light of the above considerations, a successful US containment policy toward Southeast Asia would require—

a. Avoiding a situation where one or another major power, especially the USSR, achieves military dominance of the region;

b. Continuing US military presence in the general area to provide "balance" against the Soviet military presence in Vietnam;

c. Maintaining strong US security ties to South Korea and Japan in order to underline the fragility of Soviet power projections into Southeast Asia;

d. Supporting ASEAN states in carrying out successions in the coming years;

e. Engaging US influence to strengthen democratic processes and ensure political stability, social justice, and economic growth in the Philippines;

f. Ensuring continued economic growth in ASEAN by permitting continued access for Southeast Asian goods to markets in the United States and other Western countries;

g. Gradually strengthening ASEAN institutions, working toward regional unity while avoiding any premature movement toward a military alliance;

h. Continuing to display Western interest in Southeast Asia through such devices as the annual foreign ministerial meetings; and

i. Maintaining a reasonable degree of Western unity in policy toward Vietnam, emphasizing the necessity of Vietnamese withdrawal from Cambodia but leaving the door open to reconciliation and a weaning of Vietnam away from its Soviet embrace.

The current strategic equation in Southeast Asia is hardly cast in concrete. All major participants retain room for maneuver. The very pace of Southeast Asia's progress will ensure some change in perceptions in the future. These changes will bring new risks and new opportunities for participants in the political struggles. Chances are that this competition will continue to be essentially a diplomatic one. Soviet miscalculation of the USSR's interests and the degree of risk entailed in securing a gain is always possible, if unlikely. It is at least as conceivable that the USSR and Vietnam will come to a parting of the ways, opening up new opportunities for Western advantages to be brought into the equation.

In this situation, containment from a US perspective must adopt a highly differentiated approach, one that employs a variety of foreign policy tools. It must appreciate that the West will continue to hold most of the cards in Southeast Asia—and will need to play them wisely.

Note

1. *U.S. Commitment to SEATO*, Hearings before the Committee on Foreign Relations, US Senate, 93rd Congress, 2nd Session, 6 March 1974 (Washington: US Government Printing Office, 1974), p. 4.

23

African Strategies of Containment

Henry S. Bienen

THE USSR WAS NOT AN AFRICAN POWER when George Kennan developed the containment doctrine after World War II. Russia had historical ties with Ethiopia and had tried to undermine Western European influence on the African continent in the nineteenth century.[1] But aside from interventions in Ethiopia, Russian influence was not much evident in Africa, especially in Black Africa. While Soviet analysts and policymakers were increasingly interested in African nationalist movements from the 1920s on, the Soviet Union was not an important actor in the process of decolonization or in the establishment of new states as African countries became independent

Henry S. Bienen is James S. McDonnell Distinguished University Professor at the Woodrow Wilson School of Public and International Affairs, Princeton University, where he is also the Director of the Center of International Studies and Professor of Politics and International Affairs.

in the late 1950s and 1960s. By the mid-1970s, however, Soviet interventions were to directly or indirectly affect the outcomes of struggles between nationalist groups within Angola and between Ethiopia and Somalia in the Horn of Africa.

In fact, the Soviet Union had become an important actor on the African scene by the 1960s. It became involved in the Congo crisis during the early 1960s, and it provided diplomatic support for many African states which wanted to distance themselves from the West, such as Ghana and Guinea. Also from about that time, the USSR was able to gather support from many African states for its positions in the United Nations and in other international forums. By 1977, the African continent was receiving about 60 percent of Soviet arms deliveries to noncommunist developing countries.[2] Moreover, Soviet military advisers were spread throughout Africa along with East German military personnel and significant numbers of Cuban combat troops, the latter heavily concentrated in Angola and (secondarily) in Ethiopia. Until the expulsion of Soviet military advisers from Egypt in 1972, the USSR had a significant military presence in that country, and it had base, docking, and overflight rights in particular countries at various times, including Guinea, Somalia, Ethiopia, and Angola.

Furthermore, beginning with Congo-Brazzaville in 1963, a number of African states embraced a scientific socialist economic path in the 1960s and 1970s—some of them declaring People's Republics. Usually, the Marxist-Leninist nature of the state was affirmed by military regimes. The army rulers of Somalia announced their Marxism-Leninism in 1970; Benin's proclamation took place in 1974, Madagascar's in 1975. These countries had been under military rule for some time when Marxism-Leninism was announced, and the ideological affirmation was often highly dependent on a particular military leader. For example, Madagascar's declaration waited upon Captain Ratsiraka's ascension to power in 1975, and it was two years later that the regime created its own party (l'Avant-Garde de la Revolution Malagache) alongside others. In many states which

called themselves Marxist-Leninist, military regimes created
parties but kept tight control over them. In Ethiopia, for example, where the military took over in 1975 but did not announce
its communist nature until 1976, Mengistu dragged his heels
concerning the creation of a party, finally announcing one with
great fanfare a decade after the revolution.[3]

The ideological and social base of African communist regimes, their commitment to social change, and their relationships to the armed forces and the Soviet Union have been much
discussed by Soviet and non-Soviet observers.[4] The USSR itself
has not fully embraced as communist those regimes it calls
"Afro-Marxist" or "Afro-Communist." Some observers have referred to these states as ones of "socialist orientation," noting
that the proclamation of adherence to Marxism-Leninism is not
sufficient to turn a vanguard party into a functioning socialist
party in the absence of the necessary class basis.[5] Moreover, the
USSR has been rather guarded in its commitments to these
states, providing significant military assistance but slim economic support.[6] It resisted Mozambique's application to join
Comecon, and it could not or would not respond to the dire economic straits of Mozambique, Congo-Brazzaville, or even Angola and Ethiopia. Thus, as African countries have faced the
1980s in a context of debt, drought, and falling per capita in-
comes, the Soviet Union has witnessed an intensification of African economic ties to the West, including countries that defined
themselves as Marxist-Leninist. Economic dependence on the
West, linked with a declining security situation, led Mozambique to try for rapprochement with South Africa and the United
States, while Angola continued to negotiate with those countries
for a settlement of outstanding grievances. Only in Ethiopia
could it be said that Soviet influence had intensified by
mid-1985.

What can we make of this record in terms of the doctrine
of containment? In a superficial sense, containment of the
USSR in Africa has failed. The USSR has been able to develop
political and military ties, if few economic ones, with most

African states. In some important cases, it has determined political and military outcomes on the continent. In others, such as the Congo crises of the 1960s and Liberia after the fall of the Tubman regime in 1980, the USSR has been prevented from making inroads by Western military actions or economic aid. In Egypt, the Sudan, Ghana, Guinea, and Mali, the record of Soviet influence during the past twenty-five years has been mixed; but on balance, Soviet influence had weakened by the 1980s.

Soviet Aims and Capabilities

Neither in "The Sources of Soviet Conduct" nor elsewhere did George Kennan express concern that the USSR would try to attack the basis of Western power through the "soft underbelly" of the Third World. But many observers have contended that the USSR has a grand design to weaken the West by expanding its influence in the Third World and, specifically, by controlling resources so that it could deny oil and strategic metals to the West. Such a strategy is imputed to the Kremlin even though the USSR itself does not require African resources and does not trade extensively with the continent—being a producer of the very minerals found in Africa and especially southern Africa: platinum-based minerals, gold, uranium, and diamonds.

One could, of course, read back into Kennan's work elements of this view, since the USSR has explicit and desired goals of supremacy and is hostile to capitalist countries. Kennan also stressed that Soviet political action "is a fluid stream" that can accommodate itself to barriers and has flexible time frames within which to accomplish its goals. Its tactics may be opportunistic, but its designs are clear and unchanging.

But whatever one thinks of Soviet motives in Africa, the Soviets have not strengthened their ability to control resources—either directly on the continent or on routes over or around the African land mass, including the Cape sea routes. Of course, Soviet military capabilities, especially sea and air, have been greatly increased. The Soviet Union now has a large

Indian Ocean naval presence; it has basing rights in the Persian Gulf and Indian Ocean littorals; and it has proved its logistical abilities to move men and materials in Angola and the Horn. Short of striking at the industrial base of the USSR directly, the United States surely did not have the ability to prohibit the development of this capacity.

Yet scenarios envisioning Soviet control of the Cape routes or Soviet control of supplies through a minerals cartel and pressure on one or another Black regime in southern Africa are unconvincing. Oil supplies are easier to interdict coming out of the Gulf or at pipelines and refineries in the Middle East than around the Cape. The destruction of the White regime in South Africa and its replacement with a regime no friendlier to the United States than Angola's (which sells its production to the West through Gulf Oil) would hardly mean loss of access to South Africa's minerals. A Black-ruled South Africa would have to sell its minerals on world markets. Only if a regime were a complete client of another state, with the maintenance of its elite resting on that outside state's power, could cutoffs of supply be envisioned. There is no evidence that the USSR can establish such relationships in Africa over any period of time unless a regime's very existence is threatened by external and internal enemies. And even in Angola or Ethiopia, where such threats do exist, significant degrees of independence in foreign and domestic policymaking exist.[7]

This is not to say that an assessment of Soviet motives is irrelevant to structuring foreign policy responses in Africa. However, US responses should not be deduced from Soviet motives and goals, even if we could understand these perfectly. For one thing, the United States has interests in Africa that are outside of the framework of East-West relations. We have commitments to economic and environmental development and to human rights, independent of our concerns with the USSR, even if those concerns sometimes modify specific policy responses. Furthermore, even where Soviet-American relations are central, and even if we accept that an American policy toward any region should be strategic in its conception and understood in terms of its interrelatedness with US world policies (as the Reagan administration has argued from the start), US policies still will be more effective if they are not negative reactions to Soviet initiatives but rather are grounded in regional realities. It is therefore false and misleading to distinguish between "globalists" and "regionalists" on African policy, as was done during the Carter administration between UN Ambassador Andrew Young and Secretary of State Cyrus Vance on the one side, and National Security Adviser Zbigniew Brzezinski on the other.

American Perspectives and African Conditions

As the Reagan administration has found out, having global positions and emphasizing strategic issues does not settle foreign policy priorities; all the hard work of hammering out a foreign policy still remains to be done, whether one starts from a global or a regional perspective. Indeed, globalists and regionalists ask many of the same questions: What are the principal US interests in a given region? What is the nature and magnitude of the Soviet threat? What policies should the United States pursue to advance its interests and to deal with the USSR? But the order of priority in which the questions are asked and the weight given to the answers frequently differ. Globalists ask first about the Soviet Union's or other large powers' behavior, motivations, and threats. Regionalists usually begin by trying to define US interests in the particular region in question. They argue that globalists are frequently ignorant of conditions in a country, refuse to deal with specifics, and are given to sloganeering about regional power vacuums, "arcs of instability," and strategic needs. Regionalists also view the globalist desire to fill "power vacuums" as leading to efforts to project US power through the agency of such "regional influentials" and surrogates as Iran under the Shah, Saudi Arabia, and Nigeria. They argue that the so-called new influentials are often powers with feet of clay whose own commitment to US policies is uncertain. Regionalists claim that globalists' strategic objectives are often vaguely defined and unrelated to practical political and economic goals.[8]

The realities of international relations and of conflictive bilateral relations between states have made it difficult for the Reagan administration to persuade regional powers to define their policies in terms of the Soviet threat. Surely, it has been difficult to persuade South Africa that common opposition to Soviet and Cuban influence requires a settlement in Namibia; and it will be even harder, should the Reagan administration ever try it, to persuade South Africans that strategic concerns and world balances of power require fundamental changes in their domestic order. Nor do factions on the ground in Namibia or Angola seem to take their positions from an overarching geopolitical point of view. The Reagan administration's insistence on removal of Cuban troops from Angola as part of a Namibian settlement stems from its concern with the projection of communist power in southern Africa. However, Angola relies on Cuban troops to protect it from South Africa, and the ruling MPLA faction requires Cuban troops in its struggle with Jonas Savimbi's UNITA. Since the MPLA's first priority is retention of power, it could dispense with Cuban troops only as part of a settlement with UNITA. The Reagan administration is aware that the power struggle in Angola deeply affects the way the parties see the issue of Cuban troops, and has tried to be sensitive to their requirements. But the administration has insisted, nonetheless, on the Cuban issue—in part because it gives priority to East-West competition, in part because it believes that without the removal of Cuban troops there is no chance of South Africa's agreeing on a Namibian settlement.

Elsewhere in Africa, the Reagan administration has tempered its globalism with a sensitivity to the realities and complexities of local and regional conflict. But even as it has in practice taken account of regional complexities—or has been forced to do so—it has continued to place great emphasis on the military and security aspects of US interests in Africa. Investigating Soviet behavior in Africa to demonstrate either a "grand design" or a "targets of opportunity" theory also is not very useful. Certainly, the Soviet Union has goals and policies toward Africa, and it presumably orders them in some hierarchy. But here we must confront changed conditions since Professor Kennan set forth his ideas on containment.

To use a favorite Russian phrase, the "correlation of forces" between the United States and the USSR has changed over time, but not in any simple direction. The influence of the great powers has waxed and waned in particular places and at various times, depending first on the problems that confronted particular elites—their own survival, economic development, and military needs—and second on what the USSR or the United States was prepared to offer them. The Soviet Union can now project power to Africa; it can offer military support or threaten disruption through military assistance to groups or countries. But it has not been able to offer food, high technology relevant to Africa's needs, stable and extensive trade relations, or financial support. The very unevenness of the Soviet economy that Kennan pointed to in "The Sources of Soviet Conduct" persists and constrains the development of Soviet influence.

Thus, while the porosity, instability, and fragility of African political systems (and conflicts within the African interstate system) may allow the USSR many opportunities, Moscow has found it difficult so far to turn these opportunities into long-term and stable influence. The very conditions which open Africa to Soviet influence constrain Moscow's ability to deepen that influence and extend it to economic realms. Africa provides a context for Soviet power to be extended, but it also provides conditions in which sudden changes in influence are possible and indeed likely.

Irrespective of Soviet intentions, in other words, the Soviet Union's influence can be contained in Africa. Kennan's sense of the limits on Soviet power has been confirmed historically with respect to the African continent. There is good reason to believe that Soviet leaders know the constraints on their actions vis-a-vis Africa, although there are undoubtedly debates in the Kremlin as to the importance of factors which limit influence and the ways that the USSR should respond to them. Even if one wants to disbelieve the evidence accumulated by observers of the Soviet policy debate, Soviet tactics have shown an ability to adjust to changed circumstances—both for the better and for the worse.

Impacts on the USSR of Containment's Success

In "The Sources of Soviet Conduct," Kennan argued that "the political personality of Soviet power as we know it today is the product of ideology and circumstances." Whatever one thinks about the stability of Soviet ideological formulations, "circumstances" have certainly changed since the immediate post–World War II period. A central idea of Kennan's doctrine was that containment of foreign expansion would have domestic effects within the USSR. Since Africa has not been a primary strategic locale of either the Americans or the Soviets, it might be argued that containment in Africa is largely irrelevant to producing domestic change in the USSR. Nonetheless, events in Africa since independence should have had a sobering impact on the Kremlin's vision of a Third World moving toward communism.

There has been almost no development of an indigenous working class in Africa along lines envisioned by Lenin. The communist parties in the Sudan and South Africa, two of Africa's largest in the 1960s, have not assumed independent influence. No African states have witnessed large-scale social transformations from below through a process of revolution, although there have been revolutionary movements limited in time and place. There have been attempts at social transformation from above, usually through military regimes. The creation of state farms and large-scale state enterprises is consistent with many noncommunist and nonsocialist experiments in Africa, but this process is currently being reversed or reduced in state after state. Ethiopia is the single example of major social transformation, of what could be called an ongoing revolutionary process. Kennan postulated flexible time horizons for Soviet leaders as they looked for revolutionary change in the world, and such an outlook is the best construction today's comrades could put upon recent events in Africa.

Let us assume for the moment that those who rule the USSR do not care about domestic social change in African countries, that they care only insofar as it might create a closer community of elites across national lines, itself a dubious proposition. Let us further assume that they care about the projection of Soviet power, at least in the short and medium term, leaving revolution and social change to take care of themselves. At the least, Soviet analysts do appear to take a prudent view of their ability to affect the social base of African politics in the near future. They understand the persistence of ethnic ties, the weakness of classes, the fragmentation of elites, the nature of underdeveloped economies. They seem to understand that Soviet power and the transfer of resources directly or by proxies may affect who wins in Angola or Chad or Ethiopia, but that it is much more difficult to construct central authority after the combatants have exhausted themselves. They also seem to understand that African states fight with each other; that new African leaders can alter foreign policies more easily than leaders in countries with more developed pressure groups and official institutions for foreign policymaking; and that many new actors are competing in Africa, especially China but also India, Japan, Saudi Arabia, and Iraq. Better than we, they may understand that Cuba, as well as Libya, is on this list as an actor with its own interests and concerns.[9]

Knowing these things appears to have made the Soviet Union not only cautious about commitments to and predictions about social change in Africa, but also circumspect with regard to the potential for expansion of Soviet influence. Obviously, the Soviets have been willing to make important commitments in Africa when they have perceived either that the United States was unlikely to act (as in Angola) or when the situation on the ground favored Soviet action and would be supported broadly within Africa (as in Angola and Ethiopia). But many examples can be found where in less favorable circumstances the USSR did *not* escalate its commitments to a leader or a faction (for example, Chad, Uganda under Amin, Mozambique and Angola facing South African pressure, Sankara in Burkina Faso, or Rawlings in Ghana).

Has an understanding of its limitations influenced the Soviet Union's relationship more generally with the United States? Is it true, as it has been argued, that the general strategic decline of the United States vis-a-vis the USSR in the 1970s allowed the latter to intervene more aggressively in Africa?[10] Was this strategic reversal itself altered simply by the coming to power of Ronald Reagan, who articulated different policies but who could not quickly alter strategic military ratios? Regional defense of interests may be necessary to preserve global positions and vice-versa. But in Africa, it is difficult to see a more aggressive US posture, aside from a commitment to constructive engagement in southern Africa and an increased willingness to provide military assistance to a limited number of countries like the Sudan, whose leader fell in any case. Soviet weakness became evident in Africa, not renewed American strength.

Nevertheless, Soviet perspectives on global relationships with the United States may be influenced by perceived changes in developing countries. In the 1970s, Soviet writing stressed that the correlation of forces was changing in favor of the USSR and suggested that the USSR was dealing with the United States from positions of increasing strength. But it is hard to know who in the USSR adopted this view and how it affected decisions in strategic issues. In the end, it is impossible to be certain about the relationship of Soviet African policies—to say nothing of Moscow's policies toward the developing countries more generally—to Soviet-US relations. One simply cannot verify the proposition that success or failure, in whatever terms the USSR sees these phenomena in Africa, makes the USSR a more or less aggressive actor in Soviet-American global relations and, if so, whether such changes occur because experience alters the personality of Soviet power (as Kennan suggested) or because it alters Soviet assessments of the strength or weakness of the West.

Impacts on the United States of Containment's Failure

It is perhaps easier to understand how Soviet actions in Africa, among other places, affect US perspectives on global relations with the USSR. Certainly, specific Soviet actions in Angola and the Horn of Africa in the mid to late 1970s, as well as the invasion of Afghanistan and the Iranian revolution, fundamentally altered perspectives within the Carter administration and shifted the balance of power between different actors within it. Africa helped change the Carter administration's attitudes toward detente, not because it was intrinsically important to US strategic concerns, but because the Soviet Union was seen to be acting in spheres removed from its traditional interests in an aggressive and unrestrained way. The USSR's willingness to be involved in large-scale military support in Angola and the Horn of Africa suggested to American policymakers that the USSR was exploiting a "post-Vietnam syndrome" and American political weakness to change a regional balance of power. Thus Henry Kissinger gave weight to Soviet actions in Angola and Zbigniew Brzezinski saw detente "buried in the sands of the Oganden." Ronald Reagan's campaign attributed Soviet regional moves to a general US strategic and military weakness.

However, it was hardly American military weakness which allowed the Soviet Union to change balances in the Horn and in Angola. It is hard to see that the USSR had a grand design in the Horn. Rather, after trying unsuccessfully to straddle interstate divisions and work toward agreement between Ethiopia and Somalia, the USSR picked, in Ethiopia, the larger and more important horse, the one also backed by the community of African states. Whether the USSR was persuaded early on by the ideological *bona fides* of the Mengistu group is hard to say. The Kremlin does seem to have cared about social and political experiments in Ethiopia, but it may have cared more about the Mengistu regime's weakness and the likelihood that it would be highly dependent on Soviet military support. By contrast, lacking Ethiopia as an option, the United States could not find a good horse on the Horn. No friend of the United States for many years, Somalia was small, poor, and possessed of irredentist demands on its neighbors which were not supported by the United States or by African states. In Angola, Zaire had proved to be a weak reed for supporting Holden Roberto's FNLA,[11] and the United States could not assist it or UNITA without close collaboration with South Africa. The South African role led to widespread public support for the MPLA throughout Africa, even among states that had initially opposed it.

In these two cases, then, the USSR was able to use local conflicts to build positions of influence in situations where US options were limited, irrespective of US "will" and military capabilities. The Soviet exploitation of those opportunities did affect US views about the Soviet Union's commitment to detente, although the USSR had always argued that it had the right to support like-minded Third World states. Raymond Garthoff has argued that the United States' support of its own allies' interventions led the Soviet Union to think that the United States did not see detente as marking any radical departure from the tradition of direct, proxy, and allied interventions of the 1960s and 1970s.[12] Indeed, the Soviet Union could have pointed to French actions in the Central African Republic or Zaire's support for the FNLA in Angola, as well as to direct and indirect South African interventions in its neighbors' affairs. But aside from the United States' initial meddling in the Angolan civil war, the USSR would have been hard put to assign Washington anything like the role it had itself played in the Horn and in Angola.[13]

Of course, the USSR has always argued that American and, more generally, Western influence was acquired and exercised differently. Moscow points to the West's colonial experience and subsequent patterns of imperialist economic ties while noting that its own ability to exert influence is limited to support via proxies and military assistance. The argument has some historical merit, but it ignores the fact that large-scale military interventions are peculiarly destabilizing for relations between the superpowers. At least partially cognizant of this fact, the USSR has worked through proxies, especially Cuba, in its interventions.

Although the United States itself searched for regional surrogates under the Nixon Doctrine, African states have had a hard time achieving regional power status. Neither Zaire nor Nigeria is a stable country with a strong economic base, even though different administrations have centered their African policies on them for a time. The one true regional power at the moment is South Africa, a country with its own peculiar liabilities as an ally. More importantly, regional powers tend to try to further their own interests and concerns, often at the expense of those of the great powers. This unfortunate consideration applies to the relationship of Ethiopia to the USSR as well as that of Zaire or Morocco to the United States.

Strategies for Containment in Africa

Success or failure in Africa does matter, and the USSR's role in Angola and the Horn did have consequences. Nevertheless, American policymakers should remember that Soviet success is usually limited at best in Africa, and it comes with liabilities and costs. Not all successes are long-lived, as Soviet relations with Egypt, Somalia, the Sudan, Mozambique, and other African states show. Political relations for the USSR cannot easily be translated into either long-term military gains or economic advantages. Moreover, there is nothing ineluctable about one success bringing another in its train. There has been no wave of Soviet success in Africa; although states are unstable and fragile, dominoes have not fallen.

Conditions in Africa will continue to make possible the extension of Soviet military and political influence. African states are weak, and limited resources can affect power balances between factions within a country and between states. Because African states are becoming more differentiated by wealth and power, and because there are continued grievances among them, we can expect more interstate conflict. The Soviet Union will be able to fish in troubled waters. But so will the United States, China, and smaller powers like France, Cuba, and Saudi Arabia, as well as African ones such as Libya, Egypt, Morocco, and Nigeria. It is conflict and change that create opportunities for the USSR more than any decline in US capabilities.

That African states' political power is highly personalized requires little documentation or argument. Changes in leaders, even without fundamental changes in regime, can lead to shifts in foreign policy alignments. Both the fragility of power in Africa and the centralization of power in leaders, especially for foreign affairs, makes the influence of outside powers on Africa somewhat unpredictable.[14] Thus, although Soviet influence in Africa cannot easily be contained, if containment means keeping the USSR out of Africa, broad and deep economic influence is not likely to develop from short-term or even longer-term political gains.

As we look to the 1990s, then, the United States is not threatened by serious expansion of Soviet influence in Africa. The United States need not always be on the defensive. Indeed, Soviet positions are under direct assault by insurgents in Angola and to a lesser extent in Ethiopia. In Mozambique, insurgency coupled with South African pressure and a dire economic situation have already forced the Machel government to move away from the USSR. But the fundamental issues for Africa do not lie in East-West struggles. Nor do the fundamental choices for the United States lie in whether to merely react to Soviet moves or to be on the offensive politically and militarily where the Soviet Union is already strong.

The Soviet Union is no giant in Africa, and the United States has failed to understand its own strength there. Our comparative advantage lies not in military competition with the Soviet Union but, rather, in financial, economic, technological, and human resources which can provide markets for Africa's goods, assistance for its development, and aid during its crises. The Soviet Union has not risen and cannot rise to the challenges posed by failing African food production, rising population pressures, lagging productivity, poorly structured economies, and weak technological bases. Its economic models and strategies are part of the problem, not part of the solution.

Of course, political instability can affect developmental contexts, and political strategies are needed to counter Soviet moves. But dwelling on East-West confrontations cannot be effective in dealing with African problems either. Moreover, security for much of the African continent is as much a matter of trade, aid, population movements, transportation improvement, and debt relief as it is a matter of interstate conflict or Soviet power. And for southern African states, security is threatened by a powerful and active South Africa more than by the Soviet Union. Conflict in southern Africa, and within South Africa, will provide the major opportunity for the Soviet Union to extend its influence throughout the continent. US positions toward South Africa may turn out to be the most crucial element in containing Soviet influence in Africa as a whole. To ignore these facts is to build policies on flawed assumptions about Africa, and thus to threaten the very security we seek to protect.

Notes

1. See, among others, Edward T. Wilson, "Russia's Historic Stake in Black Africa," in David E. Albright, ed., *Communism in Africa* (Bloomington: University of Indiana Press, 1980), pp. 67–92.

2. Kenneth L. Adelman, *African Realities* (New York: Crane Russak and Co., 1980), p. 11.

3. For a discussion of military regimes and radical movements in Africa, see Henry Bienen, "Populist Military Regimes in Africa," *Armed Forces and Society* (Spring 1985), pp. 357–77.

4. See David Ottaway and Marina Ottaway, *Afrocommunism* (New York: Africana, 1980); Crawford Young, *Ideology and Development in Africa* (New Haven: Yale University Press, 1982); Carl Rosberg, Jr., and Thomas Callaghy, eds., *Socialism in Sub-Saharan Africa* (Berkeley: Institute of International Studies, 1979); Albright, ed., *Communism in Africa.*

5. A number of authors have reviewed the debates on this issue in the Soviet Union, among them Elizabeth Kridl Valkenier, "Revolutionary Change in the Third World: Recent Soviet Assessments," *World Politics,* April 1986; and Mark N. Katz, *The Third World in Soviet Military Thought* (Baltimore: Johns Hopkins University Press, 1982). I have benefitted from reading forthcoming work by Jerry Hough on this subject and Hough's "The Evolution in the Soviet World View," *World Politics* 32 (July 1980), pp. 509–30.

6. See Albright, *The USSR and Sub-Saharan Africa in the 1980s,* The Washington Papers 101, Vol. 11 (New York: Praeger, 1983, pp. 27–30).

7. These issues have been discussed at some length in Henry Bienen, "U.S. Foreign Policy in a Changing Africa," *Political Science Quarterly* 93 (Fall 1978), pp. 443–64; and Bienen, "The United States and Sub-Saharan Africa," in John P. Lewis and Valerian Kallab, eds.,

U.S. Foreign Policy and the Third World, Agenda 1983 (New York: Praeger, 1983), pp. 66–85.

8. Bienen, "The United States and Sub-Saharan Africa," p. 68.

9. See Bienen, "Soviet Political Relations with Africa," *International Security* 6 (Spring 1983), pp. 153–74.

10. This has been maintained by, among others, Walter F. Hahn and Alvin J. Cottrell in *Soviet Shadow Over Africa* (Coral Gables: Center for Advanced International Studies, University of Miami, 1976).

11. There are by now many accounts of Soviet intervention in the Angolan civil war. See Arthur Jay Klinghoffer, *The Angolan War: A Study in Soviet Policy* (Boulder: Westview Press, 1980).

12. Raymond Garthoff, *Detente and Confrontation: American-Soviet Relations from Nixon to Reagan* (Washington: The Brookings Institution, 1985), p. 671.

13. I find Garthoff's listing of interventions by the United States and its allies as compared to ones by the Soviet Union to be not convincing if the aim is to suggest that the scope and consequences of the interventions were on the same plane, at least as far as Africa is concerned.

14. Bienen, *Soviet Relations with Africa*, p. 160.

24

Updating US Strategic Policy: Containment in the Caribbean Basin

Howard J. Wiarda

L ATIN AMERICA HAS LONG BEEN of peripheral interest in global US foreign policy. Historically, our concerns have centered chiefly on the European countries, the European military
and strategic theater, and, since World War II, particularly on
the Soviet Union. In terms of priorities, we have not paid Latin
America much attention: the area ranks behind the Soviet
Union, Western Europe and NATO, the Middle East, Japan and
China, and the broader Pacific Basin in the rank-ordering of our
foreign policy concerns. Under the impact of the crisis in Central America, however, and as we ourselves become something
of a Caribbean nation, our historical disinterest has begun to
change. Latin America and our Latin America policy are now

Howard J. Wiarda is a Resident Scholar at the American Enterprise Institute
for Public Policy Research and Director of its Center for Hemispheric Studies.

being taken seriously for the first time since World War II; the area is coming under increased scrutiny from scholars, the think tanks, strategic analysts, and policymakers.[1]

The question is not just whether we have devoted sufficient attention to Latin America, however, but also whether the fundamental assumptions of the policy we have followed are adequate. Even those who firmly believe in a strong defense and who have been generally supportive of US policy in Central America can profit by reexamining the bases of US policy toward Latin America in the political, economic, and foreign assistance areas.[2] It is perhaps time now also, within the context of support for the overall goals of US foreign policy, to reexamine some of the strategic assumptions as well. The question we ask is whether the historical assumptions and fundamentals of US policy in the Caribbean Basin are still relevant and appropriate in the altered circumstances of today. For Latin America has changed greatly in the last twenty years, as have the United States and US–Latin American relations; these changes prompt us to ask whether policy must be adjusted to new realities.

Historical US Policy in Latin America

Historical US policy in Latin America—and the strategic thinking and assumptions undergirding it—have not changed greatly since Admiral Alfred Thayer Mahan (and with him, Teddy Roosevelt) first articulated a coherent and integrated policy for the region almost ninety years ago.[3] In fact, strategic policy has not changed greatly since the days of President James Monroe and the famous Doctrine that bears his name. Moreover, the fundamentals of the policy have been remarkably consistent and continuous over this long history, regardless of the party or administration in power. Only the means best to achieve these agreed-upon goals have varied.[4]

The basic bedrocks of US policy in the Caribbean Basin, the historical record shows, include the following:[5]

1. Protect the "soft underbelly" of the United States. Since we have thousands of miles of oceans to our east and west and a friendly, mostly English-speaking nation to our north, our primary strategic concern in this hemisphere has been with the small, unstable nations to our south. Indeed, it is their very smallness, weakness, and chronic instability that give rise to the fear in the United States that a hostile foreign power will take advantage of their debility to establish a base in the Caribbean region from which to launch offensives against the United States itself. Hence—particularly since the building of the Panama Canal—the United States has maintained a string of bases, radar tracking stations, and the like throughout the Caribbean.

2. Maintain access to the area's raw materials, primary products, markets, and (recently) labor supply. This objective implies supporting a policy of free trade, open markets, and easy and direct US investments. US economic activity in the area is also viewed as a way to maintain stability and discourage potential competitors.

3. Keep out hostile foreign powers, or maybe *any* foreign powers, from an area thought of as lying within *our* sphere of influence. This meant action directed against Russia, Spain, France, Britain, and Germany in the past; since World War II, it has meant excluding the Soviet Union from the area.

4. Maintain stability in ways that are supportive of the bedrock interests listed above. In general, this stricture has been interpreted to call for support of whatever government friendly to our interests happens to be in power, while also keeping lines of communication open to the moderate opposition. Maintaining stability does not necessarily mean defending the status quo; it includes sufficiently supporting change and reform to head off the possibility of instability arising out of popular dissatisfaction.

From these "basic bedrocks" of US policy in Latin America, which is in fact a long-term and historical strategy of exclusion and containment, a number of corollaries follow:

1. US policy has consistently been more concerned with those countries in Central America and the Caribbean that are "close to home" than with those more distant in South America.

2. US policy in the area has historically been crisis-oriented. That is, because ours is essentially a defensive policy in an area we have not thought of as very important, we have responded to crises after they occurred rather than developing a more positive, mature, long-term, and anticipatory policy.

3. Democracy and human rights have been accorded secondary importance. To the degree democracy and a strong human rights policy help secure stability and protect our other bedrock interests, we have encouraged them, but not usually for their own sake or as a fundamental aspect of US policy.

4. The same goes for economic and social development. We tend to emphasize these programs as a means to preserve stability when the nations of the area are threatened by Castro-like revolutions. In noncrisis times, however, our attitude is generally one of "benign neglect."

Our basic policy in Latin America, therefore, has been one of hegemony, containment, and balance of power. The question is whether these historical bases of policy, which still undergird a great deal of policy thinking today, continue to be useful and relevant under the changed conditions in which we and the Latin Americans now find ourselves.

New Realities

Three areas of change need to be analyzed. All three strongly affect the question of the continuity, relevance, and utility of US containment policy vis-a-vis Latin America. The three areas of change to be examined are changes in the United States, changes in Latin America, and changes in the inter-American system.[6]

Among many basic changes in the United States in the last twenty years, the following may be of special importance:

1. The United States since the Vietnam War is a considerably chastised nation, wary of foreign entanglements. We do not wish to be involved deeply in Central America, and we certainly do not want to commit US ground forces.

2. Because the public and Congress will not countenance new, large foreign aid programs for Latin America, we have fewer levers of influence in the region.

3. The Department of Defense is also wary of new interventions in countries where the goals are not clear, public opinion is divided, a prolonged war may result, and the military institution is likely to be discredited. It wants no more "Vietnams."

4. The US foreign policymaking process is more fragmented, chaotic, and paralyzed than before. It is now far more difficult for us to carry out a long-term, coherent, bipartisan foreign policy.[7]

5. Isolationist sentiment is strong. We want "no more second Cubas" in the Caribbean, but we are unwilling to provide the funds or programs to ensure they do not happen.

6. The United States is a weaker presence in Latin America than it was before. Our political, military, diplomatic, cultural, and economic leverage has been significantly lessened. Our capacity to act in the region has thereby been reduced.

In Latin America the following changes have occurred:

1. Latin America is more developed, modern, and sophisticated than before. We can no longer treat these as "banana republics," amenable to "quick fixes."

2. Latin America is much more assertive and nationalistic; it now listens to the United States reluctantly if at all. No longer can we easily impose our will.

3. Latin America is now much more socially and politically differentiated and pluralistic. We must deal with these new complexities.

4. The Latin American nations are now pursuing much more independent, if not nonaligned, foreign policies than before. They wish to distance themselves from the United States while not losing our assistance programs in the process.

5. Latin America's priorities are now quite different from those of the United States. Our concerns are overwhelmingly strategic; they are primarily concerned with trade and economic development.

6. Latin America is going through both a period of crisis and a period of experimentation with new forms. We frequently confuse the two tendencies while they plead for patience.

In the realm of the inter-American system, if it can still be called that, the following changes have taken place:

1. The structure of the inter-American relationship has been badly damaged through neglect, inattention, and failures to live up to its obligations—as in Central America, the 1982 Falklands/Malvinas war, and numerous other cases.

2. While the United States seems more chastised and weaker than it was twenty years ago, the larger and more militarily powerful Latin American states (Argentina, Brazil, Mexico, Venezuela, Cuba) are far stronger and are pursuing more independent foreign policies at the level of middle-ranking powers.

3. A number of new outside powers—West Germany, France, Spain, Japan, and others—have begun to play a larger role. The United States no longer has the monopoly in the area that it once had.

4. New issues—drugs, debt, human rights, democracy, protectionism, trade, migration—have begun to replace the historical strategic ones. Latin American priorities in these matters are often quite different from US priorities.

5. The United States has become more dependent on Latin America for manufactured as well as primary goods, rendering our relationship one of far more complex interdependence than in the past.

6. Latin America has greatly diversified its international ties in recent years, opening up new relations with Eastern Europe, China, and the Soviet Union among others; the United States is no longer the only country with which it has important relations.

All these trends must be factored into the new equations of inter-American relations and into our assessment of the adequacy of traditional US containment policy. To these must now be added the rising presence of the Soviet Union and of its proxy, Cuba, throughout the area.

The Soviet Presence in Latin America

Containment policy, aimed at excluding the Soviet Union from the Western Hemisphere, worked quite well until the late 1950s. There were small communist parties in most countries of the hemisphere, but they lacked popular support or a strong organizational base, and the notion of Stalinist troops disembarking on Latin America's shores was dismissed as ludicrous—as it deserved to be. In 1954 the United States intervened in Guatemala to help oust a populist-leftist government in which some communists held key posts, but until the Cuban revolution, the walls that excluded the Soviets from Latin America remained unbreachable.[8]

The Cuban revolution of 1959, Fidel Castro's declaration of Marxism-Leninism, and the incorporation of Cuba into the Soviet camp changed all that. From this point on, the Soviets would have a base in the Western Hemisphere for political as well as military operations. During the 1960s the Cubans tried, with Soviet assistance, to export their revolution to quite a number of other Latin American countries. The United States responded with what came to be called the "no second Cuba" doctrine: vigorous steps to prevent what happened in Cuba from happening in other countries.

In 1962 a new element was added to the equation with the installation in Cuba of offensive Soviet missiles pointed at the United States. In a tense confrontation, the United States forced the Soviet Union to remove the missiles from Cuba while itself agreeing tacitly not to continue seeking the overthrow of the Castro regime. With this showdown, the "no second Cuba" doctrine acquired a double meaning for the United States: the prevention of Castro-like revolutions throughout the hemisphere *and* the insistence that no Latin American country be used as a base for implanting sophisticated Soviet military hardware with an offensive capability that might threaten the United States. Where, precisely, the lines are drawn remains unclear, but certainly the United States is unwilling to accept the presence of MiG fighter planes in Nicaragua.

The response of the United States to the Cuban revolution was massive. For the first time since World War II, we began paying serious attention to Latin America. We quarantined Cuba, broke relations, and imposed a trade embargo against the island. We launched the Peace Corps and the Alliance for Progress, as well as a host of other development-related programs, as a way of heading off the growth of revolutionary sentiment. We initiated training programs in civic action and counterinsurgency for the Latin American militaries, and we assisted several countries in defeating their Cuban-inspired and -assisted guerrilla movements. The United States itself, when these other measures failed, intervened militarily in the Dominican Republic in 1965 to prevent what it thought was a Cuban-like revolution from succeeding.

These efforts were remarkably successful in medium-range terms. The embargo against Cuba kept that country isolated and economically unsuccessful, which meant that Cuba never became an attractive model for the other Latin American countries. By the late 1960s, especially with the death of Ché

Guevara in Bolivia, the Cuban-like guerrilla movements had been all but eliminated in most countries. Even though all its assumptions were wrong concerning the Latin American middle class and the capacity of the United States to bring democracy to the region, the Alliance for Progress bought us some time (not a glorious basis for policy, but for the United States a useful and pragmatic one) and helped avoid more Cubas.[9] By the end of the 1960s, the threat seemed sufficiently minimal and Latin America sufficiently "safe" for the United States to revert to its traditional policy of "benign neglect."

The inattention to Latin America in the early-to-mid-1970s was understandable but ultimately mistaken in long-range terms. Preoccupied by Vietnam and Watergate, we virtually ignored Latin America for most of the decade. We thus missed opportunities in the early 1970s to influence the course of events in El Salvador, Guatemala, and Nicaragua that would have prevented those countries from becoming such problem cases later on. Our foreign assistance dropped markedly. The number of US personnel and programs in Latin America was greatly reduced. In not paying attention to the area, we thus sacrificed most of the levers of influence that we had once had. Meanwhile, those "new realities" discussed earlier became accomplished facts, rendering obsolete quite a number of our traditional security doctrines. When Latin America blew up again in the late 1970s (Nicaragua, Grenada, El Salvador), we were quite unprepared for it.[10]

In the meantime, some new ingredients, some other "new realities," had been added. Principally, these involved the rising Soviet presence in the region. During the 1970s, the Soviet Union had become a major actor in Latin America. Its normal state-to-state relations with almost all the countries of the area had increased enormously. Using Cuba as its "aircraft carrier," the Soviet Union has become a significant military presence in the Caribbean. Soviet trade and commercial relations have grown dramatically; the Soviet Union is, for example, Argentina's largest export customer. In Peru the Soviets have military

Containment: Concept and Policy

equipment, training programs, and a significant presence. Soviet cultural and diplomatic activities have increased, and so have Soviet political and subversive efforts. The Soviet Union is by no means an equal of the United States in Latin America, but its influence and presence are clearly on the rise.[11]

Not only is the Soviet Union a rising presence, but its tactics and strategies have also become far more sophisticated. It is less heavy-handed and more subtle, playing for the long term while not ignoring possibilities for the short term. It ingratiates itself with democratic regimes while simultaneously seeking to push them toward nonalignment (and in some cases, continues to aid armed opposition forces seeking their overthrow). It uses aid, scholarships, military programs, and trade rather deftly. It has a different strategy for different kinds of countries, following a flexible course rather than some rigid ideological formula. Meantime, it has imposed order, coherence, and unity of direction on otherwise disparate guerrilla groups. It cleverly uses Cuba and now Nicaragua as its proxies, while also directing and overseeing a sophisticated division of labor among its fellow communist bloc countries. The Soviets have become far more clever at manipulating opinion in Western Europe and the United States.[12]

Nevertheless, limits also exist on the Soviet role in Latin America. The Soviets still do not function especially well in that context, and Latin America is not particularly sympathetic to a communist system. What the Soviets have been able to do quite cleverly and successfully, however, is to attach themselves to popular revolutionary movements ostensibly designed to promote national independence and social justice throughout the region, and to play upon and take advantage of Latin America's rising nationalism and anti-Americanism. The Soviets do not wish to challenge the United States unnecessarily in a part of the world that is only of peripheral importance to them and where the United States enjoys overwhelming local advantage. Within these limits, nonetheless, the Soviet gains in the last fifteen years have been impressive.[13]

The US response to the new Soviet initiatives was to resurrect the older containment policy. We have "rolled back" the revolution in Grenada through military intervention, and we have put immense pressures—military, political, economic, and diplomatic—on the Sandinista regime in Nicaragua, though the exact goals there remain ambiguous. We threatened to "go to the source" by, presumably, eliminating Cuba as a root cause of the troubles in Latin America. We proclaimed, at least in the early months of the Reagan administration, that the conflict in El Salvador was an East-West struggle; and there were some hints, almost certainly exaggerated, that the Cold War might be decided or turned around there. Our military-strategic buildup in the region has been immense.[14]

A strong case can be made that this military buildup was necessary, and it is certainly to be preferred to the handwringing, pious, blame-it-on-ourselves, and do-nothing character of the previous administration. The question that needs answering, however, is whether the kind of traditional containment policy we have followed is any longer adequate in the changed circumstances, in the "new realities," of today. The answer is that it is not; that it badly needs updating and greater sophistication; that we need to go, as in the title of one of the better books on the subject, "beyond containment";[15] and that the Reagan administration recognizes this and has begun to move in the new directions that are absolutely necessary if our policies in Latin America are to be successful.

"Economy of Force": Containment Policy in Latin America

An important part of American strategic policy in Latin America is based on the notion of what strategic planners call "economy of force." That is, the strategy correctly assumes that the Soviet Union is the country with which the United States is most likely to be engaged in any future conflict. But then it goes on to assume that such a conflict, were it to break out, would most likely occur in Central Europe or perhaps the Middle East. In such an eventuality, the United States would want to rush all its resources to the locus of the conflict as soon as possible. It would not want to have its forces tied down, paralyzed, or bottled up in some peripheral arena of conflict by some "third-rate" power like Cuba. That is how the Caribbean region is viewed: as an area in which the United States would not want to have its forces preoccupied with some local skirmish or tied up by a local adversary when strategically more vital needs lie elsewhere. Hence, if the Caribbean and Central America can be kept free of communist regimes and revolutions, if only an "economy of force" can be used to pacify that area, then US resources can be concentrated where the real conflict is—presumably on the plains of Central Europe.[16]

The economy of force strategy has in the past been fairly successful. The United States has managed to isolate Cuba and keep it from meddling in the internal affairs of very many other nations. We have limited Cuba's capacity to export its revolution to other countries. On a small island, Grenada, a "quick 'n' easy" intervention got rid of the local Marxist-Leninist regime and replaced it with one that would not attempt to sow revolution in the other small islands. In Nicaragua, through our support of the resistance forces (the so-called contras), we have tied down the Nicaraguan armed forces which had been enormously built up since the revolution, kept Nicaragua from spreading its revolution to its neighbors, and employed a mercenary army as a way of avoiding any commitment of US ground forces.

But the "economy of force" strategy has a number of problems and conceptual flaws. For one thing, it continues to treat Latin America as a side show, peripheral to the main action. Many analysts, however, are convinced that continuing to ignore Latin America or treat it as if it were of only peripheral importance is precisely what helps give rise to revolutions and anti-Americanism in Latin America, and that this attitude is at the root of our policy difficulties there. Second, it underestimates the domestic difficulties of sustaining a long-term proxy war in Central America, of carrying out a coherent policy over time given the play of domestic interest groups and opposition forces; and it overestimates the capacity of the United States to intervene with military force where necessary.[17]

Third, it assumes that Europe will be the main theater in a general war and that the type of war to be fought will be rather like the last one, involving tank and ground forces, and perhaps some limited tactical nuclear weapons, in the heartland of the Continent. One hates to resurrect that old saw about generals always fighting the last war, but in this instance, that seems again to be the case. A strong argument can be made that such a high-technology but more or less conventional war in the European center is the *least likely* kind of war we will be called on to fight. Far more likely are murky guerrilla struggles of the kind we are now witnessing in Central America or that we have previously seen in Cuba, Vietnam, Angola, and elsewhere. Unfortunately it is these more irregular wars that the United States, even with all its verbal commitments to counterinsurgency training and preparation over the last twenty years, is the least well-equipped and trained to deal with.[18]

The Evolution of Administration Policy

The Reagan administration got off to a rather shaky start in dealing with Latin America. In part, its difficulties stemmed from efforts to resurrect the unrefined containment policy of the past rather than creating the more subtle policy that later evolved and that is absolutely essential for US success. That is, the administration saw Cuba and the Soviet Union as the prime causes of the insurrection in Central America, it pictured the conflict in exclusively East-West terms, and it tended to view the problem and its solution in a purely military way. One recalls not only the early and sometimes unfortunate statements of administration spokesmen to this effect, but also their denigration of other related aspects of the problem. For example, Napoleon Duarte, now president of El Salvador, was once told by a National Security Council official that the United States was not very interested in agrarian reform in El Salvador and, in fact, thought it damaging to the economy. And the administration's first nominee to the post of assistant secretary of state for human rights and humanitarian affairs suggested that, if confirmed, he intended to abolish the job and office for which he was being considered. Those are not prudent and politically viable ways to conduct a successful Latin American foreign policy.

The administration has come a long way since those early weeks, and has fashioned a much more sophisticated and multifaceted approach. In part, the changes have been due to reactions from the Congress, the media, our allies, and public opinion, which have forced the administration to compromise and temper its policies. In part, the changes have been due to bureaucratic politics and rivalries within the government, and to the reassertion over time by State Department and foreign policy professionals of their expertise and more moderate views. And in part, the changes have been the result of a learning process that has occurred within the administration itself, stimulated by public opinion polls as well as by the more middle-of-the-road views and expertise found in the think tanks and other bodies that have generally been supportive of the administration. These and other influences have forced the administration back to a more moderate and mainstream foreign policy position.[19]

The administration now sees Central America as both an East-West *and* a North-South issue. It understands the indigenous roots of revolution in the area, as well as the capacity of the Cubans and Soviets to fan the flames of revolution, to exacerbate a crisis that already exists, and to take maximum advantage of the situation to embarrass the United States in its own backyard and score gains for themselves. US policies are now multifaceted rather than unidimensional. New US tactics are both more tempered and moderate *and* more refined than the older, sometimes heavy-handed orientation, which led to too many policy gaffes and thereby often defeated the purposes it sought to fulfill.

The administration's response has similarly been increasingly pragmatic. It now understands the need to balance its military-strategic emphasis with a real concern for democracy and human rights. It sees the requirement to pour in social and economic assistance as well as military aid. It supports agrarian reform and other programs of change as a way of securing long-term stability in the area and diminishing the appeals of communism. It has learned to work indirectly, behind the scenes, and through third parties rather than by means of the either-or confrontational strategies of the past. It has built up the US military presence in the area but also recognizes the dire need of these countries for economic recovery. It has put enormous political, economic, and military pressures on the Sandinista regime but has also kept open the possibilities for diplomatic negotiation. The policy now is far more sophisticated and subtle than in those early days.

The concrete manifestation of these more sophisticated strategies may be found in the Caribbean Basin Initiative and in the Kissinger Commission recommendations. The Caribbean Basin Initiative is a forward-looking assistance program combining official foreign aid with encouragement of private investment, not very much different from Kennedy's Alliance for Progress. The Kissinger Commission report contains similar recommendations for a judicious blend of public and private assistance, economic and military aid, strategic, democratic, and human rights concerns. It is a complex, multifaceted package that reflects the new, more moderate and sophisticated stance of the administration; and the Commission itself was an instrument in forging a more tempered and balanced strategy. The Kissinger Commission report is, in fact, now administration policy in Central America, even though not all of its recommendations have been formally enacted into law by the Congress.[20]

Toward an Updated Containment Strategy

The containment strategy, and the companion "economy of force" doctrine, would seem in the present, more complex circumstances to be woefully outdated—at least as these strategies were practiced in their traditional forms.[21] The containment strategy was based on an earlier conception of the global conflict as exclusively bipolar, grounded on mutual understandings of "spheres of influence," derived from the idea that both superpowers could and would police their own backyards, organized exclusively around an East-West axis, and based on the principle that whatever disruptions occurred in one superpower's own backyard must be due to the machinations of the other. There are still considerable elements of truth in all these assertions, but as a complete and sufficient explanation for the recent upheavals in Central America, they are quite inadequate.

In Central America, the problems have proved to be far more complex, deep-rooted, and intractable than the administration first thought. It is clear that quite a number of these problems cannot be resolved as easily, quickly, or cheaply as originally envisaged. The fundamental problem, however, in dealing with Central America remains a conceptual one.[22] We are still relying on policies and strategies having to do with great power tactics, containment, geopolitical position, spheres of influence, and balance of power that, in Latin America, badly need to be rethought and updated. Some of these strategies are anachronistic; others need to be reconceived. The fact is, they were designed for an earlier and simpler era and they no longer have the same relevance in today's Latin America. The new realities in Latin America—a changed and generally weaker US role, a new assertiveness and independence on the part of the Latin American nations, a desperate desire on the part of the Latin American peoples for development and social justice, the presence of other outside actors in the area, the changed inter-American system, and so on—all imply the need for a fundamental re-evaluation of policy.

Space does not permit a complete analysis of the policy package that ought to be pursued, but we can at least provide some guidelines.[23] To begin, we need to be *engaged* in Latin America with empathy and understanding, instead of viewing it as a side show. We need to examine and understand thoroughly the changed conditions of Latin America outlined here, and their implications for foreign policy. We need to develop our capacities to understand Latin America in its own terms and context, rather than through our own biased and often ethnocentric lenses.[24] We need to normalize and regularize our relations with the area and put them on a mature basis, rather than paying Latin America only fleeting attention in times of crisis. We need a sophisticated and multifaceted program for the area, as proposed by the Kissinger Commission but so far only partially implemented. We need to be flexible in meeting the challenges of the area, which will require far more capability and training in responding to guerrilla war. And we require a re-assessment of strategic thinking and tactics to reflect the changed conditions and new realities of the region and our position there. On this basis, a prudent, realistic, and more sophisticated policy can be developed.

Specifically, we need far more training in limited and irregular war capacity and counterinsurgency, in both rural and urban settings. We certainly need better language and area studies programs in our foreign policymaking agencies, not just in Spanish and Portuguese but also in such native Indian languages as Quechua and Aymará. We need a policy that incorporates expanded cultural and student exchanges, economic and debt aid, a vigorous human rights program, investment and trade, assistance for social modernization, support for democratization, and greater contacts between US and Latin American groups—as well as attention to strategic and military aspects. We need to understand and come to grips realistically with the rising Soviet-Cuban presence in the area and the Soviets' and Cubans' new, more sophisticated tactics. And we need to develop programs, such as the med-vac ones, to deal with Latin America's problems on the ground, close to the people, in terms the Latin Americans will both know and appreciate. In these ways, we need to update and modernize our containment strategy, keeping it viable as a policy for the United States in Latin America for the decades ahead, but adjusting it to the new realities outlined here and giving it a new formulation.

Notes

The research assistance of Janine Perfit and Frank Vega is gratefully acknowledged; thanks are also due to Dr. Iêda Siqueira Wiarda, who offered helpful commentary on an earlier version of this paper.

1. These themes are elaborated in Howard J. Wiarda, *In Search of Policy: The United States and Latin America* (Washington: The American Enterprise Institute for Public Policy Research, 1984).

2. Wiarda, ed., *Rift and Revolution: The Central American Imbroglio* (1984), *The Crisis in Latin America: Strategic, Economic and Political Dimensions* (1984), *The Alternative Futures of Latin America* (1985), *Human Rights and U.S. Human Rights Policy* (1982), and *The Crisis in Central America* (1982), all published by the American Enterprise Institute. See also, by the author, "At the Root of the Problem: Conceptual Failures in U.S.-Central American Relations," in Robert Leiken, ed., *Central America: Anatomy of Conflict* (New York: Pergamon Press, 1984) pp. 259–78.

3. See especially Mahan, *The Interest of American Sea Power, Present and Future* (Boston: Little, Brown, 1898).

4. J. Lloyd Mechan, *A Survey of United States–Latin American Relations* (Boston: Houghton-Mifflin, 1965).

5. From Wiarda, "The United States and Latin America: Change and Continuity," in Alan Adelman and Reid Reading, eds., *Confrontation in the Caribbean Basin* (Pittsburgh: Center for International Studies of the University of Pittsburgh, 1984) pp. 211–26.

6. A more complete discussion is found in Wiarda, *Latin America at the Crossroads: Development Strategies for the 1990s* (Washington: A Report Prepared for the Inter-American Development Bank, 1985) chap. 5.

7. The author has treated this subject in more detail in "The Paralysis of Policy: Current Dilemmas of U.S. Foreign Policy-Making" (Washington: American Enterprise Institute, Occasional Paper, 1985).

8. Cole Blasier, *The Giant's Rival: The USSR and Latin America* (Pittsburgh: University of Pittsburgh Press, 1983).

9. We need a reassessment of both the successes and the failures of the Alliance in this light.

10. See the discussion in Wiarda, ed., *Rift and Revolution,* esp. the Introduction.

11. Jiri Valenta and Virginia Valenta, "Soviet Policies and Strategies in the Caribbean Basin," in Wiarda, ed., *Rift and Revolution.* An updated version is forthcoming in Mark Falcoff and Howard J. Wiarda, *The Communist Challenge in Latin America* (Washington: American Enterprise Institute, 1986).

12. Ernest Evans, "Revolutionary Movements in Central America: The Development of a New Strategy," in Wiarda, ed., *Rift and Revolution,* and, in revised form, in Falcoff and Wiarda, eds., *The Communist Challenge.*

13. Wiarda, "Soviet Policy in the Caribbean and Central America: Opportunities and Constraints," in Falcoff and Wiarda, eds., *The Communist Challenge.*

14. An assessment, by the author, is "Aftermath of Grenada: The Impact of the U.S. Action on Revolution Prospects in Central America," in Herbert Ellison and Jiri Valenta, eds., *Grenada and Soviet/Cuban Policy, Internal Crisis and U.S. Intervention* (Boulder, Colo.: Westview Press, 1985).

15. Aaron Wildavsky, ed., *Beyond Containment: Alternative American Policies Toward the Soviet Union* (San Francisco: Institute for Contemporary Studies, 1983).

16. Robert Kennedy and Gabriel Marcella, "U.S. Security on the Southern Flank: Interests, Challenges, Responses," in James R. Greene and Brent Scowcroft, eds., *Western Interests and U.S. Policy Options in the Caribbean Basin* (Boston: Oelgeschlager, Gunn and Hain, for the Atlantic Council, 1984) pp. 187–242.

17. For a full discussion see Wiarda, "The Paralysis of Policy."

18. See the discussion of the former American commander in El Salvador, Colonel John Waghelstein, in "Post Vietnam Counterinsurgency Doctrine," *Ft. Leavenworth Military Review,* May 1985.

19. These changes are analyzed in a forthcoming book by the author, tentatively entitled *Finding Our Way? Toward Maturity in U.S.–Latin American Relations* (Washington: American Enterprise Institute, 1986).

20. See the *Report of the President's National Bipartisan Commission on Central America* (New York: MacMillan, 1984), as well as Wiarda, ed., "U.S. Policy in Central America: Consultant Papers for the Kissinger Commission," special issue of *AEI Foreign Policy and Defense Review* 5, No. 1 (1984).

21. For discussion, see George F. Kennan (writing as 'X'), "The Sources of Soviet Conduct," *Foreign Affairs* 25 (July 1947); John Lewis Gaddis, "Containment: A Reassessment," *Foreign Affairs* 55 (July 1977), pp. 873–87; Eduard Mark, "The Question of Containment: A Reply to John Lewis Gaddis," *Foreign Affairs* 56 (January 1978), pp. 430–40; Charles R. Wolf, Jr., "Beyond Containment: Redesigning American Policies," *Washington Quarterly* 5 (Winter 1982), pp. 107–17; Louisa S. Hulett, "Containment Revisited: U.S.-Soviet Relations in the 1980s," *Parameters* 14 (Autumn 1984), pp. 51–63; Barry R. Poser and Stephen Van Evera, "Defense Policy and the Reagan Administration: Departure from Containment," *International Security* 8 (Summer 1983), pp. 3–45; Robert W. Tucker, "In Defense of Containment," *Journal of Contemporary Studies* 6 (Spring 1983), pp. 29–49; and K. N. Lewis, "Reorganizing U.S. Defense

Planning to Deal with New Contingencies: U.S.-Soviet Conflict in the Third World," (Santa Monica: RAND Corporation, 1982).

22. The analysis in this paragraph follows closely the similar conclusion of G. Pope Atkins, "U.S. Policy in Central America: International Conditions and Conceptual Limitations," paper presented at the Annual Convention of the International Studies Association, Washington, DC, 8 March 1985.

23. Further details on what I have termed a "prudence model" of US policy in Latin America are presented in Wiarda, *In Search of Policy*, chap. 8. For an analytic discussion that places this strategy in the context of other alternative views, see Harold Molineu, "Latin American Politics and the U.S. Connection," *Polity* 18 (Fall 1985), pp. 167–75.

24. For a full discussion, see Wiarda, *Ethnocentrism in Foreign Policy: Can We Understand the Third World?* (Washington: American Enterprise Institute, 1985).

Part Four

Containment's Future

25
Containment in a New Era

Donald S. Zagoria

D ESPITE THE DOUBTS OF MANY, in power and out, the fact is
that the West has been extremely successful in containing
Soviet power during the past forty years. And much of that success can be attributed to remarkable men such as George
Kennan, Dean Rusk, Clark Clifford, Eugene Rostow, Alex
Johnson, Walt Rostow, and others who were gathered at the National Defense University for the conference on "Containment
and the Future."

Moreover, there is no reason why we should not continue
to be successful in the years ahead, when we will be faced with
a continuing Soviet challenge, though under quite different circumstances. But if we are to be successful in containing Soviet
power, we will have to avoid the counsels of both extremes in
the United States: those who allege that containment is too
passive, who oversimplify and exaggerate the Soviet challenge,
who regard every negotiation and every agreement with

Donald S. Zagoria is Professor of Government at Hunter College and the
Graduate Center of the City University of New York. He is also a Fellow at
the Harriman Institute for Advanced Study of the Soviet Union at Columbia
University.

Moscow as a sign of weakness; and those who fear that containment is too dangerous in a nuclear age, who minimize the Soviet challenge, who long for an end to the competition, and who
rationalize and explain every Soviet advance.

People who know the Soviets best have no doubt that they
are a formidable adversary, determined to alter in their favor
what they call the "correlation of forces." The Chinese call the
Soviets "hegemonists" with a "southern strategy" designed to
outflank Europe. The North Koreans—when they were freer to
speak their minds—called the Russians "dominationists."
Seweryn Bialer talks of the "unrelenting drive of the Soviet
leaders to sustain and advance Soviet power in the global
arena," and he and many others speak of the insatiable Soviet
appetite for "total security."[1] Zbigniew Brzezinski calls Soviet
global strategy a "unique organic imperialism" sprung out of
territorial insecurity.[2] Hans Morgenthau would call them "imperialist" because they are dissatisfied with the existing distribution of power in the world.[3] We would be wise not to ignore
these assessments.

The Soviets are not only an expansionist power, but they
are also highly secretive, relentless, and ruthless. With a
younger, more stable leadership, and global military reach, they
could be even more formidable in the years ahead.

To be sure, as Kennan noted, we ourselves face a variety
of challenges, from the environment to the deficit, in addition to
that of the Soviet Union. But no American president has been
able to escape from the Soviet challenge even though several
have tried.

There is no question but that the containment of Soviet expansion will remain the proper strategy for the United States in
dealing with the Soviet Union, and that it will be necessary far
into the future. Such a containment strategy is not incompatible
with arms control or limited detente or even cooperation on
some issues of common concern. But the Soviet Union is and
will remain our most important challenger. And in many ways it

is a stronger and far more effective challenger than it was twenty or thirty years ago.

The nature of the containment problem has changed because the world has changed. The real question we should be asking is how to adapt the containment strategy to the new global environment of the 1980s and beyond. Containment I was successful from 1945 to 1985 because it confronted the challenge of restoring the balance of power shattered by World War II. If Containment II is to be successful, it will have to confront the new problems of growing Soviet military power and power projection, regional conflicts, Third World instability, and chronic Soviet opportunism designed to alter important regional balances in their favor.

Containment I: Reasons for Success

By the 1960s, the three pillars of Containment I were already in place. First, there was a continuing US diplomatic and military presence on the Eurasian continent and a NATO alliance of free nations committed to checking Soviet expansion. Second, there was a strong and resurgent Europe. Third, there was an independent China. I would add a fourth element: an economically strong and dynamic Japan allied to the United States. By the 1970s, there was added to these factors the success of many of the NICs, or newly industrializing countries, particularly in Asia, so that by the end of the seventies the Asia-Pacific region had become our principal trading partner and, alongside Europe, an important second zone of US strategic influence. All of this ensured the success of Containment I. The Soviet Union was unable to dominate any of the major power centers in North America, Europe, or Asia, and the balance of power shattered by World War II was restored on terms highly favorable to the West.

In addition to these critical factors accounting for the success of Containment I, I would add a few others. Crude and counterproductive Soviet behavior has been one of the West's best allies. To a considerable extent, the Soviet Union has contained itself. From the Korean War to the Berlin blockade to the shooting down of an unarmed Korean airliner, and from Poland to Afghanistan, crude Soviet actions have helped to galvanize the West and drive many countries closer to the United States. As a result of the war unleashed by North Korea with Soviet acquiescence, the US defense budget tripled or quadrupled. Similarly, the Soviet invasion of Afghanistan led to six or seven years of steady increases in the US defense budget. Soviet military pressure on the Chinese border and on the territories disputed with Japan has been partly responsible for driving both China and Japan closer to the United States. And the Soviet-supported Vietnamese invasion of Cambodia has unified the noncommunist countries of Southeast Asia (ASEAN) behind Thailand and prevented the further expansion of Soviet influence in that important region.

Another important factor has been the declining appeal of the Soviet model for a centrally planned economy. Both inside and outside the communist world, the limits of the Stalinist model of economic development are highly visible. Everywhere in the communist world, economic reform is on the agenda. In China, that reform has already gone quite far, and China's "open door" policy has potential consequences that no one can yet fully foresee. China's reform has even had an important impact on North Korea and Vietnam, and it is bound to have an influence throughout the Third World.

Another factor accounting for the success of Containment I has been the Soviet Union's difficulty turning influence into control, especially in regions far removed from it geographically. Despite arms supplies, friendship treaties, and the Cuban-Yemeni-North Korean-East European "international brigade," the Soviet Union is still a long way from controlling any of its key Third World clients such as Syria, India, and Iraq. And it still lacks much influence in other important Third World states like Egypt, Saudi Arabia, Iran, Indonesia, and Nigeria.

The Soviet Union is engaged in an experiment, trying to turn influence into control in the smaller Marxist-Leninist states (such as Angola, Afghanistan, Nicaragua, and Ethiopia) through the formation of "vanguard communist parties," which it hopes will subordinate themselves to Moscow. But the prospects for this happening outside of nearby Afghanistan are not very bright. Indeed, as Jerry Hough points out, recent Soviet writing includes quite a number of pessimistic arguments that most of the alleged Marxist states in the Third World are unstable and unable to build "socialism" because of their backward conditions; in addition, they represent a huge drain on Soviet resources.

The best strategy for Third World countries to adopt, moreover, is not one of "leaning to one side" in the superpower rivalry. Rather, it is one of balancing between the superpowers in order to obtain the favors of both. China is now playing this game more effectively than ever before, and India looks like it may move in this direction under its new prime minister, Rajiv Gandhi.

Finally, Containment I was successful because China became not only independent but actively opposed to Soviet expansion, particularly in Asia, where it continues to support the resistance in both Afghanistan and Cambodia. As China becomes stronger under the impetus of its four modernizations, it will be in a position to resist Soviet expansion in Asia even more effectively.

Containment II: The Challenges

When we turn from the success of Containment I to the problems we face in containing Soviet expansion in the future, the picture is more complex. The most disturbing new elements in the picture are, first, the enormous growth of the Soviet military, particularly its power projection capabilities; second, regional conflicts, such as the Arab-Israeli conflict, and the chronic instability in the Third World which the Soviets ceaselessly seek to exploit; third, growing divisions within the Western alliance about how to deal with the Soviets; and finally, the breakdown of the US domestic foreign policy consensus which characterized the critical part of the early postwar period.

About the growth of Soviet military power, there is little to add to what is or should be widely known. The Soviets have built an impressive array of military capabilities for every conceivable contingency. Moscow considers its achievement of nuclear parity with the United States as its single most important accomplishment of the postwar period, one that has sobered the "imperialist world" and made it reluctant to intervene in various local conflicts. The Soviets are determined to attain not only nuclear parity on the global scale, but what they call parity in the European and Asian theaters as well. A Soviet general recently told an American academic that the Soviet Union was determined to have "parity" in Asia, a region where it is well behind in the overall "correlation of forces," indicating that the Soviets are very much aware of the importance of military power in determining regional balances.

It is in this context that we must view the Soviet deployment of SS–20s in Europe and Asia, the recent modernization of Soviet air and naval capabilities in the Pacific, the permanent Soviet naval deployments in the Indian Ocean and the South China Sea, and the indications that the Soviets have begun to build large aircraft carriers. The global balance of power is now determined to a considerable extent by regional balances. We will have to pay more attention to this phenomenon, because the Soviets will ceaselessly try to use military and other forms of power to alter these balances in their favor.

It is in the Third World that the Soviet challenge is likely to be most serious during the coming years. The main Soviet challenge to the West now and for the foreseeable future is not that Moscow is likely to launch a direct attack on the United States or its allies, but rather that it is determined to exploit global turbulence in order to weaken the United States and to expand its own interests. The Soviet Union, in other words, is a scavenger of global instability.

Moscow seeks global status neither by head-on nuclear war—which is too dangerous—nor by peaceful socioeconomic competition—for which it is unfit to compete. As Brzezinski says, the only way open to it is "that of attrition and gradual disruption of stable international arrangements so that the U.S. suffers directly and indirectly. The most effective way of pursuing such a strategy of disruption is to achieve and maintain sufficient military power to deter U.S. reactions and to intimidate U.S. friends in those strategically vital areas which possess the greatest potential for a dynamic shift in the global balance."[4] These areas are, of course, the Middle East, the Persian Gulf, and Southwest Asia. Moreover, the Soviets are bound to have increasing opportunities in the Third World in the years ahead. The pressures of growing population, massive social, economic, and political inequality, and growing literacy are likely to contribute to radicalism, fundamentalism, and other anti-Western ideologies.

I am particularly concerned with what Gregory Massell calls the suicide of the pro-Western oligarchs. In Vietnam under Thieu, Iran under the Shah, Nicaragua under Somoza, and now the Philippines under Marcos, the collapse or threatened collapse of pro-Western authoritarian governments has had or threatens to have grave consequences for the West. The victory of a radical nationalist or Marxist element in the Philippines and the ejection of the United States from its important naval and air bases at Subic and Clark would profoundly change the psychological, and therefore the strategic, situation in the Pacific. Similarly, the radicalization of Egypt or Indonesia could dramatically alter the situation in other key regions. Yet anti-Americanism is growing in the Middle East. And even in such a staunch ally as South Korea, a substantial number of students are receptive to Marxist and neo-Marxist theories of "dependency."

The situation on our doorstep is also alarming. The Mexican population is doubling every eighteen years or so, and it is a real question whether this phenomenon, combined with the debt problem and other pressures, will not eventually lead to an explosion. Were the United States to be confronted with a hostile Mexico and a hostile Central America, our own strategic situation would change markedly.

Even if we are relatively fortunate, and anti-Western movements in the Third World do not grow, the Soviets are likely to have increasing opportunities for political advance even among the more moderate states. Because they are losing faith in the United States as a friend and protector, and because they are losing hope that the Reagan administration has the will or the skill to play honest broker between Arabs and Israel, many moderate Arab states are already edging away from the United States and making overtures to the radical Arab camp, to Europe, and to the Soviet Union. Many of these moderate Arab states see current US policy as one of general neglect of their interests. In the Persian Gulf, Oman and the United Arab Emirates have already established diplomatic ties with Moscow, and Jordan has said that it will have to consider buying arms from the Russians if it cannot get them from the United States.[5]

Containment II: A Strategy

In sum, the Third World is the "weak link" of the West, and any strategy for Containment II will have to come to terms with this fact. Such a strategy will require a mix of many elements. As Sir Francis Pym suggests, there ought to be an increasing transfer of economic resources to the Third World. There also needs to be increasing pressure for economic and political reform there. We must have a better early warning system for signs of growing unpopularity of pro-Western governments. And when the warning sounds, we must take early action, not wait for crises to occur. If the radicals win, the United States should try to come to terms with them when this is possible. When it is not, we should support the opposition. Of course, the

use of our power needs to be discriminating, and there are limits
on our ability to influence such situations. But often that influence can be far from negligible.

Finally, we need a strategy to promote regional integration.
As Akira Iriye points out, the problem of containment in Asia is
essentially one of fostering regional stability through integration. We should nourish ASEAN and seek to foster regional organizations and institutions elsewhere. To paraphrase Peter Jay,
good regionalism is good containment.[6] Where there is effective
regionalism there will be fewer opportunities for predatory outside powers like the Soviet Union to exploit regional conflicts.

A third problem for Containment II is the growing difference within the Western alliance over how to cope with the Soviet Union. It is virtually impossible these days to hear a
European, even a conservative European, talk about the Soviet
Union in the same way as a conservative American. Within
Europe, important elements in the Social Democratic Party of
Germany and the Labor Party of England are calling for withdrawal from NATO. All of this is bound to stimulate Soviet ap-
petites, and the Russians are likely to step up their efforts to
split the Western alliance. It was, as the Soviets say, "no accident" that the new Soviet leader, Mikhail Gorbachev, met with
French President Mitterand on the eve of his meeting with President Reagan and sought to get Mitterand to sign a joint condemnation of the US Strategic Defense Initiative.

Finally, there is the problem of the lack of a foreign policy
consensus at home for dealing with the Soviet Union. An important reason why we were successful in Containment I was
that, for most of the early postwar period, we had a bipartisan
foreign policy. If we are to be successful in Containment II, we
will have to develop some procedures for institutionalizing
bipartisanship. Some sensible suggestions have been made for
how to accomplish this goal. Why, for example, could it not become standard practice for incoming presidents to appoint secre-
taries of state and defense who are broadly acceptable to both

major parties? It might also be advisable to have a permanent bipartisan commission on the Soviet Union attached to the National Security Council. Such a commission could be charged with fashioning a bipartisan policy toward Moscow. The model for such a group would be the Scowcroft Commission, which was able to articulate a strategic weapons policy that was broadly acceptable. It will also be important for each president to develop a close working relationship with the leaders of the opposition party in the Congress.

Containment II: The Outlook

Despite the rather serious problems we face in the era of Containment II, I remain cautiously optimistic that we will be successful. Part of the reason for this confidence is that the United States has now reversed its military decline of the 1970s. The other reason for my confidence has to do with the flawed nature of Soviet power. Taken together, I think these factors signify that the late 1980s and the 1990s are not likely to be a promising decade for the Soviet Union in its drive to become an effective challenger to the United States.

First, the trends in the strategic competition are becoming increasingly unfavorable for Moscow. A series of US strategic modernization programs—the MX, perhaps the "Midgetman," the new, more accurate Trident missiles, the revived B–1 bomber, the advanced technology (Stealth) bomber, the Pershing II, as well as ground-, sea-, and air-launched cruise missiles—will soon enhance the American nuclear arsenal. Moreover, as Arnold Horelick has pointed out, "superior U.S. technology in such areas as sensors, computers, computer programming, signal processing and exotic kill mechanisms being harnessed in connection with President Reagan's Strategic Defense Initiative is bound to increase Soviet anxiety about the possible shape of the strategic balance in the years ahead."[7]

Second, the Soviet Union faces severe economic and social stagnation at home. Some Soviet specialists describe it as a systemic crisis, but it is important to understand its true nature. It is not a crisis of survival. The Soviet economy is not going to fall apart; there is not going to be a new Russian revolution. But there is a crisis of efficiency; and some Soviet intellectuals have been warning that, if present trends are not soon reversed, the "Polish disease"—disaffection within the working class—could spread to the Soviet Union.

The new Soviet leader, Mikhail Gorbachev, has suggested that the Soviet Union, unless it improves its technology and economic productivity, may not be able to maintain its present strategic position in competition with the West, a point Dimitri Simes makes as well. In a brutally frank report delivered on 10 December 1984, three months before he became General Secretary of the Soviet Communist Party, Gorbachev attributed the "slowdown of growth in the late 1970s and early 1980s" to the "stagnant retention" of "outmoded production relations." He warned that the ills of the system were of "truly tremendous scale" and that it would be a "titanic task" in terms of innovation and complexity to deal with them. What was at stake, he concluded, was nothing less than the need to make sure that the Soviet Union could "enter the new millenium worthily, as a great and flourishing power." And, in an unusually candid admission, he conceded that because of Soviet economic failures, the West was winning not only the economic and technological race, but the ideological competition as well. As recently as 11 June 1985, Gorbachev added to this dire warning. He said that "urgent measures" were required to improve the economy because he could not cut social programs or reduce defense expenditures in the face of the "imperialist threat." He may yet be forced to do one or the other.

Declining trends in the strategic competition and severe economic difficulties at home are not Gorbachev's only problems. The Soviet Union is still bogged down in Afghanistan, and it faces a continuing crisis in Poland. Elsewhere in Eastern Europe, its economically hard-pressed satellites want greater independence and increased trade with the West. Some of them want to experiment with Chinese- and Hungarian-type economic reforms. A harshly worded *Pravda* article on 21 June 1985 has reacted to these developments by warning Eastern Europe of the dangers of "revisionism" and even of "Russophobia."

Trends outside the empire are no more reassuring. In the Far East, the Soviet Union is increasingly "odd man out." In Europe, despite clumsy Soviet efforts to prevent the deployment of the Pershing IIs and cruise missiles, the deployments have proceeded on schedule. In the Persian Gulf, Iran has halted its natural gas deliveries to the Soviet Union and continues to broadcast revolutionary Islamic propaganda to Moscow's Muslim republics. Meanwhile, Iraq has been establishing closer economic ties with the West. In the Third World more broadly, Moscow faces armed insurgencies in almost all of its desperately poor client states. Finally, the American economy continues its recovery and President Reagan has launched the most sustained US military buildup since World War II.

None of this means that Gorbachev is going to opt out of the international competition with the United States. But the problems he faces are formidable and deep-rooted; they cannot be solved quickly. It could take a decade or more just to begin a turnaround in the ailing Soviet economy.

Do these developments mean that Gorbachev will want a long period of calm in relations with the United States while he concentrates on his internal and imperial problems? We should find out if this is in fact the case, and we need to test Soviet intentions to do so. Of course, we should have no illusions about a return to detente. The rivalry between the superpowers will continue. But while we continue our necessary efforts to contain Soviet power, there may be an opportunity for arms control and for some easing of tensions, as called for by Alton Frye. Under the present circumstances, this is the best we can hope for. But it is not insignificant, and we must let neither visions of the ideal nor fears of the unreal inhibit whatever progress an imperfect world may allow.

Notes

1. "Andropov's Burden: Socialist Stagnation and Communist Encirclement," address to the Twenty-fifth Annual Conference, International Institute for Strategic Studies, 8 September 1983, Ottawa, Canada.

2. "The Soviet Union: World Power of a New Type," ibid.

3. "Imperialism," chap. 5 in *Politics Among Nations,* 5th Revised Edition (New York: Alfred A. Knopf, 1978), pp. 48–76.

4. "The Soviet Union: World Power," IISS address.

5. *The Wall Street Journal,* 24 December 1985.

6. Peter Jay, "Regionalism as Geopolitics," *Foreign Affairs, America and the World 1979* 58 (No. 3, 1980), pp. 485–514.

7. Arnold Horelick, "The Return of Arms Control," *Foreign Affairs, America and the World 1984* 63 (No. 3, 1985), p. 527.

26

Socio-Cultural Imperatives for a New Containment Policy

James H. Billington

A LMOST EVERY SERIOUS OBSERVER says that the United States needs a steady, rational policy toward the USSR in order both to avoid miscalculation on the Soviets' part and to sustain unity among our allies. Yet the oscillations in US policy toward the USSR have continued and perhaps increased in the two decades since the fall of Khrushchev. Whereas the Soviet Union has consistently had a foreign policy far more effective than its basic system, just the opposite is true of America. As a society, America has experienced continuing growth and re-markable dynamism—without, however, finding an effective foreign policy.

Although each of the three most recent chief American policymakers has displayed certain strengths in dealing with the Soviets, each has also encountered difficulties. Nixon developed both a new relationship with China as a check against Soviet power and a framework for negotiating directly with Soviet leaders. Yet detente may have encouraged the American public

James H. Billington is Director of the Woodrow Wilson International Center for Scholars and Chairman of the Advisory Committee to the graduate program at the Georgetown University School of Foreign Service.

to expect too much, and it failed either to provide real incentives for Soviet restraint or to project higher ideals to the post-Stalinist generation.[1] Carter's human rights emphasis projected such an ideal; but his contradictory signals interrupted the continuity of the negotiating process with the Soviet leaders, and the SALT treaty he *did* negotiate could not be sold domestically after the invasion of Afghanistan.

If the net effect of the Nixon-Ford era was to heighten the Soviet elite's sense of condominial self-importance, the net effect of the Carter policies was to make the Soviet leaders angrier at (though not more afraid of or deterred by) their American adversary. Reagan, by institutionalizing the increased defense effort of the late Carter years and adding the Strategic Defense Initiative, or SDI, has introduced an element of genuine fear into the Soviet leadership while sustaining the human rights emphasis. He may have made long-range gains by indirectly encouraging forces for change within the rising generation of Soviets, but the initial stridency of his challenge created short-term problems for American policy by stimulating nationalistic elements in the Soviet population to support militaristic policies.

The Soviet-American Relationship

To determine how best to undertake the difficult task of developing constructive new initiatives, we need to examine afresh the basics of how the USSR in fact relates to the United States. Neither the Russian Empire nor the USSR has ever been at war with the United States. Relations in the eighteenth and nineteenth centuries were distant, but generally amicable. Even today the USSR does not pose to the United States a direct geopolitical threat of the classic kind—a threat of conquest or direct intimidation from a contiguous power. The USSR poses, rather, a special, complex threat deriving from its unique if varying capacity to—

  (1) Destroy the United States directly in minutes or hours with missiles and nuclear weapons;

(2) Reduce the United States to vassalage in a matter of months or years, by establishing geopolitical dominance of Eurasia through conventional attack and imperial politics; or

(3) Bleed us to death and eventually reduce us to vassalage over the next few decades by becoming an increasingly dominant force in the Third World.

With such awesome *capabilities,* the classic question of Soviet *perceptions* and *intentions* becomes even more important. The new political generation in the USSR will have difficulty scaling back the heightened political expectations its predecessor has built up along with its military arsenal during the last two decades; and the risk of reaching a point of no return on the way to war is aggravated by the radically different ways in which Soviet and American leaders perceive reality.

This perception gap is *not,* I believe, greatest in that area most immediately menacing to both the USSR and the United States: the nuclear missile face-off (threat number 1 above). Both sides have a rational grasp of the basic nuclear facts and dangers, which can be perceived in both statistical and visceral ways that transcend cultural or ideological blinders. The perception gap is almost certainly much greater in the area of potential geopolitical dangers to our Eurasian allies (threat number 2 above). There is a tendency, rooted deep in Russian history, for Soviet leaders genuinely to perceive as defensive the kinds of aggressive action or preemptive threat that seem clearly offensive to us and our allies.

But the area in which the perception gap may be widest—and the risk of real war greatest—is in the unallied and turbulent two-thirds of the globe we call the Third World (threat number 3 above). There is a radically different perception not just of the facts at issue in the Third World but also of the forces at work and the basic legitimacy of outside involvements. Ironically (but perhaps mercifully), the danger of war is almost certainly greatest in that area of threat in which there is the least direct and immediate danger to the two superpowers and the greatest chance of avoiding their automatic involvement. But, for precisely these seemingly reassuring reasons, we may continue to neglect this crucial area of danger—and the perception gap may continue to widen, even as Soviet involvement deepens and the number of proxies and potentially uncontrollable independent actors increases.

An important if elusive factor in Soviet-American relations is the peculiarity of national psychology on both sides. Particularly important are the quite different ways in which each of these multiethnic, continent-wide civilizations on the periphery of Europe feels itself to be different from traditional European powers and, in fact, unique in the world. To oversimplify, Russians tend to feel uniquely persecuted and long to be respected; Americans tend to feel uniquely favored and wish to be loved. The Puritan Anglo-Saxon base of America infused its public culture with a sense of respect for the individual based on law, but left the culture with an awkwardness about public manifestations of love; the Orthodox Russian base of Soviet culture provided communal love in almost embarrassing excess, but was weak in conferring individual self-respect in the public realm.

As their global reputations slipped in the course of the 1970s, each country turned to a new leader who spoke to these special needs. In Andropov, the USSR produced a specialist in persecuting its internal opposition from an institution, the KGB, that commanded awesome respect; in Reagan, America produced a specialist in communicating its sense of national favor using the techniques of an institution, the cinema, that inspires confidence based on affection. Revived nationalism in each superpower added in turn to the difficulty each experienced in communicating with the other, while generating a certain restiveness in Eastern as well as Western Europe among allies who find it difficult to understand their respective dominant powers.

Soviet attitudes toward the United States derive in important ways from the historical attitudes of Russian leaders toward the West. Those attitudes include tendencies to see the West as a unitary enemy dedicated to exploiting Russia, but one which is morally weak and politically divisible. At the same time, there is the well-known sense of Russian inferiority, combined with a certain love-hate dependence on the USSR's principal Western adversary. Many of these attitudes result from the fact that Russia does not have a secure sense of its own cultural identity, has repeatedly been attacked from both East and West, and has for much of its history lacked clear external boundaries or well-defined internal civil procedures. The United States has replaced the Germany of the late nineteenth and early twentieth centuries (and the France of the late eighteenth and early nineteenth centuries) as the essential "West" that Russians must both publicly confront and privately learn from.

There are, then, very deep cultural difficulties in US-USSR communication, differences reinforced by the Reagan administration's focus on redressing the strategic military balance. Such US action may be necessary to check the Soviet leaders' inertial belief that they could continue to make foreign policy gains free of cost. But projecting power in missiles and space programs risks revalidating to the Russian people precisely the image of a hostile West seeking material predominance that they so love to hate.

Opportunities for a More Sophisticated Approach

Although we have as yet little experience with Mikhail Gorbachev, it is at least clear that the new generation of leadership in the USSR is committed to far-reaching economic changes. These, in turn, could lead (albeit unintentionally) to dramatic changes in the Soviet political system. The objective need for systemic economic reform legitimizes demands for change within the political oligarchy; and the cumulative effect of massive deferred maintenance at a time of domestic economic stagnation will make it increasingly clear that projected economic targets cannot be met without systemic change.

Sociologically, there is an almost unimaginable contrast in basic formative influence between Soviet leaders of the past twenty years and those of the next twenty. The generation of Brezhnev-Andropov-Chernenko was formed in the Stalin era of massive purges, violent social upheaval, and world war, whereas that of Gorbachev grew up in the postwar, post-Stalinist era of unprecedented peace and (by Soviet standards) rising prosperity and educational levels.

Finally, this volatile socioeconomic context is politically energized by the intensity and depth of the striving (begun during the 1960s and 1970s within the nonpolitical educated population) to continue the artificially arrested process of de-Stalinizing the USSR, in order to satisfy the thirst both for more efficiency and for a non-Stalinist Russian national identity. Although the dissident tip of the iceberg has been virtually eliminated since the repression began in 1979, there is a far larger, presently submerged mass of sentiment for serious reform within the establishment. A thirst for basic restructuring is evident in writings on a host of intellectual and social questions—and occasionally in direct reform proposals leaked to the press (such as the Novosibirsk documents). Indeed, the extremely protective way in which the geriatric Stalinist elite so long resisted bringing post-Stalinist leaders into top-level positions reflects—at least partly—the classical reactionary oligarchy's instinctive fear that, when both policy and personnel changes have been so long delayed, they are likely to be far-reaching.[2]

Given the continued militance of Soviet leaders on foreign policy, America faces the difficult task of speaking simultaneously both to outer power and to inner searching. Although the latter is largely concentrated among (though not confined to) the better-educated professional leaders, that group includes many of those exercising major line responsibility in the government and economy within the Gorbachev generation. This reality requires a much more clearly defined and differentiated dialogue with the USSR than we have yet had: tough and specific with the outer forces of power, but broad, exploratory, and even generous with the younger forces for innovation and change.[3]

Such a differentiated approach is not an easy order for a democratic society that always wants a simple, monolithic line of policy, preferably with a chronologically guaranteed outcome. But such a distinction is essential for a sustainable policy that will avoid either of two oversimplified but persistent American delusions about the USSR. The first is that liberalization is somehow built into the process of national development and should be helped along by more accommodating attitudes toward the present leaders. The second is that the Soviets' continuing hostility somehow reflects built-in historical characteristics of immutable Russian (or Bolshevik) attitudes, for which there is no remedy except continuous confrontation by external force. We must, in my view, clearly reject the implied determinism of either of these views and accept the element of instinctive insight in each.

In fact, Soviet leaders are hostile to us not primarily because of Russian history or even communist ideology, but because they are the political beneficiaries of one of the greatest state-committed atrocities of this century: Stalin's demonic purges of his own people in general and of the most talented political and intellectual leaders in particular. The Brezhnev-Chernenko generation compounded the crime by stopping Khrushchev's process of de-Stalinization, which might have opened up possibilities for modification of orthodoxy and creative innovation. The Gorbachev generation may not need to bear the guilt or perpetuate the paranoia of those whose careers were built on the genocidal policies of the 1930s, but their legacy will be difficult to shake.

The main hope of the surviving Stalinists for a full-blown transmission of their repressive form of rule to the next generation currently lies in their efforts to convince their subjects that now, as in the 1930s, there is a growing external danger so great as to justify a partial return to Stalinism. Particularly since the harshly repressive turn of 1979, Soviet leaders have increasingly been using the high Stalinist tactic of fanning domestic fears that "the West" threatens the identity—perhaps even the existence—of Russia itself. The recent blossoming of pictures of Stalin on Soviet automobiles indicates that the popular appeal of this seemingly repellent tactic may be greater than we like to think. As a result, there is at present both a need (because the old guard is actively fueling a growing chauvinistic mystique in the USSR) and an opportunity (because of the possibility of a different outlook among the successor generation) for important fresh American initiatives.

Priorities in Policy Objectives

To effectively move the USSR in a direction less threatening to the United States, any such initiatives must satisfy a daunting list of substantive and formalistic requirements:

(1) Substantively, the United States must check the Soviet external power thrust without providing material for the internal legitimation of the Stalinist oligarchs.

(2) At the same time, we must provide a message of rational hope for those interested in more basic structural reforms and positioned to push them forward.

(3) The *content* of US proposals must be dramatic and substantive enough to be widely perceived as serious even in the USSR.

(4) The *form* these proposals take must be sufficiently comprehensible within Russian culture and universal enough in tone that they will not be perceived as the prepackaged ultimatums of a rival culture.

This extremely difficult task has yet even to be attempted by American leaders. Many of the requirements are in obvious tension with each other. President Nixon had an instinctive feel for 3 and 4, but not for 1 and 2; Carter at various times stressed

1 and 2, but not 3 and 4. Reagan's concentration on 1 has raised the stakes, increasing both the danger and the opportunity for the United States. Can we—and, if so, how do we—further a strategic policy toward the USSR that is intrinsically constructive, presumptively sustainable in our own political system, and perceived as stable and "serious" by friend and foe alike?

A clear sense of what we really want of the USSR has always been missing from American foreign policy. The simple objective of containing Soviet external expansion is modest and inherently appealing. But it is, in the last analysis, a cop-out from dealing with a country whose external behavior results so largely from its ideology. Moreover, responsible American leadership has the right and obligation to try to help any nation capable of destroying us to develop moral and structural restraints against doing so. The Helsinki Final Act makes important parts of Soviet internal policy matters of formal international commitment by the Soviet government, and these human rights questions are an important part of the moral consciousness of the coming generation in the USSR.

Should we, then, act on the assumption that the USSR will not be capable of moderating its external behavior until the Soviet empire either transforms into something like a liberal democracy or disintegrates into a number of independent national entities? Such an assumption (which would have to be made explicit in our kind of society) would present the Soviet leadership—never more Great Russian than now—with what has historically been most difficult for Russians to accept: the external imposition of a foreign ideal. The more we presume to prescribe and proclaim our blueprint for their future, the more we encourage their reactionary xenophobia. American policy necessarily must focus primarily on modifying Soviet policies toward the *outside* world. But important changes are likely only if there is also evolution *within* the USSR. Important changes must be defined by Russians for Russians, not thought of by us as somehow representing imperfect approximations of ourselves.

There are, I think, three preliminary steps we must take in order to reach higher ground. They constitute both a logical sequence and a moral ordering of priorities. Each step depends on the preceding one for its effectiveness; each demands that we overcome currently fashionable illusions. We must find the courage to accept the full measure of responsibility we bear for preventing thermonuclear war, reducing the risks of any violent confrontation, and beginning to develop a new global agenda.

Preventing thermonuclear war is too serious a matter to be dealt with either by continuing business as usual or by simply proliferating token approaches. In view of the unprecedented nature of our accumulating destructive possibilities, bold pacifist gestures or unilateral moves toward disarming probably deserve more serious consideration than they usually get. It is not enough simply to answer "better red than dead" with "better neither than either." The deeper point is that becoming red is in fact more likely to lead to becoming dead. No wars have been more violent, no conflicts more bitter in the postwar era than those among communists (witness the Cambodian holocaust); and this reality is the logical fruit of a system that, as we noted above, produced the largest genocide that any political oligarchy has directed against its own people in modern history. In the welter of social science research on war, one fact is clear: democracies rarely fight democracies.

In preventing nuclear war there has, of course, been some record of success. Deterrence has kept thermonuclear peace for almost forty years. The greatest danger of nuclear war in the short term almost certainly comes from the possession of nuclear weapons by an insecure Soviet oligarchy free of all accountability to its own people. The priority task for preventing nuclear war at the present time thus still may be to make sure that the Soviet leaders believe in the reality of our deterrent power and will.

But if this task is necessary, it is emphatically not sufficient—and not just for the familiar reasons that accumulated weapons tend ultimately to be used, or that new delivery technologies may be destabilizing, or even that greater complexity and numbers of weapons means a heightened probability of accidents and breakdowns in command and control. The real danger is the growing tendency to make weapons the measure of everything else in international relations. Paradoxically, even those who focus on reducing, freezing, or otherwise creatively restructuring the arsenal may involuntarily complicate the problem. Even if adopted, such measures may amount only to technological carvings on the totem pole, symbolic actions that do not go to the heart of the main problem, which is the growing risk that other kinds of violent confrontation could involuntarily lead to nuclear war. Unless the unifying ideals for our own people transcend the ultimately materialistic ones of prosperity measured in productivity and security measured in weapons, our kind of civilization may subtly, unrecognizably become ever more fixated on the thermonuclear totem in a garrison state. America as we have known it will be in its terminal travails, the only real question being whether we end with a bang or a whimper—burning in space or freezing in place.

Reducing the risks of violent confrontation may well be the area of US-Soviet relations in which creative new initiatives can most immediately be taken. Serious American theologians are increasingly saying that vast nuclear arsenals can only be justified if the time during which war is deterred is used creatively to build the structure of a peace sustainable without them. This task can be advanced in at least four ways, each step moving ahead by building on the one before:

(1) Strategic arms talks with the USSR should increasingly focus directly on the final objective of eliminating *all* thermonuclear, chemical, and biological weapons. This objective cannot, of course, be immediately accomplished—but neither can the lesser objectives of most recent arms reduction talks. In this television age, a dramatic concentration on the ultimate objective would begin to suggest a ritual of shared renunciation rather than of rival totem worship.

(2) Our own conventional military forces should be built up in conjunction with our allies' so that the subnuclear geopolitical threat in Eurasia is minimized and a greater deterrent created against the Soviet Union's use of its conventional military strength for conquest or intimidation. This need argues for, among other things, conscription—perhaps as part of a national commitment for young Americans.

(3) Soviet authorities should be engaged in an institutionalized process to create "rules of the game" in the Third World that will lessen the risk of confrontation through proxy activities, arms shipments, or terrorism. The existence of such a process could subtly undermine that part of the Soviet bureaucracy that services a variety of subversive undertakings inherited from either Imperial Russia or the Communist International—and could help deter new Soviet "venture capital" investments in oversea movements that disrupt peaceful evolution or that directly threaten us.

(4) In the commercial and educational spheres, the United States should initiate a major new set of overtures to the emerging post-Stalinist generation. These programs should be aimed just below the high political level and structured so as to reach a broad cross-section of the emerging professional elites while avoiding the custody of the Moscow *apparatchiks* who now so dominate contacts with this country.

A final way to break the hypnotic fascination of the arms race (and the xenophobic conservatism it helps foster in the USSR) is to begin to develop a new global agenda, opening a multinational dialogue about what kind of world we want to see by the year 2000. Such a dialogue should be not just another intra-Western intellectual exercise in "globaloney," but an effort to involve the Soviets with Western leaders in a serious forum sufficiently remote from immediate policy issues to permit the Soviets to begin climbing off their outmoded ideology without asking them directly to reject it. A dialogue of this kind has the great advantage of being limitable to younger people who will themselves live in the twenty-first century.

We are in one of those rare periods when the USSR is facing long-deferred policy choices that could determine the Soviet course for the rest of this century. To hold their system together and give it fresh dynamism, they must infuse it either with new fear through repressive chauvinism or new hope with scope for incentives. Our policy must be to do all we can to further the latter possibility. Because the Soviets have difficulty taking initiatives in times of transition, we must take some. It is surely in our interest—as leaders of the free world who must provide vision and example to our friends—to do so boldly and comprehensively rather than reluctantly and piecemeal.

Global Values and the Soviet System

We can do more to help set a new agenda if we speak to the Soviets in terms that do not so much tout *our* particular institutions as affirm more *universal* values, values that could point to a variety of Russian futures less dominated by external threats. Freedom, for example, is a universal ideal in our time, but parliamentary democracy and private property may not be. The emergence in the USSR of a relatively autocratic system that nevertheless widens civic participation, human rights, and local control over productive forces would be conducive to greater concentration on domestic development rather than on the projection of global power. Changes of this kind would enable a new generation of Soviet leaders to follow the old Byzantine pattern of changing the *content* of their policy without changing the *form*—and thus avoid undergoing the cultural indignity of acknowledging a foreign model.

For the immediate future, we will need to remain tough and specific in our negotiations with the USSR, conveying continuing firmness to them while sustaining unity with our allies. But we may have more reason for hope about long-range change in the USSR now than in the immediate postwar period—not just for reasons of internal development, but also because of some surprising external ideological currents that may not leave even a relatively isolated Soviet society unaffected. I would mention only four, each of which suggests that history in the late twentieth century may move in new and unpredictable directions which are basically more compatible with the American than with the Soviet model. The latter has lost all its subjective appeal to anyone outside the Soviet Union who is free to make a choice, and these currents may even make the Soviet model objectively inadequate within the USSR itself by the end of the century.

The first of these four rather neglected currents of our time is replacement of revolution by evolution as the pattern of social change and source of political legitimation. It has always been a sloppy cliche, and may now be an anachronism, to say that we live in an age of revolution. The inventory of Leninist victories does not seem very impressive given the length of the postwar era, the extent of its disruptive change, and the size of the Soviet investment in subversion. This observation holds despite some successes in extremely authoritarian societies like Cuba, Ethiopia, and Nicaragua, and in the transition from the French colonialism in Southeast Asia and from the Portuguese in southern Africa.

The real dynamism in social, economic, and political development during recent years has lain in constructive evolution toward democracy rather than in destructive revolution leading to dictatorships. In Western Europe and Japan, South Asia, southern Europe, and South America, democratic evolution rather than totalitarian revolution has increasingly been the means of bringing dramatic change and fresh legitimation to stagnant societies. As the revolutionary fire burns itself out on peripheral killing fields, the Parisian establishment which first lit and long tended the flame has decisively turned away from it in one of the most dramatic of recent intellectual developments. As historians inventory the horrors perpetuated in the name of rival revolutionary ideologies, humanity seems increasingly inclined to look to evolution rather than revolution for fresh beginnings.

The most profound and perhaps prophetic challenge to a Soviet-type regime in Eastern Europe has come not from any revolutionary (or counterrevolutionary) elite driven by ideology but from a spontaneous popular movement in Poland calling not for power but for radical *evolutionary* change. The more likely model for radical evolutionary change in the Soviet Union is the Hungarian—probably as adapted by the Chinese, who, of course, turned to evolution as a specific alternative to, and repudiation of, the revolutionary spasm of the Cultural Revolution. Because of the Russian fascination with large-scale foes, China (like America) may have more potential as a hidden model than might otherwise seem logical.

A second powerful force in the world that is operating now in a way it was not in the immediate postwar period is the rising importance of education and communication within a far more sophisticated populace. The increase in the educated among peoples of the world may be a more portentous development than the global population explosion itself. Although deliverance via education is not automatic (as Nazi Germany reminds us), the spreading taste for unrestricted pursuit of truth powerfully challenges systems like the Soviets' that claim to encapsulate truth in state policy or a state newspaper.

A third force at work in the world that may seem almost the opposite of the preceding one is the return of the sacred, which seems strangely to advance along with the thirst for secular learning. Far from becoming irrelevant in our time of rapid modernization, religion has in many parts of the world become a resurgent part of that change. The most original and most unforeseen new developments of the last decade in the Third World and the communist world—respectively, the rise of Khomeini in Iran and Solidarity in Poland—were both examples of political movements deeply rooted in a prophetic monotheistic faith. Much of that which is genuinely innovative in the conservative politics of North America and the radical politics of Latin America can similarly be traced to religious sources. Once again, this may be a force that the Soviets can at times manipulate to their political advantage abroad, but not over the long term at home. The force of religion could provide a positive element within the otherwise ominous nationalist revival currently taking place in the USSR, with the 1988 millennium of Russia's conversion to Christianity possibly serving as a quiet catalyst.

A fourth force at work in the world is the widespread desire among peoples to assert their own cultural and ethnic uniqueness and identity, even at a time of increased technological interdependence. This development poses, of course, grave problems for the multinational Soviet imperium, but it also opens up new possibilities for productivity if the Soviet leaders can bring themselves genuinely to decentralize and to increase local autonomy.

In summary, then, if America can maintain Western unity and provide tough but not provocative leadership in the difficult times ahead, the Soviets might at last genuinely transform their system. George Kennan's forty-year-old prophecy might thus be fulfilled somewhat later and in a different way than originally anticipated—by a radical evolution drawing both on older Russian traditions and on recent outside experiences. Encouraging change will require a combination of toughness and imagination on our part, and a willingness for short-term sacrifice in the free world. Something might come of it that is presently unforeseen by either us or the Soviets, but which would draw them back from the dangerous international politics of the recent past. It would be ironic if, in the next century, those who have known what it was like to live without liberty come to value that old ideal more than those who simply took it for granted in this one.

Notes

1. There is a certain nostalgia now for the policies of the Nixon-Ford era—fueled by the articulateness of Nixon's return to public discourse, and by the enduring popularity of Ford and Kissinger. It is also to some extent a vehicle for expressing dissatisfaction with the policies of both Carter and Reagan. But, however one ultimately judges the Nixon-Ford policies, there does seem to have been an underlying illusion of condominium with the USSR that was bound to fall apart, both because it was based on nineteenth-century models not sustainable in this age and because the relative power of both superpowers vis-a-vis other rising forces in the world is steadily declining.

2. I described at length my reasons for believing in the strength and vitality (though not yet the political "clout") of this process of ferment within the USSR in an article in the *Washington Post*, 14 November 1982.

3. I argue for this distinction in another article in the *Washington Post*, 20 November 1983.

27
Containment and the Shape of World Politics, 1947–1987

Richard H. Ullman

CONTAINMENT—AS AN EXPLICIT, SELF-CONSCIOUS STRATEGY —was very much a product of the international environment of the early postwar era, when the United States enjoyed both unrivaled power and unrivaled standing in "the opinions of mankind." It was therefore scarcely surprising that Americans, like George Kennan, who gave such thought to the shape of the international system should see in this fortunate circumstance a way of containing the outward expansion of the only other member of the system capable of posing both a military and an ideological challenge.

Today, with military capabilities more diffused and pretensions to ideological ascendancy more subject to skeptical questioning, the goal of containing Soviet power within a given geographic sphere is more difficult to achieve. Nevertheless, containment survives as a strategy and, indeed, as the

Richard H. Ullman is Professor of International Affairs in the Woodrow Wilson School of Public and International Affairs, Princeton University.

organizing concept against which both US administrations and their critics measure quite disparate strands of foreign policy. Yet—as Kennan never tires of saying—precisely because the state system has proved to be so much more resilient than˙ it seemed in the 1940s, American policymakers can well afford to be more relaxed as they assess the ebbs and flows of Moscow's influence.

Kennan and the Shape of Europe

In fact, Kennan's famous 'X' article of 1947 gave little explicit attention to the shape of world politics, either as the international system existed at the time or as it might evolve over the coming decades. Neither is that surprising; Kennan's focus then was on "The Sources of Soviet Conduct," and by his reckoning that conduct was driven primarily by domestic imperatives. Soviet conduct could certainly be affected at the margin, however. Indeed, the margin—literally, the geographic borders between the Soviet empire and the non-Soviet world—was where Kennan would bring to bear "a policy of firm containment, designed to confront the Russians with unalterable counter-force at every point where they show signs of encroaching upon the interests of a peaceful and stable world."[1] For Kennan, the Soviet Union in 1947 was "by far the weaker party" compared to "the Western world in general." However, he worried that the United States might prove itself incapable of exercising sufficient moral leadership to hold the West together until the time when the amply apparent strains within Soviet society would "eventually find their outlet in either the break-up or the gradual mellowing of Soviet power."

An astute commentator has observed that, so far as he could discover, never once in a long career had Kennan "brought himself to pen the word 'superpower.' " That might be, Barton Gellman suggests, because Kennan has always disliked the notion of bipolarity, instead seeking a return to a multipolar balance of power such as the one prevailing before World War I.[2] Indeed, for him a central purpose of American foreign policy after World War II was the restoration of a balance of power in Europe and Asia. The basis for that balance had been shaken, if not shattered, by the war and the vacuum of power created by the defeat of Germany and Japan. To restore a balance, therefore, it would be necessary for the United States actively to assist in these nations' economic and psychological revival, together with that of the industrial democracies that had fought them, so that none of those centers of strength should fall under the domination of a power hostile to the United States—meaning the Soviet Union.

The purpose of containment, therefore, was to provide a shield behind which the societies of Western Europe and Japan could gather the physical and mental resilience necessary to resist communism. In 1947 and later, Kennan clearly regarded the Soviet threat as more political and psychological than military. He had no doubt that the United States was militarily superior to the USSR. It was not ravaged by war. Its economy was vastly more productive and its people more energetic. What concerned him, he said in the 'X' article and in many other forums, was whether Americans had the political and psychological maturity for a task that was both so demanding and at the same time so quotidian as the calm "exertion of steady pressure over a period of years."[3]

The decade that followed saw not only the restoration to economic and political health of these key industrial centers, but also their organization—largely but not entirely under US auspices—into an alliance aimed at containing Soviet power. Judged by any reasonable standards, the effort was quite successful—much more so, indeed, than many critics expressed at the time. Eastern Europe was "lost"; so, apparently, was China. But these geopolitical outcomes were very much the products of strategic choices made during the war; nothing within the power of US policymakers in the postwar years could have changed them.

As Kennan has reminded us ever since, however, the United States might have prevented the division of Germany.

But the Truman and Eisenhower administrations chose not to explore seriously Moscow's proposals regarding the possibility of trading Germany's unification for its demilitarization and neutralization. Rather than run the risk that the unified, neutralized German state might fall under Soviet influence and, eventually, control, they preferred instead to settle for the certain half loaf of a Federal Republic firmly embedded in the Western military alliance and economic community. This decision (in fact, a series of incremental decisions), more than any other that the West had it in its power to make, froze the postwar international system into the geopolitical shape that has endured until today. Once Germany was divided between communist and noncommunist states that were themselves not only the principal forward bastions for Soviet and American armed forces but also potent (if compliant) military powers in their own right, the division of Europe into two relatively rigid blocs was a foregone conclusion.

That division, in turn, has been one of the two dominant features of international politics since the late 1940s. Although the US-Soviet competition has been global and, especially over the last two decades, has seemed to be most intense in the various theaters of the Third World, it is Europe that has always been the ultimate prize. The line between East and West in Europe has been the focus of the two most powerful permanently stationed aggregations of military force ever assembled. Hypothetical European contingencies have shaped the military doctrines of the two superpowers and have been the major factors driving both the procurement and the deployment of weapons themselves. And while the spark that ignites armed conflict between Washington and Moscow may originate elsewhere, it will only find the forcing winds and the tinder that can fan it into World War III if it reaches Europe.

The Impact of Nuclear Weapons

The other dominant feature of the international political landscape has been the existence of nuclear weapons, the potential source of the most fearsome flames of war. Although not used in anger since 1945, nuclear weapons pose a menace that has been integral to the division of Europe and, indeed, to the rigidity of international politics. The division of Germany took place while the United States enjoyed a nuclear monopoly; although Soviet forces east of the Elbe considerably outnumbered American, British, and French forces in the Western occupation zones, one reason they chose against offering armed opposition to Western measures and programs was certainly the US possession of an atomic trump.

There is an important sense, it should be noted, in which nuclear weapons and the division of Europe are antithetic. Bloc formation is part of a classical pattern of collective security in which states join alliances in order to magnify their military power. Yet nuclear weapons make such blocs irrelevant. As nuclear superpowers, the United States and the Soviet Union do not need allies to safeguard the physical security of their homelands. Indeed, it is now generally accepted that, because Washington and Moscow need to extend security guarantees to their allies, the European alliances raise rather than reduce the risks the superpowers run. On the Western side, that problem is the essence of what has come to be called "NATO's nuclear dilemma"—how the United States can make credible its commitment to retaliate, with nuclear weapons if necessary, against either a nuclear or a massive conventional attack upon its European allies, when honoring such a commitment would likely bring down nuclear weapons on its own territory. For the Soviets, geographical proximity to their allies may make the dilemma less pointed, but it is nonetheless real.

NATO (and perhaps also the Warsaw Pact) has thus been rent by two contradictory impulses. One, coming especially from the United States, has been to raise the nuclear threshold so that the awful decision to use nuclear weapons might never have to be faced. That has meant struggling to find the economic resources and political will to field conventional forces capable of delaying a nuclear response to the outbreak of war long enough to reach a diplomatic resolution of the conflict. The second impulse, arising mainly from the Europeans, has been to question the worth of large expenditures on additional conventional forces, since any war in Europe is likely to be nuclear from the outset. This second position seems credible when one considers that (a) NATO could match Warsaw Pact conventional forces only with an enormous effort, (b) nuclear weapons will remain the real deterrent to war in any case, and (c) many Europeans would rather risk the low probability of nuclear war than do anything that might make it more likely that a war of any kind (even conventional) would be fought on their territory.

Thus, while nuclear weapons have obviously reinforced the dominant roles the United States and the Soviet Union have played within their alliances, they have also increasingly been a solvent that has unstuck the glue in once-tight relationships. Washington's allies ask themselves whether they are really more safe with US nuclear weapons on their territory or adjacent waters. (New Zealand is the most recent, but not the first, to answer that question in the negative. It is, however, the first to be threatened with ostracism by Washington.[4]) Moscow's allies are more mannerly than to voice objections to Soviet nuclear policy in public. It is known, however, that Czechoslovakia and East Germany, and no doubt Hungary and (although not directly affected) Romania, were unhappy with the Kremlin's decision to respond to NATO's 1983 deployment of intermediate-range nuclear forces (INF) in Western Europe with corresponding deployments in Eastern Europe.

China, of course, is the *cause célèbre* that exemplifies the corrosive effect of nuclear weapons on the Kremlin's alliances. The initial rift between Moscow and Beijing was caused by Soviet refusal to supply nuclear weapons technology at a time when the People's Republic felt threatened with a US nuclear attack and wanted its own retaliatory capability, not uncertain guarantees from an uneasy ally. Unlike Moscow's Eastern European allies, China could break away because of its sheer size and because no Soviet troops were stationed on its territory. It could therefore present the Soviets with a *fait accompli*.[5]

Scorekeeping in the Third World

During the early 1970s, when Richard Nixon and Henry Kissinger were shaping the agenda for American foreign policy, analysts were preoccupied with the question of whether the international system should still be regarded as bipolar. *Emergent* multipolarity was the term favored in the White House. We now know, however, that even with the qualifying adjective, the term was premature. During the intervening years the other potential centers of power—Western Europe, Japan, and China—have not gained in relative strength by comparison with the superpowers. Yet neither do we today have bipolarity of the kind that prevailed during the 1950s, when the United States and the USSR not only wielded predominant military power but also presided over much more unified blocs of allies. (Lack of unity may today seem more characteristic of Washington's alliances than Moscow's. But recall that analysts once routinely referred to the "Sino-Soviet bloc.") What we now have is an international system in which the two superpowers still possess preeminent military capabilities, but one in which they do not control events to anything like the extent they did a generation ago. And each—especially the United States, but also the Soviet Union—has considerably less ability to induce its allies to march to its drum, particularly when the route of the march leads "out of area," beyond the European theater in which each alliance prepares to confront the other.

Yet despite these changes in the structure of international politics, there has been strikingly little diminution in the pervasiveness of the "scorekeeper" mentality that has characterized both superpowers over the entire period since 1945. Each consistently behaves as if the defection of any state with which it has been aligned would be a blow to its security. That is obviously true, for good political and military reasons, regarding what might be called the core allies—NATO and Japan for the

United States, and the Warsaw Pact and (once) China for the
Soviet Union. But the superpowers have also behaved as if it
were true for states whose political alignment should matter
much less—for example, in recent years, Afghanistan and Central American states. In these instances, the military forces of
the states involved count for little. Afghan forces can contribute
nothing of significance to Soviet security, nor could they seriously threaten it. The same is true for US security and the combined military forces (not to mention those of any one state) of
Central America. In fact, it is arguable that even as bases for the
rival superpower these territories are overrated: in peacetime
they would be costly to supply and maintain; in the event of war
they could easily be neutralized; and the communications and
surveillance activities that might be conducted from them are
being carried on adequately from existing facilities nearby.

It is, however, the political consequences of possible de-
fections in these peripheral states that actually seem to worry
Moscow and Washington more than their practical effects. The
Soviets have never stated the motivations for their invasion of
Afghanistan, but high among them apparently was the fear that
if a fundamentalist Islamic regime ever came to power in Kabul
it would exercise a potentially destabilizing attraction on Soviet
Muslims across the border. That is, in fact, a not unreasonable
supposition. Certainly, it seems more reasonable than the assumptions that evidently underlie the Reagan administration's
policy in Central America—that Marxist-Leninist regimes
among the small, fragile states in the isthmus would exert a
falling-domino effect upon other Latin American states, or that
their coming to power would release a horde of refugees that
would beset our own borders.

The scorekeeper mentality has far more pernicious effects
on the United States than it does on the Soviet Union. That is
because ascribed wins and losses abroad—"Who lost Patagonia?" as William Bundy once put it[6]—become the stuff of our
competitive politics at home. And in order to gain popular and
congressional support for measures designed to prevent new

"losses," presidents explicitly make implementation of those measures a test of the credibility and reliability of the United States as an ally. Not surprisingly, foreigners—and foreign leaders—sometimes appear to take the presidents at their word. Thus when President Reagan asserts, as he so often does, "what happens in Latin America and the Caribbean will not only affect our nation but also will shape America's image throughout the world. If we cannot act decisively so close to home, who will believe us anywhere?" his message is played back, as it was last spring in a message to the US Congress from a group of well-known European conservatives: "If you fail in Nicaragua, we must ask, where will you fail next? If freedom and democracy are not worth defending in your own hemisphere, where are they worth defending?"[7]

This process is pernicious *not* because foreign friends and adversaries are likely to believe that a US administration's failure to draw a line in the sand of some Third World country means that it or its successors will fail to stand by a core ally under attack. Such perceptions do not seem widespread. For example, there is no evidence that US allies in Europe and Asia viewed Washington's "abandonment" of South Vietnam in 1975 as the start of a process of unraveling, and began to trim their own sails accordingly. Rather, they saw it as the end, at last, to a wasteful diversion of strength and effort away from those interests—assuming that US presidents once saw South Vietnam as a "vital interest"—that were "more vital" still. What *is* pernicious, however, is that American administrations and publics begin to believe their own rhetoric. Then the process of attempting to forestall revolutionary change in the name of containment becomes an undifferentiated goal that appears applicable everywhere, and by which Americans measure their own foreign policy performance. Stanley Hoffmann once observed that the appropriate metaphor for much of contemporary international relations was the labor of Sisyphus, whose endless effort to roll a gigantic rock uphill had long since ceased to have any meaning outside itself. The image seems especially appropriate for American foreign policy in the Third World.[8]

Moreover, the metaphor fits despite what is often cited as the greatest structural change in international power relationships since the basic shape of the postwar world order was set—the achievement by the Soviet Union over the last twenty-five years of a capability to project conventional military force rapidly over long distances. That capability is still not equal to that of the United States, but it is respectable. More important, it developed from virtually nothing. Yet it is striking how little difference to the course of events Moscow's new capability seems actually to have made. The standard list of Soviet interventionary successes includes Angola, where Soviet-supported Cuban troops installed a Marxist regime, and Ethiopia, where they saved one. Yet each involved a highly special set of circumstances—a situation approaching stateless anarchy in the first and a state repulsing an old-fashioned cross-border invasion in the second. In neither case did it seem remotely likely that the United States or its allies would introduce military forces of their own.

Except for these instances (indeed, even *in* these instances), Moscow has behaved with caution. Its apparent threat to send airborne troops to rescue the beleagured Egyptian Third Army Corps near the Suez Canal in 1973 evaporated when the Nixon administration placed US forces on worldwide alert. On perhaps three occasions it has provided clients with air defenses manned by Soviet personnel, but only when there was no likelihood that attacking aircraft would be American.[9] And although it has supplied a variety of clients on a variety of continents with weapons and military training, such efforts long predated and certainly have not been dependent upon the enhancement of Moscow's own interventionary capabilities. As an arms supplier, also, Moscow has acted cautiously—refusing, for example, to send to some clients weapons so advanced as to alter a regional balance or (as in the case of Nicaragua) to furnish Washington an excuse for attacking its client. Aside from the communist regimes of Eastern Europe, which have always depended for ultimate survival upon the threat of direct Soviet military intervention, the only other Soviet clients who may feel reasonably certain that Soviet forces will be at their side in substantial numbers if they are endangered are the regimes in Afghanistan and Vietnam—the former by virtue of physical proximity, the latter because it is threatened by China, not the United States. Even the Cubans, who have carried more than their share of Moscow's mail, know they will almost certainly have to fight alone if they get into a shooting war with Washington.

If American political leaders could only adopt a time horizon longer than four (or two!) years, they might find that they have every reason to take a more relaxed view of the Soviet threat to US interests in the Third World. In particular, they would not feel compelled to make every instance of Soviet involvement an explicit test of the credibility and reliability of the United States. To urge such a longer view is not to counsel complacence. But it is to recognize that many of the Third World regimes targeted by revolutionaries enjoying a greater or lesser degree of Soviet support have been so thoroughly weakened by their own previous domestic failures as to be able to remain in power only by means of massive repression, massive US assistance, or both. And it is to suggest that even revolutionaries who come to power with (or because of) Soviet support are unlikely to wish to be dependent upon Moscow afterward. America's experience with the People's Republic of China should teach that a supposed satellite beyond the Kremlin's direct reach is not likely to remain a satellite unless immediate enemies—especially the United States—impinge so directly upon it that its leaders see no alternative. Cuba under Fidel Castro would surely not have evolved into a liberal democracy, but its orientation might have been very different had US policy not made it dependent upon Moscow for economic survival.

Containing in the Third World

It is in this realm of US policy toward Third World revolutionary regimes that containment still presents questions rather than answers. In Europe and Northeast Asia the lines have been clearly drawn ever since George Kennan's time. What is at issue in these geographic zones are the methods that should be used by the United States, in conjunction with its allies, to respond to "traditional," overt border-crossing aggression. That is far from a trivial issue, involving as it does quite difficult questions about the kinds of military forces America's allies should buy, doctrines and strategies for conventional defense, the role of nuclear weapons, and so forth. But there is virtually no debate over what might constitute aggression or how responsibility for aggression might be determined. Nor is there any need for such a debate.

In the Third World, however, these are highly debatable questions, and the answers will not come easily. Indeed, it is unclear whether "aggression"—either through conventional military means or, as is much more likely, through the entire spectrum of activities that constitute unconventional warfare—might not define the range of impermissible behavior too narrowly. Certainly, it seems too narrow for the Reagan administration, which has on occasion expressed the view that even if revolutionary regimes like the Sandinistas "let their neighbors alone" they might nevertheless, merely by existing in their present form, still destabilize their regions. And if questions such as these are unresolved, so also are ones regarding the means by which containment should be pursued.

In dealing with such matters, the United States now finds itself often quite alone. That is one result of a far-reaching structural change in the international system—the coming to independence since 1960 of the great majority of states that were once colonies of the European powers. Rich and powerful among the poor and weak, the United States has increasingly been on the losing end of lopsided votes in international forums. However, in questions involving political change in the Third World, the United States often finds itself estranged not only from the Third World majority but also from its principal allies.[10]

Here is a profound departure from what might be called orthodox containment. For from being able to orchestrate coherent
counterpressure to what it assesses to be Soviet expansionism,
the United States often has great difficulty in persuading its allies that in a given instance there is even a need for action. Differences in analysis began with the Vietnam War, when
successive administrations in Washington were unable to convince the allies to accept their diagnoses of the nature of the
conflict, of the stakes involved for the West, or of the appropriate Western responses. It was then that anti-
Americanism—augmented because of the way in which the
United States chose to fight the war—spread beyond fringe-Left
parties in Europe and Japan.

Such differences in assessment have extended since the late
1960s to the Middle East as well. Publics and governments in
Europe and Japan do not share the American commitment to Israel, and have been generally skeptical of the claim, put forward
by several presidents, that the Arab-Israeli conflict should be
viewed as part of the larger East-West conflict. And the years
since 1973 have seen the slightly bizarre spectacle of the United
States appearing much more concerned about the possibility of
Soviet disruption of Persian Gulf oil supplies than the governments of Western Europe and Japan, whose societies are vitally
dependent on those supplies.

Differences in assessment between Washington and its allies extend, of course, to Latin America, particularly to Central
America. But in one important respect, Central America has
been dissimilar. The Reagan administration has made no more
than token efforts to convince its partners that they should share
its concern regarding the consequences for US national security
(and, by extrapolation, the security of the Western alliance) of
an insurgent victory in El Salvador or of the survival of the
Sandinistas in Nicaragua. That many observers do not share the
administration's concern has been amply demonstrated. Indeed,
some NATO allies have continued to send aid to the Sandinistas

at the same time the United States has been trying forcibly to overthrow them.

These divergences of view have outraged many Americans—in and out of government, and in Congress in particular—but they are scarcely surprising. Indeed, it would be surprising if they did not exist. States view one another through the prisms of their own domestic politics. And at the center of political controversy in virtually every state are assessments of risk, estimates of the potential harm that other states might cause, and choices among the range of measures that should be taken to forestall that harm. But assessments of risk are also related to capability. When a state no longer has the power to defend what it once defined as an interest, it will begin to define its interests differently. Some interests that were once thought to require active military protection may seem no longer to need it; others may cease to be regarded as interests at all. Risks a polity knows it cannot forestall will often seem less dangerous than those it thinks it can.[11] Alone among the Western allies, the United States defines its interests—and threats to those interests—in global terms because it alone has the ability to project military power throughout the globe.

Causes for Containment

What, then, is left of containment nearly forty years after the 'X' article? The observations thus far are not intended to suggest that containment of the Soviet Union is no longer a valid objective for US foreign policy. But we should be clear what it is we are trying to contain. There is no dispute over the contention that "classic" aggression with military forces—by the Soviets themselves or by their allies—should be resisted if it cannot be deterred. Here the record is good. The security system represented by the core alliances organized by the United States has clearly been successful. We will probably never know whether over the course of four decades Soviet leaders have ever seriously contemplated attacking westward from the Elbe or eastward across the Straits of Japan, but we know that they have not done so.

Indeed, in this restricted but scarcely unimportant sphere of what might be called orthodox military containment, the few apparent failures do not support a conclusion that the policy itself has failed. Forces allied to Moscow moved into South Korea in 1950 and into Cambodia in 1979, but only after the first country (not then a US ally) had explicitly been defined as outside the United States' defense perimeter and after the regime that ruled the second had become a universally loathed pariah. In the first instance, the United States learned—but also taught—a costly lesson. In the second, it seems clear that in invading Cambodia, Vietnam was pursuing purposes historically very much its own, not Moscow's; for a complex of reasons, Washington properly drew the line at the border of its regional ally, Thailand. A murkier instance was Angola in 1975. There, as we have already noted, the Soviets supported one faction in a civil war, taking advantage of unique circumstances—the combination of the absence of any recognized authority and the previous invasion of the country by South African forces.

Finally, there was Afghanistan. The forces that invaded in December 1979 were Moscow's own, not proxies. However, no matter how literally one might take the notion of "confront[ing] the Russians with unalterable counter-force at every point where they show signs of encroaching upon the interests of a peaceful and stable world," the facts of geography made any immediate Western military response out of the question. Yet those same facts make Afghanistan, in the most literal sense of the word, peripheral. The most the West could do—and has done fairly effectively since 1979—was to arm the Afghan resistance. Military containment will not stand or fall on the record of that very special situation.

It may be argued, however, that "orthodox" military containment makes for easy cases. Much more difficult—and prevalent—are those instances in which there has been no border-crossing movement of regular military forces, but rather a pattern of Soviet-supported subversion, infiltration, and insurgency. North Vietnam's long campaign against South Vietnam was such an example, only at the end becoming an "orthodox" war. Another example is the current effort by insurgent forces to overthrow the government of El Salvador. There have been many more. In some, the Soviet role has been minimal, no more than that of a minor supplier of weapons and training to one or more insurgent factions.[12] In other instances Soviet support may have been decisive—though it is obviously difficult to say for certain.

These cases of "unorthodox" war are the instances in which, if the United States chooses to intervene, it is likely to find itself doing so either alone or, as occurred in Vietnam, with only token assistance from allies.[13] Then, ironically enough, George Kennan's 1947 emphasis on the American domestic political landscape once again becomes the primary factor. If the United States is going to make any but a brief, Grenada-style military effort abroad, the danger must be clear and present and the stakes must be apparent. Otherwise, as Secretary of Defense Caspar W. Weinberger implied when he defined the conditions under which he would recommend the use of American military force, the political consensus necessary to sustain even an operation involving only small numbers of fighting men would not be forthcoming.[14] This is a limitation that no administration is likely to overcome through "public education."

Containment and its Alternatives

Weinberger's strictures contrast sharply—in practice, if not in theory—with the appeal for an assertive "nationalist-unilateralist" foreign policy, "activist" rather than "reactive," made recently by Irving Kristol in the name of a "self-consciously ideological . . . new conservatism." Kristol and his neoconservative friends want to take the gloves off in the conflict with the Soviet Union. Among the gloves are "all those 'foreign entanglements' our State Department has so assiduously contrived over the past forty years," including NATO, the Organization of American States, and even the United Nations. They are, Kristol says, "ineffectual barriers against 'aggression' ... but very effective hindrances to American action."[15]

In proclaiming the end of the era of "liberal internationalism," Kristol foresees no return to "old-fashioned, nationalist isolationism." Yet surely that would be the likely result of the unilateralism he proposes. Freed of the emotional and even cultural linkages inherent in the structure of post-1945 international institutions, Americans might well decide that the only value worth much exertion is the physical security of the United States (and—just perhaps—of Israel), and that in an era of seemingly ever more versatile nuclear weapons, little can happen beyond the nation's borders that will really jeopardize that security. The "support of the American people and their elected representatives" that Weinberger regards as crucial would not be forthcoming for the politically forceful—and militarily force-wielding—policies required by Kristol's vision of an ideologically assertive United States.

There is irony here. The contemporary international system finds the United States at the center of a web of entanglements that arguably provides it with no additional security and which, indeed, adds vastly to the burdens American taxpayers are asked to bear. (The commitment to NATO, especially, powerfully shapes and makes more costly the US military force structure.) To critics like Kristol, these entanglements mandate compromises that open doors for the expansion of Soviet influence and, potentially, control. Effective containment therefore requires that we free ourselves of the necessity of paying attention to the hopes and fears of others and march to our own drums. Yet there is every likelihood that an increasingly self-centered United States might conclude that very little of the rest of the world really "matters." In such a political climate, containment would come to seem less and less relevant as a goal for American foreign policy.

Like Sisyphus with his rock, the United States seems stuck with the present structure of world politics. Changing the ground rules that underlie that structure—as those who would rid us of our entanglements would do—would not be likely to result in a nation more capable of shrinking the domains of the world's evil empires; sustaining the requisite domestic political support for doing so would be an impossible task. We are therefore stuck as well with a version of containment that has also become part of the system's ground rules. That version offers us and our partners ample insurance against some of the risks that we perceive. Before we attempt fundamentally to alter the quality of that insurance, we should carefully examine the quality of our perceptions.

There are, to be sure, many facets of the present US-Soviet relationship that lie beyond what we have come to think of as containment. One is the realm of negotiations. "Orthodox" containment, as it was articulated during the first decade or so following World War II, placed very little emphasis on negotiations between Washington and Moscow. The USSR was considered to be virtually impermeable; the purpose of containment was to erect a barrier (what an earlier generation called a *cordon sanitaire*) behind which the Soviet state might evolve in more benign directions. Yet over the past two decades, by seeking explicit agreements, American administrations have attempted to shape not only Soviet external behavior but also Soviet society itself. These efforts have as a matter of course included negotiations on limiting arms, on military intervention (e.g., in the Middle East), and on relations with Third World clients (e.g., arms sales). But they have also extended to human rights (e.g., Jewish emigration) and to important dimensions of the Soviet internal economy (e.g., grain imports).

Thus far, US-Soviet negotiations have given rise only to fairly modest results. Yet that poor record is due in considerable measure to the way negotiations have been conducted on the American side. All too frequently, bureaucratic infighting and congressional pressures have led US negotiators to lack clear objectives or to be unable to make real concessions. In the realm of arms control, especially, they have often had little to put on the table: the military services and the nuclear weapons laboratories have been tenacious in making sure that future options ·are not closed off and that weapons already in the inventory are not bargained away. That has also been true of efforts to constrain the military roles of the two superpowers in the Third World—for example, negotiations during the Carter administration on limiting transfers of conventional arms or demilitarizing the Indian Ocean.[16] During Ronald Reagan's first term, the idea of any negotiations at all with the "evil empire" was virtually anathema; the administration was anxious not to offend its militant Right-wing supporters, including Kristol and other neoconservatives. And although Reagan in his second term appears to be less motivated by such domestic political considerations, he nevertheless has firmly rejected offers of potentially far-reaching concessions from Moscow when they seemed likely to interfere with his administration's plans for new defensive and offensive nuclear weapons.[17]

Indeed, the record of US-Soviet negotiations points up a fundamental change in the structure of international relations over the last four decades: containment is now a two-way street. In order to restrict Soviet options—for that is what containment means—American policymakers must now accept limitations on their own. That applies to nearly every strand of Soviet behavior that Washington would like to change, from deploying new missiles in Europe to supporting insurgent movements in the Third World to easing restrictions on Soviet citizens seeking to emigrate. Reciprocity does not mean that limitations must be identical, however. The road to human rights concessions runs not through matching concessions by Washington (there are none to make, nor are Soviet leaders concerned about "human rights" in the United States) but, as Gerald Ford's administration learned, through guarantees on trade and credits.

There are those who would say that the very need for reciprocity points up the ultimate bankruptcy of containment as practiced by every American administration since Franklin Roosevelt's. Rather than containment, they say, the preferred approach should have been to destroy Soviet power before it could grow: containment has only served to preserve (or even to nurture) the Soviet state rather than to alter it.[18] The observation may be valid; it is also irrelevant. So drastic an enterprise, no matter how accomplished, would have required an American nation and leaders radically different in character from what we knew in 1947 and have known since.

As George Kennan himself has often pointed out, the United States has been far from adept at "employing force for rational and restricted purposes"; wars, once begun, have tended to become crusades, as did the two world wars.[19] But preventive war against a major adversary (as distinguished from, say, the war against Spain of 1898, or the invasion of Grenada in 1983) has never been part of the American repertoire. It is impossible to imagine a president ordering one—or the political system complying. Containment is indeed the antithesis of preventive war. And the critics of containment have yet to suggest an alternative strategy that is within the capability of the American political system, or is even remotely as well suited for enabling the United States to cope with the world as it was in 1947—or as it is today.

Notes

1. George F. Kennan (writing as 'X'), "The Sources of Soviet Conduct," *Foreign Affairs* 25 (July 1947), p. 581.

2. Barton Gellman, *Contending with Kennan: Toward a Philosophy of American Power* (New York: Praeger, 1984), p. 43.

3. From a draft lecture prepared by Kennan for delivery on 20 February 1947, quoted in ibid., p. 133.

4. From the outset of the NATO alliance, Denmark and Norway have both refused to allow nuclear weapons on their territory in peacetime, and the United States honors this preference—while at the same time adhering to a longstanding policy of not discussing the location of US nuclear weapons. Denmark and Norway do, however, allow visits of nuclear-powered or nuclear-armed vessels to their ports.

5. It is worth noting, also, that China's separation came by stages. The initial phase of the dispute was closely followed (indeed, overlapped) by the Cultural Revolution, which surely seemed so unpromising to Western interests that the USSR did not feel directly threatened. By the time China had unambiguously turned to the West, its independence from Moscow was so well established that no Soviet "rescue" was remotely possible.

6. William P. Bundy, "Who Lost Patagonia? Foreign Policy in the 1980 Campaign," *Foreign Affairs* 58 (Fall 1979), pp. 1–27.

7. This particular Reagan quotation (there have been many like it) was from an address to a group of Cuban exiles on 20 May 1983; *The New York Times*, 21 May 1983, p. 4. The 88 Europeans (and an Australian, former Prime Minister Malcolm Fraser) took a full-page advertisement in ibid., 18 April 1985, p. B28.

8. Stanley H. Hoffmann, *The State of War* (New York: Praeger, 1965), p. 49.

9. The first instance was the so-called Egyptian-Israeli "War of Attrition," in 1970, when the USSR shored up Egyptian air defenses with Soviet pilots flying MiG-21 interceptors and ground crews manning surface-to-air missiles (SAMs). The second occurred following Israel's total destruction of Syrian SAMs in Lebanon in 1982; Moscow is said to have set up several batteries of long-range SAM-5s in Syria, wholly manned by Soviet crews. The third instance is present-day Angola, where the Soviets are said, in mid-1985, to have set up defenses against South African air attacks.

10. On this theme, see Sanford J. Ungar, ed., *Estrangement: America and the World* (New York: Oxford University Press, 1985).

11. For a discussion of differences of assessment as an issue in Anglo-American relations, see Richard H. Ullman, "America, Britain, and the Soviet Threat in Historical and Present Perspective," in Hedley Bull and W. Roger Louis, eds., *The 'Special Relationship': Anglo-American Relations since 1945* (London: Oxford University Press, 1986).

12. That was the case, for example, in the guerrilla war against Ian Smith's white minority regime in Rhodesia. Moscow supported Joshua Nkomo's ZAPU forces. In the end, they lost to Robert Mugabe's ZANU, which had China's support; but even had they won, it is unlikely that Moscow would have had any significant influence in the Zimbabwe that emerged from the war.

13. Australia, New Zealand, and South Korea—none except, perhaps, the last with any enthusiasm—sent contingents to assist the United States in Vietnam, a marked contrast from the Korean War, in which the "United Nations Command" included many American allies.

14. Secretary Weinberger's speech to the National Press Club on 28 November 1984 was excerpted in *The New York Times* the following day and printed in full, with minor modifications, in the form of an article, "The Use of Force and the National Will," in *The Baltimore Sun,* 3 December 1984.

15. Irving Kristol, "Foreign Policy in an Age of Ideology," *The National Interest,* No. 1, Fall 1985, pp. 6–15.

16. See, e.g., Strobe Talbott, *Endgame: The Inside Story of SALT II* (New York: Harper and Row, 1979), pp. 164–80; and Raymond L. Garthoff, *Detente and Confrontation: American-Soviet Relations from Nixon to Reagan* (Washington: The Brookings Institution, 1985), pp. 755–63.

17. Thus, preceding and during Reagan's summit meeting with new Soviet Party Chairman Mikhail S. Gorbachev at Vienna in November 1985, the White House seemed summarily to dismiss Soviet proposals that, in exchange for US shelving of plans to develop new antimissile defenses, Moscow would agree to 50-percent reductions in strategic offensive forces. And following the summit, the administration—asserting that Soviet assurances could not be trusted—even more bluntly rejected a Soviet proposal for a comprehensive ban on nuclear weapons testing that seemed to depart substantially from Moscow's previous unwillingness to allow intrusive on-site inspections. (See *The New York Times,* 22 November 1985, p. A12, and 20 December 1985, p. A13.)

18. For an extreme version of this argument, see "Containment: A View from the Kremlin," an address by Senator Malcolm Wallop to the symposium, "Containment and the Future," 7 November 1985, National Defense University, Washington, D.C., reprinted in *The Congressional Record,* Senate, 20 November 1985, pp. S16050–53.

19. See, e.g., Kennan's *American Diplomacy 1900–1950* (Chicago: University of Chicago Press, 1951), chaps. 4 and 5 (the quotation is on p. 84).

28

Inching Beyond Containment: Detente, Entente, Condominium— and Orchestraint

Alton Frye

T HOUGH LONG IN DOUBT, the success of detente cannot be questioned. The former adversaries have broken through their suspicions and misunderstandings to a level of communication and good feeling that would have been undreamed of a few short years ago. Students and tourists, businessmen and officials flock eagerly—and by the thousands—between the two countries. Commerce has begun to flourish, and, although early expectations for economic relations were too high, the communist state's astonishing shift toward policies which incorporate greater latitude for individual initiative and material incentives has won the admiration of most Americans. Even in the sensitive areas of nuclear technology and military hardware, there are the beginnings of cooperation.

Alton Frye is Washington Director and Senior Fellow of the Council on Foreign Relations.

Politically, where once the two governments eyed each other with unrelieved skepticism, predisposed to hostility, their leaders now receive each other with unfeigned warmth and cordiality. Where each side not long ago read the other's every gesture as a calculated maneuver for advantage, each now lavishes on the other the benefit of every doubt. Frictions which used to justify martial preparation and ominous rhetoric are now managed as minor irritants which cannot be allowed to impede the steady course of amity. So intent are the two nations on forging a durable friendship, that even the truly serious disputes between them are shunted aside for the time being. It is, after all, a measure of sturdy relations that lingering time bombs may be described forthrightly so long as they are tied to slow-burning fuses of indefinite length.

Mirabile dictu! Detente is indeed alive and well—between China and America. As the wag puts it, from the era of "ping-pong diplomacy" to that of "Deng Xiaoping-pong" diplomacy, the ball has been bouncing right in Chinese-American relations. There could scarcely be a greater contrast with the faltering, on-again off-again attempts to achieve similar results between the United States and the Soviet Union. What accounts for the difference?

Culture? It is not clear that Americans are better equipped to cope with Oriental authoritarians than with Eurasian ones; the *hauteur* bred by centuries of Chinese civilization is as difficult to handle as the insecurity chronically displayed by Soviets. The absence of significant bilateral disputes? On the contrary, the festering disagreement over Taiwan is closer to a territorial *casus belli* than any issue between Washington and Moscow. A history of friendly association? America's missionary impulse did run to China and not to Russia, but that link evoked no affection in the heart of Mao Tse-tung's followers—while millions of Soviet and American citizens recall with satisfaction their wartime alliance against Hitler. Russia remains an enigma, but, unlike the People's Republic of China, it has never drawn American blood as an enemy of the United States.

The search for a new path which Washington and Moscow might follow together leads one to examine a central puzzle of modern history. How do enemies among nations become friends, or at least tolerable acquaintances? Answers to that question fit together in strange and contradictory fashion. Not only Chinese-American, but also German-American, Japanese-American, and Italian-American relations offer suggestive cases. Within the span of a few years, nations striving to annihilate each other came to see their very survival as dependent on intimate collaboration. In several instances, however, improved relations followed total military defeat of one state, and, in the European cases, powerful ethnic and cultural ties worked to reinforce the desire for better relations. A cynic would be tempted to say that the lesson of history is, "war cures enmity." But we know the other half of that truth—it also breeds it—and no one could propose to relieve the recurrent strains in Soviet-American relations by active combat.

In some degree, the explanation for wholesome US relations with those former enemies is the Soviet Union itself. The fears and animosities generated by Soviet policy in the last four decades have formed a critical bond in the ties of other nations. Their shared anxiety about the Soviet Union has brought them into much closer association than might otherwise have been likely. "The enemy of my enemy is my friend" has proven to be a cardinal principle of contemporary world politics. If hot war is no acceptable alternative to cold war, a more refined option could be to find surrogate enemies to share, common threats to overcome, dangers that can only be met through mutual action.

This may seem an excessively negative approach to relations between nations. Americans are prone to accentuate the positive, looking for opportunities; the presidential optimism of our day captures this national trait in high degree. Yet a focus on risk and hazard is a realistic reflection of the downbeat and wary tone that has marked most of the diplomatic experience between the United States and the Soviet Union. At a still more elementary level, that focus builds upon a central finding of psychological research, namely, the Maslow hypothesis that the most powerful motivations in human behavior flow from a sense of values threatened.[1] Governments and nations are not individuals, but the task of reconciling differences among them can usefully begin with concern for the psychological qualities of the individuals who lead them. The premise here is, if one can define threats to shared values in ways to which both Soviet and American leaders can respond, there will be opportunities to resolve some of them by cooperative action.

There are familiar explanations for the perpetual difficulties between Moscow and Washington. They are the only true superpowers, able to compete on a global scale. They alone pose threats of ultimate destruction to one another. As the preeminent states of the capitalist and communist worlds, their obligations to lead their respective ideological camps bring them into continuing controversy with each other. These factors have continuing force. They both complicate and make more urgent the effort to dampen conflict between Soviets and Americans. The two countries' status and relations are unique in ways which create special impediments to the kind of transformation wrought in other bilateral relationships.

Each superpower serves as the devil in the other's efforts to rally the faithful. At the same time, it is worth remembering that, however coercive Soviet policy toward satellite states may be, some independent governments value ties to Moscow for the same reason others turn to the United States, namely, to have a powerful friend against nearby enemies. The dynamic that opened circuits from Washington to Beijing by way of Islamabad also did so between New Delhi and Moscow. Syria has leaned toward the Soviet Union not because of ideological affinity but because of straightforward reasons of state. Time and again, states with grievances against the United States (or, more often, against friends of the United States) have discerned advantage in a Soviet connection, whether or not they wished to be part of any bloc.

The critical question for Soviet and American statesmen is whether they serve their own nations best by emphasizing an open-ended contest for secondary allies in the complex balance of power, or by forging direct accommodations with the primary party, the other superpower. For decades the two governments have oscillated between these options, but the relentless quest for favor among lesser states has easily overpowered explorations of ways to tone down the Cold War. Yet a balanced assessment of previous efforts in that direction is prerequisite to considering current possibilities for new departures in superpower relations.

The Record of Detente

Simon Serfaty has aptly characterized the duality of America's efforts to apply containment while probing for the possibilities of detente: "neither policy has ever existed without the other . . . neither is truthfully remembered; both are conveniently imagined."[2] For some analysts, the record reads, "detente is a fraud" and "balance of power politics is the only option." In fact, the record is too complex to support such sharp conclusions. It points toward several, more shaded judgments. The first is that a stable balance of power is the necessary starting point for attempts at detente. The second is that preserving a stable balance is a principal function of any detente. Properly construed, detente will be for both Soviets and Americans an instrument to maintain their position in the balance of power. Otherwise, accommodation would be tantamount to surrender.

A third judgment is that detente works better in some areas than in others, and that it sometimes benefits third parties more than the superpowers. This thought is captured by the remark that "Europeans expected less from detente and got more, while Americans expected more and got less." Frankly put, a number of governments have at times feared improved relations between the superpowers, reflecting the fact that other states have in some respects been the beneficiaries of superpower rivalry. The bidding contest between Moscow and Washington has enabled some states to extract concessions from both superpowers even while stressing loyalty to one. Yet intervals of reduced tension have opened different opportunities for such states. It is probably accurate to say that most allies on both sides have come to prefer detente to its alternatives. Moods and attitudes vary over time, but, for some years now, the basic disposition among American allies in Europe has been toward reviving and extending the detente experiment of the Nixon years.

Is the problem, then, mainly one of unrealistic expectations among Americans? The widespread perception that detente was oversold in the 1970s undoubtedly conveys a public view that, for a combination of domestic political considerations, policymakers deliberately inflated expectations about the likely fruits of improved relations with Moscow. But, judged in the longer sweep of history, if Americans expected more from detente than was reasonable, they gained more than they realized. A legislator once admonished a witness that he was making progress more difficult by refusing to recognize its achievement. The observation applies to many critiques of detente.

Though a term of the seventies, *detente* loosely describes a phenomenon of every administration since Franklin Roosevelt's. From the Eisenhower years onward, the search for normal relations with Moscow has ebbed and flowed, but consistently returned with heightened intensity. The litany of failures in the process—from Hungary 1956 and Czechoslovakia 1968 to Angola 1976 and Afghanistan 1979, from the abortive Paris summit of 1960 to the stalemate over SALT II in 1980—is well known and frequently recited. Too often neglected, however, are entries on the other side of the ledger.

The Austrian State Treaty of 1955 was a signal achievement of superpower diplomacy. Responding to President

Eisenhower's initiative, and going against the grain of prior Soviet practice and international legal doctrine, the two sides managed to craft a de facto open skies regime which, through space-based observation systems, enhanced strategic stability immeasurably. The difficult passage through the Cuban missile crisis was followed by the 1963 Limited Nuclear Test Ban Treaty and significant steps to open scientific and cultural exchanges. Even in the depths of the Vietnam conflict, the two governments found a basis for cooperation in the Nuclear Non-Proliferation Treaty of 1968, and in other pacts which shored up mutual restraint in outer space and Antarctica.

The Nixon years brought extraordinary political progress. The four-power Berlin accord muted one chronic source of friction. The superpowers began the continuing process of strategic arms negotiation, achieving low limits on strategic defense set by the ABM Treaty of 1972 and raising the prospect of far-reaching restraints on offensive forces. An important gain was the agreement designed to prevent incidents at sea between the two sides' naval forces. The Threshold Test Ban Treaty and the Peaceful Nuclear Explosions Agreement of 1974 nudged verification procedures toward cooperative measures and useful exchanges of data, procedures further extended in the inconclusive negotiations for a comprehensive nuclear test ban in the later seventies. The Ford-Brezhnev agreement at Vladivostok and the Helsinki Final Act pointed toward further progress in containing the growth of strategic weaponry and in lowering tensions in Europe. The SALT II agreement of the Carter period advanced toward actual reductions in the number of strategic launchers and toward qualitative restraints, capping the number of warheads permitted on individual missiles and limiting the total number of MIRVed systems (those with multiple independently targetable reentry vehicles). The Soviets joined the London Suppliers Club to explore ways to regulate civilian trade in nuclear materials and systems in order to contain the spread of weapons capabilities.

Many interpret these episodes as examples of wishful thinking, naive American gestures exploited by clever Soviet leaders to steal a march on the West by creating the impression that "peace had broken out." They stress commitments not fulfilled in the Helsinki process, provisions bent or broken in arms control agreements, and obligations for restraint in other areas honored mainly in the breach. They give little credit for agreements whose major terms have been applied in good faith, ignoring the problems which would have grown worse in the absence of efforts at mutual restraint.

To assess the prospects for success in the mid-eighties, one needs to ask both why superpower efforts to address mutual problems have so often faltered and whether the burdens imposed by past failures provide new incentives to resolve them now. On the first question, conventional wisdom veers toward the conclusion that the detente of the seventies did not bite deeply because the two governments saw it as a cover for continued pursuit of their geopolitical ambitions. Weighed against those ambitions, the profits of detente seemed too skimpy to warrant greater self-restraint in other areas of competition.

That view is plausible, but it takes too little account of the particular sequence in which the Nixon-Brezhnev efforts began to unravel. As Raymond Garthoff has documented, mutual disappointments and suspicions mounted so rapidly that the thrust of detente was almost immediately weakened.[3] An important issue is whether the Soviet behavior which Americans found so objectionable would have occurred if the hoped-for trade benefits with the United States had materialized; if the Jackson-Vanik amendment had not undermined quiet diplomacy to facilitate Jewish emigration; if the United States had not pursued its own anti-Soviet campaigns in the Persian Gulf region, the Far East, and elsewhere; if American leadership had not been so dislocated by Watergate and Vietnam. Had detente become a growing tree instead of a shriveled twig, would Moscow have found dabbling in Africa such a temptation, infringements of

Helsinki worth the political cost, superfluous military expenditures justifiable?

Similarly, Moscow needs to consider its responsibility for the stunted form detente assumed. What advantage did it find in purchasing heightened tension with the United States by adventurous diplomacy in Somali and Ethiopia; by gratuitous support in Angola of those Cuban surrogates, bound to inflame American opinion; by virulent anti-American propaganda beamed to Iran during the protracted US ordeal there; by playing so close to the edges of arms control agreements that it placed its own good faith under a cloud? Would not the Soviet Union be more secure today if its attempt at intimidating NATO's European allies had not provoked deployment of Pershing II and cruise missiles; if its large-scale strategic and conventional deployments had not undermined support in the United States for the SALT II Treaty; if its bullying tactics in Poland had not once more highlighted the oppression of Eastern Europe; if its bloody intervention in Afghanistan had not outraged the world?

Obviously, perceptions about such matters differ greatly within and between the superpowers. Both governments need to reflect upon them critically—and self-critically. A careful evaluation of the abortive experiment of the Nixon-, Ford-, Carter-Brezhnev period can go far toward making possible more substantial success in the Reagan-Gorbachev phase now unfolding.

The purpose here is not to replace skepticism with naivete. It is to ask whether these efforts to change central features of Soviet-American relations were fundamentally misdirected or well-conceived policies which were overwhelmed by other factors—extraneous political crises, inopportune shifts in leadership, technological developments out of phase with political initiatives, impatience for immediate and comprehensive success in a process that required years to bear full fruit. Most importantly, do these and similar initiatives of past decades constitute building blocks for future policy, or must any attempt to construct more wholesome relations discard them and begin anew?

Prelude to a New Detente

The view here is that there is much on which to build. The danger in damning prior measures of detente as wholesale failures is that it will contaminate arrangements and policies that are vital to larger innovations. Change has occurred within and between the two superpowers, and one must recognize its significance if further change is to be steered in mutually beneficial directions. It is a far different world when a Republican president explicitly renounces the goal of "military superiority" embraced by his own party platform. It is a far different world when the men who guide both governments testify that "nuclear war can never be won and must never be fought." For in those altered professions lies the acknowledgment that "victory" is not an option, that neither superpower can prevail over the other. The two sides have barely begun to act on the implications of that finding: perpetual cold war is futile, its attendant risks unjustifiable, and the search for viable political and strategic understandings between Moscow and Washington an inescapable duty of statecraft.

A chain of logic descends from these theses which lead to the conclusion that both governments are, in fact, animated by a common dread of nuclear war.

- Avoiding nuclear war requires a stable strategic balance, which in turn dictates mutual restraint in the development, deployment, and use of nuclear weapons.

- Because the risk of escalation to nuclear war arises in any military conflict between the superpowers, avoiding conventional war is a vital interest of the two parties.

- The risk of conventional war is in turn regulated by a massive balance of forces deployed on the central front in Europe, but it is less well controlled in numerous Third World settings where Soviet and American political interests may draw the superpowers into direct conflict.

- Other risks to the superpowers arise from the possible spread of nuclear weapons capabilities to additional states; neither has confidence that the acquisition of nuclear weapons by others will induce sufficient responsibility to guarantee that they will not be used in regional conflicts, perhaps increasing the danger that the superpowers will be drawn into war.

These are core values shared by the two powers. All of them could, in principle, be served best by explicit arrangements between Moscow and Washington, together with other states where appropriate. Despite complaints about the superpowers' excessive preoccupation with arms control, it is not surprising that they find their vision of other possible common interests obscured by the paralyzing hazards accompanying the nuclear competition.

In important respects, these core values provide a surrogate for the "common enemy" that has helped forge positive shifts in other relationships between adversaries. But the operational question is how far the common dread of nuclear war can be exploited to move the United States and the Soviet Union toward collaboration. To what extent will other interests lead the superpowers to risk these shared values? Specifically, can the two governments be persuaded to subordinate their broader political competition to the requirements of central strategic stability?

One difficulty we face is language. The very term *detente* carries a certain opprobrium in some quarters. It was ruled out of legitimate political discourse in the United States by a moderate president defending himself against charges of softness on the Soviets. Because of what happened in Soviet-American relations during the 1970s, it carries an aura of overblown rhetoric and undersatisfied expectations. Its longstanding service as a slogan in Soviet propaganda makes it heavy baggage for

Americans to bear in trying to formulate a policy readily identifiable with US national interests. Even the phrase, *hard-headed detente,* sensible though it sounds, labors under the unhelpful handicap of trying to salvage a controversial noun by dressing it up with a presumably more palatable adjective. *Containment without isolation* appeals to some, but is rather bulky in English and condescending in Russian. We need to free consideration of Soviet-American relations from rusty rhetoric and dilapidated symbols.

Let us, then, restate the objectives one might propose for an altered relationship between the superpowers and give it a different name. The goal recommended here is a relationship in which the superpowers acknowledge that their own interest requires them (1) to give priority to the Soviet-American relationship, (2) to orchestrate their behavior in key respects, and (3) to exercise sufficient restraint bilaterally and otherwise to protect that central relationship against disruption. Until we contrive a more felicitous term, one may call such a relationship *orchestraint.*

A minimalist view would hold that little can be expected beyond a measure of self-control on both sides, directed at avoiding strategic war, whether by inadvertence, escalation, or miscalculation. A maximalist goal would be to shape a form of condominium in which, in the interest of suppressing danger to themselves, the superpowers would bargain directly—not only on bilateral issues but also on arrangements to be imposed on other states whose disputes threaten to ignite wider war.

Measures of Orchestraint

In some respects, the two countries are already well beyond the minimalist standard. They have not managed to elaborate and enforce general codes of conduct, but they have created some standards for strategic behavior and have ratified important de facto developments, notably the prevailing use of national technical means to keep an eye on each other. Their acceptance of such means has produced interesting by-products, for instance in the Soviet Union's alert of the United States regarding possible preparations for a nuclear test in South Africa. They have curbed the longstanding games of "chicken" between their navies and moved to modernize the "hot line" set up in the 1960s.

The fact that some arms control provisions have not been fully or faithfully implemented should not blind one to the fact that many have been. Since 1972, the two sides have dismantled hundreds of strategic launchers to remain within aggregate limits. Not all of those weapons were obsolete, a fact confirmed by the continued service of retired missiles as boosters for space launches. Many would have remained on station, if for no better reasons than bureaucratic inertia and determination not to yield something for nothing. The superpowers have not violated the fractionation rule by multiplying warheads on individual missiles beyond levels set in the SALT II Treaty, even though the agreement was not ratified. Evidence suggests reasonable compliance with the 150-kiloton ceiling on underground detonations set by the Threshold Test Ban Treaty—again despite its nonratified status. The record is mixed, but it is not barren.

At the other end of the spectrum, no leader on either side has even proposed anything remotely resembling a superpower condominium. As a general proposition, the improbability of condominium is apparent. Neither Moscow nor Washington is likely to trade known, trustworthy relations with friends for a reckless embrace of its principal adversary. Perhaps the closest thing to a step in that direction was the 1969 Soviet probe for US acquiescence in the event of a possible attempt to destroy the embryonic Chinese nuclear capability. The hint was quickly rebuffed by American negotiators, but it raised the question of whether the two sides might agree to deny other states entry into the nuclear weapons club. That would have amounted to a kind of "functional condominium" to cope with a specific problem, as distinct from the kind of shared power over territory normally conjured up by the term.

Far different is another concept designed to universalize nuclear deterrence as a means of discouraging the spread of nuclear weapons to other countries. It contemplates joint superpower action to deter proliferation by offering to make available to any victim of nuclear attack the means for proportionate reprisal. Without having to build a nuclear arsenal of its own, a potential victim could in theory be shielded against nuclear threat or attack by the deterrent value of promised access to the superpowers' arsenals. A Soviet-American commitment to respond in this way to additional proliferation could be a far more potent antiproliferation policy than the negative and positive security assurances they have tendered in various forms to nonnuclear states. Although the idea has evoked interest in intellectual circles in both countries, it has not been explored in intergovernmental channels. Whatever its theoretical merits and demerits, a proposal of this nature has no promise unless the superpowers first make major strides toward muting the tensions between them. It is worth noting, however, that the record of cooperation on proliferation issues and the clear sense in Moscow and Washington that they stand in a similar posture toward potential proliferators identify this issue as one on which collaboration might be carried to its maximum lengths.

Along the spectrum from minimal arrangements to the hypothetical option of condominium lies a broad array of possibilities for orchestraint, including elements of more active engagement verging on entente. They include political and economic measures, as well as additional security arrangements affecting numerous states. Beyond the strategic arms proposals occupying center stage, conventional ideas include confidence-building measures and mutual force reduction in Europe, steps to relieve friction over human rights issues, expanded East-West trade, and concerted action to deal with a large number of regional trouble spots and problems—Afghanistan, Nicaragua, El Salvador, Angola-Namibia, the Iran-Iraq war, the Arab-Israeli conflict, continuing violence in Southeast Asia and South Africa, renegade states like Libya, and the division of Korea.

It is here that the real business of world politics will be transacted. The need is not so much for new options on the menu of superpower diplomacy as for fresh approaches to identified problems. Of special significance may be the fact that Moscow and Washington are edging into regional political discussions simultaneously with summit preparations on strategic arms issues. Across-the-board progress on regional disputes is not in the offing, but three regions stand out as ripe for superpower orchestraint: Central America, Afghanistan, and the Middle East.

Spheres of Cooperation

However offensive the phrase *sphere of influence,* Central America and Afghanistan invite analysis as contemporary instances of that classical property of world politics. That is why a number of experienced observers have suggested,[4] usually *sotto voce,* that there may be a basis for an arrangement involving (1) US restraint in supporting the guerrillas in Afghanistan as part of a movement toward political settlement of the invasion—civil war there, perhaps under United Nations auspices; and (2) Soviet restraint in backing Cuban-Nicaraguan-Salvadoran guerrilla activities in Central America, coupled perhaps with Contadora-type agreements to promote democratic processes in the region in conjunction with disengagement of foreign military elements.

Such a bargain will be difficult to contrive and could not readily be acknowledged by either superpower, but it deserves priority attention. The United States cannot in conscience abandon freedom fighters in Afghanistan, but it is in no position to help them prevail; if the *mujahedin* are offered reasonable terms to seek national reconciliation in the context of Soviet military withdrawal, the United States cannot in conscience exploit the circumstances for geostrategic purposes by encouraging guerrilla recalcitrance. There are good reasons to believe that the Soviets have found their Afghanistan involvement longer and more burdensome than expected and, although they can continue to bear it, they could welcome a compromise that met their concern for border security without requiring permanent Soviet military operations in the country.

By the same token, the Soviets will not easily relinquish the opportunity to nettle the United States in its own hemisphere. Nor will they wish to appear hesitant in applying the doctrine of national liberation movements to Central America. But the Soviet Union cannot expect wider comity with the United States so long as it is thought to be a prime sponsor of troubles on America's doorstep. An intriguing and suggestive remark came from former Foreign Minister Andrei Gromyko when he told former Secretary of State Alexander Haig, in a moment of exasperation, that "Cuba is your problem." If the statement means anything, it surely reveals an awareness that Moscow's capacity to operate through intermediaries in the Western Hemisphere has definite limits. Bringing its leverage into play to lower the level of violence in Central America, whether spawned by Cuba or not, could buy the Soviet Union considerable credit in the high political accounts of superpower relations.

The circumstances of the Middle East are quite different, and far past the stage when either power could assume the prerogatives of a tacit sphere of influence. It is not clear what specific initiatives the two could take to help terminate the simmering blood bath between Iran and Iraq, but the topic should be on the bilateral agenda. A more concrete opportunity may exist in the intermittent peace process that has gone to seed after the flowering of Camp David. The United States has found it difficult to coax that process forward; it has sternly resisted the notion that the Soviet Union, so often seen as a disruptive presence in the area, should take an active role.

Several reasons argue for a reassessment of that policy. Foremost among them is the fact that King Hussein has framed the latest Jordanian-Palestinian overtures with a view to Soviet involvement in an international conference, out of which direct

Arab-Israeli negotiations would emerge. That framework reflects a credible judgment that, especially as Syria's principal patron, the Soviets already possess essential influence over key aspects of any political movement in the region; better to have them inside the tent than out, said the Bedouin sage, Lyndon Johnson.

From the American perspective, there are additional reasons to rethink the matter. The exclusion policy dates from the years before Anwar Sadat transformed the situation by expelling Soviet military personnel from Egypt and making his historic journey to Jerusalem. The earlier assumption that Iraq was gravitating into Moscow's orbit no longer holds. There are tantalizing hints of Soviet willingness to resume diplomatic relations with Israel. There are, to be sure, hard arguments in *Realpolitik* terms for resisting Soviet participation, but the occasion could well provide a crucial test of Moscow's willingness and capacity to play a constructive role in working for a more expansive detente.

The Soviets are in the Middle East, but in a weakened condition. There may not be a better time to run the risk of experimenting with their presence in the peace process. That is all the more true when, if they prove unhelpful, other options will remain available and attractive. Inviting the Soviets into the process would throw light on how the new leaders in Moscow view their responsibilities to help manage international conflict. It would also meet their longstanding complaint that exclusion from the Middle East process denies them recognition as a great power with legitimate interests in the region. In or out of the formal procedures, Moscow can impede or facilitate them; it may be more inclined to facilitate them if it is an active party—and if the process is linked to the larger attempt to shape an affirmative superpower relationship.

These key regional conflicts illustrate cases in which the superpowers need to enrich the narrower conceptions of detente applied in the past. For frictions over such Third World issues have fed back into the central relationship in ways which cast doubt on its true direction. Collaboration in these realms, needless to say, cannot substitute for progress on bilateral strategic and political issues or on the Eurocentric problems which consume so much of their attention. But, apart from its intrinsic importance, such collaboration could make the central agenda less vulnerable to disruption.

Arms Control Opportunities

Of that central agenda, only the essentials can be mentioned here. President Reagan and General Secretary Gorbachev may well have the greatest opportunity in history to strike a basic bargain, maintaining strategic stability while reducing nuclear weapons. Granted that pitfalls exist, there are numerous paths toward such stability through reductions, and honest negotiation can discover the ones most agreeable to the parties. Nibbling at the edges of the problem will not suffice. What is called for is a package deal, incorporating useful precedents from the SALT and Test Ban negotiations and making fair trade-offs between the concerns and advantages of both nations.

At the heart of the bargain, evidently, must be a mutually acceptable arrangement relating strategic defensive activities to the proposed offensive force reductions. Mr. Reagan has stressed that the immediate task is to end the erosion of the 1972 ABM treaty, and that any research on the Strategic Defense Initiative should take place within the terms of that agreement. He has also said that, if the research is successful, the United States would share the resulting technology with the Soviet Union. Under those criteria, it should be possible to clarify the boundary between permissible research and prohibited development, perhaps specifying certain activities which could only take place under joint supervision. For, as former National Security Adviser Robert McFarlane assured the British in 1985, the US government recognizes that any eventual transition to greater reliance on defenses would require the cooperation of the Soviet Union. Whatever the ultimate fate of SDI and its Soviet coun-

terpart, cooperation in defining the future defense regime will
have to begin now if actual force reductions in offenses are to
be achieved.

That task has grown more problematic as the administration has coupled its declaratory commitment to abide by the
ABM treaty with dubious interpretations of its provisions.
Clearly, the treaty cannot survive self-serving interpretations of
convenience by either party. And equally clear is the certain
failure of attempts to resurrect superpower negotiations on offensive force reductions if there is bad faith in managing the existing treaty regime on strategic defenses. Excessive zeal in
catering to the president's interest in research on strategic defense by subverting the ABM treaty, which he is sworn to respect, may cast a cloud over his good faith and jeopardize his
goal of achieving real reductions in offensive weapons—at the
very moment when he has elicited significant movement in the
Soviet bargaining stance. Evidently, the two sides will have to
clarify these interpretive issues.

Among the myriad details involved in the strategic arms
negotiations, three questions are overriding. The first concerns
the boundaries for strategic defense activities. Interestingly, private discussions with knowledgeable Soviets reveal considerably more forthcoming attitudes about strategic defense research
than official positions convey. The large portion of the SDI devoted to surveillance, acquisition, tracking, and kill
assessment—multi-purpose technologies which are difficult to
monitor—might well be acceptable to the Soviets, provided
there were adequate constraints on other critical technologies.
Specifically, agreement not to test in space large-scale lasers
and other weapon components might encourage Soviet acquiescence in a wide range of research on other elements of strategic
defense. Similarly, in order to maintain confidence that neither
side was seeking to break out of defensive restraints—in other
words, to give effect to President Reagan's pledge that any
eventual transition to greater reliance on strategic defense
should be cooperative—the two sides might limit the size and

potential of power sources approved for deployment in space, subject to mutual visitation rights and possibly to exceptions for joint systems. In principle, amendments to the ABM treaty could focus restraints on a few identifiable technologies, leaving considerable latitude for the kind of research Mr. Reagan wishes to authorize for the benefit of his successors. There should be no impediment on America's part to such a selective approach, for *regulating* SDI in no way amounts to *abandoning* SDI. Larger uncertainties surround the degree to which General Secretary Gorbachev would be willing to narrow his wholesale opposition to SDI.

The second critical question bears on the relationship between superpower and third-country nuclear forces. Although the complexities surrounding these latter forces are severe, they should never have been allowed to confound Soviet-American arms diplomacy. Gorbachev's gambit of offering to the British and the French separate discussions on European nuclear forces points up an untenable situation. The Soviets and Americans cannot negotiate about the nuclear forces of other countries, but neither can they disregard their existence in determining the scale and character of possible reductions in superpower deployments. Over the years of SALT, START, and INF, this issue has been finagled in various ways, obscured in side deals and tacit trade-offs, but never addressed forthrightly. It now demands a straightforward approach, for the simple reason that without one, substantial reductions in the major powers' forces are unlikely.

While those powers cannot constrain the weapons of other states, they can make explicit a common standard for their own response to any expansion of those weapons that jeopardizes possible reductions in Soviet and American deployments. That standard might take the form of an agreement that, in reducing forces to a specified level of delivery vehicles and warheads, each superpower reserves the right to retain additional forces equivalent to any third-country deployments above a fixed percentage of that level. Such an arrangement would be equitable, but more importantly, it would embody a political reality that must be advertised: neither superpower will continue reductions for long if other states increase their nuclear forces indefinitely. An agreement along these lines would create a powerful political stake for third countries in the process of superpower reductions. It would be a weighty responsibility for any of them to trigger suspension of that process by excessive buildups of their own. And a provision of this nature could pave the way for formal negotiations with Paris, London, and Beijing at a later stage. Both France and Britain have indicated that they would be willing to consider how best to contribute to arms reductions, once the superpowers have actually embarked upon a reductions program.

The third overriding question goes to the scope and content of offensive reductions. It is obvious that incorporating precedents, criteria, and counting rules previously negotiated could do a great deal to expedite such a bargain. Gorbachev's confirmation that Moscow accepts the necessity to lower both launcher numbers and warhead totals steers discussion in the right direction. Making warhead reductions workable will require reasonable counting rules, which SALT II provides for ballistic missiles. That agreement also offers a basis for avoiding an endless wrangle over how to treat weapons carried by bombers: it equates bombers not equipped for cruise missiles with single-warhead ICBMs. Given the different characteristics of those systems, that is a fair standard, and it could prove critical for balanced reductions. Just as Soviet missile throw-weight is likely to exceed that of the United States in a reduced force posture, American bomber advantages are likely to persist. For both sides, these residual capacities would provide useful hedges against a collapse of the agreement, in which case missiles could add warheads and bombers, cruise missiles.

Because both countries have begun to add air-launched cruise missiles to some of their bombers, a central task will be to relate constraints on ALCM-carrying bombers to reductions in ballistic missile warheads. Again, SALT offers a suggestive counting rule of twenty weapons for ALCM bombers, compared to the maximum of ten warheads permitted on heavy ICBMs. One possibility would be to set a delivery vehicle sub-ceiling to cover both heavy bombers carrying ALCMs and heavy ballistic missiles. Equating the two for purposes of the sub-ceiling would balance the larger number of slow-reaction cruise missiles on bombers, which face active defenses, against half that number of fast-reaction weapons on heavy ballistic missiles. Analysts can argue forever about the specifics of any formula, but political inventions of this kind will be necessary if the two sides are to phase down their very different strategic postures. Integrated handling of bombers and heavy missiles might make feasible reductions of central strategic forces to the 7,000-weapon range, if not to the 6,000-"charge" total reportedly proposed by Moscow.

Needless to say, no reductions will take place if either government feels they will undermine stability. Ideally, the two sides would describe a long-term evolution away from relatively vulnerable MIRVed systems and toward more survivable single-warhead ballistic missiles. It is an open question whether development of counterforce-capable SLBMs will proceed so rapidly as to rob the parties of the potential benefits to stability envisaged by the Scowcroft Commission. Relaxing limits on the number of small, single-warhead ICBMs permitted under a reduced ceiling—perhaps by allowing a trade of one MIRVed ICBM for two single-warhead missiles—would be prudent. In any case, the decisive fact is that the dynamics of reductions will impose greater discipline and new incentives on both military establishments. In a smaller force, the premium will be on survivability. To a considerable extent, one can rely on rational military planners to attend to that requirement as forces are compelled to shrink.

In short, the new fluidity in the strategic arms control process demands fresh and imaginative efforts to craft a viable reductions program. There are many ways to exploit this opportunity and many ways to reconcile the differing inclinations the parties bring to the negotiation. To do so, however, will require a better sense of timing than either government has usually shown. The unfolding force growth and technological excursions now impending lend urgency to the mission.

Success in striking a deal on the central strategic balance can open the door to moderation of political and military stresses in Europe as well. Intermediate nuclear forces will have to be treated in the strategic accords, but conventional and tactical forces will remain on the agenda in the Conference on Security and Cooperation in Europe and the Mutual and Balanced Force Reduction talks. Those negotiations have long been stymied because they are dependent variables in the overall equation. Resumption of productive diplomacy on strategic forces should improve the chances of forward movement in both CSCE and MBFR. The candidates are plentiful—more substantial confidence-building measures, phased pull-backs of tactical nuclear weapons and armored forces on both sides, incremental reductions in manpower, perhaps provisions to reduce the ambiguities and potential instabilities associated with dual-capable systems. The parties' habitual disagreement over the actual numbers of forces in the theater may now be susceptible to resolution by creative blending of recent Soviet and Western proposals. No program to cultivate a spreading orchestraint can prosper without concrete innovations in the European security arena.

The Need for Action

This paper does not pretend to set forth a comprehensive and systematic scheme for settling the Cold War once and for all. What it aspires to do is advance a more hopeful perspective on previous efforts to move beyond that unhappy era—and a more ambitious outline for the effort to forge a credible and durable relationship between the superpowers. As the two governments embark on that ineluctable challenge, wariness is in order; a sense of futility is not. Their predecessors wrought better than they have been given credit for; they have provided many building blocks with which to erect a sturdier structure. Their successors are unlikely to have a better opportunity than they themselves have now. Unless today's incumbents act decisively they will bequeath a sad legacy: mounting military deployments, increasing economic distress, prolonged political tensions, and decreasing security for the nations they serve.

Lingering questions abound. Are the Soviet and American peoples mature enough to acknowledge that the failures of detente are shared failures, shortcomings for which both sides bear responsibility? Do leaders on both sides have a clear enough view of past mistakes and frustrations in the relationship to avoid them in the future? Do they perceive the more positive legacies of detente, on which they can begin to erect a sturdy strategic and political orchestraint? Or do the arrival of Gorbachev and the departure of Gromyko portend a turning away from emphasis on US-Soviet relations, either in despair or opportunism? Can the "surrogate enemy"—the shared dread of nuclear catastrophe—motivate Soviet and American governments to subordinate their ongoing political competition to the discipline of orchestraint? Answers to these questions will only emerge from a lengthy period of active engagement between the superpowers.

When Ronald Reagan completes his term of office, he will have presided over nearly one-fifth of the nuclear age. Mikhail Gorbachev, who will be younger in the year 2000 than Mr. Reagan is today, may hold power for a third of it or longer. How will they make use of their stewardship? On the answer to that question hinges not only their place in history, but the course of history itself.

Notes

1. Vernon Van Dyke applies Maslow's thesis to the behavior of nations in *Pride and Power* (Champaign/Urbana, Ill.: University of Illinois Press, 1964).

2. Simon Serfaty, "Introduction: Neither Detente Nor Containment," in Serfaty, ed., *U.S.-Soviet Relations,* FPI Policy Study Groups, School of Advanced International Studies, Johns Hopkins University, August 1985, p. 2.

3. Raymond Garthoff, *Detente and Confrontation: American-Soviet Relations from Nixon to Reagan* (Washington: Brookings Institution, 1985).

4. See, for example, Zbigniew Brzezinski, "Afghanistan and Nicaragua," *The National Interest* 1 (Fall 1985), pp. 48–51.

29
Containment: Choices and Opportunities

Dimitri K. Simes

S INCE THE SECOND WORLD WAR, US policy toward the Soviet Union has been dominated by containment. Containment has been practiced with different degrees of intellectual
and rhetorical clarity, with differing mixtures of foreign policy
tools, and with varying degrees of vigor. Yet, regardless of the
personal preferences and ambitions of American presidents,
there has been neither an escape from containment nor a way to
go much beyond it.

President Jimmy Carter brought to office a hearty disdain
for containment. During his presidency he managed to expand
containment rhetorically, if not quite in reality, to the Persian
Gulf. Conversely, President Ronald Reagan initially talked
about putting Soviet communism "on the ash heap of history."
His advisers included individuals who argued that US policy

Dimitri K. Simes is Senior Associate, Soviet Foreign Policy, Carnegie Endowment for International Peace; Professorial Lecturer, School of Advanced
International Studies, Johns Hopkins University; and Adjunct Professor, Columbia University.

should be aimed at transforming—or at least considerably modifying—the Soviet system. But on the eve of the 1985 Geneva summit with Mikhail Gorbachev, in an interview with the BBC, Mr. Reagan took the position that there is not "any reason why we can't coexist in the world—[and] where there are legitimate areas of competition, compete. But do it in a manner that recognizes that neither one of us should be a threat to the other."

The evolution of the attitudes of Mr. Carter and Mr. Reagan is another reminder that containment is more than a policy option. The very structure of the world environment, the increasing dependence of Soviet foreign policy upon military exploitation of global trouble spots, and the character of the US political process turn containment into more than a necessity—it has become a fact of life.

The Roots of Containment

The complexity of the international system notwithstanding, in terms of power the world is still bipolar. Even regardless of Moscow's intentions, the emergence of global Soviet power presents a major structural problem for the United States. The mere projection of Soviet force into new regions inevitably imposes constraints on American conduct. The appearance of a new and formidable actor changes the power equilibrium to the United States' disadvantage. It encourages American foes, it concerns American allies, and it forces US policymakers to take into account the possibility of Soviet counteraction. Accordingly, even a relatively benign or temporary expansion of Soviet presence cannot but limit US freedom of geopolitical maneuver.

That does not mean, of course, that any spread of Soviet influence anywhere and in any case should automatically cause alarm in Washington. What it does mean is that such a spread is inherently against US interests and cannot be perceived with indifference.

Of course, Soviet advances are not universally accomplished through benign means. And while in a number of instances, most notably in Indonesia, Egypt, and Somalia, Soviet presence has proven to be short-lived, in many others it has demonstrated considerable staying power. Moreover, even a temporary Soviet role in turbulent areas may result in a real threat to important US interests. There would have been no Somalian invasion of the Ogaden desert without a roughly $2 billion Soviet investment in Mogadishu's military machine. And the outcome of the conflict would, in all likelihood, have been quite different if the USSR had not switched sides and supported Ethiopia.

In the Middle East, Soviet military assistance and superpower patronage enabled Egypt and Syria to attack Israel in October 1973. Soviet support of the Arabs did not preclude President Anwar Sadat's breaking from Moscow. Nevertheless, it triggered a situation in which US forces had to be put on alert. American relations with the Arab world experienced a painful if temporary setback. More ominously, there was a dramatic rise in oil prices which did damage not just to the Western economy, but also to the very social fabric of industrial democracies and the cohesion of NATO.

Perceptions are an integral part of international reality. And when the Soviets and their proxies successfully act as arbiters of Third World disputes—even when these disputes and the regions they take place in are not of great strategic significance to the United States—America's credibility as a superpower inevitably suffers in the process. Furthermore, the definition of what is of strategic significance cannot be divorced from the role played by a competing superpower. An area not terribly crucial to the United States in itself can quickly acquire importance if, as in the example of Angola, if offers facilities for the Soviet navy and air force, hosts (for whatever reason) 35,000 Cuban expeditionary troops, or becomes the recipient of major quantities of sophisticated Soviet weapons.

It is doubtful that any diplomatic arrangement could persuade the Soviets to downplay military and security assistance as their principal policy tools in the Third World. Moscow is well aware that the Soviet model of development has lost much of its appeal, that Soviet technology and consumer goods are of inferior quality, and that Soviet ideology and, more broadly, Soviet culture are of extremely limited attraction.

Thus, when the Soviet leadership is asked by the United States to limit the rivalry in the Third World to a strictly peaceful competition, the perception in the Kremlin is that they are being asked to compete with both hands tied behind their back. There was a time in the late fifties and early sixties when, under Nikita Khrushchev, Moscow held romantic illusions about the great common revolutionary goals shared by the USSR and newly independent nations. Those illusions are gone. By now the Politburo is perfectly aware that it is regional turmoil that provides opportunities to expand and maintain Soviet influence and that military force, coercion, and security assistance offer the best chances for success.

Surely, Mikhail S. Gorbachev and his associates have to balance the quest for global influence against other Soviet priorities. These include avoiding an all-out confrontation with the United States and deriving benefits of economic cooperation with the West. But the quest, even if pursued in a careful and calibrated fashion, exists. And it allows the United States little choice but containment.

Containment is also a domestic political imperative in the United States. The US political process, despite its periodic masochism, has little tolerance for Soviet geopolitical advances. Americans envision their worldwide mission to be the promotion of democracy and free enterprise. When any country moves into the US sphere of influence—especially when such a move is at least partially the outcome of the Soviet Union's own actions rather than the free will of the people in question—that move inevitably triggers a strong public outcry in the United

States. As President Carter discovered, downplaying Soviet geopolitical advances can carry a heavy political price. Although it was the Soviet invasion of Afghanistan that made Mr. Carter a convert to containment, he certainly was under strong pressure for some time to respond to Soviet Third World exploits in a more vigorous manner.

Containment Choices

Containment is an integral part of any effective and sustainable policy toward the Soviet Union. It is not, however, adequate as a policy in itself. On the one hand, there is always the question of which broader political objectives containment should enhance and support. On the other, the appropriate tools to carry out these objectives must be determined.

Today, realistically, a qualified containment of Soviet power in areas truly vital to US security may be taken for granted. Containment is not automatic, of course. But if an adequate American effort is made—and a national consensus in favor of such an effort exists—both Western Europe and the Far East are beyond Soviet reach. The conventional superiority of the Soviet Union in Europe is not sufficient to assure the Kremlin of a successful blitzkrieg, particularly since Soviet military planners cannot be quite certain whether Eastern European armies would be more of an asset or a liability in the event of a protracted conflict in the European theater. The relatively smooth and painless deployment of US missiles in Europe, despite a major Soviet propaganda drive, served to demonstrate NATO's will and cohesion. And a near collapse of Eurocommunism has contributed to the domestic stability of European democracies. These considerations are all in addition to whatever uncertainty the remnants of extended deterrence can still generate in the Soviet mind.

The political and military situation in the Far East is no more conducive to Soviet military adventures than in Europe. Japan's rearmament under the Nakasone government, coupled with the political stabilization and modernization of China, severely limits opportunities for Soviet probing. The relatively orderly expansion of democracy and economic growth in South Korea is another contributing factor. All in all, despite major improvements in the Pacific fleet and other categories of Soviet forces, containment in the Far East appears to be as solid as ever.

In the Persian Gulf the situation is more murky. Unlike in Europe and the Far East, there is no neat dividing line between the two systems of alliances. A number of pro-Western regimes feel vulnerable to Islamic fundamentalism and left-wing radicalism. The image of the United States as a principal sponsor of Israel contributes to anti-American sentiment and makes governments friendly to Washington subject to intensely emotional, even violent criticism.

Yet the ability of the United States to project power in the Gulf is superior to that of the USSR and will continue so as long as Iran maintains its distance from Moscow. Also, this region is not quite on the periphery of the Soviet Union, and the Soviets tend to act with greater care at longer distances from their borders. Moreover, the Soviet leadership has already demonstrated its tacit respect of US interests in this region by taking the position (both publicly and privately) during the hostage crisis in Tehran that the United States has legitimate security and economic concerns in the Gulf. Of course, the Politburo would not accept an attempt by the United States to bring the Persian Gulf into the American orbit through a unilateral use of force. And the Soviets have claimed that they must be included in any arrangement to guarantee security of the Gulf. To illustrate its seriousness, Moscow has continued providing assistance to Iran, expanded its naval facility in South Yemen, established diplomatic relations with Oman, and made approaches to Saudi Arabia.

However, the Soviet Union does not seem to have given much priority to creating mischief in the Gulf. Because of lack of an opportunity, innate caution, or a reluctance to invest scarce resources, the Soviet Union has maintained a rather low-key posture in the region. The oil glut made the United States less exposed to turbulence in the Gulf, while probably signaling to the Soviet Union that chances to create major mischief were limited for the time being. Without predicting the future direction of Mr. Gorbachev's foreign policy, it is fair to observe that his leadership to date does not seem overly enthusiastic about making additional high-risk Third World commitments. Assertive retrenchment, rather than a search for new involvements, appears to be the name of the game for Moscow in the Middle East.

In summation, unless there is a drastic change of circumstances in the region, or of priorities in the Kremlin, the United States should be in a position to sustain containment in the Persian Gulf.

The real dilemma for the United States is whether to go beyond a containment policy limited to Western Europe, the Far East, and the Persian Gulf. Common sense suggests that global containment of communism, or even, more narrowly, of the Soviet Union, cannot be foolproof. An attempt to put a straight jacket on the Soviet empire could produce an embarrassing gap between perceived US interests and the power to protect them. An indiscriminate commitment to stopping the Soviets in the Third World could involve the United States in more Vietnams, shattering the American domestic consensus in favor of tough-minded policy toward the USSR in the process. And spreading US resources too thinly may result in failing to constrain Moscow where it really matters.

But if global containment of the Soviet Union cannot reliably work everywhere, does it follow that the only alternative is selective containment in areas of vital interest to the United States? To start with, a containment strictly limited to the defense of a few particularly important regions is about as unrealistic a notion as the idea of a foolproof global containment. If the Soviet Union is allowed to acquire geopolitical momentum, and if US credibility as a superpower could be damaged in the process, how long would it take before the American ability to implement even more modest containment schemes would be questioned by friends and foes alike? And containment, after all, is very much in the eye of the beholder. It reflects not only the balance of forces but also the balance of perceptions.

Second, an appreciation that the United States has neither the resources nor the will to take a stand at every point of Soviet penetration does not mean that the only other option in areas of less than vital interests is passivity. If the Soviets are making advances in areas where the United States does not have vital interests or where local circumstances do not favor a major American involvement, an appropriate US response may still be limited action.

The purpose of such action would be not necessarily to win but rather to upgrade the costs for the Soviet Union. Global powers cannot be effective if they agree to become involved only when there is a realistic chance to achieve victory. It may be sufficient to make an experience so costly to a rival that he would be deterred from repeating it elsewhere. And the rule of thumb is that if you make a low-key contribution to those opposing your rival in a variety of trouble spots, somewhere your clients are bound to have a success.

That is how the USSR has supported numerous so-called national liberation movements for decades. The Kremlin was rarely certain that any one of them in particular would come to power. It was enough to know that some were likely to deliver on the Soviet investment. Also, the Soviets were comforted by the thought that they had to invest less in these movements than the West had to spend, both financially and in terms of political capital, to cope with them. Keeping a rival busy that cheaply is not a bad geopolitical strategy.

Consequently, there is no necessary contradiction between pursuing global containment and avoiding indiscriminate commitments. Vital interests require vigorous defense, including, if necessary, the use of military force. Peripheral interests justify marginal investments. But the sum total of marginal United States investments can considerably restrain the Soviet geopolitical drive.

Should the ultimate purpose of containment be limited to this objective? Those who believe in "containment without confrontation" would caution against more ambitious designs. They would argue that success of containment is partly dependent upon Soviet cooperation. If the Soviets view containment as a part of a broader strategy to deny them superpower status—to say nothing about encouraging instability inside their empire—they may respond with unpredictable violence.

Nevertheless, it is fairly obvious that instability inside the Soviet orbit inevitably strains Moscow's assertiveness. The Soviet preoccupation with just protecting itself and its own makes containment easier to implement. Reasonable people may disagree over what the United States can realistically do to put the Soviet Union on the defensive in its own sphere of influence, and they may debate the consequences of destabilization for East-West relations. But it is hard to see how limiting the Soviets' freedom of maneuver in dealing with the Eastern Europeans and other clients could be contrary to American interests, including those which fall under the requirements of containment.

An effective containment does not have to be—moreover, simply cannot be—merely defensive. It has to be incorporated as an indispensable element of a more general policy of disciplining the Soviet power—disciplining it to the greatest possible degree—not only outside, but also inside the Soviet sphere of influence.

The Tools of Containment

The tools of containment may be somewhat artificially divided into three categories: coercion, abdication, and cooperation. In the eighties, the Western arsenal of coercion, in addition to the traditional tools of extended deterrence and maintenance of the system of alliances, was complemented by a number of resistance movements in areas under Soviet influence. There is a growing sentiment that these movements represent not only an inherently moral cause but also a promising foreign policy instrument. At the same time, an argument that support of these movements would represent an ethical and political blunder is gaining strength. The rebels are often not quite knights on white horses—witness the contras in Nicaragua. Moreover, some argue that few rebels are likely to prevail and that aid to them would only result in greater Soviet military involvement— witness Afghanistan. Also, some of these movements are supported by outcast governments and are guilty by association— witness UNITA in Angola.

Such arguments cannot be easily dismissed. But they only point up the impossibility of engaging the Soviet Union in a vigorous geopolitical competition without incurring some moral and political costs. Each situation, of course, should be assessed individually. But the lens through which these situations are viewed must be colored by a recognition that stopping, and where possible reversing, Soviet advances is a dominant political and moral imperative for the United States.

Another tool of coercion is the new potential for mobility and maneuver of NATO forces in Europe. The only credible extended deterrence in Europe in this era of nuclear parity is a deterrence based upon some conventional retaliatory capability against non-Soviet Warsaw Pact territory. The ability to retaliate in Eastern Europe inevitably—whether NATO intends it or not—creates some doubt in Moscow regarding Western intentions in the event of another Prague Spring. To extend a token of deterrence—even a mere token—slightly beyond the great dividing line between the two alliances is an opportunity too great to miss.

Using the tools of abdication requires US determination not to help the Soviet Union manage its empire with Western assistance. Again, the practical choices are not easy. What about starvation in Ethiopia? What about the Polish people, who would suffer if their government defaults? Using innocent civilians as pawns in the geopolitical rivalry is inherently contrary to the American ethos.

Yet, in disregarding the option of abdication the United States fails to exploit one of the most important Soviet vulnerabilities, namely, the economic and social failure of the Russian-style model of communism. Those who choose to be allied with the Soviet Union should be prepared to expect the associated internal costs.

Finally, there are the tools of cooperation. A useful, if somewhat artificial, distinction can be made between those intended to contribute to a climate of relative interdependence which supplements the basic rivalry with useful shock absorbers, and those essentially designed to promote US geopolitical interests. In the first category is direct trade with the Soviet Union; in the second are economic arrangements with and aid to Eastern European and other countries (Mozambique, for example) which are striving for a modicum of foreign policy autonomy from Moscow. The latter are not terribly controversial. There are good reasons to offer a reward to governments prepared to distance themselves from the Kremlin. The former raise some tough questions. Mutually beneficial, unsubsidized, nonstrategic trade is unobjectionable in its own right. The real issue is how much leverage the West can buy with it as long as the USSR is denied what it wants most: high technology and major, long-term, subsidized investment. To accommodate the Soviet desire runs the risk of contributing to Soviet military power and to the attractiveness of the Soviet model. But the failure to accommodate Soviet requests significantly reduces one potential for political leverage.

Up to now, economic cooperation has failed to have a major impact on Soviet political ambitions. It has created some valuable bonds between the two sides, but the bonds have been useful only at the margins of managing the rivalry in a more rational and controllable fashion. The lesson of the past forty years is that containment cannot be based on anything but a forceful unilateral effort. Today, conditions for such an effort are uniquely favorable. But, as in the past, the absence of this effort—the refusal to make critical (even if unpleasant) choices—can cost dearly.

30

Containment, Peace, and the Charter

Eugene V. Rostow

T HERE IS A DISQUIETING GAP between official statements of
US foreign policy, on the one hand, and, on the other, current American literature on the subject and the implicit foreign
policy agenda suggested by the pattern of American budgets,
actions, and failures to act in world politics. Moreover, the gap
is widening.

Except in one important particular, the official foreign policy of the United States is firm in the faith of the gospel according to President Truman and Secretary of State Acheson. That
creed was announced nearly forty years ago. It has been followed and developed by the United States and its allies with
varying degrees of energy, imagination, and success ever since.
President Reagan's distinctive amendment to the policy, if it be-
cames a reality, should increase its effectiveness.

Eugene V. Rostow is Distinguished Visiting Research Professor of Law and
Diplomacy at the National Defense University and Professor Emeritus and
Senior Research Scholar at Yale.

But the major theme of the non-official literature and of actual practice is one of retreat from the Truman-Acheson foreign policy. Those who advocate retreat speak in many voices. They rarely tell us how far to retreat. Sometimes they do not speak at all, but simply act. They all have different hobby horses and put special emphasis on different points. Some are less opaque than others. But all their counsel points in the same direction.

What the chorus is saying, over and over again, is that the United States is over-committed; that after Korea and Vietnam the American people will not tolerate military adventures much beyond Martha's Vineyard and Pearl Harbor; that we cannot afford the security expenditures required to keep up with the Soviet Union and its allies, and that our own allies are not doing their share in the common effort. Therefore, the prophets of retreat tell us, we should cut our military budgets; reduce our forces in Europe, the Middle East, and Asia; and gradually pull back to our own shores. Some advocate an even more bizarre policy, which they call "unilateral internationalism"—a program which would apparently require the United States, freed of the tiresome obligations of alliance diplomacy, to protect its worldwide security interests single-handed.

The arguments for retreat are reinforced by the state of the nuclear balance and by the magnitude and momentum of the Soviet nuclear buildup. For many Americans and Europeans, that phenomenon alone is enough to justify policies of withdrawal, neutrality, and accommodation, which they fondly imagine are available to Europe, Japan, and the United States as an alternative foreign policy. The nuclear-oriented apostles of retreat start with the arresting proposition, first put forward by General De Gaulle, that great powers do not commit suicide for their allies. They continue by pointing out that the Soviet-American nuclear balance is such that the United States could never make good on its guarantees; that "extended deterrence" is now a myth and perhaps always was a myth; that Soviet nuclear strength makes it impossible for the United States and its allies to use conventional force in defense of their interests; and therefore that the West should accept the inevitable and make the best deal it can with the Soviet Union.

This paper rejects the arguments for an American retreat to isolation root and branch, in all their protean variety. Its thesis is that, for the most permanent and fundamental reasons of national security, the United States cannot and must not retreat, but on the contrary must go forward. The Truman-Acheson foreign policy should not be abandoned but be renewed and improved in the light of the changes which have occurred since the late forties. The Western objective in this effort, based on prudent policies of allied solidarity, should be not only containment of Soviet expansion achieved by aggression, but also genuine peace with the Soviet Union.

The United States is not over-committed; its commitments correspond to its geopolitical interests in a world political system where only the United States can lead the coalitions required to protect the world balance of power. The American people are not in the least hysterical in the aftermath of Korea and Vietnam; every election and every serious poll shows that they are staunch, patriotic, and ready as always to support the national interest if their leaders have the courage to lead and the ability to explain what is required and why. Of course we can afford the costs of national security, and of course our allies are doing their share—far more than most people realize. In any event, the performance of our allies is irrelevant. We have guaranteed their security for reasons of our own national interest, not of philanthropy. As a nation, we cannot afford to allow vast centers of power like Western Europe and Japan to fall under hostile control. And it is ridiculous to imagine that we are incapable of the marginal effort required to maintain our capacity for nuclear retaliation, the basis for extended deterrence as well as the deterrence of nuclear attacks on the United States itself.

Mr. Gorbachev says his foreign policy goal is what he calls a "modus vivendi" with the United States. By this revealing

phrase he seems to have in mind a political condition which
would be something less than peace, but less tense than that of
the moment. In short, Mr. Gorbachev is proposing yet another
agreement of detente like those which led to such bitter disappointments for the United States after Soviet-American procla-
mations of improved relations in the "spirit" of Geneva in 1955
and Camp David in 1959; the moment of euphoria following the
Cuban missile crisis of 1962; and the summit meetings and
other Soviet-American agreements achieved by President Nixon
during 1972 and 1973. What Mr. Gorbachev's modus vivendi
means is that the United States and its allies should remain
passive while the Soviet Union outflanks them by means of aggressive campaigns of expansion conducted throughout the
Third World. A Soviet-American modus vivendi now would
rather be an ignis fatuus, which the Oxford dictionary defines as
a fire of swamp gas, a delusive and bewitching fire leading the
unwary into pools and ditches.

The realistic objective for Western policy toward the Soviet
Union is not a modus vivendi but peace itself. A condition of
peace between the United States and the Soviet Union would require each side to abide scrupulously by the rule of the United
Nations Charter against aggression, which President Reagan
made the centerpiece of his speech before the United Nations on
24 October 1985. Such a goal is well within the capacity of the
coalitions and potential coalitions led by the United States in the
Atlantic and Pacific basins, the Middle East, and Southern Asia.
It would build on the strength and good sense of President
Truman's containment policy—which has served the nation well
in the years since 1947—but go beyond it in pressing for peace
with the Soviet Union, rather than waiting patiently for the Soviet Union to realize how foolish and costly its present policies
are. A Western policy built on this principle is the only way to
end the Cold War, which could easily get out of hand in any
one of a dozen flash-points around the world.

Containment at the Outset

It is important to recall that the policy of containment was not the first but the second postwar policy of the West toward the Soviet Union. The first American policy proposal was one of full cooperation with the Soviet Union in repairing the physical damage of the war and restoring the state system in accordance with the principles of the United Nations Charter. That goal remains and will remain a lodestar of American and Western foreign policy, to be pursued despite all obstacles.

The policy of containment was announced in 1947, two years after the end of the Second World War. During those two years, the hopes and dreams of the war period about the possibility of achieving relations of continued cooperation with the Soviet Union turned to ashes. Above all, it became clear that the Soviet Union had no intention of abiding by the rule against aggression which is the foundation of the state system organized under the banner of the United Nations Charter.

During the war, Soviet-Allied relations were characterized by episodes of nearly unbelievable Soviet hostility. The governments of the United States, Great Britain, and France thoroughly understood the nature of Soviet policy. There was great foreboding within the Western governments and a correspondingly intense determination to make every possible effort to sustain and improve the wartime pattern of Soviet-Allied collaboration. There were high hopes throughout the West that the Soviet government would choose to continue its wartime association with the Western allies. More particularly, it was hoped that the Soviet Union would join its erstwhile allies in managing the state system much as the great powers cooperated in the Concert of Europe during the nineteenth century. Soviet diplomats commented later that if the San Francisco Conference had been delayed for a year, the United Nations Charter would never have been signed. There is nothing mysterious about their observation. As Stalin told Ambassador W. Averell Harriman near the end of the war, during a conversation in which Harriman was trying to persuade Stalin to accept an American postwar reconstruction loan under the Lend-Lease Act, "We have decided to go our own way."

Stalin's policy was carried out with a vengeance. The Soviet government attempted to seize Greece and the northern provinces of Iran, threatened Berlin and Turkey, and intervened in Czechoslovakia. It brusquely rejected the Marshall Plan and the Baruch Plan, which offered the Soviets reconstruction loans and nuclear cooperation; took over Eastern Europe, repudiating its promises to hold free elections in that critical area; refused to discuss or modify its policy of indefinite expansion either in Europe or elsewhere in the world; and rejected any and all proposals to create the decisive great power peacekeeping forces called for by the Charter.

Facing these bleak realities, the West decided to adopt the course of deterring and containing Soviet aggression, and defeating it when necessary, rather than eliminating in a more conclusive way the Soviet Union's capacity to commit aggression. For reasons which reflect the finest features of our national character and of Western culture at large, the Western nations undertook to follow the advice of George Kennan's classic article in *Foreign Affairs*—to contain Soviet expansion and give the benign influence of Russian high culture time to mellow the Soviet leadership, in the hope that one day the Soviet Union would give up its imperial ambitions and settle down to cooperate with the other powers in keeping the peace.

Thus in 1947 the West launched the policy of containment—the foundation for an ambitious foreign policy of economic and social progress, of political solidarity, and of international cooperation in the control of nuclear weapons and nuclear technology.

For two decades, the Western foreign policy developed by President Truman and Secretary of State Acheson was moderately successful, except in the area of achieving effective

international control of nuclear weapons and nuclear technology. It was the engine of reconstruction and economic growth in
the capitalist world, the Third World, and the world of communist states, and this policy sustained an impressive cultural and
political renaissance in many parts of the globe. But from the
beginning, it failed in its most fundamental goal—the restoration of the state system as an effective check on aggression. The
West hesitated before the challenge of enforcing the Charter
rules against Soviet aggression in Eastern Europe. With some
success, it moved to defeat Soviet-supported aggression in the
Third World, only to discover that successful instances of Western defense—in Berlin and Korea, for example—did not deter
further aggression, but simply led to an increase in the intensity
and scale of violence the next time. The Soviet Union did not
mellow in the sunshine of Russian high culture, as George
Kennan had anticipated. On the contrary, its program of expansion and aggression became steadily worse. Finally giving up
hope of achieving Soviet compliance with the Charter rules anywhere, the United States came to rely more and more on what
we supposed were bilateral Soviet-American codes of crisis
management and crisis prevention.

Nuclear Weapons and the Illusion of Crisis Management

The increasing concentration of Western thought on problems of
crisis management rather than of foreign policy was a register of
defeat—an admission that the expectation of peace of the early
postwar period had faded, and that we were in fact living under
siege within a contracting perimeter, responding to attack—
sometimes—in ways we hoped would be effective without pro-
voking all-out war. What are the supposed canons of crisis management and crisis prevention on which we have relied to
minimize ultimate risks?

The first and most basic is that the armed forces of each superpower not fire at the armed forces of the other. Manifestly,
such a rule should make it easier for each side to avoid nuclear
war by inadvertence or escalation. The only major exception to

that rule, so far, has been the Cuban missile crisis of 1962, when the United States boarded and turned back a Soviet vessel bound for Cuba. The Soviet government did not use armed force to interfere with the allied airlift which saved Berlin in the late forties, nor with the flow of supplies and troops to allied forces in Korea and Vietnam. It has, however, used force with deliberate brutality to sabotage the arrangements for inspection established in Germany immediately after the Second World War.

In the West, many students and officials once thought that there would be a second tacit rule of prudence in the conduct of the Cold War—that each side would respect certain special security interests of the other. Thus the West did not interfere with the Soviet sphere of influence in Eastern Europe. But it soon became clear that the Soviet Union would not reciprocate. Instead, it tried to take over Greece, Cuba, Iran, Turkey, and other countries or areas which we thought they had agreed were in our sphere of influence.

During the last twenty years, there have been a number of efforts to develop crisis management and crisis avoidance techniques. The "hot line," permitting rapid and direct communication between the two heads of government, is one example. Another is the Standing Committee on Accidents at Sea, which has had a positive influence on the number of collisions and near collisions between Soviet and American naval vessels.

The attempt to obtain Soviet-American agreements which could control nuclear weapons in the interest of peace is the most conspicuous of all the American efforts to achieve Soviet-American arrangements for crisis management and crisis avoidance.

We went through a long period of trial and error in trying to discover the significance of nuclear weapons in war and diplomacy.

In 1945 and 1946, some Americans thought that a single waggle of our nuclear finger would dissuade the Soviet Union from any kind of adventure. Perhaps this was the case in the first crisis of the Cold War, that in Northern Iran in 1946. But as the Soviet Union persisted in probing our responses to their experiments in expansion, it soon became clear that there were many situations in which we would not use or threaten to use nuclear weapons. In those situations, the Soviets could use conventional forces to accomplish their purposes, confident that if we resisted at all, we would do so only locally, and only with conventional forces.

During the fifties, John Foster Dulles announced the doctrine of "massive retaliation," threatening a nuclear response against the Soviet Union as a means of deterring or resisting Soviet-based aggression in important but secondary theaters of Soviet expansion. The doctrine was stillborn. It was soon apparent that the United States was not likely to use nuclear weapons against the Soviet Union even in situations like Korea or Vietnam, although, after several bitter years of warfare, two credible nuclear hints did bring the Korean War at least to an armistice. But the same procedure did not work in Vietnam, at a time when the Soviet-American nuclear equation was more nearly in balance and Sino-Soviet rivalry for political leadership in the area had become acute.

During the 1960s, the doctrine of "flexible response" was articulated to govern the role of the nuclear weapon in the defense of Europe and other vital American security interests. It remains the theoretical basis of our policy for the military use of the nuclear weapon.

The Cuban missile crisis remains in many ways the most illuminating and instructive of all the Soviet-American confrontations since 1945. The nuclear element in the crisis was conspicuous, and its implications remain pertinent. Indeed, the United States has pressed the Soviet Union ever since to accept rules that might ensure the deterrent stability of the Soviet-American nuclear balance. To the American mind, the Cuban missile crisis dramatized the explosive potentialities of nuclear anxiety and demonstrated the utility of agreements or understandings that might minimize uncertainty about the nuclear forces and intentions of the other. We took it for granted that the Soviet leadership took the same view of the problem.

The focal point of the crisis—eighteen months after the Bay of Pigs fiasco—was the secret Soviet plan to deploy intermediate-range nuclear weapons on Cuban soil. The United States had announced publicly that it would not tolerate the Soviet emplacement of "offensive" weapons in Cuba. The Soviet Union had denied both publicly and privately that it was preparing to make such a deployment, but it was doing so. The United States, with the support of the Organization of American States and of its NATO allies, assembled an expeditionary force of 250,000 troops in Florida, established a partial blockade of Cuba, and intercepted a Soviet vessel approaching the island with a load of missiles. After a round of hectic diplomatic exchanges, agreement was reached and the missiles were withdrawn, although Castro was left in power.

On what legal basis did the United States use a limited amount of force in self-defense? There was no armed attack on the United States, and no threat of an armed attack, nuclear or otherwise. The nuclear balance in 1962 was so favorable to the United States that a direct Soviet attack was inconceivable. Cuba had the legal right to request Soviet assistance in defending itself against possible attack—a concern which had a certain plausibility in the aftermath of the Bay of Pigs affair. Yet the United States argued, and the Western world generally agreed, that a sudden, secret, and deceptive change in the Soviet-American nuclear balance was in itself an illegal act of force justifying a legally appropriate American response—that is, a limited and proportional use of enough force to cure the Soviet breach of international law. It is important to emphasize, as Albert and Roberta Wohlstetter pointed out at the time, that the threat in Cuba against which the United States was reacting was primarily political in character, a threat designed to weaken the alliance systems of the United States by means of nuclear intimidation.

The American threat to invade Cuba with conventional forces was credible to the Soviet Union because of the state of the Soviet-American nuclear balance in 1962. The principal moral of the Cuban missile crisis is that Western conventional forces can be used only with the implicit protection of a believable American capacity to retaliate with nuclear weapons if the Soviet Union should intervene. Thus in 1983, when the United States, France, Italy, and Great Britain landed forces in Lebanon, some experienced American foreign policy experts criticized the move because it might lead to a nuclear confrontation with the Soviet Union. The critics were in error on the facts, but their argument brings out the relationship between the state of the nuclear balance and our capacity to use conventional force. In Lebanon as in Cuba, Korea, and Vietnam, the United States could use conventional force because we had the capacity to retaliate against the Soviet Union if it interfered. The allied debacle in Lebanon was not a response to Soviet nuclear threats. The allies simply failed to take advantage of an important strategic opportunity.

The Illusion of Arms Control

The link between the nuclear balance and the capacity of the West to use conventional force is the heart of the nuclear problem, politically as well as militarily. Unless the United States retains a strong nuclear retaliatory capacity, it will be unable to carry out the foreign and defense policies it must pursue to protect the nation's security interests in world politics.

The future of America's nuclear retaliatory capacity is the key issue—indeed the only issue—with which Soviet and American negotiators have been wrestling since the beginning of the nuclear arms control talks in 1969. The goal of the Soviet Union in these talks has been to attain unchallengeable superiority in intermediate-range and intercontinental land-based ballistic missiles—thus far the most accurate and destructive nuclear weapons, and the weapons least vulnerable to defenses of any kind. Such an advantage, the Soviet experts believe, would destroy the deterrent credibility of American nuclear guarantees and lead the United States to withdraw its forces from Europe, the Mediterranean, and the Far East, adopting a posture of neutrality in the event of an attack on American allies or other interests. Nuclear arms agreements ratifying such a Soviet advantage would facilitate the achievement of the Soviet Union's main strategic objective—the separation of the United States from Europe and the consequent subjugation of Western Europe, Africa, the Mediterranean, and the Far East.

In 1972, when the SALT I agreements were signed, the United States and the Soviet Union had approximately the same number of warheads on intercontinental land-based ballistic missiles, and the United States had a comfortable lead in sea-based and airborne forces. The American capacity for nuclear retaliation was beyond question. In 1985, the Soviet Union had a lead of more than 3.5 to 1 in the number of warheads on ICBMs and a lead of more than 4 to 1 in the throw weight of these weapons. Its sea-based and airborne nuclear forces have made comparable if less spectacular gains. In addition, it had a near monopoly on advanced intermediate-range land-based weapons threatening targets in Europe, Japan, China, and the Middle East. These shifts in the Soviet-American nuclear balance raised serious doubts about our ability to deter attacks against security interests most fundamental to the balance of power—the independence of Japan, China, Western Europe, South Korea, and the Middle East.

The prospect of a Soviet first-strike capacity—a capacity to destroy a large part of our retaliatory forces with 25 or 30 percent of their ICBMs alone—is proving to be a political influence of incalculable power, pushing the United States toward the mirage of isolation and its allies toward the corresponding mirage of neutrality and accommodation. No one in the West has the slightest inclination to find out whether the arcane calculations of a Soviet first-strike capacity would prove accurate if put to the test.

As the Scowcroft Commission concluded in 1983, the United States cannot permit the Soviet-American nuclear imbalance to continue. There are only three ways in which nuclear stability, predictability, and deterrence might be restored: (1) a crash American building program involving MX, Midgetman, cruise missiles, Pershing II, and other nuclear delivery systems; (2) the development of defensive weapons which might transform the nuclear equation by requiring 80 or 90 percent rather than 25 or 30 percent of the Soviet nuclear force to execute a first strike; or (3) an arms control agreement with the Soviet Union based on the principle of Soviet-American deterrent retaliatory equality.

The only significant difference between the Soviet Union and the United States in the Geneva nuclear arms talks between 1981 and 1983, and in the new round of the talks which began in 1985, concerns this crucial issue—that of Soviet-American equality. The United States has pressed for agreements based on the principle of equality, offering amendment after amendment in the hope of inducing the Soviet Union to compromise; the Soviets have adamantly refused, holding out for what they call "equality and equal security," a phrase that would entitle them to a force equal to the sum of all the other nuclear forces in the world. The Soviet goal in the negotiations is to induce the United States to acknowledge the Soviet Union's "right" to nuclear superiority. That is why they have pressed for the inclusion of British and French forces in the INF talks, although they know that those forces are no threat to the far superior Soviet arsenal but exist for quite different national purposes. And they hold out for agreements based on the principle of equal *reduction*—so far, primarily in launchers rather than in warheads or throw weight—not reduction to equal *levels*. The Soviet approach both in the 1981–83 INF and START negotiations and thus far in the new round of three-sided nuclear arms negotiations in Geneva would make the crucial Soviet advantage in land-based ballistic missiles even bigger and more intimidating than it is now. And they have the temerity to demand an end of American research and development of defensive weapons, although they themselves are spending more on defense against nuclear weapons than on the manufacture of offensive ones.

But the public reports on the substance of the new round of negotiations show considerable movement, at least in the form of the Soviet positions. The basic Soviet proposal adopts the structure of the American START position which has been on the table in Geneva since 1982. It calls for a reduction of what Mr. Gorbachev calls the number of "nuclear charges" to equal levels on both sides—we must make sure that the word "charges" means warheads, not launchers—with a sub-limit providing that no more than a given fraction be in any one category. The American position remains what it has been in principle, although it has been modified in detail. It is that the unit of account in the negotiations should be warheads and their destructive quality, not launchers, and that the outcome must be equality between the two sides, not a Soviet right to a first-strike capacity. Naturally, the significance of these changes in the Soviet position are being carefully explored.

Of course the Soviet advantage in land-based missiles may erode in time if the new weapons for our Trident submarines turn out to be as accurate and as formidable as expected. Again, cruise missiles or other small, accurate, and mobile weapons may guarantee nuclear stalemate, and the development of defensive weapons may in the long run completely transform the nuclear equation as it stands today. But for many years we shall continue to depend upon deterrence through the threat of retaliation with offensive weapons.

The nuclear arms situation of the last twenty years cannot continue indefinitely. It may be that the variables in the nuclear equation are becoming so numerous, so mysterious, and so complex that the Soviet Union will come to agree that the nuclear component of world politics cannot be managed without Soviet-American cooperation. We have no alternative but to try for such a goal, but the record since the 1960s offers little ground for optimism. The Soviet objective in arms control negotiations, like the rest of Soviet foreign policy, has been not stability but instability, not equality with the United States but domination over the United States, not mutual deterrence but American acceptance of a Soviet capacity for nuclear blackmail. There is no objective reason for expecting the Soviet leadership to change its position soon.

But even if we should wake up one morning and discover that the Soviet Union had agreed to a good arms control agreement—an agreement based on the principle of Soviet-American equality in deterrent power, taking offensive and defensive weapons into account—we should have accomplished little. There is no sense in an arms control agreement which promises immunity from nuclear war but in effect licenses conventional war without limit. Since the most likely cause of nuclear war is escalation from conventional war, such an agreement would be a deception from the start. The United States and other Western powers would have to maintain a secure retaliatory nuclear capacity in any event, just as they do now.

The Illusion of a Modus Vivendi

Obviously, the United States cannot continue to muddle along in the pattern of pure containment. Forty years is long enough to wait for George Kennan's prophecy of a Soviet mellowing to materialize. The postwar era is over. The ice is breaking in the state system, and the present is one of those rare historic moments of choice, like President Truman's creative term of office.

If we put aside counsels of despair and surrender, there are two approaches to the problem of Soviet-American relations which have some plausibility at the present time—the approach of a new agreement of detente, a modus vivendi, as Mr. Gorbechev calls it; and the approach of peace itself, a determination on the part of the Western nations to insist that the Soviet Union give up the practice of aggression and live within its legitimate borders like other states, in conformity to the rules of the United Nations Charter. Secretary of State Acheson put the issue sharply a generation ago in responding to a Soviet proposal for a nonaggression pact with the United States—a hardy perennial in Soviet diplomatic practice. "We already have a nonaggression pact with the Soviet Union," Acheson said. "It is called the Charter of the United Nations. Any special agreement between us could only weaken and qualify the influence of the Charter, and we must not follow that road."

Henry Kissinger has put forward the most cogent and realistic sketch of a possible reduction of tensions through a new modus vivendi agreement with the Soviet Union. It is well worth examining in detail:

> For too long, the Western democracies have flinched from facing the fundamental cause of tensions, the ground rules the Soviets have succeeded in imposing on the international system. Everything that has become Communist remains forever inviolate. Everything that's non-Communist is open to change: by pressure, by subversion, by guerrilla action, if necessary by terror. These ground rules if not resisted will inexorably shift the balance of power against the democracies.[1]

Mr. Kissinger's article admirably defines the central dilemma of Western foreign policy. He does not concentrate on how to achieve a nuclear arms control agreement with the Soviet Union or on other secondary issues. Instead, he directs attention to the primary problem: what to do about the continuing process of Soviet expansion accomplished by the illegal use of force. Unfortunately, the remedy Mr. Kissinger prescribes would make the crisis worse.

As Mr. Kissinger points out, the Soviet Union is pressing us to accept the singular thesis that it is above the law against aggression applicable to all other states. Soviet expansion achieved by direct and indirect aggression is changing the world balance of power. And, unless countered, the increasing Soviet advantage in land-based ballistic nuclear missiles and other nuclear weapons will soon make it impossible for the Western nations to resist Soviet aggression through the use of conventional forces. Facing these pressures, the West, rather than accepting the true character of Soviet policy, has "flinched" and is still flinching. For the moment, the West is mesmerized, like a bird confronted by a snake.

As a result, Mr. Kissinger tells us, the international order is lurching toward a systemic breakdown like that of August 1914. He concludes that unless the Soviet Union and the United States reach agreement soon on viable rules for peaceful coexistence, a major confrontation between the two is nearly inevitable, a confrontation neither side could expect to control. The reason such an outcome is so likely, Mr. Kissinger believes, is that the existing ground rules for Soviet-American coexistence are both unacceptable and dangerous.

Thus far, Mr. Kissinger is on solid ground. My disagreement with him concerns the next stage of his argument. To eliminate the threat of an uncontrollable crisis in a nuclear setting, Mr. Kissinger recommends a secret Soviet-American negotiation to achieve "specific agreements that define the true vital interests of each side and the permissible challenges to them." Mr. Kissinger writes, "In the past such agreements have been confined to generalities that created an illusion of progress. Let us now work on a concrete and definite program."

A substantial fraction, perhaps a majority, of Western opinion agrees with the judgment behind Mr. Kissinger's proposal, i.e., that we lack the power and the will to require the Soviet Union to live in peace with its neighbors in accordance with the United Nations Charter. People of this persuasion therefore seek a "pragmatic" modus vivendi with the Soviet Union. They advocate a spheres-of-influence agreement which would define a Soviet-American relationship short of peace but less explosive than that of the last forty years, a deal which they hope would head off the climax Mr. Kissinger rightly perceives as nearly inevitable if present trends continue. Mr. Nixon, for example, calls such a relationship "hard-headed detente."[2]

No American could possibly object to a Soviet-American understanding that would reduce tensions and make the international environment less fragile. Indeed, American and Western opinion has greeted with relief and enthusiasm each proclamation since Yalta that the Soviet Union and the Western powers have achieved such an understanding. But the record of Soviet international behavior makes it obvious that the advocates of yet another modus vivendi agreement with the Soviet Union are whistling in the wind. In the small, dangerous, interdependent, and volatile nuclear world of the late twentieth century, there is no possible state of "detente" halfway between war and peace. Eager as the West is for "detente" and truly "peaceful coexistence" with the Soviet Union, more than forty years of diplomatic frustration make it apparent that the West can accept no definition for these terms except peace itself—that is, the rules of the United Nations Charter purporting to govern the international use of force.

Two classes of reasons compel this conclusion: reasons of experience and reasons of analysis.

The United States and the Western nations as a group have reached modus vivendi agreements with the Soviet Union many times since the summit meetings at Tehran, Yalta, and Potsdam. They have all failed. Some were general in their language but many were extremely concrete and specific. For example, the Soviet-American agreement of October 1962, negotiated by Governor Harriman, was crystal clear. In that agreement, the Soviet Union promised us that North Vietnam would withdraw its troops from Laos and respect the neutrality of that unhappy land. Many students of the Indochinese wars believe that President Kennedy's failure to insist on the enforcement of the 1962 Laos agreement led straight to the Vietnam tragedy.

The Indo-Chinese Agreements of January and March 1973 were comparably "concrete and definite." They purported to provide a great-power guarantee for the enforcement of the Laos Agreement of 1962 and for the rights of self-determination of the South Vietnamese people. Similarly, the Nixon-Brezhnev agreement of May 1972 not only promised Soviet-American cooperation in managing future crises peacefully but categorically assured us of Soviet support for efforts to achieve peace in the Middle East in accordance with Security Council Resolution 242. The Soviet Union breached the Middle Eastern feature of the 1972 agreement a month before it was signed by promising Sadat full support for the Yom Kippur War of 1973. And it treated all the other agreements mentioned here as scraps of paper before the ink of their signatures was dry. A high-ranking Soviet official referred to one of the most important of these agreements—the Indo-Chinese Agreements of 1973—as a typical attempt by an American president to deceive American public opinion.

Nothing could have been more "concrete and definite"—or more important—than the assurance of free elections in Eastern Europe given us by the Soviet Union at Yalta and Potsdam. President Kennedy once told a Soviet interviewer that there could be no peace between the Soviet Union and the United States until those promises were carried out. But they have not been carried out. One could list other modus vivendi agreements: the McCloy-Zorin agreement, the Helsinki Final Act, the statements issued after summit meetings without number. They have all had the same melancholy fate.

It is hard to imagine why the Soviet Union should be more willing now than in the past to fulfill agreements of this kind. The Soviets are still enlarging their lead over the West in most categories of military power. Despite political setbacks in Egypt and in China, they continue to gain politically in many important areas of the world. And they remain convinced believers in the un-Marxist view that the future of world politics will be determined by the correlation of military forces.

But analysis reveals an even more fundamental reason why proposals that we try to negotiate a new "detente" arrangement with the Soviet Union are devoid of promise. There is no way in which the United States and the Soviet Union could define and agree to respect each other's national security interests until the Soviet Union gives up its dream of empire.

The most basic national security interest of the United States is to prevent any one power from controlling the full Eurasian land mass, a reservoir of power which the coastal and island states, including the United States, Great Britain, and Japan, could not hope to defeat. But the manifest goal of Soviet foreign policy *is* to gain control of the Eurasian land mass—to achieve hegemony both in Europe and in Asia, and therefore to impose its will in Africa, Latin America, the Middle East, and many other parts of the world. The present foreign policy objectives of the United States and the Soviet Union cannot be reconciled by negotiation, however secret and ingenious.

The United States has always been conscious of its geopolitical interest in opposing hegemonic power in Europe and in Asia. When Napoleon invaded Russia, Thomas Jefferson saw at once, despite his strong sympathies with France and the French revolution, that a French victory over Russia would endanger the United States. The same perception led the United States to fight two world wars in order to prevent Germany from dominating Western Europe and Russia. And we helped organize NATO in 1949, and have participated in its activities ever since, to keep the Soviet Union from achieving the same end. The identical principle led us to fight in four Asian wars since 1898 and, more recently, to protect the security of Japan, China, South Korea, Taiwan, the Philippines, Australia and New Zealand, Thailand, and Pakistan. Modern Japan is obviously a vital security interest of the United States exactly as Western Europe is, and for the same reason: to keep so great a center of power independent. Korea is both important in itself and vital to the defense of Japan. Europe could be outflanked and neutralized from Soviet bases in the Middle East. The United States and its allies and associates must oppose hegemonic power in Asia and the Middle East as well as in Europe. The world, after all, is round.

In trying to deal with the dynamic process of Soviet expansion, now extending to every corner of the globe, can any geographical areas be listed in advance as beyond the possible security concerns of the United States? In recent years we have perceived significant if not vital threats to our national interest in Central Africa, Afghanistan, South Yemen, and Thailand, as well as in Central America and East Asia. In the context of the Soviet Union's flexible strategy of expansion, these perceptions were well founded. As Alexander Hamilton pointed out in Number 23 of the *Federalist,* the circumstances which may threaten the safety of nations are infinitely varied. They cannot be defined in advance with precision. We should avoid the temptation to try.

The United States and most other nations of the world want an open state system of sovereign and independent states, conducting their affairs autonomously in accordance with the rules of international law. The Soviet Union is still pursuing a course of indefinite expansion achieved by aggression, a policy which can end only in dominion or disaster. The relation between the United States and the Soviet Union is therefore like that between Great Britain and the nations which bid for dominion between the sixteenth and twentieth centuries: Spain in the time of Philip II, France from the age of Louis XIV to that of Napoleon, and Germany in the first half of this century. Now, in a global state system which is no longer Euro-centered, the Soviet Union is seeking mastery with the aid of the nuclear weapon and, more specifically, with the political aid of a visible and plausible first-strike capacity against the United States. Of necessity, the United States must be what Great Britain was for so long, the arbiter of the world balance of power. There is no other nation or combination of nations which could offset the Soviet nuclear arsenal and other aspects of Soviet military power as a paralyzing and neutralizing political force.

A modus vivendi of the kind Mr. Kissinger recommends would involve a narrowing of our present defense perimeter, perhaps a radical retreat. At a minimum, it would result in an agreement through which the Soviet Union would promise to withdraw from the Western Hemisphere in exchange for the neutralization of Western Europe and Japan, and therefore the withdrawal of the United States from the Middle East and Southern Asia.

But we cannot retreat to a narrower perimeter of defense without allowing a catastrophic and nearly irreversible change in the world balance of power to take place. In the nuclear age, peace really is indivisible. The "Balkans" detonating the contemporary state system could be Baluchistan, Afghanistan, Iran, Korea, or Southern Africa, as it once was Sarajevo, Manchuria, Abyssinia, and Spain. If the United States tries to retreat to isolation and neutrality, a Soviet-dominated world system would emerge automatically. It is a fantasy to suppose that such a system would tolerate American individualism and American freedom.

Restoring the Charter Rule of Peace

If the foreign policy we have employed since 1946 has resulted in a great increase in the power and aggressiveness of the Soviet Union and a corresponding decline in the security of the United States and the Western world, and if a new modus vivendi agreement would have even less promising prospects than its predecessors, what should be done to rectify the situation?

The cure for the crisis, in my judgment, is to create or re-create the state system in whose stability and successful functioning every state has an equal and inescapable interest, the state system posited by the United Nations Charter. Such an international order could only be based on a stable balance of world power. There are no shortcuts to this goal, no cheap substitutes for directly addressing the problem of Soviet aggression. Spheres-of-influence agreements, arms-control agreements, economic carrots and sticks, and other half-measures are snares and delusions unless they are backed by arrangements of collective security to protect the balance of power.

A first step to this end, after suitable consultations, would be to supplement President Truman's policy of containment, the cornerstone of Western foreign policy since 1947. Concretely, this would require President Reagan to inform Mr. Gorbachev that unless the Soviet Union gives up its policies of aggression, the United States and its allies will have to reconsider their own commitment to the Charter rules.

The Soviet practice of aggression is eroding the political foundations of Article 2(4) of the United Nations Charter, the basic organizing principle of the state system since the Congress of Vienna. The rule prohibits any international use of force against the territorial integrity or political independence of a state, save for purposes of individual or collective self-defense. As a rule of law and a political principle, this prohibition must be generally respected or it will not be respected at all. The state system cannot function under a double standard. Unless the Soviet Union gives up the practice of aggression, it cannot expect other states to regard Article 2(4) of the Charter as the eleventh Commandment. Adlai Stevenson said a generation ago that we will not stand by and be nibbled to death. When Alexander M. Haig was secretary of state, he warned that continued Soviet violations of Article 2(4) would deprive the provision of all influence over the behavior of states. And Secretary of State Shultz commented in February 1985, in a speech at the Commonwealth Club of San Francisco, that it was ridiculous for the Soviet Union to claim a right to send arms and men to fight against the authority of a state and then object if the United States did the same thing.

Erosion of legal strictures against the use of force is not a development the United States wants. On the contrary, it would violate every precept for which the United States has labored in world politics for two centuries. But it will come, inevitably, if world politics are governed by instincts of self-preservation rather than by the rule of law.

The step recommended here is not to be undertaken lightly. It would be worse than useless if it were considered a bluff. And it will not be easy or cheap to carry out. But, in my view, it is the only course available to the United States and the West. The Soviet Union will not be swayed from its course by sweet reason alone. It will undertake to live under the Charter rules only when it is convinced that all the alternatives are less attractive.

President Reagan's address of 24 October 1985 to the United Nations General Assembly takes a long step toward making this policy explicit. It describes the basic cause of tension between the Soviet Union and the rest of the world with indispensable clarity and candor: the cause of tension is Soviet aggression throughout the world, the president said, not simply the problem of reaching a nuclear arms agreement. The arms race and the special intricacies of the nuclear weapon are not causes but symptoms of the underlying problem. The president invited the Soviet Union to join the United States in seeking to settle some of the most acute conflicts now raging around the world in accordance with Article 2(4) of the United Nations Charter, which he quoted.

The Soviet-American summit meeting of November 1985 generated enormous political pressures on President Reagan. Those pressures reflected the natural yearning of the Western peoples for an end of the Cold War. It remains to be seen whether the president will yield to those pressures by accepting Mr. Gorbachev's offer of a modus vivendi, or whether he will continue to insist that there is no possible basis for true detente between the Soviet Union and the United States except reciprocal respect by both nations for the rule of the United Nations Charter against aggression.

A policy to achieve peace cannot be fulfilled in a moment, or in six months. There is much damage to be overcome before it could become effective. But the most important component of social cohesion, as social philosophers in the tradition of Montesquieu and Ortega y Gasset have perceived, is not a shared past but a shared vision of the future. Lord Carrington recently warned that the greatest weakness of the Western alliances today is precisely that they lack a shared vision of the future and agreement on practical means for achieving it.

The nature of the choice before the United States, its NATO and ANZUS allies, Japan, China, and the many other nations which share the American desire for a genuine peace was well formulated some years ago by Sinnathamby Rajaratnam, then deputy prime minister of Singapore, in these terms: "Unless the Soviet challenge is made the core of United States foreign policy and met with the same resolve and sense of realism that the Soviets bring to their cause, then a Pax Sovietica is a high probability in the 80's. This is not what we in Asia want, but if that is the only item on the shelf that is what we shall have to settle for."

Notes

1. *Los Angeles Times*, 5 May 1985.

2. Richard M. Nixon, *Real Peace, A Strategy for the West*, first published in a privately printed edition, 1983.

31

The Rise and Fall of
Containment: Informal Remarks

Norman Podhoretz

L ET ME BEGIN with two perspectives on containment which I
consider essential to understanding its history and its appli-
cability to our current circumstances. First, containment should
be seen as a national reaction to the lesson of Munich. Second,
as such, it was successful in enlisting bipartisan support during
the first years of its existence. There was deep, abiding, national support for a policy that seemed to be at once morally
ennobling, politically viable, and conducive to the most vital of
American and Western values. It was because the lesson of
Munich—that is, the lesson that appeasement leads to war and
that tardy resistance to totalitarian aggression is the road to war
or defeat or both—had been absorbed by virtually all elements
in our political culture that this new anti-Munich policy was not
only conceived but also received with such enthusiasm.

Norman Podhoretz is the Editor-in-Chief of *Commentary* magazine, a Member
of the Council on Foreign Relations, and a Member of the Boards of the Committee on the Present Danger and the Committee for the Free World.

Fundamentally, containment was based on two simple propositions—simple, but by no means uncontroversial, in 1947 and still today. The first of these propositions was that there was a "clear and present danger," a Soviet threat, to the free institutions of the West. The second proposition, equally simple and perhaps less controversial then than it is today, was that only American power could successfully cope with or "contain" that threat.

The resistance to these two propositions came both from the Left and from the Right. On the Left, it was denied that there *was* a threat. The Soviet threat was seen as the figment of a paranoid anticommunist American imagination. It was denied that the Soviet Union had aggressive or expansionist intent and asserted that any Soviet actions which seemed aggressive or expansionist were really defensive responses to American provocation. This challenge to containment's view of Soviet behavior found political expression through the leadership of Henry Wallace and the Progressive Party in their 1948 presidential campaign against Harry Truman. I was an undergraduate at Columbia University during that campaign, and a supporter of Wallace. I was still too young to vote, but I remember attending a Wallace rally on the Columbia campus, chaired by the late Mark Van Doren, then the single greatest literary star on the Columbia faculty. A young and surprisingly skinny Norman Mailer appeared, to make a pitch for Wallace's candidacy. A folk singer named Pete Seeger (some things never change) was there to entertain us.

We were told that Henry Wallace would get 10 million votes. In the end, in fact, he got under a million. Because Wallace failed so badly and was so humiliated at the polls, the position that he represented was discredited as a serious point of view in the mainstream of American politics. That pretty well took care of the Left-wing attack on the fundamental premises of containment. The phenomenon that has come to be rather loosely known as McCarthyism then conducted what might be called a mopping-up operation.

There was also a Right-wing attack on containment. We need only remind ourselves that the young Richard Nixon spoke of Secretary of State Acheson's "Cowardly College of Communist Containment," and actually accused Dean Acheson of being soft on communism. (Younger people today think of Richard Nixon—with some justification, incidentally—as having grown a bit soft on communism himself. Younger people are also amazed to hear that John F. Kennedy successfully attacked Nixon for being soft on Cuba in the 1960 presidential campaign, and that it was Kennedy who was the hard-line candidate in that contest. Some things *do* change: look at the Democratic Party today.) But the young Nixon spoke for the wing of the Republican Party which believed that the trouble with containment was not that it misconstrued the nature of the Soviet threat, but that it misconstrued the nature of the strategy needed to meet that threat. In other words, they attacked containment for being timid and defensive. What the Right wing was calling for in those days was a policy that used to be known as rollback or liberation.

Rhetorically, rollback or liberation maintained a lively existence until the election of Dwight Eisenhower. Richard Nixon, of course, was Eisenhower's vice president, and John Foster Dulles, the great exponent of rollback and liberation, was his secretary of state. It would have been reasonable, if naive, to suppose that they were about to embark on a policy of rollback or liberation. In fact, the Eisenhower administration did no such thing. As its response to the Hungarian revolution of 1956 vividly demonstrated, it had no intention of practicing anything remotely resembling a policy of rollback of Soviet power.

Eisenhower's failure to follow Right-wing Republican tactics meant that the policy of containment as developed by the young George Kennan—or Kennan I, as I sometimes call him—became a bipartisan policy, representing a broad national consensus. The nation was willing to support the idea that American political, economic, and if necessary military power should be used in order to hold the Soviet Union behind the lines that had been set at the end of the Second World War. As an earnest of our seriousness, we had sent troops into Korea, the invasion of which was seen as a direct challenge to the policy of containment. We spent blood (more than 33,000 American lives) and treasure, and there was very little dissent from the decision to go into Korea in the name of containing Soviet or communist expansionism. (Indeed, no distinction was being made, at that point, between the two.)

Detente and the Lessons of Vietnam

As we all know, this happy consensus was destined to be destroyed by the Vietnam War. Some of us believe that American intervention in Vietnam was mandated by the same intellectual imperatives that had mandated the intervention in Korea. I, myself, have argued that our intervention in Vietnam was an act of imprudence. But in principle, going into Vietnam was entirely consistent with the policy of containment, both as defined in the abstract and as embodied in concrete action by the Truman and Eisenhower administrations. So Kennedy made the decision to go in (though these days, listening to some of the people who were in that administration, you would never know it; they contend that somebody else took us into Vietnam—I don't know who, but the way they tell it, it was not Kennedy).

Defeat in Vietnam, of course, destroyed the consensus that had crystallized around containment. If containment was the policy developed in response to the lesson of Munich, it was destroyed in its turn by the lesson of Vietnam. For an entire generation, and indeed for virtually the entire political culture, Vietnam replaced Munich as the grand symbol of "Never Again." Just as the world had pledged almost unanimously that there would be No More Munichs, so the guiding principle in the United States now became No More Vietnams.

What, exactly, was the lesson of Vietnam? When we marked the tenth anniversary of the fall of Saigon recently, the debate over that question reemerged, still unresolved among us. But in the seventies, the lesson of Vietnam was widely taken by our political culture to be not that going into Vietnam might have been an imprudent, reckless, or unwise application of a fundamentally sound strategy, but rather that the strategy— namely, containment—had been wrong from the beginning. In fact, the lesson went even further than that. The lesson was putatively that the entire basis of American policy in relation to communism and the Soviet Union since 1947, since the enunciation of the Truman Doctrine and the publication of the 'X' article in *Foreign Affairs,* had been fundamentally flawed. Vietnam, it was thought, had torn the mask off that policy and exposed it as based on illusion at best and on evil intent at worst. The alleged illusion concerned the Soviet threat which—so it was said—had been wildly exaggerated. We had gone into Vietnam in response to a threat that did not exist.

Vietnam was also very widely thought to teach the lesson that American power, whose purposes had seemed to be good, benevolent, and even noble, was in fact morally deficient. American power had been deployed in support of immoral and indeed criminal ends. And not only was it morally flawed, it was also operationally flawed. The supposedly greatest power on earth couldn't even win a war against those characters running around in black pajamas. So what was our power worth?

Here, in the starkest possible terms, was the traumatic disintegration of the national consensus we had enjoyed since 1947 on the main issue in our foreign policy. In response, a Republican administration led by the same Richard Nixon who had spoken of the Acheson "Cowardly College of Communist Containment" developed an alternative policy which was built on the principle of strategic retreat. I think it is fair, in the historical context I'm trying to sketch here, to say that detente represented, at least in the minds of Richard Nixon and Henry Kissinger, an effort to salvage as much of containment as possible under conditions that made the continued pursuit of such a policy impossible.

This is the heart of what came to be called the Nixon Doctrine. What did the Nixon Doctrine, coming almost exactly twenty years after the Truman Doctrine, say? The Nixon Doctrine said that the United States would no longer use its own military power to contain Soviet expansionism. Let me observe that in the minds of Nixon and Kissinger, the Soviet threat was still recognized, acknowledged, and held to be serious. In that sense, detente did not represent a departure from or an abandonment of containment's vision of the Soviet Union: the Soviet threat was there, it was real, and it was serious. But it could no longer be dealt with directly through the use of American military power, either deterrent power or the actual deployment of American forces. Substitutes for American power had to be found, and what the Nixon Doctrine proposed was the appointment of surrogate powers to do the job in various regions of the world. We could help them with military aid, economic aid, and political support, but we would leave the fighting to them. Who were they? Iran under the Shah in the Persian Gulf and in the Middle East generally, and, more significantly as it would turn out, China in the Far East.

In the opening to China, which I see as part of this new policy of strategic retreat, the Nixon Doctrine was in effect defining the enemy to be contained not as communism but, rather, as the Soviet Union, defined as a traditionally expansionist nation-state. There was a change in understanding here: a threat at once ideological and military became one that could be assimilated into the traditional terms of great power conflict and diplomacy. Is the Soviet Union comparable to Wilhelmine Germany, or is it comparable to Nazi Germany? Are we trying to avert World War I, or are we trying to avert World War II? The debate over which analogy really applies seems to some people an academic and even frivolous argument. To me, it goes to the heart of the matter.

In the years between 1947 and 1968, we implicitly looked upon the Soviet Union as comparable to Nazi Germany; the threat emanating from the Soviet Union was viewed as comparable to the threat that had come from Nazi Germany. When I say *we* I don't just mean the foreign service or the politicians, but also the intellectual community, which was in those days very heavily influenced by such works as Hannah Arendt's *The Origins of Totalitarianism,* a book whose entire point was to portray the Soviet Union as a mutation of the same species as Nazi Germany. Its thesis was that totalitarianism was a new phenomenon in history. Nazi Germany was one expression of it, the Soviet Union another; they were exactly comparable, morally and politically.

Containment in its first phase, I believe, implicitly accepted that view of the Soviet Union. The difference under detente was not to deny that the Soviet Union was a threat but to deny that the Soviet Union was *that kind* of threat. Some academic defenders of detente (Stanley Hoffmann of Harvard, for example) explicitly invoked the analogy of Wilhelmine Germany. Helmut Sonnenfeldt, when he was counselor of the State Department under Henry Kissinger, used the same image. In this view, the Soviet Union was an expansionist power, but not a revolutionary actor on the world scene trying to create a new international order in which it would enjoy hegemony. It was, rather, an ambitious outsider seeking an equal place for itself in the imperial sun, like Wilhelmine Germany. That's what the new understanding of the Soviet Union alleged that the Soviet Union was—at least among those who were willing to grant that the USSR represented any kind of threat at all.

But however one looked at the Soviet Union, there was general agreement that American power was no longer capable by itself, or even with help from US allies, of coping with that threat. We were weakened and demoralized, and neither Congress nor the media nor the relevant political constituencies were willing to back the kind of forceful policies, or the level of defense spending, that would be required to continue classical containment. Therefore, a retreat was necessary, along with the creation of substitute power in the form of surrogates—the policy of the Nixon and Ford administrations. By the time we got to Jimmy Carter—that is, Carter in the first three years of his administration—there was a further slide down this particularly slippery slope, because at this point we began hearing from high officials of the administration—indeed, from the president himself and his secretary of state—that there was no Soviet threat at all.

And here you had, for the first time, a really serious mainstream challenge to one of the two fundamental pillars on which classical containment had rested. High officials of the Carter administration—and also, I would say, the vast majority of academic specialists in the universities and the foreign policy institutes—were now saying that the Soviet Union, whatever it might or might not have been in the past, had become a status quo power. That view persisted up until the invasion of Afghanistan. Secretary of State Cyrus Vance said in a speech, which I hope he has lived to be ashamed of, that President Carter and Leonid Brezhnev shared the same values and aspirations. And the president himself congratulated the nation on having overcome what he called its "inordinate fear of communism," a remark which led some to ask what an ordinate fear of communism might look like.

Not content with denying that there was a Soviet threat, not content with this radical assault on one of the two fundamental premises of containment, the Carter administration went even further into a fantasy that should have shaken—but I fear did not shake—the military. The administration said that military power had become or was becoming obsolete in our time as compared with other forms of power, suggesting that the use of military power, whether for deterrent purposes or actually for shooting purposes, was, in almost any situation, no longer to be regarded as necessary. That dictum completed a thorough and radical departure from containment.

Reagan and the Lessons of the Post-Vietnam Era

History sometimes has a way of impinging upon the false or deluded consciousness of those who attempt to shape it, and so it did in the Carter administration. First, I think, came an event that did not directly impinge on the Carter *Weltanschauung* itself, but which had consequences for it—namely, the fall of the Shah of Iran and the rise of the Ayatollah. In failing to do what was necessary to prop up the Shah when he was under assault, we as a nation simply abandoned the Nixon Doctrine. If one of the main surrogates for American power could not depend on American support when he was in trouble, and in trouble as a result of a challenge from anti-American forces, then the whole doctrine was nonsense. It simply exposed itself as a brilliant scheme on paper and nonsense in action. No matter how many speeches anyone made to the contrary it was clear that surrogates were not an adequate substitute for our own power.

But if the fall of the Shah discredited the Nixon Doctrine, it was the invasion of Afghanistan that discredited the Carter view of the Soviet Union. Here the president himself, unlike many people, was willing to admit that he had been wrong. He said that in a single week he learned more about the Soviet Union than he had known in his whole life before. Evidently, Mr. Carter had actually believed that the Soviet Union was not a threat, that military power was obsolete, and that Mr. Brezhnev, as Secretary of State Vance had declared, subscribed to the same values as we did. But then the Soviet Union rudely contradicted him by sending more than 75,000 troops into Afghanistan, the first use by the Soviet Union of its own troops outside the Warsaw Pact territory since the early postwar period. Mr. Carter was at least honest enough to recognize that he had been mistaken about the Soviet Union, though some of us wondered how much the political education of Jimmy Carter had cost the country in the previous three years.

At the same time, his eyes, and the eyes of a lot of other people, were opened to another illusion—namely, that the

Soviet Union was only interested in parity with us in nuclear weaponry. People who had resisted the warnings of groups like the Committee on the Present Danger about the Soviet military buildup suddenly, in the post-Afghanistan climate, began to entertain the possibility that they might have been wrong, that Paul Nitze and Eugene Rostow and a few others might indeed have been right in their Churchillian warnings that the Soviets were trying to achieve not parity but strategic superiority.

In his fourth year, remarkably, even Jimmy Carter emerged as a born-again hawk. I say born-again because he had actually been a hawk once upon a time. Not that graduating from Annapolis would necessarily make you a hawk. (I don't know what it is about Annapolis. West Point and the Air Force Academy don't seem to produce anything like those semi-pacifist retired admirals who keep running around the country preaching disarmament.) Still, Carter had been a very enthusiastic supporter of the Vietnam War in his younger days, and his conversion to a dovish position came late. After the Afghanistan invasion, as a born-again hawk, he came out for a big increase in the defense budget. He withdrew SALT II from the Senate. He instituted a grain embargo against the Soviet Union. He even enunciated a new Presidential Doctrine. Ten years after the Nixon Doctrine, we were given the Carter Doctrine, in which the president said that the United States would use any measure up to and including military force to prevent an outside power—and everybody understood whom he meant—from taking control of the oil fields of the Persian Gulf region. Many presidents have been haunted by the ghosts of past strategies, past policies; and Jimmy Carter was clearly haunted by the ghost of Harry Truman, the ghost of containment past. (Of course, Carter never had an opportunity to show us what he might have done if he had been reelected. Judging from the way he has talked out of office, he would have lapsed again into born-again appeasement—if one wanted to be polite, one might call it detente.)

At any rate, by 1979 it seemed as though we were back again to 1947, and in some ways as a nation we were. If you study the polls from 1979–80, you find an extraordinary degree of support for serious increases in defense spending—up way over the 70 percent mark, which on an issue like that is unprecedentedly high. Alarm over the Soviet threat also moved sharply upward around the same time. In addition, there emerged what was called a new patriotism or a new nationalism, which had a good deal to do with frustration and rage over the hostage crisis in Iran. There was a feeling that it was because we had allowed ourselves to become weak that we were being attacked and humiliated in such a way. In a sense, then, the state of public opinion was not dissimilar to the state of public opinion in 1947–48, with Iran and Afghanistan now serving as the galvanizing events, just as the coup in Czechoslovakia and the threat to Greece and Turkey had done then.

Ronald Reagan clearly was swept into the White House on the tide of this new public feeling both about the Soviet threat and about the need for a reassertion of American power: not just a military buildup, but a concerted effort to reverse a felt decline in American power of every kind, an effort to rediscover and to recapture the lost sources of American greatness. Reagan seemed the best leader for such an effort. The subliminal and sometimes even the explicit message of Jimmy Carter's candidacy was that the decline of American power was inexorable, inevitable. There was nothing we could do about it. A mature people, which is what he exhorted us to be, would make its peace with this decline. Reagan said no: the decline of American power was a result of bad policy, and he knew how to reverse it. What the American people said in electing Reagan in 1980 was that they were not quite ready to be "mature" and to accept decline as inexorable. They wanted another shot at national greatness.

But ghosts also haunted Reagan. In his first couple of years in office, the ghosts of the young Richard Nixon, of Douglas MacArthur, and of John Foster Dulles (before he became secretary of state) floated through the White House. The ghostly doctrine of rollback or liberation haunted Reagan's rhetoric when he spoke of the Soviet Union as an "evil empire" and when he said that communism would be consigned to the ash heap of history. This kind of talk instilled a good deal of hope in people like me and aroused hysteria in a lot of other people. Fortunately for them, and unfortunately for me, the ghost of rollback haunted only Ronald Reagan's rhetoric. It did not go so far as to haunt his actual policy.

There, a different ghost took over: the ghost of detente, the ghost of an older Richard Nixon. It was, to be sure, detente as Mr. Nixon now began defining it in speeches and articles— detente of the hard-headed variety, not, as he saw it, of the soft-headed variety that Carter had adopted. Once, when criticizing something I had written about detente, Helmut Sonnenfeldt said, "You don't understand; detente to us meant an iron fist in a velvet glove." If that were the case, what Mr. Nixon, Mr. Sonnenfeldt, and others were now saying was that Jimmy Carter had removed the iron fist, leaving only a velvet glove good for nothing but stroking. In that context, we might say that the Reagan administration, at least in its rhetoric, was trying to put the iron fist back into the glove, though in its actual policies it did a bit of stroking itself.

I think one could make a very solid and well-documented case for the thesis behind this playful metaphor. Even the tough policies of the Reagan administration, whether rhetorical or real, are entirely consistent with the theory of detente as spelled out by the post-presidential Richard Nixon, and in some of the writings of Henry Kissinger, because their conception of detente did indeed involve a component of power. Detente had to be policed, and the only policeman available was the United States. So if the Soviet Union stepped out of line, we had to be prepared to growl or do something—call an alert, send a ship, send a tank—do something. But as Nixon and Kissinger see it, because Watergate had destroyed executive authority and because Congress wouldn't supply the means with which, say, to help

Savimbi in Angola, this necessary component of the strategy was eliminated, frustrating Kissinger's design and leaving Carter with a policy that was, for all practical purposes, equivalent to appeasement.

In that sense, the Nixonian tradition came back into the Reagan administration's policies. But it was done with a view toward reestablishing some system of incentives and penalties that would serve to restrain Soviet behavior and, in turn, make it possible for Reagan to arrive at an accommodation similar to the one that had been outlined in the Basic Principles of Detente agreed to by Nixon and Brezhnev in Moscow in 1972 (which, however, the Soviets immediately began to violate).

The Lessons of Mr. X

All these ghosts still are haunting our efforts to define a sense of ourselves and a sense of our responsibilities in relation to the Soviet threat. The truth of the matter is that we have not returned to the spirit of 1947. We have not returned to the clarity of 1947, and we have not returned to the state of national will that we were able to mobilize in 1947. Since 1979, we as a nation have been floundering in search of a policy or a strategy: in search, as I would put it in less technical terms, of some clarity about who we are, what our responsibilities as a nation are, and what it is we're trying to accomplish.

Why should we be floundering in this way? What is the problem? Let me suggest that the problem is fundamentally not political but what I would call, in the broad sense, cultural.

I am an unreconstructed and unrepentant admirer of the 'X' article, the George Kennan of 1947—Kennan I—and just as severe a critic of the George Kennan of today, Kennan II. D. H. Lawrence once gave this advice to literary critics: "Never trust the teller," he said, "trust the tale." The tale in this case is "The Sources of Soviet Conduct," Mr. Kennan's famous *Foreign Affairs* article. Now, I believe that this article, which develops the two fundamental principles of containment and the principles around which a national consensus mobilized so enthusiastically, remains valid. I would go so far as to say that it is more valid today than it was back in 1947. We are floundering because we have permitted ourselves to forget what Mr. X taught us in 1947, namely, that what he called "Russian expansive tendencies" "cannot be charmed or talked out of existence." They can only be restrained—and these are Mr. Kennan's words—"by the adroit and vigilant application of counter-force at a series of constantly shifting geographical and political points corresponding to the shifts and maneuvers of Soviet policy." We have forgotten the wisdom and realism behind that view of the Soviet Union, and I believe that Mr. Kennan himself has forgotten it. We are floundering because we have also forgotten the purposes to which we once dedicated American power. These, too, were outlined in the 'X' article, which defined the objective of the policy of containment as being to promote "tendencies which must eventually find their outlet in either the breakup or the gradual mellowing of Soviet power."

How are we to bring ourselves to remember these principles? We can begin by recognizing that Mr. X was right in everything but his timing. The Kennan of 1947 thought it would take only ten or fifteen years for containment to result in the breakup or mellowing of Soviet power—not an eternity of confrontation, but ten or fifteen years. Ironically, of course, fifteen years brought us to the intervention in Vietnam and the beginning of the breakup of *American* power.

But even though Kennan's timing was off, his prediction was right. What he said, turning the Marxist tables on the Soviet Union, was that the idea of the internal contradictions—by which the capitalist world was supposedly doomed—was much more applicable to the Soviet Union. Internal contradictions would make it impossible for the Soviet Union to exist in the same form indefinitely, provided that its "expansive tendencies," which Kennan saw as a kind of safety valve or escape from those internal contradictions, were contained. If the Soviets were held behind the post–World War II line, the pressures would build up, and a mellowing or breakup would gradually result.

Now, I think we have to recognize that mellowing is an impossibility for the Soviet Union; to expect it is to expect a political class to commit suicide. This is a class which owes its legitimacy to its commitment to the Leninist mission in the world at large, and which therefore cannot forsake that commitment without calling its own legitimacy into question. Whether they subjectively believe in communism or not doesn't matter. Some people say there are no communists left in the Soviet Union—perhaps that's true. Perhaps they don't believe in communism. But communism, let me say, believes in them. There is no way that they can maintain themselves in power if they repudiate the Leninist commitment. And here I would ask, from their point of view, do they have any good reason to do so?

I think, then, that to look forward to a mellowing of Soviet power is to harbor an illusion. On the other hand, to look forward to the breakup of the Soviet empire is to look forward not only to a reality but to what I would argue is a virtual inevitability. There are some people who think that of all the empires in history—the Assyrian, the Babylonian, the Greek, the Roman, the British—only the Soviet empire is eternal. But the Soviet empire is no more eternal than any other empire known to history. It will break up some day. The question is, when and under what circumstances?

Once, we understood what our role in that process ought to be. We understood it in the post-1947 period under the tutelage of men like George Kennan. I think we need to recapture the courage to follow a strategy that would promote the tendencies which are now much more richly developed than they were in 1947 and that might lead to a breakup of the Soviet empire. I don't have to spell out what those tendencies are: the demographic problems, the economic problems, and so on. Concretely, what would such a strategy look like? I think it would look not all that different from the strategy that was outlined by the 'X' piece itself, updated to meet certain new realities.

First, we would have to be determined not to allow Soviet military power to outstrip our own. I rank this as the very minimum, as a first priority, and as the necessary foundation for all the other steps we might take. We would have to maintain a healthy military balance. I would like to see us actually achieve superiority, but at the very least, we need to prevent the Soviets from achieving superiority. The second thing we should be doing is helping the various anti-Soviet insurgencies that are now operating on the periphery of the empire—in Afghanistan, in Angola, in Nicaragua. The third would be to practice economic denial, as much of it as possible, in dealing with the heartland of the empire, so as to exacerbate the economic crisis within.

The fourth, which I do not put last because I think it has the lowest priority—in fact, I think it may have the highest priority—is to recapture our sense of what this struggle is all about. I believe it is a struggle with the primary remaining mutation of the totalitarian curse which has been the twentieth century's distinctive contribution to the history of despotism and tyranny. Our willingness to assume the responsibility to defeat the other principal example of this accursed contemporary species of tyranny—namely, Nazi Germany—was matched by an equally courageous and morally noble determination in 1947 to set ourselves against the triumph of the Soviet Union (even though, for tactical, prudential reasons, we had made an alliance with the Soviets when the Nazi threat was the more urgent "present danger"). We have to teach ourselves once again that we're not in this struggle in order to establish some kind of classical nineteenth-century balance of power or to serve dubious theories of *Realpolitik*. We are involved, rather, in a clash of civilizations, and it is a clash that will not, as Mr. X said, be charmed or talked out of existence. This means we have to learn once again to talk about communism and what communism means, and in what sense it represents a mortal curse and a threat.

Will anyone support such a policy? Are there any politicians willing to sponsor it? I don't know; very likely not. Nevertheless, I find myself going back over and over again to the concluding words of the 'X' article, which, again, I think are at least as applicable to our situation as a people today as they were in 1947. Indeed, they are more applicable, given the kinds of changes—spiritual and cultural as well as political, economic, and military—that have occurred. Kennan spoke with the eloquence that he so inimitably commands no matter what position he's arguing. He said that "the thoughtful observer of Russian-American relations" would find no "cause for complaint in the Soviet threat." And then he concluded with these words:

> [T]he thoughtful observer. . .will rather experience a certain gratitude to a Providence which, by providing the American people with this implacable challenge, has made their entire security as a nation dependent on their pulling themselves together and accepting the responsibilities of moral and political leadership that history plainly intended them to bear.

I can think of no better contemporary exhortation to the people of the United States (and indeed of the Western world generally) than those magnificent words.

32

Epilogue:
The Future of Containment

John Lewis Gaddis

L ET ME BEGIN BY CALLING to your attention a recurring problem in strategy: it is what we might call the "Moliere syndrome," because it is best exemplified in the character from *Le
Bourgeous Gentilhomme* who is amazed to discover that, without realizing it, he has been speaking prose all his life.

Containment is something with which most people in the
national security community have spent most of their lives. It
has become a thoroughly familiar—if not always engaging—
presence. We have become so accustomed to it that we rarely
stop to consider what its precise goals are supposed to be, or indeed whether we would even recognize them if they were attained. We run the risk, like Moliere's protagonist, of having
practiced "containment" quite successfully all along, but without realizing it.

One good cure for the "Moliere syndrome" is history: if
one wants to get a sense of how far we have come, and of what

we have accomplished, it helps to recall from whence we started. And that brings me back—not wholly by accident—to George Kennan, and the remarkable series of lectures he delivered to students at the National War College during the earliest days of the Cold War; lectures, by the way, that give a far clearer and more coherent view of his strategy than the much-quoted but unfortunately misleading 'X' article.

In those lectures, Kennan put forward three fairly clear objectives for containment. These were (a) to restore the international balance of power, thereby preventing the Soviet Union from exploiting power vacuums left by the defeats of Germany and Japan; (b) to reduce the Soviet Union's ability to project influence beyond its borders through the international communist movement; and (c) ultimately to bring about, through a combination of inducements and deterrents, a modification in the behavior of the Soviet leadership toward the outside world which would cause it to learn to live with, rather than to seek to eliminate, diversity.

How well has it worked? Are we, today, at the stage where we can say that at least Kennan's original objectives for containment have been attained?

As Kennan himself points out in his contribution to this volume, the first objective—restoration of a balance of power—has more than been accomplished. The prospect of the Soviet Union's coming to dominate other vital centers of industrial-military power in the world—a possibility that seemed very real at the end of World War II—has obviously not come to pass. Indeed, we have gone a good deal beyond that goal: the past forty years have seen greater stability in the positions of the great powers relative to each other, and to the rest of the world as well, than at any other point since the now wistfully remembered eras of Metternich and Bismarck. That stability is all the more remarkable for the fact that no one consciously designed it—we had no Congress of Vienna or Paris Peace Conference to set it up—and that we have gotten by quite nicely without any Metternichs or Bismarcks to manage it.

Kennan himself would insist, I am sure, that what we have evolved is not a balance of power at all, but a balance of terror. Certainly, a case can be made that only the existence of nuclear weapons on both sides has made this stability possible; certainly, we could all agree that this is a profoundly risky way to maintain that condition. But Kennan's concern with the nuclear question may cause him to overlook certain of the non-nuclear components of postwar stability: the inherent simplicity of a bipolar over a multipolar configuration of power in the world; the fact that for all their ideological rivalries, Russians and Americans have had no great historical antagonisms and, indeed, alone among major world powers, have never fought one another in war; the fact that our respective economies are relatively independent, and that wars most often arise among nations that are economically interdependent; the fact that we have both shown ourselves capable of modifying ideological militancy to bring it into line with state interests; the fact that nothing in our respective cultures or traditions glorifies war as a necessary or desirable end. Nuclear weapons have been an important stabilizing mechanism, to be sure, but the stability we have attained does not depend wholly upon them.

Would this stability have evolved if there had been no strategy of containment? No one can say, of course, but given the difficulty the Soviet Union has historically had in defining the limits of its own security interests, containment cannot have been wholly irrelevant to the process. As the historian Vojtech Mastny has suggested,[1] containment may well have reinforced rather than detracted from stability by telling the Russians where to stop when they themselves could not quite make up their minds.

How stable is the balance of power today? If one accepts, as it seems to me any good strategist must, the proposition that power comprises a good deal more than simply military hardware, then the balance seems relatively stable: the possibility of either superpower gaining a decisive advantage over the other in all of the dimensions that go to make up power—military, political, economic, ideological, psychological, cultural—seems quite remote. Nor has anyone identified third parties who seem capable of challenging the superpowers in all of these categories anytime soon.

There is a cloud on the horizon, though, having to do with the Soviet Union's increasing and by now disproportionate emphasis on the military components of power. Critics of containment have seen this as a source of great strength for the Russians, and as reason to doubt whether containment as we have practiced it in the past continues to serve our interests. I myself am inclined to see it as an admission of weakness: as a painful acknowledgement of the fact that the only means left to the Soviet Union for projecting influence in the world is military, its attractiveness in all other respects having so noticeably waned. And if the history of the Cold War tells us anything at all, it is that there is no necessary correlation between the military power one has and the capacity one has to influence events in the rest of the world.

What happens to the balance of power when a superpower suddenly realizes that the forces of history are no longer on its side, and when it begins to perceive that the only means it has left to try to reverse the decline are military? It would be a fine thing if history always arranged for the simultaneous and symmetrical decline of great powers: equilibrium could then be maintained, all the way down to impotence and senility. But history is rarely so accommodating. The greatest threat to the balance of power in the remainder of this century, it seems to me, is likely to come from visions of decline, not hegemony. And what this volume suggests is that it is the Russians who are more likely to have these visions than we.

This, then, raises the interesting question of whether, if our interest into the twenty-first century is to preserve the remarkably stable balance that has grown up over these past forty years, we ought to be pursuing strategies aimed at widening the gap that already exists between the overall power positions of our two countries. Might we not find it in our interests over the next several decades to shift our strategies for dealing with the Soviet Union from containment to some form of sustainment? Far be it from me to attempt to answer such an inflammatory question, but I will at least leave it there to be pondered.

Kennan's second objective for containment was to reduce the Soviet Union's capacity to project influence beyond its borders through the activities of the international communist movement. Here the "Moliere syndrome" has affected our perceptions to an even greater extent, for if containment has been successful in any respect, it has been in this one.

It is difficult, sometimes, to remember fears long since overcome. But there was a time, once, when people actually lay awake nights worrying about an international communist conspiracy centrally directed from Moscow. Many people will recall the films, shown in high schools throughout the land, depicting the earth from outer space, with great bloated arrows rising ominously from the Kremlin to splash down in various Third World countries, turning each of them a lurid shade of red.

Now, the Soviet Union doubtlessly still would like to dominate as many of those countries as possible. Many of them to this day still have communist governments. But it is the linkage between these two things that has been broken: Moscow's capacity to dominate other countries solely through the mechanism of ideology is today virtually nil; communism itself as practiced outside the Soviet Union is so diverse a phenomenon as to be virtually meaningless. Any movement that encompasses within it the likes of Kim Il-sung, Fidel Castro, Nicolai Ceaucescu, and Deng Xiaoping is no movement at all: it is a diaphonous fog. The West has won the ideological Cold War; and yet, afflicted as we tend to be by the "Moliere syndrome," we have hardly taken notice.

One can, to be sure, raise the objection that all of this would have happened in any event, even if there had been no strategy of containment: the sun does not really rise just because the rooster crows. But that is just the point: the test of an effective strategy is the extent to which it can align itself with things that are going to happen anyway. It is a striking testimony to the foresight of Kennan and his colleagues on the Policy Planning Staff—and special mention should be made of John Paton Davies' contribution in this respect—that they anticipated how much more durable nationalism was going to be than communism, and that they were able to frame policies aimed at taking advantage of this phenomenon; policies, we now know, that were followed more often and with greater consistency in the ensuing years than many of us had once thought.

There is, of course, great irony in this, because one of the charges most often made against "containment" was that it accepted too passively the status quo: it was not interested, critics asserted, in "rolling back" areas of Soviet control. But if one understands "roll-back" as the employment of economic, psychological, and other nonmilitary means to undermine the appeal of Soviet ideology, then there is much to be said for the view that "containment," far from neglecting this strategy, both originated and implemented it. The result—with a good deal of help, of course, from the Russians themselves—has been a fragmentation of adversaries; an outcome thoroughly consistent with what one would expect an effective strategy to bring about.

Kennan's third objective for containment was to change the behavior of the Soviet leadership toward the outside world: to deter action inconsistent with American interests and, at the same time, to reward action of which we approved. If this sounds suspiciously like linkage, let me simply point out that Henry Kissinger invented a name, not a concept. But has it worked? Of all the objectives Kennan set out for containment, this is the one about which the largest amount of disagreement still exists.

Certainly, the Soviet Union is a very different place from what it was when Kennan first went to Moscow in 1933, or when he served there briefly—and more dramatically than he would have wished—as ambassador in 1952. The terror has largely disappeared; the cult of personality has been largely dismantled; the government's capacity to assess events in the world outside is far more sophisticated than it was in Stalin's day. Contacts with the United States, whether of a political, economic, cultural, or academic nature, proceed on a scale and with a frequency that would have been inconceivable as recently as a quarter century ago. Nor are Soviet leaders as remote and distant as they once were: the first Reagan-Gorbachev summit was the eleventh to take place since Stalin's death.

At the same time, and despite all these changes, few Americans would feel comfortable today dispensing with containment altogether. The Soviet Union still has difficulty defining the limits of its security interests; it still is remarkably casual about the security interests of others. Nor is the insecurity that motivates such expansionism by any means dead: Kennan's analysis in the 'X' article of how the regime's lack of self-confidence creates the need to picture the outside world as hostile remains as valid as it was when it was written four decades ago. So what has containment achieved in modifying Soviet behavior?

One answer is that it has gradually narrowed the Kremlin's propensity to take risks. Expansion still occurs—Afghanistan demonstrates that clearly enough—but not the kind of expansion that risks direct confrontation with the United States. Despite the collapse of detente, we have not seen, in recent years, risk-taking on the order of what Stalin attempted by blockading Berlin or authorizing the North Korean attack on South Korea, or what Khrushchev tried to accomplish by rattling rockets, issuing ultimatums, and finally putting missiles in Cuba, or even what Brezhnev might have had in mind by threatening to send troops to settle the 1973 Middle East war.

728   Containment: Concept and Policy

Another thing that containment has accomplished has been to buy time for a group of prosperous, self-confident, and not easily intimidated states to arise along the periphery of the Soviet Union, and this, too, is beginning to modify Soviet behavior. It has gradually become clear that "Finlandization" is not all that easily accomplished—even among the Finns themselves—and that something a bit more subtle than, say, an SS-20 deployment may be required if Moscow is going to promote its interests beyond the Soviet Union's borders.

Finally, containment has created a willingness on the part of the Russians—in certain areas—to settle differences with the United States on the basis of negotiations: that, too, is a major change since Stalin's era. These negotiations have not always worked out to each side's satisfaction; most often because they have not been equally consistent with each side's interests. But where interests have been congruent—and there are a fair number of cases where that has been the case—negotiations have produced lasting and mutually beneficial results.

There is a problem, though, with this business of Soviet behavior modification, and it is one Kennan warned against years ago in the lectures he delivered at the National War College. The foreign policy of the Soviet Union, he pointed out, is only partially a response to internal circumstances; it is affected as well by the foreign policy of the United States. Washington could not expect to take actions the Russians might perceive as threatening without having them respond in kind. A diplomatic resolution of differences required restraint—and a sensitivity to the consequences of actions—on both sides.

This, it seems to me, is where we need to ask ourselves some hard questions. Are we completely clear in our own minds as to what we expect of the Russians? Are we completely clear as to who is supposed to be making American foreign policy in the first place? No one who has taken the time to read Raymond Garthoff's recent and painfully thorough account of the collapse of detente can be satisfied with the way in which we have dealt with those questions over the past decade and a half.[2]

Our real problem is that we have never given much thought to how we would like the Cold War to end. Not long ago, this question came up at a meeting in Washington. A distinguished retired diplomat replied instantly—and quite instinctively—"Oh, it hadn't occurred to us that it would end."

Surely this is a mistake. Human nature being what it is, international rivalries, like those among individuals, are likely to be with us for a very long time. But the Cold War between the United States and the Soviet Union is only one of many international rivalries: it is, therefore, a discrete historical episode. It had a beginning, and it will have, in some form and at some point, an end. It is an indication of how accustomed we have become to the Cold War that we find it so difficult to envisage what that end might be, but there will surely be such an end, and it is perhaps not too early to begin thinking about how, and on what basis, we might like it to take place. Otherwise, our strategy fails the most elemental test: that of having a clearly defined objective.

I suggested at the outset that the "Moliere syndrome"—the habit of doing things without realizing it—is a pervasive affliction. Let us hope that it is pervasive enough to infect the latest round of Soviet-American summits, and that as a result we will all be amazed to find ourselves closer than we had ever suspected to being able to relegate the Cold War—and containment—once and for all to those custodians of ancient quarrels and defunct controversies, the historians. Speaking as one who has been accused, from time to time, of having a certain vested literary interest in perpetuating the Cold War and containment, I should like the record to show that I, for one, would ardently welcome such an outcome. After all, if historians really are going to have the last word, they do have to live long enough to get around to it. And none of us are getting any younger.

Notes

1. Vojtech Mastny, *Russia's Road to the Cold War: Diplomacy, Warfare, and the Politics of Communism, 1941–1945* (New York: Columbia University Press, 1979).

2. Raymond L. Garthoff, *Detente and Confrontation: American-Soviet Relations from Nixon to Reagan* (Washington: Brookings Institution, 1985).

The Editors

Terry L. Deibel is Professor of National Security Policy and Associate Dean of Faculty at the National War College. He worked on this volume while on sabbatical as Resident Associate at the Carnegie Endowment for International Peace. He also has been an International Affairs Fellow of the Council on Foreign Relations with the Bureau of Politico-Military Affairs, Department of State. His positions before coming to the National War College include Assistant Professor of International Affairs at the School of Foreign Service, Georgetown University, and Budget Examiner in the International Programs Division, Office of Management and Budget. For ten years, he was a Member of the Board of Trustees, Ohio Wesleyan University. He received a B.A. from Ohio Wesleyan University and an M.A., an M.A.L.D., and a Ph.D. from the Fletcher School of Law and Diplomacy, Tufts University. He has a Diplome from the Institute of Advanced International Studies, University of Geneva.

John Lewis Gaddis is Distinguished Professor of History at Ohio University. His teaching positions have included Assistant Professor of History at Indiana University Southeast, Visiting Professor of Strategy at the US Naval War College, and Bicentennial Professor of American Studies at the University of Helsinki. A recent winner of the Guggenheim Fellowship, he has received other grants and fellowships from the National Endowment for the Humanities and the American Council of Learned Societies; he also was awarded the Bancroft Prize for History for *The United States and the Origins of the Cold War*. Author of numerous articles and books on containment, including *Strategies of Containment*, Professor Gaddis is currently at work on a biography of George Kennan. He received a B.A., an M.A., and a Ph.D. from the University of Texas.

Index

Abdullah, Prince (of Afghanistan),
471
ABM Treaty (1972), 645, 656,
657–58
mutual vulnerability in, 373–74
The Absolute Weapon (Brodie), 268
Acheson, Dean, 33, 35, 57, 705
delineating of defensive perimeter
by, 7, 122
foreign policy of, 9, 128, 677–79,
682
UN Charter and, 692
Adenauer, Konrad, 175
Adler-Karlsson, Gunnar, 178–79
Afghanistan. *See also* Third World
communist party in, 467–72
containment policy's use in, 119,
121, 124–29, 131, 457–77
negotiations for Soviet withdrawal
from, 472–77
resistance in, 467–72
Soviet bases in, 476
Soviet departure from, 446–47
Soviet involvement in, 28, 119,
121, 124–29, 131, 151, 169,
221, 240, 272, 280, 326,
340, 342, 349, 364, 365,
407, 408, 420, 428–29, 433,
622, 629, 647, 674, 711–12
US backing of rebels in, 462–67
Africa. *See also* Horn of Africa; individual countries in
containment strategies for, 541–56

Soviet aims and capabilities in,
544–46
Soviet bases in, 324–25, 327–28
US perspectives of, 546–49
Alliance for Progress, 566, 567
Alliances, 189. *See also* individual
treaties
Carter-Reagan, 206–10, 211
as containment instruments, 190
containment's application and,
195–97
containment's future and, 210–11
containment theory and, 191–95
Eisenhower-Dulles, 202–6
Truman-Acheson, 197–202
Almond, Gabriel A. *See The Ameri-
can People and Foreign Policy*
Amanullah, King (of Afghanistan),
459
*The American People and Foreign
Policy* (Almond), 70
Amin, Hafizullah, 458, 463, 465–66
Amin, Idi, 551
Andropov, Yuri, 299, 473, 600
Angola. *See also* Africa; Third
World
containment policy's use in, 119,
121, 124, 126–31
containment's failure in, 277, 278
Soviet influence in, 28, 121, 124,
126–31, 222, 240, 272, 324,
542, 545, 547, 550–52, 624,
675

733

European Economic Community
(EEC), 371
Export Administration Act. *See* Ex-
port Control Act
Export Control Act (1949), 164,
167–68, 174

Fahd, King (of Saudi Arabia), 471
Falklands war, 564
Far East. *See also* individual coun-
tries in
Soviet influence in, 669–70
Federal Reserve (Fed), 142
independence of, 138
money policy of, 146, 147–48,
150
"Flexible response" doctrine, 685
FNLA, 553
Force d'Action Rapide, 247, 248
Ford-Brezhnev agreement, 645
Ford, Gerald, 598
Angola and, 128
containment policy of, 13, 119
national economy and, 149,
151–52
reciprocity and, 633
Foreign Policy Leadership Project,
86, 88
Forrestal, James, 25
40 Committee, 126
Four-power Berlin accord, 645
Fricaud-Chagnaud, Georges, 247
Frye, Alton, 594

Gabrilov, Stanislav, 473
Gaddis, John Lewis
analysis of Kennan by, 191–92,
384, 388, 389–90
containment theories of, 104–7,
312, 315, 347, 432–33
economic capabilities and,
135–36, 138, 140

Gallup organization, 69, 70, 76, 80,
82, 83, 98, 101
Garthoff, Raymond L., 464, 466,
553, 646
detente and, 728–29
Gavin, James, 267
Gellman, Barton, 209, 616
General Agreement on Tariffs and
Trade (GATT), 143, 148, 371
Geneva Conference (1954), 203
Geneva summits (1981, 1983, 1985),
666, 689, 690
Germany, 27. *See also* Eastern
Europe; Europe; Western
Europe
containment and, 276–77
division of, 618
future of, 394–95
Kennan's views of, 384–85
Ghandi, Rajiv, 587
Gorbachev, Mikhail, 506, 666, 668
arms control and, 656, 658–59,
662, 690
dialogue with U.S. by, 43, 369
economic policies of, 179–80,
183, 366
foreign policy of, 303–7, 372,
591, 594
"modus vivendi" and, 679–80, 700
Soviet changes under, 601–3
Soviet technology and, 593
Gorshkov, Sergei, 322
Greece
aid to, 58, 59, 94
NATO entry by, 425
Grenada, 229, 272
US invasion of, 279, 569
Gromyko, Andrei, 654
Guevara, Che, 566–67
Gulf Cooperative Council (GCC),
444
Gulf of Tonkin Resolution (1964),
124, 129

Containment

Concept and Policy

Text and display lines in Times Roman and Italic
Book and cover design by Thomas Gill
Cover mechanical and illustrations by Laszlo L. Bodrogi

Special thanks to the Carnegie Endownment for
International Peace for its support of Terry L. Deibel,
Resident Associate there, during the editing of
the papers published in these volumes.

NDU Press Editor, Thomas Gill
Editorial Clerk, Carolyn Valentine

SYMPOSIUM COORDINATORS

Colonel Giles Harlow, USAF
Director, External Programs

Dr. Harold W. Holtzclaw
Director, Symposia

Lieutenant Colonel Robert Walker, USAF
Director, Operations

Dr. Terry Deibel
Program Advisor, National War College

Lieutenant Colonel M. D. Krause, USA
National War College Coordinator

Ambassador J. Bruce Amstutz
Industrial College of the Armed Forces Coordinator

Master Sergeant G. C. Huff
Symposia Noncommissioned Officer